IT'S HERE!

PRENTICE HALL
SCIENCE

FINALLY, THE PERFECT FIT.

NOW YOU CAN CHOOSE THE PERFECT FIT FOR ALL YOUR CURRICULUM NEEDS.

The new Prentice Hall Science program consists of 19 hardcover books, each of which covers a particular area of science. All of the sciences are represented in the program so you can choose the perfect fit to *your* particular curriculum needs.

The flexibility of this program will allow you to teach those topics you want to teach, and to teach them *in-depth*. Virtually any approach to science—general, integrated, coordinated, thematic, etc.—is possible with Prentice Hall Science.

Above all, the program is designed to make your teaching experience easier and more fun.

ELECTRICITY AND MAGNETISM
Ch. 1. Electric Charges and Currents
Ch. 2. Magnetism
Ch. 3. Electromagnetism
Ch. 4. Electronics and Computers

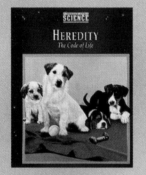

HEREDITY: THE CODE OF LIFE
Ch. 1. What is Genetics?
Ch. 2. How Chromosomes Work
Ch. 3. Human Genetics
Ch. 4. Applied Genetics

ECOLOGY: EARTH'S LIVING RESOURCES
Ch. 1. Interactions Among Living Things
Ch. 2. Cycles in Nature
Ch. 3. Exploring Earth's Biomes
Ch. 4. Wildlife Conservation

PARADE OF LIFE: MONERANS, PROTISTS, FUNGI, AND PLANTS
Ch. 1. Classification of Living Things
Ch. 2. Viruses and Monerans
Ch. 3. Protists
Ch. 4. Fungi
Ch. 5. Plants Without Seeds
Ch. 6. Plants With Seeds

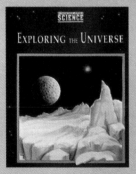

EXPLORING THE UNIVERSE
Ch. 1. Stars and Galaxies
Ch. 2. The Solar System
Ch. 3. Earth and Its Moon

EVOLUTION: CHANGE OVER TIME
Ch. 1. Earth's History in Fossils
Ch. 2. Changes in Living Things Over Time
Ch. 3. The Path to Modern Humans

EXPLORING EARTH'S WEATHER
Ch. 1. What Is Weather?
Ch. 2. What Is Climate?
Ch. 3. Climate in the United States

THE NATURE OF SCIENCE
Ch. 1. What is Science?
Ch. 2. Measurement and the Sciences
Ch. 3. Tools and the Sciences

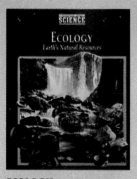

ECOLOGY:
EARTH'S NATURAL RESOURCES
Ch. 1. Energy Resources
Ch. 2. Earth's Nonliving Resources
Ch. 3. Pollution
Ch. 4. Conserving Earth's Resources

MOTION, FORCES, AND ENERGY
Ch. 1. What Is Motion?
Ch. 2. The Nature of Forces
Ch. 3. Forces in Fluids
Ch. 4. Work, Power, and Simple Machines
Ch. 5. Energy: Forms and Changes

PARADE OF LIFE: ANIMALS
Ch. 1. Sponges, Cnidarians, Worms, and Mollusks
Ch. 2. Arthropods and Echinoderms
Ch. 3. Fish and Amphibians
Ch. 4. Reptiles and Birds
Ch. 5. Mammals

CELLS:
BUILDING BLOCKS OF LIFE
Ch. 1. The Nature of LIfe
Ch. 2. Cell Structure and Function
Ch. 3. Cell Processes
Ch. 4. Cell Energy

DYNAMIC EARTH
Ch. 1. Movement of the Earth's Crust
Ch. 2. Earthquakes and Volcanoes
Ch. 3. Plate Tectonics
Ch. 4. Rocks and Minerals
Ch. 5. Weathering and Soil Formation
Ch. 6. Erosion and Deposition

MATTER: BUILDING BLOCK OF THE UNIVERSE
Ch. 1. General Properties of Matter
Ch. 2. Physical and Chemical Changes
Ch. 3. Mixtures, Elements, and Compounds
Ch. 4. Atoms: Building Blocks of Matter
Ch. 5. Classification of Elements: The Periodic Table

CHEMISTRY OF MATTER
Ch. 1. Atoms and Bonding
Ch. 2. Chemical Reactions
Ch. 3. Families of Chemical Compounds
Ch. 4. Chemical Technology
Ch. 5. Radioactive Elements

HUMAN BIOLOGY AND HEALTH
Ch. 1. The Human Body
Ch. 2. Skeletal and Muscular Systems
Ch. 3. Digestive System
Ch. 4. Circulatory System
Ch. 5. Respiratory and Excretory Systems
Ch. 6. Nervous and Endocrine Systems
Ch. 7. Reproduction and Development
Ch. 8. Immune System
Ch. 9. Alcohol, Tobacco, and Drugs

EXPLORING PLANET EARTH
Ch. 1. Earth's Atmosphere
Ch. 2. Earth's Oceans
Ch. 3. Earth's Fresh Water
Ch. 4. Earth's Landmasses
Ch. 5. Earth's Interior

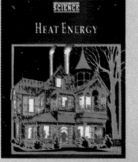

HEAT ENERGY
Ch. 1. What Is Heat?
Ch. 2. Uses of Heat

SOUND AND LIGHT
Ch. 1. Characteristics of Waves
Ch. 2. Sound and Its Uses
Ch. 3. Light and the Electro-magnetic Spectrum
Ch. 4. Light and Its Uses

A COMPLETELY INTEGRATED LEARNING SYSTEM...

The Prentice Hall Science program is an *integrated* learning system with a variety of print materials and multimedia components. All are designed to meet the needs of diverse learning styles and your technology needs.

THE STUDENT BOOK

Each book is a model of **excellent writing and dynamic visuals**—designed to be exciting and motivating to the student *and* the teacher, with relevant examples integrated throughout, and more opportunities for many different activities which apply to everyday life.

Problem-solving activities emphasize the thinking process, so problems may be more open-ended.

"Discovery Activities" throughout the book foster active learning.

Different sciences, and **other disciplines, are integrated throughout** the text and reinforced in the "Connections" features (the connections between computers and viruses is one example).

TEACHER'S RESOURCE PACKAGE

In addition to the student book, the complete teaching package contains:

ANNOTATED TEACHER'S EDITION

Designed to provide **"teacher-friendly"** support regardless of instructional approach:

■ **Help is readily available** if you choose to teach thematically, to integrate the sciences, and/or to integrate the sciences with other curriculum areas.

■ **Activity-based learning** is easy to implement through the use of Discovery Strategies, Activity Suggestions, and Teacher Demonstrations.

■ Integration of all components is part of the teaching strategies.

■ For instant accessibility, all of the teaching suggestions are wrapped around the student pages to which they refer.

ACTIVITY BOOK

Includes a **discovery activity for each chapter**, plus other activities including problem-solving and cooperative-learning activities.

THE REVIEW AND REINFORCEMENT GUIDE

Addresses **students' different learning styles** in a clear and comprehensive format:

■ Highly visual for visual learners.

TEACHER'S RESOURCE PACKAGE

FOR THE PERFECT FIT TO YOUR TEACHING NEEDS.

■ Can be used in conjunction with the program's audiotapes for auditory and language learners.

■ More than a study guide, it's a guide to comprehension, with activities, key concepts, and vocabulary.

ENGLISH AND SPANISH AUDIOTAPES

Correlate with the Review and Reinforcement Guide to aid auditory learners.

LABORATORY MANUAL ANNOTATED TEACHER'S EDITION

Offers **at least one additional hands-on opportunity per chapter** with

answers and teaching suggestions on lab preparation and safety.

TEST BOOK

Contains **traditional and up-to-the-minute strategies for student assessment.** Choose from performance-based tests in addition to traditional chapter tests and computer test bank questions.

STUDENT LABORATORY MANUAL

Each of the 19 books also comes with its own Student Lab Manual.

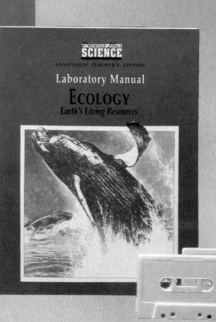

ALSO INCLUDED IN THE INTEGRATED LEARNING SYSTEM:

- Teacher's Desk Reference
- English Guide for Language Learners
- Spanish Guide for Language Learners
- Product Testing Activities
- Transparencies

- Computer Test Bank (IBM, Apple, or MAC)
- VHS Videos
- Videodiscs
- Interactive Videodiscs (Level III)
- Interactive Videodiscs/ CD ROM
- Courseware

All components are integrated in the teaching strategies in the Annotated Teacher's Edition, where they directly relate to the science content.

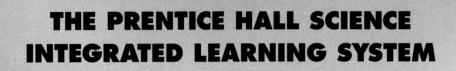

THE PRENTICE HALL SCIENCE
INTEGRATED LEARNING SYSTEM

The following components are integrated in the teaching strategies for
EXPLORING PLANET EARTH.

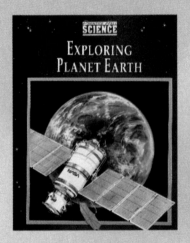

- **Spanish Audiotape**
  English Audiotape

- **Activity Book**

- **Review and**
  Reinforcement Guide

- **Test Book—including**
  Performance-Based Tests

- **Laboratory Manual,**
  Annotated Teacher's Edition

- **Product-Testing Activities:**
  Testing Bottled Water

- **Laboratory Manual**

- **English Guide for**
  Language Learners

- **Spanish Guide for**
  Language Learners

- **Transparencies:**
  Ocean Floor Features
  Ocean Wave Characteristics
  Long-Distance Surface
    Currents
  Rip Currents
  The Water Cycle
  S and P Waves
  Landscape Regions

- **Videos/Videodiscs:**
  Earth's Atmosphere
  Wind and Air Currents

- **Videodiscs:**
  Aquatic Ecosystems:
    Freshwater Wetlands and
    Freshwater
  Aquatic Ecosystems:
    Estuaries and Marine

- **Interactive Videodiscs:**
  Investigating Science:
    Treasures From the Deep
  Planet Earth: The Force
    Within
  ScienceVision: TerraVision
  On Dry Land: The Desert
    Biome
  ScienceVision: EcoVision
  The Blue Planet

- **Interactive Videodisc/**
  CD ROM:
  Amazonia

INTEGRATING OTHER SCIENCES

Many of the other 18 Prentice Hall Science books can be integrated into **EXPLORING PLANET EARTH.**
The books you will find suggested most often in the Annotated Teacher's Edition are EXPLORING THE
UNIVERSE; CHEMISTRY OF MATTER; SOUND AND LIGHT; CELLS: BUILDING BLOCKS OF LIFE;
HUMAN BIOLOGY AND HEALTH; ECOLOGY: EARTH'S LIVING RESOURCES; EXPLORING EARTH'S
WEATHER; DYNAMIC EARTH; HEAT ENERGY; MATTER: BUILDING BLOCK OF THE UNIVERSE;
PARADE OF LIFE: MONERANS, PROTISTS, FUNGI, AND PLANTS; ECOLOGY: EARTH'S NATURAL
RESOURCES; PARADE OF LIFE: ANIMALS; and ELECTRICITY AND MAGNETISM.

INTEGRATING THEMES

Many themes can be integrated into **EXPLORING PLANET EARTH.**
Following are the ones most commonly suggested in the Annotated Teacher's Edition: ENERGY, SCALE
AND STRUCTURE, SYSTEMS AND INTERACTIONS, PATTERNS OF CHANGE, and STABILITY.

For more detailed information on teaching thematically and integrating
the sciences, see the Teacher's Desk Reference and teaching strategies throughout
the Annotated Teacher's Edition.

For more information, call 1-800-848-9500 or write:

 P R E N T I C E   H A L L

Simon & Schuster Education Group
113 Sylvan Avenue Route 9W
Englewood Cliffs, New Jersey 07632
Simon & Schuster A Paramount Communications Company

Annotated Teacher's Edition

Prentice Hall Science
Exploring Planet Earth

Anthea Maton
Former NSTA National
    Coordinator
Project Scope, Sequence,
    Coordination
Washington, DC

Jean Hopkins
Science Instructor and Department
    Chairperson
John H. Wood Middle School
San Antonio, Texas

Susan Johnson
Professor of Biology
Ball State University
Muncie, Indiana

David LaHart
Senior Instructor
Florida Solar Energy Center
Cape Canaveral, Florida

Maryanna Quon Warner
Science Instructor
Del Dios Middle School
Escondido, California

Jill D. Wright
Professor of Science Education
Director of International Field
    Programs
University of Pittsburgh
Pittsburgh, Pennsylvania

Prentice Hall
A Division of Simon & Schuster
Englewood Cliffs, New Jersey

ISBN 0-13-400607-0

3 4 5 6 7 8 9 10   97 96 95 94

Contents of Annotated Teacher's Edition

To the Teacher

Welcome to the *Prentice Hall Science* program. *Prentice Hall Science* has been designed as a complete program for use with middle school or junior high school science students. The program covers all relevant areas of science and has been developed with the flexibility to meet virtually all your curriculum needs. In addition, the program has been designed to better enable you—the classroom teacher—to integrate various disciplines of science into your daily lessons, as well as to enhance the thematic teaching of science.

The *Prentice Hall Science* program consists of nineteen books, each of which covers a particular topic area. The nineteen books in the *Prentice Hall Science* program are

The Nature of Science
Parade of Life: Monerans, Protists, Fungi, and Plants
Parade of Life: Animals
Cells: Building Blocks of Life
Heredity: The Code of Life
Evolution: Change Over Time

Ecology: Earth's Living Resources
Human Biology and Health
Exploring Planet Earth
Dynamic Earth
Exploring Earth's Weather
Ecology: Earth's Natural Resources
Exploring the Universe
Matter: Building Block of the Universe
Chemistry of Matter
Electricity and Magnetism
Heat Energy
Sound and Light
Motion, Forces, and Energy

Each of the student editions listed above also comes with a complete set of teaching materials and student ancillary materials. Furthermore, videos, interactive videos and science courseware are available for the *Prentice Hall Science* program. This combination of student texts and ancillaries, teacher materials, and multimedia products makes up your complete *Prentice Hall Science* Learning System.

About the Teacher's Desk Reference

The *Teacher's Desk Reference* provides you, the teacher, with an insight into the workings of the *Prentice Hall Science* program. The *Teacher's Desk Reference* accomplishes this task by including all the standard information you need to know about *Prentice Hall Science*.

The *Teacher's Desk Reference* presents an overview of the program, including a full description of each ancillary available in the program. It gives a brief summary of each of the student textbooks available in the *Prentice Hall Science* Learning System. The *Teacher's Desk Reference* also demonstrates how the seven science themes incorporated into *Prentice Hall Science* are woven throughout the entire program.

In addition, the *Teacher's Desk Reference* presents a detailed discussion of the features of the Student

Edition and the features of the Annotated Teacher's Edition, as well as an overview section that summarizes issues in science education and offers a message about teaching special students. Selected instructional essays in the *Teacher's Desk Reference* include English as a Second Language (ESL), Multicultural Teaching, Cooperative-Learning Strategies, and Integrated Science Teaching, in addition to other relevant topics. Further, a discussion of the Multimedia components that are part of *Prentice Hall Science*, as well as how they can be integrated with the textbooks, is included in the *Teacher's Desk Reference*.

The *Teacher's Desk Reference* also contains in blackline master form a booklet on Teaching Graphing Skills, which may be reproduced for student use.

Integrating the Sciences

The *Prentice Hall Science* Learning System has been designed to allow you to teach science from an integrated point of view. Great care has been taken to integrate other science disciplines, where appropriate, into the chapter content and visuals. In addition, the integration of other disciplines such as social studies and literature has been incorporated into each textbook.

On the reduced student pages throughout your Annotated Teacher's Edition you will find numbers within blue bullets beside selected passages and visuals. An Annotation Key in the wraparound margins indicates the particular branch of science or other discipline that has been integrated into the student text. In addition, where appropriate, the name of the textbook and the chapter number in which the particular topic is discussed in greater detail is provided. This enables you to further integrate a particular science topic by using the complete *Prentice Hall Science* Learning System.

Thematic Overview

When teaching any science topic, you may want to focus your lessons around the underlying themes that pertain to all areas of science. These underlying themes are the framework from which all science can be constructed and taught. The seven underlying themes incorporated into *Prentice Hall Science* are

Energy
Evolution
Patterns of Change
Scale and Structure
Systems and Interactions
Unity and Diversity
Stability

The primary themes in this textbook are Energy, Patterns of Change, Scale and Structure, Systems and Interactions, and Stability. Primary themes throughout *Prentice Hall Science* are denoted by an asterisk.

A detailed discussion of each of these themes and how they are incorporated into the *Prentice Hall Science* program are included in your *Teacher's Desk Reference*. In addition, the *Teacher's Desk Reference* includes thematic matrices for the *Prentice Hall Science* program.

A thematic matrix for each chapter in this textbook follows. Each thematic matrix is designed with the list of themes along the left-hand column and in the right-hand column a big idea, or overarching concept statement, as to how that particular theme is taught in the chapter.

CHAPTER 1

Earth's Atmosphere

*ENERGY	• The energy of the sun makes life possible on Earth. The energy of the sun also contributes to the formation of characteristic layers in the atmosphere.
EVOLUTION	• The composition of the Earth's atmosphere has changed greatly over time.
*PATTERNS OF CHANGE	• Over billions of years, the atmosphere has been altered by the organisms that live on Earth. The composition of today's atmosphere remains relatively constant.
*SCALE AND STRUCTURE	• The Earth's atmosphere can be divided into four layers: the troposphere, stratosphere, mesosphere, and thermosphere.
*SYSTEMS AND INTERACTIONS	• Many of the gases in the atmosphere are cycled through living systems. These gases return to the atmosphere when organisms die and decay.
UNITY AND DIVERSITY	• Different layers in the atmosphere contain varying amounts of certain gases.
*STABILITY	• Today, the percentages of the gases found in the atmosphere remain relatively constant.

CHAPTER 2

Earth's Oceans

*ENERGY	• The energy of the wind causes the formation of waves. • The energy of an earthquake can produce a tsunami, a huge "wave" that carries much destructive energy with it.
EVOLUTION	• Ocean life has changed over time. Today, the life zones in the ocean support organisms that are adapted to the environmental conditions that exist there.
*PATTERNS OF CHANGE	• The amounts and kinds of dissolved materials in the ocean are variable. Salts and other dissolved materials are carried to the oceans by rivers and streams, deposited in the ocean by volcanic activity, and dissolved in the oceans by wave activity.
*SCALE AND STRUCTURE	• The Earth's oceans can be divided into three life zones: intertidal zone, neritic zone, and bathyal zone. • The Earth's crust is thinner under the ocean than on land.
*SYSTEMS AND INTERACTIONS	• Water in the atmosphere is cycled through the Earth's oceans. The sun's energy causes water to evaporate into the atmosphere, leaving salts behind. This pure water falls on land and then returns to the oceans in rivers and streams and as runoff.
UNITY AND DIVERSITY	• The Earth's crust that lies under the ocean has higher mountains and deeper valleys than the crust on land. • Different water temperatures and density areas in the ocean contain varying amounts of certain gases and other dissolved materials.
*STABILITY	• The salinity of ocean water remains within a relatively narrow range. It varies from 33 to 37 parts per thousand and averages 35 parts per thousand.

CHAPTER 3

Earth's Fresh Water

*ENERGY	• The energy of the sun provides the energy to drive the water cycle that replenishes Earth's supply of fresh water.
EVOLUTION	
*PATTERNS OF CHANGE	• During the water cycle, water undergoes evaporation, condensation, and precipitation.
*SCALE AND STRUCTURE	• Water molecules have polarity. This property enables water to act as a solvent for many different substances. Because water can dissolve so many different substances, it is called the universal solvent.
*SYSTEMS AND INTERACTIONS	• Water evaporates from the ocean, leaving salts behind. This water becomes part of the atmosphere. Eventually this water forms precipitation. • There is a constant movement of water from the ocean to the land and back to the ocean.
UNITY AND DIVERSITY	• All life on Earth depends on a supply of fresh water.
*STABILITY	• The amount of water and salts in the ocean remains constant. Water that evaporates from the ocean is returned to the ocean by rivers and streams as runoff.

CHAPTER 4

Earth's Landmasses

*ENERGY	
EVOLUTION	• Over time, the surface of the Earth has been altered by natural forces, as well as by the actions of people.
*PATTERNS OF CHANGE	• The Earth's landmasses have different characterististics. These characteristics are often caused by climate conditions.
*SCALE AND STRUCTURE	• The landscape of the Earth varies greatly. Mountains, plains, and plateaus exist on the Earth. These landscape features are characterized, in great part, by their altitude above sea level.
*SYSTEMS AND INTERACTIONS	• Mountains can form in several ways. They may form when magma from within the Earth pushes its way to the surface. Mountains can also form when parts of the Earth's crust are folded or broken.
UNITY AND DIVERSITY	• There are various ways to show the Earth's surface in maps and on globes. Different projections distort the Earth's features in different ways. Topographic maps show surface features of the Earth.
*STABILITY	• The Earth rotates 15° per hour. The Earth has been divided into a series of 24 time zones, each consisting of 15°.

CHAPTER 5

Earth's Interior

*ENERGY	• The energy released during an earthquake generates seismic waves. These waves have been used by scientists to gather information about the Earth's interior.
EVOLUTION	• Over time, the crust of the Earth changes as materials produced within the Earth's interior come to the surface.
*PATTERNS OF CHANGE	• Pressure and temperature increase as you approach the Earth's center.
*SCALE AND STRUCTURE	• There are four layers in the Earth's interior. • Most of the mass and volume of the Earth is contained within the mantle.
*SYSTEMS AND INTERACTIONS	• Iron in the Earth's inner core is believed to be the source of the Earth's magnetic field.
UNITY AND DIVERSITY	• The Earth's inner core is made mostly of iron and nickel. • The mantle and the crust contain other elements in addition to iron and nickel.
*STABILITY	• Conditions of temperature and pressure within the layers of the Earth's interior remain relatively stable.

Comprehensive List of Laboratory Materials

Item	Quantities per Group	Chapter
Aquarium tank or deep-sided pan	1	4
Beakers, small	2	5
Cardboard	1 medium-sized piece	4
Clay, modeling	250 mL	3
	1 large block	4
Containers, shallow	2	1
Cornstarch	15 g	5
Glass, clear	1 pane	4
Graduated cylinder, 500-mL	1	3
Gravel	250 mL	3
Medicine dropper	1	5
Metric ruler	1	4
Paper cups, small	4	3
Pencil, glass-marking	1	4
Plastic tubes of different lengths that contain sediment samples and salt water	several	2
Sand	250 mL	3
Stirring rod, metal, or spoon	1	5
Stopwatch or clock with sweep second hand	1	1
Thermometers	10	1

EXPLORING PLANET EARTH

Anthea Maton
Former NSTA National Coordinator
Project Scope, Sequence, Coordination
Washington, DC

Jean Hopkins
Science Instructor and Department Chairperson
John H. Wood Middle School
San Antonio, Texas

Susan Johnson
Professor of Biology
Ball State University
Muncie, Indiana

David LaHart
Senior Instructor
Florida Solar Energy Center
Cape Canaveral, Florida

Maryanna Quon Warner
Science Instructor
Del Dios Middle School
Escondido, California

Jill D. Wright
Professor of Science Education
Director of International Field Programs
University of Pittsburgh
Pittsburgh, Pennsylvania

Prentice Hall
Englewood Cliffs, New Jersey
Needham, Massachusetts

Prentice Hall Science

Exploring Planet Earth

Student Text and Annotated Teacher's Edition
Laboratory Manual
Teacher's Resource Package
Teacher's Desk Reference
Computer Test Bank
Teaching Transparencies
Product Testing Activities
Computer Courseware
Video and Interactive Video

The illustration on the cover, rendered by Keith Kasnot, shows a research satellite in Earth's orbit.

Credits begin on page 184.

SECOND EDITION

ISBN 0-13-400599-6

2 3 4 5 6 7 8 9 10   97 96 95 94 93

Prentice Hall
A Division of Simon & Schuster
Englewood Cliffs, New Jersey 07632

STAFF CREDITS

Editorial:	Harry Bakalian, Pamela E. Hirschfeld, Maureen Grassi, Robert P. Letendre, Elisa Mui Eiger, Lorraine Smith-Phelan, Christine A. Caputo
Design:	AnnMarie Roselli, Carmela Pereira, Susan Walrath, Leslie Osher, Art Soares
Production:	Suse F. Bell, Joan McCulley, Elizabeth Torjussen, Christina Burghard
Photo Research:	Libby Forsyth, Emily Rose, Martha Conway
Publishing Technology:	Andrew Grey Bommarito, Deborah Jones, Monduane Harris, Michael Colucci, Gregory Myers, Cleasta Wilburn
Marketing:	Andrew Socha, Victoria Willows
Pre-Press Production:	Laura Sanderson, Kathryn Dix, Denise Herckenrath
Manufacturing:	Rhett Conklin, Gertrude Szyferblatt

Consultants

Kathy French	National Science Consultant
Jeannie Dennard	National Science Consultant
Brenda Underwood	National Science Consultant
Janelle Conarton	National Science Consultant

CONTENTS

EXPLORING PLANET EARTH

CONCEPT MAPPING

Throughout your study of science, you will learn a variety of terms, facts, figures, and concepts. Each new topic you encounter will provide its own collection of words and ideas—which, at times, you may think seem endless. But each of the ideas within a particular topic is related in some way to the others. No concept in science is isolated. Thus it will help you to understand the topic if you see the whole picture; that is, the interconnectedness of all the individual terms and ideas. This is a much more effective and satisfying way of learning than memorizing separate facts.

Actually, this should be a rather familiar process for you. Although you may not think about it in this way, you analyze many of the elements in your daily life by looking for relationships or connections. For example, when you look at a collection of flowers, you may divide them into groups: roses, carnations, and daisies. You may then associate colors with these flowers: red, pink, and white. The general topic is flowers. The subtopic is types of flowers. And the colors are specific terms that describe flowers. A topic makes more sense and is more easily understood if you understand how it is broken down into individual ideas and how these ideas are related to one another and to the entire topic.

It is often helpful to organize information visually so that you can see how it all fits together. One technique for describing related ideas is called a **concept map**. In a concept map, an idea is represented by a word or phrase enclosed in a box. There are several ideas in any concept map. A connection between two ideas is made with a line. A word or two that describes the connection is written on or near the line. The general topic is located at the top of the map. That topic is then broken down into subtopics, or more specific ideas, by branching lines. The most specific topics are located at the bottom of the map.

To construct a concept map, first identify the important ideas or key terms in the chapter or section. Do not try to include too much information. Use your judgment as to what is really important. Write the general topic at the top of your map. Let's use an example to help illustrate this process. Suppose you decide that the key terms in a section you are reading are School, Living Things, Language Arts, Subtraction, Grammar, Mathematics, Experiments, Papers, Science, Addition, Novels. The general topic is School. Write and enclose this word in a box at the top of your map.

SCHOOL

Now choose the subtopics—Language Arts, Science, Mathematics. Figure out how they are related to the topic. Add these words to your map. Continue this procedure until you have included all the important ideas and terms. Then use lines to make the appropriate connections between ideas and terms. Don't forget to write a word or two on or near the connecting line to describe the nature of the connection.

Do not be concerned if you have to redraw your map (perhaps several times!) before you show all the important connections clearly. If, for example, you write papers for Science as well as for Language Arts, you may want to place these two subjects next to each other so that the lines do not overlap.

One more thing you should know about concept mapping: Concepts can be correctly mapped in many different ways. In fact, it is unlikely that any two people will draw identical concept maps for a complex topic. Thus there is no one correct concept map for any topic! Even though your concept map may not match those of your classmates, it will be correct as long as it shows the most important concepts and the clear relationships among them. Your concept map will also be correct if it has meaning to you and if it helps you understand the material you are reading. A concept map should be so clear that if some of the terms are erased, the missing terms could easily be filled in by following the logic of the concept map.

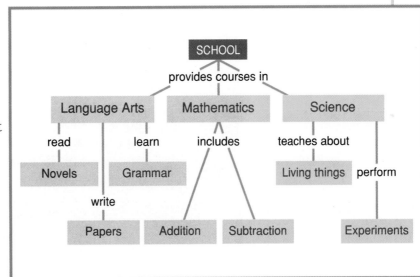

Exploring Planet Earth

TEXT OVERVIEW

In this textbook students are introduced to the various components and structures that make up the Earth. They first study the composition and layers of the Earth's atmosphere and the makeup of the magnetosphere. Then they investigate water on the Earth, dealing first with the oceans and ocean-life forms and then with fresh groundwater and surface water. Students go on to explore the Earth's landmasses, and they learn about topography and mapping. Finally, they are introduced to the Earth's interior and learn about the core, mantle, and crust.

TEXT OBJECTIVES

1. Discuss how the composition of the Earth's atmosphere has changed over time.

2. Describe the layers of the atmosphere and describe the magnetosphere.

3. Identify the properties, life zones, and motions of the Earth's oceans.

4. Explain how the Earth maintains a supply of fresh water.

5. Name the Earth's continents and describe the characteristics of mountains, plains, and plateaus.

6. Describe the types of maps made of the Earth and explain how to interpret such maps.

7. Name and describe the properties of the Earth's layers.

EXPLORING PLANET EARTH

As the *Voyager* spacecraft began its epic journey among the planets of the solar system, it sent back a portrait of the Earth and its moon. During its 13-year voyage, the sturdy spacecraft was to send back thousands of stunning images of the outer planets and their moons before disappearing into the depths of space. But of all the planets and moons on *Voyager*'s travels, Planet Earth is unique.

▲ From the moon, Earth appears as a watery blue planet with swirls of white clouds.

▲◄ This photograph of clouds near the top of the Matterhorn in Switzerland illustrates two features of Earth—landmasses and an atmosphere. Of all the planets, only Earth contains liquid water.

 8 ■ I

INTRODUCING EXPLORING PLANET EARTH

USING THE TEXTBOOK

Begin your introduction of the textbook by having students examine the textbook-opening photographs and captions. Before students read the textbook introduction, ask them the following questions.

• **What are the most noticeable features of Earth in the photograph taken by** *Voyager?* (The blue water and the white clouds.)

• **What is significant about these two visible features of Earth?** (The blue water points out that Earth is the only planet with liquid water and that the white clouds are a reminder of Earth's atmosphere, which is also unique.)

• **Why are water and an atmosphere important?** (Without them, life as we know it could not survive on this planet.)

Have students read the textbook introduction on pages I8 and I9.

• **Why is Earth the planet that interests us the most?** (It is our home, where we live.)

• **Why is Earth's uniqueness both a wonderful and a frightening thing?** (Wonderful because it has evolved the way it has and, therefore, we have evolved the way we have; frightening because there are no other worlds where we could live as we do here.)

CHAPTERS

Of all the planets in our solar system, only Earth has oceans and rivers of liquid water on its surface. And only Earth is surrounded by a blanket of breathable air. In the pages that follow, you will learn about the Earth's oceans, its freshwater lakes and rivers, and the atmosphere that surrounds it. You will also learn about Earth's landmasses—its mountains, plains, and plateaus. And you will take a journey to the center of the Earth to study its interior.

Voyager has given us a valuable glimpse of the worlds that make up the sun's family. In this textbook, you will explore the world that interests us most—our home, Planet Earth.

Raging Iguassu Falls in Brazil demonstrates how Earth's surface is changed by moving water. ▶

Discovery *Activity*

Neighborhood Mapping

Use a large sheet of plain, white paper and colored pencils to draw a map of your neighborhood. Show the location of houses, schools, libraries, streets, and other local features, as well as any natural features such as bodies of water. Include a scale and a key to indicate direction on your neighborhood map.

■ Trade maps with a classmate. Can you find your way around using your classmate's map? Can your classmate use your map to find a specific location in your neighborhood?

■ What features make a map useful?

CHAPTER DESCRIPTIONS

1 Earth's Atmosphere In Chapter 1 the composition of the atmosphere is discussed, and the characteristics of the various layers of the atmosphere are explained. The chapter closes with a description of the makeup of the Earth's magnetosphere.

2 Earth's Oceans The oceans of the world are discussed in Chapter 2. The properties of ocean water are presented. The topography of the ocean floor is then described, along with ocean-life zones and methods of ocean-floor mapping. Finally, the motions of the ocean and their effects are discussed.

3 Earth's Fresh Water The major sources of fresh water are discussed in Chapter 3. The contribution of groundwater to such sources of fresh water is described. Finally, the property of water as a solvent is treated.

4 Earth's Landmasses In Chapter 4 the names and characteristics of the Earth's continents are presented. The characteristics of mountains, plains, and plateaus are also discussed. The advantages and disadvantages of various types of maps are explained, and methods for interpreting topographic maps are described.

5 Earth's Interior Chapter 5 deals with the layers of the Earth. The properties of the inner core, outer core, mantle, and crust are described, and the Moho is discussed. Seismic waves are also introduced, as indicators of the Earth's inner structure.

• **Why do you think it could be important for you to know about Earth's oceans, lakes and rivers, landmasses, and atmosphere?** (Accept all answers. Lead students to understand that these are the things that make up Earth, and they are important to Earth and important to us. They are the things that we all must work to protect so that Earth will survive and, therefore, we will survive.)

DISCOVERY ACTIVITY

Neighborhood Mapping

Begin your introduction to the textbook by having students perform the Discovery Activity. Suggest to students that while they are drawing their maps, they keep in mind the needs of their future users. How can they organize and illustrate their maps so that they will be easy to use? If necessary, review the functions of a map scale and key with students. When students have finished their maps

and traded them with a classmate, give students specific places to find or routes to follow using their partner's map. For example, can they find their way from home to school? Can they locate the nearest public library or grocery store? Ask students to note things they like and do not like about the map to use in a later discussion about useful map features.

Chapter 1 — EARTH'S ATMOSPHERE

SECTION	HANDS-ON ACTIVITIES
1–1 A View of Planet Earth: Spheres Within a Sphere pages I12–I15 Multicultural Opportunity 1–1, p. I12 ESL Strategy 1–1, p. I12	**Activity Book** CHAPTER DISCOVERY: Plants and the Atmosphere, p. I9 **Teacher Edition** Air Pressure, p. I10d
1–2 Development of the Atmosphere pages I15–I24 Multicultural Opportunity 1–2, p. I15 ESL Strategy 1–2, p. I15	**Student Edition** ACTIVITY (Discovering): Clean Air Anyone? p. I22 ACTIVITY BANK: A Model of Acid Rain, p. I166 **Laboratory Manual** Finding the Percentage of Oxygen in the Atmosphere, p. I7
1–3 Layers of the Atmosphere pages I25–I33 Multicultural Opportunity 1–3, p. I25 ESL Strategy 1–3, p. I25	**Student Edition** ACTIVITY (Discovering): The Temperature Plot, p. I26 LABORATORY INVESTIGATION: Radiant Energy and Surface Temperature, p. I36 **Laboratory Manual** Effect of the Atmosphere on Cooling Rates of the Earth's Surface, p. I11 **Teacher Edition** Density, p. I10d
1–4 The Magnetosphere pages I34–I35 Multicultural Opportunity 1–4, p. I34 ESL Strategy 1–4, p. I34	**Activity Book** ACTIVITY: Plotting Radio Reception, p. I21
Chapter Review pages I36–I39	

OUTSIDE TEACHER RESOURCES

Books

Goody, Richard, and James C. Walker, *Atmospheres*, Prentice-Hall.

McCormac, B. M., ed. *Atmospheres of Earth and the Planets*, Reidel Pub.

McEwan, M. J., and L. F. Phillips. *The Chemistry of the Atmosphere*, Halstad.

Riehl, H. *Introduction to the Atmosphere*, McGraw-Hill.

Audiovisuals

The Air Around Us, filmstrip with cassette, CRM/McGraw-Hill

The Atmosphere and Its Effect, filmstrip with cassette, Eye Gate

OTHER ACTIVITIES	MEDIA AND TECHNOLOGY
Student Edition ACTIVITY (Reading): Explorers of the Atmosphere—and Beyond, p. I15 **Activity Book** ACTIVITY: Land, Water, and Air Temperature Changes, p. I17 **Review and Reinforcement Guide** Section 1–1, p. I5	**Video** A Breath of Fresh Air (Supplemental) **Interactive Videodisc** The Blue Planet **English/Spanish Audiotapes** Section 1–1
Activity Book ACTIVITY: Composition of the Atmosphere: A Graphic Model, p. I29 **Review and Reinforcement Guide** Section 1–2, p. I9	**Video/Videodisc** Earth's Atmosphere **English/Spanish Audiotapes** Section 1–2
Student Edition ACTIVITY (Calculating): How Thick Are the Atmosphere's Layers? p. I28 **Activity Book** ACTIVITY: It's Getting Colder, p. I13 ACTIVITY: Examining Temperature Patterns in the Atmosphere, p. I15 ACTIVITY: Global Wind Patterns, p. I23 ACTIVITY: Temperature and Pressure Patterns in the Troposphere, p. I27 **Review and Reinforcement Guide** Section 1–3, p. I13	**Video/Videodisc** Wind and Air Currents Global Forecasting (Supplemental) **English/Spanish Audiotapes** Section 1–3
Review and Reinforcement Guide Section 1–4, p. I15	**English/Spanish Audiotapes** Section 1–4
Test Book Chapter Test, p. I9 Performance-Based Tests, p. I119	**Test Book** Computer Test Bank Test, p. I15

*All materials in the Chapter Planning Guide Grid are available as part of the Prentice Hall Science Learning System.

The Atmosphere in Motion, 16-mm film or video, Encyclopaedia Britannica

CHAPTER OVERVIEW

Earth is the third planet from the sun and the largest of the inner planets. It is the only planet that supports living things. The Earth's three main features are most important to life. These are the ground you walk on, the water you drink, and the air you breathe.

The Earth's atmosphere was once very different from what it is today. The earliest atmosphere consisted primarily of two gases that are harmful to most kinds of life: methane and ammonia. Then, chemical reactions triggered by the sun produced nitrogen, carbon dioxide, and hydrogen. Later, the ozone layer that surrounds the Earth formed, and oxygen was added to the atmosphere as ocean plants carried on photosynthesis. The present atmosphere contains mostly nitrogen and oxygen, as well as small amounts of carbon dioxide and other gases.

The atmosphere is divided into four main layers: the troposphere, the stratosphere, the mesosphere, and the thermosphere. Each layer has special characteristics; for example, the temperature and the density of air change with altitude. Beyond the atmosphere is the magnetosphere, a region affected by the Earth's magnetic field.

1-1 A VIEW OF PLANET EARTH: SPHERES WITHIN A SPHERE
THEMATIC FOCUS

The purpose of this section is to introduce students to the major features of the Earth. The Earth's circumference at the equator is about 40,075 kilometers. Its three main features are the ground, the water, and the air.

The ground, or lithosphere, is part of the Earth's crust, or solid outer shell. The lithosphere includes all landmasses and the crust under the waters. The water of the Earth's surface is called the hydrosphere. The hydrosphere includes all the bodies of water, as well as the waters of the polar icecaps, icebergs, and glaciers. The air surrounding the Earth is called the atmosphere.

The themes that can be focused on in this section are energy and scale and structure.

*Energy: The energy of the Sun makes life possible on Earth.

*Scale and structure: The Earth and its environment may be studied in three major parts: land, water, and air.

PERFORMANCE OBJECTIVES 1-1

1. Describe some of the Earth's vital statistics, such as its diameter and equator.
2. Discuss the three main features of the Earth: its rocky lithosphere, its watery hydrosphere, and its gaseous atmosphere.
3. Explain how the equator divides the Earth into two hemispheres.

SCIENCE TERMS 1-1

equator p. I12
hemisphere p. I12
lithosphere p. I13
hydrosphere p. I13
atmosphere p. I15

1-2 DEVELOPMENT OF THE ATMOSPHERE
THEMATIC FOCUS

The purpose of this section is to explain the development of the Earth's atmosphere. Students will learn that about 4 billion years ago, the Earth's atmosphere consisted of two deadly gases—methane and ammonia—as well as some water vapor. Several hundred million years later, a series of chemical reactions triggered by sunlight caused nitrogen, hydrogen, and carbon dioxide to form.

Students will learn how the breakdown of water vapor in the upper atmosphere produced the ozone layer. They will also learn how the process of photosynthesis, the process plants use to make food, added oxygen to the atmosphere.

The themes that can be focused on in this section are evolution, systems and interactions, and patterns of change.

Evolution: The composition of the Earth's atmosphere has changed greatly over time.

*Systems and interactions: Many of the gases in the atmosphere are cycled through living systems. These gases return to the atmosphere when organisms die and decay.

*Patterns of change: Over billions of years, the atmosphere of Earth has been altered by the organisms that live there. The composition of today's atmosphere remains relatively constant.

PERFORMANCE OBJECTIVES 1-2

1. Describe the composition of the Earth's early atmosphere.
2. Explain how chemical reactions in the atmosphere produced nitrogen, hydrogen, and carbon dioxide.
3. Describe the formation of the ozone shield.

SCIENCE TERMS 1-2

ozone p. I17

1-3 LAYERS OF THE ATMOSPHERE
THEMATIC FOCUS

The purpose of this section is to introduce students to the four main layers of the atmosphere: the troposphere, the stratosphere, the mesosphere, and the thermosphere. Students will learn that the atmosphere is divided into these layers according to major changes in temperature.

Students will learn about the ozone layer that exists in the stratosphere. The ozone layer is important because it protects the Earth from the sun's ultraviolet rays.

The themes that can be focused on in this section are unity and diversity and stability.

Unity and diversity: Different layers in the atmosphere contain varying amounts of certain gases.

*Stability: Today, the percentages of the gases found in the atmosphere remain relatively constant.

PERFORMANCE OBJECTIVES 1–3

1. Describe the composition of the four main layers of the Earth's atmosphere.
2. Explain why ozone is important to life on Earth.

SCIENCE TERMS 1–3

air pressure p. I25
troposphere p. I26
convection current p. I27
stratosphere p. I27
jet stream p. I27
mesosphere p. I28
thermosphere p. I30
ionosphere p. I31
ion p. I31
exosphere p. I32

1–4 THE MAGNETOSPHERE
THEMATIC FOCUS

The purpose of this section is to introduce students to the magnetosphere. The magnetosphere, which is located in the upper atmosphere, is the area of the Earth's magnetic field.

Students will learn that the magnetosphere is made up of positively charged protons and negatively charged electrons. These charged particles are concentrated into belts, or layers, of high radiation called the Van Allen radiation belts.

Students will discover the cause of the auroras, or northern and southern lights. When a solar flare occurs, the magnetosphere is bombarded by a large number of charged particles from the sun. As these particles collide with other particles in the upper atmosphere, light is given off.

The themes that can be focused on in this section are scale and structure and systems and interactions.

*Scale and structure: The Earth's atmosphere can be divided into four layers: the troposphere, the stratosphere, the mesosphere, and the thermosphere. Beyond the atmosphere is the magnetosphere, a region made up of electrically charged particles.

*Systems and interactions: Solar flares on the sun bombard the magnetosphere, producing the northern and southern lights.

PERFORMANCE OBJECTIVES 1–4

1. Describe the Earth's magnetic field.
2. Describe the Van Allen radiation belts.
3. Explain how the aurora borealis and aurora australis are caused.

SCIENCE TERMS 1–4

magnetosphere p. I34
Van Allen radiation belts p. I35

Discovery *Learning*

TEACHER DEMONSTRATIONS MODELING

Air Pressure

In this demonstration the relationship between temperature and air pressure will be illustrated. For the demonstration you will need a can with a lid, water, some ice, and a hot plate.

Fill the can with water to a height of about 3 centimeters. Leave the can uncovered. Using the hot plate, heat the can until the water begins to boil After several minutes, place the lid tightly on the can. Turn off the hot plate and rub both sides of the can with ice. The can should collapse. After students have observed the demonstration, as these questions.

• **What do you think caused the can to collapse?** (Answers may vary, but the correct answer is that the decrease in temperature caused a decrease in air pressure inside the can.)
• **Does this suggest to you a relationship between temperature and pressure?** (As temperature decreases, pressure decreases.)
• **Can you apply this principle to some everyday situations?** (Possible answers include these: Tire pressure is lower in the winter than in the summer; carbonated beverages tend to explode or bubble over if left in the sun; aerosol spray cans can explode if exposed to high heat.)

Density

For this demonstration you will need 40 marbles (beans or jelly beans may be substituted), a small saucer, and a large plate or tray.

Divide the marbles into two groups of 20 each. Ask students to imagine that each marble represents a particle of air. Place one group of 20 marbles in the small saucer. Put the marbles as close together as possible. Then place the other 20 marbles on the large plate or tray, spreading the marbles out as far as possible.

• **In which container is the density of marbles greater?** (In the small saucer.)
• **Why?** (There are many more marbles per unit of space.)

Explain that air particles near the Earth's surface can be compared to the marbles in the saucer, whereas air particles many kilometers above the Earth's surface can be compared to the marbles in the large plate or tray.

• **Based on your observations, can you explain why a mountain climber might need an oxygen mask at high altitudes?** (At high altitudes there is less air in a given amount of space. Because air contains oxygen, there would also be fewer oxygen molecules that are available.)

CHAPTER 1
Earth's Atmosphere

INTEGRATING SCIENCE

This earth science chapter provides you with numerous opportunities to integrate other areas of science, as well as other disciplines, into your curriculum. Blue numbered annotations on the student page and integration notes on the teacher wraparound pages alert you to areas of possible integration.

In this chapter you can integrate social studies (p. 12), earth science and astronomy (pp. 12, 28, 32), physical science and solutions (p. 13), language arts (p. 15), physical science and the electromagnetic spectrum (pp. 17, 31), life science and photosynthesis (p. 18), life science and human physiology (p. 19), life science and ecology (pp. 21, 24), earth science and meteorology (pp. 21, 25), earth science and geology (p. 22), mathematics (pp. 26, 28), physical science and heat (pp. 27, 31), life science and health (p. 33), physical science and matter (p. 34), and physical science and light (p. 35).

SCIENCE, TECHNOLOGY, AND SOCIETY/COOPERATIVE LEARNING

The ozone layer in the stratosphere protects all life on Earth by absorbing harmful ultraviolet radiation from the sun. But in the troposphere, ozone makes the air unhealthy for people and animals to breathe and may stunt the growth of some plants.

Ozone pollution is caused when hydrocarbons escape into the air through evaporation or burning and mix with other

INTRODUCING CHAPTER 1

DISCOVERY LEARNING

▶ *Activity Book*

Begin your introduction to this chapter by using the Chapter 1 Discovery Activity from the *Activity Book*. Using this activity, students will discover some ways that green plants affect the Earth's atmosphere.

USING THE TEXTBOOK

Because the atmosphere is invisible, it is something that we often take for granted. Without the gases, temperature control, and moisture that the atmosphere provides, however, humans could not live on Earth. One reason that life as we know it does not exist on other planets is that these planets lack an atmosphere that is similar to ours.

Begin by having students observe the beautiful cloud photograph that opens the chapter.

• **Can you describe what you see in this picture?** (Towering clouds against a blue sky. The formation of the clouds gives the feeling of rising far up into the atmosphere.)

• **Are clouds all the same, or do they differ?** (Most students will have noticed that clouds come in a variety of shapes and are found at different altitudes. Some will point out that rain clouds appear darker than the clouds in the chapter-opener photograph.)

Earth's Atmosphere

Guide for Reading

After you read the following sections, you will be able to

1–1 A View of Planet Earth: Spheres Within a Sphere
- Describe some of the major features of the Earth.

1–2 Development of the Atmosphere
- Identify the gases found in Earth's atmosphere.
- Describe the Earth's early atmosphere and the processes that changed it over time.
- Explain the nitrogen, and the carbon dioxide and oxygen cycles.

1–3 Layers of the Atmosphere
- Compare the various layers of the atmosphere.

1–4 The Magnetosphere
- Describe the features of the magnetosphere.

People have walked on the surface of the moon. Machines have landed upon and scratched at the surface of Mars. Rockets have carried satellites on photographic missions into the darkness of space beyond the farthest reaches of our solar system. These voyages of exploration represent great leaps that took the minds—and sometimes even the bodies—of humans far from the comforts of their Earthly home.

Yet people forget that Earth too is a wondrous planet on a fantastic voyage. In just one year's time, Earth will make a complete trip around the sun—taking you, your family and friends, and the remainder of humanity on a fabulous journey. In many ways, Earth is like a giant spacecraft transporting a special cargo of life.

Why is Earth the only planet in our solar system uniquely able to support life? In this chapter you will learn about the Earth's atmosphere—the special envelope of air that surrounds our planet home as it journeys through space. The atmosphere is one reason there is life on Earth.

Journal *Activity*

You and Your World Have you ever thought about being an astronaut? What kind of training do you think you would need to become an astronaut? In what ways do you think life in space would be different from life on Earth? Draw a picture in your journal of what you think it would be like to float in space and describe some of the conditions you would expect to encounter.

◄ *Towering clouds are a familiar sight in the Earth's atmosphere.*

• **Have any of you ever ridden above the clouds in an airplane?** (Answers will vary.)

• **Did the clouds you saw resemble the clouds in the photograph?** (Answers will vary.)

• **Did you find that the airplane ride tended to be bumpy or smooth as you flew over clouds?** (Answers may vary, but a flight above the clouds is usually smooth.)

Tell students that two early explorers of the atmosphere were James Glaisher and Henry Coxwell. These two men investigated the atmosphere in 1862 by ascending in a hot-air balloon!

The story of Glaisher and Coxwell can serve as a good motivational tool to introduce the topic of the atmosphere. Point out that these two daring scientists were attempting to study the atmosphere with the only means available to them—an airborne balloon.

---

pollutants from industrial plants and automobile exhausts. When sunlight hits this mixture, a complex chemical reaction occurs, and ozone is produced.

Because ozone poses a health hazard, the Environmental Protection Agency (EPA) has set 120 parts per billion as a maximum level of ozone that can be in the air. Communities with ozone levels above the maximum must develop and follow a strategic plan specifying how they will control the factors that contribute to their ozone problem.

Controlling ozone pollution will not be easy or inexpensive. Special control equipment is often very expensive, products without hydrocarbons may cost more and require consumers to look at the label before they buy, and many people do not want to inconvenience themselves by carpooling or taking public transportation.

Cooperative learning: Using preassigned lab groups or randomly selected teams, have groups complete one of the following assignments.
• Design a T-shirt that illustrates the dual nature of ozone—helpful in the stratosphere and harmful in the troposphere.
• Have groups write a five-line poem titled "Ozone." Groups should write "OZONE" vertically on the page and then begin each line with one of the letters in the spelled title. Each line must include some fact about ozone.
• See Cooperative Learning in the *Teacher's Desk Reference.*

JOURNAL ACTIVITY

You may want to use the Journal Activity as the basis of class discussion. Before students begin writing, discuss some differences between life on Earth and in space. Students will probably know that there is no breathable atmosphere in space. Students should be instructed to keep their Journal Activity in their portfolio.

1-1 A View of Planet Earth: Spheres Within a Sphere

MULTICULTURAL OPPORTUNITY 1-1

Have students summarize the history of space exploration, making sure to include the achievements of men and women from different countries. Suggest that they make a chart listing the dates of the manned space missions, the names of the astronauts (called cosmonauts in the Soviet Union), and their achievements.

The list could include the first person in Earth orbit, Soviet cosmonaut Yuri A. Gagarin; the first American in space, Alan B. Shepard, Jr.; the first people to set foot on the moon, Americans Neil A. Armstrong and Edwin E. Aldrin, Jr.; the first African-American in Space, Guion S. Bluford, Jr,; the first Canadian in space, Marc Garneau.

Students should be sure to list the following women: from the Soviet Union, Valentina Tereshkova, the first woman in space, and Svetlana Sanitskaya, the first woman to walk in space; from the United States, astronaut Sally K. Ride, the first American woman in space.

ESL STRATEGY 1-1

Make sure students understand the meaning of *sphere.* When discussing the equator's division of the Earth into two hemispheres, explain that *hemi* is a Greek word meaning "half."

Dictate the following activities and ask LEP students to work with an English-speaking partner in preparing their answers.

1. Name the two hemispheres and locate them on a globe. (Northern and Southern hemispheres.)
2. List the three main features of Earth. (Land, water, air.)
3. Give the scientific words that have these meanings: rock-sphere, vapor-sphere, half-sphere, water-sphere. (Lithosphere, atmosphere, hemisphere, hydrosphere.)

Figure 1–1 *Dolls such as these are part of Russian folk heritage. In what way are these dolls similar to planet Earth?*
②

12 ■ I

1-1 A View of Planet Earth: Spheres Within a Sphere

Have you ever seen a carved doll like the one in Figure 1–1? This doll holds some surprises within its painted wooden shell. When it is opened you can see that what appeared to be a single doll is actually a series of dolls, snugly nesting one within the other. These sets of dolls are made in Russia and are part of the folk heritage of the Russian people.

In some ways, the Earth is similar to this set of dolls. What appears to be a simple structure is, upon close examination, found to have many hidden layers of complexity. And along with this complexity comes a kind of awe-inspiring beauty.

Size of the Earth

Exactly how large is planet Earth? Its size can be described by two measurements: its diameter and its circumference. The diameter of the Earth (or the distance from the North Pole to the South Pole through the center) is about 12,740 kilometers. When compared with Jupiter, the largest planet in the solar system with a diameter of 142,700 kilometers, the Earth may not seem to be very large at all. But the Earth is the largest of the inner planets— ② Mercury, Venus, Earth, and Mars—in the solar system. The diameter of Mars, for example, is only about one-half the diameter of the Earth.

The circumference of the Earth, or the distance around the Earth, is about 40,075 kilometers at the **equator.** The equator is an imaginary line around Earth that divides Earth into two **hemispheres.** These hemispheres are called the Northern Hemisphere and the Southern Hemisphere. In which hemisphere do you live? ①

Features of the Earth: The Lithosphere, Hydrosphere, and Atmosphere

The word earth has many meanings. It can mean the ground you walk on or the soil in which plants grow. Most importantly, the word Earth can mean

---

TEACHING STRATEGY 1-1

FOCUS/MOTIVATION

• **How do you know the Earth is round?** (Accept all logical answers.)
• **Why are people interested in seeing the Earth from space?** (Accept all logical answers.)
• **What do you think the Earth would look like from space?** (Accept all answers.)

CONTENT DEVELOPMENT

Point out that the Earth is divided by an imaginary line called the equator. Explain that the equator is approximately halfway between the North and South poles. The equator divides the Earth into halves, called hemispheres. The half that is north of the equator is the Northern Hemisphere. The half that is south of the equator is the Southern Hemisphere.

Figure 1–2 *In this shot of Earth from space you can see the atmosphere, land areas, and oceans. How much greater is the Earth's circumference than its diameter?* ③

your planet home. Looking at the Earth from space—actually a relatively new way to view the planet—you can appreciate its extraordinary beauty. You can also observe the three main features that make up your "home."

Photographs from space show that the Earth is a beautiful planet indeed. From space the Earth's land areas can be seen easily. The outlines of continents, in the past seen only as two-dimensional drawings on a map, become real when photographed by satellite cameras. From space, the oceans and other bodies of water that cover much of the Earth can clearly be identified. In fact, about 70 percent of the Earth's surface is covered by water. From space, the Earth's atmosphere can be observed, if only indirectly. The clouds in the photograph in Figure 1–2, floating freely above land and water, are part of the normally invisible atmosphere that surrounds the Earth.

The three main features of the Earth are the land, the water, and the air. The land areas of the Earth are part of a solid layer of the Earth known as the crust. Land areas include the seven continents and all other landmasses. Such land areas are clearly visible as part of the Earth's surface. But there is also land that is not visible—land that exists beneath the oceans and beneath the continents. You will learn more about this solid layer of the Earth in Chapter 4. Scientists call all the land on Earth the **lithosphere,** a word that means "rock-sphere." Why do you think this is an appropriate name? ④

The water on Earth makes up the **hydrosphere.** (The prefix *hydro-* means water.) The hydrosphere includes the Earth's oceans, rivers and streams, ponds and lakes, seas and bays, and other bodies of water. Some of the hydrosphere is frozen in the polar ice caps at the North and South poles, as well as in icebergs and glaciers.

You might be surprised to learn that about 97 percent of the hydrosphere is composed of salt water. The most common salt in salt water is sodium chloride, which you are more familiar with as table salt. You might think that the remaining 3 percent

---

FACTS ABOUT THE EARTH

Average distance from sun
About 150,000,000 kilometers

Diameter through equator
12,756.32 kilometers

Circumference around equator
40,075.16 kilometers

Surface area
Land area, about 148,300,000 square kilometers, or about 30 percent of total surface area; water area, about 361,800,000 square kilometers, or about 70 percent of total surface area

Rotation period
23 hours, 56 minutes, 4.09 seconds

Revolution period around sun
365 days, 6 hours, 9 minutes, 9.54 seconds

Temperature
Highest, 58°C at Al Aziziyah, Libya; lowest, -90°C at Vostok in Antarctica; average surface temperature, 14°C

Highest and lowest land features
Highest, Mount Everest, 8848 meters above sea level; lowest, shore of Dead Sea, 396 meters below sea level

Ocean depths
Deepest, Mariana Trench in Pacific Ocean southwest of Guam, 11,033 meters below surface; average ocean depth, 3795 meters

I ■ 13

and drink comes from rain and the fresh water trapped as ice.

• **How will we get the fresh water that is trapped as ice?** (Accept all answers, but lead students to suggest melting into lakes and streams.)

Media and Technology

In its liquid state, water makes planet Earth unique in our solar system. Water also makes life on Earth possible. In the Interactive Videodisc called Planet Earth: The Blue Planet, students explore the links between Earth's oceans and its weather. The movement of water, as rain, from the oceans to the lands sustains life. Students will also explore the role people play in changing climate patterns that have existed on planet Earth for many millennia.

● ● ● ● **Integration** ● ● ● ●

Use the discussion of the chemical composition of the hydrosphere to integrate solution chemistry into your lesson.

CONTENT DEVELOPMENT

Explain that the three main features of the Earth are the ground the students walk on, the water they drink, and the air they breathe.

• **What do you guess the ground is?** (Accept all logical answers.) Explain that the ground is the solid outer shell, or crust, of the Earth. Tell the students that scientists call the crust the lithosphere, which means "stony." The crust consists of all rocks, stones, and landmasses above and below the waters of the Earth.

● ● ● ● **Integration** ● ● ● ●

Use the discussion of the planets in the solar system to integrate concepts of astronomy into your lesson.

CONTENT DEVELOPMENT

Point out that the water of the Earth's surface is called the hydrosphere. The hydrosphere includes the oceans, rivers, polar icecaps, and all other water. Explain that most of the water on the Earth is salt water. The fresh water that we use

ACTIVITY
READING

EXPLORERS OF THE ATMOSPHERE—AND BEYOND

Skill: Reading comprehension

In this activity students are asked to read *The Right Stuff* by Tom Wolfe, a historical account of the early space program in the United States.

Point out that many "explorers" of the atmosphere have never left Earth! Using satellites and probes in space, scientists in such fields as communications, weather prediction, and astronomy have contributed important insights to our understanding of the atmosphere.

Integration: Use this Activity to integrate language arts into your science lesson.

Figure 1–3 *These unusual rock formations in Canyonlands National Park, Utah, are part of the Earth's crust.*

Figure 1–4 *Don't let this creek in California fool you. Most of the Earth's fresh water is locked up in the great polar ice caps. Here you see the southern polar cap in Antarctica. To which sphere does the Earth's fresh and salt water belong?* ①

14 ■ I

of the hydrosphere is fresh water that can be used by humans for a variety of purposes. You would not be correct, however. Almost 85 percent of the fresh water on Earth exists as ice locked up in the great polar ice caps. That leaves about 15 percent of the 3 percent as liquid fresh water. And keep in mind that this liquid fresh water is not evenly distributed over the Earth. The deserts of the Earth have very little fresh water, whereas the tropical areas have a great

---

1–1 (continued)

REINFORCEMENT/RETEACHING

Emphasize to students that the lithosphere includes not just Earth's visible land, but also the ocean floor. If all Earth's water were removed, the oceans would appear as huge basins in Earth's crust.

INDEPENDENT PRACTICE

▶ *Activity Book*

Students can investigate the effects of heat on soil and water in the Chapter 1 activity called Land, Water, and Air Temperature Changes.

INDEPENDENT PRACTICE

Section Review 1–1

1. The land, the water, and the air.
2. Three percent is fresh water, but only 15 percent of that is available for drinking. So, only 0.45 percent (15 percent of 3 percent) of the hydrosphere is available for drinking.
3. The atmosphere.
4. Accept all logical responses. Testing the composition of the atmosphere would be a reasonable guess.

REINFORCEMENT/RETEACHING

Review students' responses to the Section Review questions. Reteach any material that is still unclear, based on students' responses.

CLOSURE

▶ *Review and Reinforcement Guide*

Have students complete Section 1–1 in the *Review and Reinforcment Guide.*

deal. Remember also that it is liquid water that makes life on this planet possible. Without water, no life would exist on Earth.

The oxygen that you breathe is found in the last great sphere that makes up planet Earth, the **atmosphere** (AT-muhs-feer). The atmosphere is the envelope of gases that surrounds the Earth. The atmosphere protects the Earth and also provides materials necessary to support all forms of life on the Earth. In the next three sections, you will learn more about Earth's atmosphere. In later chapters, you will learn about the other spheres of planet Earth.

1–1 Section Review

1. What are the three main features of the Earth?
2. What percentage of the hydrosphere is fresh water? What percentage of the hydrosphere is available for drinking?
3. What is the envelope of gases that surrounds the Earth called?

Connection—*Astronomy*

4. *Viking* was the name of the lander that explored the surface of Mars. One of its primary missions was to determine if life existed there. What one test do you think *Viking* performed in order to get an answer to this question?

1–2 Development of the Atmosphere

When astronauts walk in space, they must wear space suits. The space suits provide a protective covering. They enclose the astronauts in an artificial environment, providing them with comfortable temperatures as well as with moisture and oxygen. Space suits also protect the astronauts from harmful ultraviolet rays given off by the sun. In a similar way, the atmosphere of the Earth provides protection for you. And it also provides some of the materials necessary to support life on Earth.

ACTIVITY READING

Explorers of the Atmosphere—and Beyond

The last half of the twentieth century has witnessed the fulfillment of many dreams. During this time, brave women and men have taken the first tentative steps in exploring space. You might like to read *The Right Stuff*, by Tom Wolfe. This book details early attempts by the United States to explore the frontiers of air and space travel, and contains the "stuff" that dreams are made of.

Guide for Reading

Focus on these questions as you read.

▶ *How does the atmosphere on Earth today compare with the atmosphere long ago?*

▶ *What gases are present in the atmosphere?*

I ■ 15

TEACHING STRATEGY 1–2

FOCUS/MOTIVATION

Ask the following question and have students raise their hands in response:

• **Which of you would like to be an astronaut?**

Then ask this question.

• **Why do you think you would want to be an astronaut?** (Accept all answers. Possible responses include for adventure and to increase scientific knowledge.)

CONTENT DEVELOPMENT

Point out to students that astronauts who have viewed Earth from space have said that it should be called Planet Ocean. And it is true that the ocean makes up more of Earth's surface than anything else—about 70 percent of Earth is covered by water. Under the ocean is a layer of rocky crust about 8 km thick. This same rocky crust extends to about 32 km under the major landmasses, or continents.

1-2 Development of the Atmosphere

MULTICULTURAL OPPORTUNITY 1-2

Have students investigate atmospheric pollution in different parts of the world and compare the problems with those in their own community. They may want to use newspaper and magazine articles from the library in their research, as well as listening to weather reports. Suggest that students make brief presentations on plans developed in different areas to combat air pollution. Interested students may want to develop additional plans of their own.

ESL STRATEGY 1-2

Write the descriptions listed below on the chalkboard and have students write down the words described. Allow them to use their textbooks to find the terms described.

• A gas used directly from the atmosphere by plants and animals. (Oxygen.)
• A gas needed by living things to make proteins. (Nitrogen.)
• Absorbs harmful ultraviolet radiation from the sun. (Ozone layer.)
• Seventy-eight percent of Earth's atmosphere contains this gas. (Nitrogen.)
• Two poisonous gases in Earth's early atmosphere. (Methane and ammonia.)
• Second most abundant gas in Earth's atmosphere. (Oxygen.)
• A gas necessary for respiration and combustion. (Oxygen.)
• A gas used by green plants to make food. (Carbon dioxide.)

After students finish finding the words for the descriptions above, have them play "Jeopardy." The category is Earth's Atmospheric Gases. A student reads one of the descriptions, and another student supplies the word that matches it.

Geochemists studying the evolution of the Earth's atmosphere have found evidence that the atmosphere 80 million years ago contained about 50 percent more oxygen than it does today. Scientists analyzed small air bubbles trapped in amber, the hardened resin of coniferous trees, to determine what the Earth's ancient atmosphere was like.

Pieces of amber were placed inside a vacuum chamber. The amber was cracked, allowing the ancient air to escape and be analyzed. The scientists' analysis revealed that the ancient air contained 32 percent oxygen. Today's air contains about 21 percent oxygen. These findings are preliminary, and more amber samples will have to be analyzed before ideas about the evolution of our atmosphere are changed.

If the scientists' findings are supported by additional research, the questions of how and why the atmosphere changed will become the focus of even more scientific research.

1-2 (continued)

FOCUS/MOTIVATION

Obtain a photograph of an astronaut in a spacesuit.
- **What do you think a spacesuit does for an astronaut?** (Answers may vary. Guide students to recognize that a spacesuit provides protection from extremes in temperature and from harmful ultraviolet rays. It also provides the astronaut with necessary gases such as oxygen, as well as moisture.)

Introduce the idea that the Earth's atmosphere provides a comfortable and safe environment for living things. Without the atmosphere, the Earth would be a harsh, dry place where nothing could live. Point out that the purpose of an astronaut's spacesuit is to simulate the Earth's atmosphere.

CONTENT DEVELOPMENT

Emphasize to students that scientists know about the Earth's early atmosphere

Cameras and other instruments aboard space satellites have provided much data about the structure and composition of the present atmosphere. From this information, and from other studies, scientists have developed a picture of what the Earth's atmosphere may have been like billions of years ago. Scientists are certain that the atmosphere of the Earth has changed greatly over time. And they believe that the present atmosphere is still changing! What are some of the conditions that may be responsible for changes in the atmosphere?

The Past Atmosphere

It is theorized that the Earth's atmosphere 4 billion years ago contained two deadly gases: methane and ammonia. Methane, which is made up of the elements carbon and hydrogen, is a poisonous compound. Ammonia, also poisonous, is composed of the elements nitrogen and hydrogen. There was also some water in the atmosphere 4 billion years ago.

As you well know, the air is no longer deadly. In fact, you could not live without it. How did this important change in the atmosphere occur?

To explain this change, it is necessary to picture the atmosphere 3.8 billion years ago. At that time, sunlight triggered chemical reactions among the methane, ammonia, and water in the air. As a result

Figure 1-5 *Scientists use a variety of tools to study the atmosphere, including weather balloons and satellites orbiting in space. Gases trapped in the ice caps thousands of years ago provide scientists with a glimpse of Earth's ancient atmosphere.*

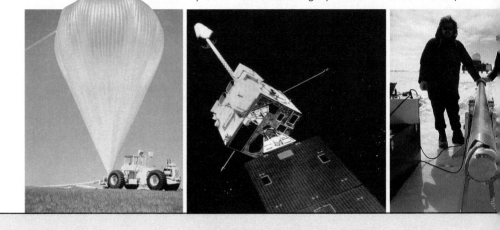

because of dust found in Greenland and other polar regions.
- **Why do you think dust from the early atmosphere would be found in these areas?** (In polar regions, ice acts as a preservative, keeping the dust intact and fixed in one place.)
- **Why would it be unlikely to find ancient dust elsewhere on the Earth?** (Factors such as wind and rain, as well as erosion and deposition, would tend to act on the dust. The dust would probably combine with other substances or be washed away. Even if the dust were to retain the same chemical composition, it would be more difficult to isolate.)

GUIDED PRACTICE

Skills Development

Skill: Making predictions

Write the following names and formulas on the chalkboard: Methane: CH_4, Ammonia: NH_3, Water: H_2O.

Figure 1–6 *An artist's idea of what the Earth may have looked like billions of years ago. What two deadly gases were common in the ancient atmosphere?* ①

of many chemical reactions, new materials formed in the atmosphere. Among the new materials were nitrogen, hydrogen, and carbon dioxide. The methane and ammonia broke down, but the water still remained.

Hydrogen is a very lightweight gas, so lightweight in fact, that it escaped the pull of the Earth's gravity and disappeared into space. That left nitrogen in greatest abundance, as well as carbon dioxide and water vapor. In the upper parts of the ancient atmosphere, sunlight began to break down the water vapor into hydrogen and oxygen gases. The lightweight hydrogen gas again escaped into space. But, the atoms of oxygen gas began to combine with one another to form a gas known as **ozone.** Eventually a layer of ozone gas formed about 30 kilometers above the Earth's surface.

The ozone layer is sometimes referred to as an "umbrella" for life on Earth. This is because the ozone layer absorbs most of the harmful ultraviolet ① radiation from the sun. Without the protection of the ozone layer, few living things could survive on Earth.

Before the ozone layer formed, the only living things on Earth were microscopic organisms that lived far below the surface of the oceans. Here these

Answers

① Methane and ammonia. (Applying concepts)

Integration

① Physical Science: Electromagnetic Spectrum. See *Sound and Light*, Chapter 3.

BACKGROUND INFORMATION
OZONE

In large quantities, ozone is a poisonous gas with a sharp, disagreeable odor. So it is vital that the ozone "umbrella" be high above the Earth.

When small quantities of ozone form on the Earth during a thunderstorm or near electric motors, the sharp odor is sometimes mistaken for "clean air"—which is why certain towns and neighborhoods have names such as Ozone Park.

Ozone is more reactive than oxygen, and it has the ability to break down many compounds. For this reason, ozone is valuable in water and sewage treatment, where it is used to destroy bacteria.

• **If these three substances were to break down and/or combine, what might form?** (Accept all answers.)

Next, write the following names and formulas on the chalkboard: Nitrogen: N_2, Hydrogen: H_2, Carbon dioxide: CO_2.
• **How many of you predicted the formation of these substances?** (Answers will vary.)

Point out to students that by a series of chemical reactions triggered by sunlight, the gases methane, ammonia, and water vapor in the Earth's atmosphere broke down and combined to form nitrogen, hydrogen, and carbon dioxide.

CONTENT DEVELOPMENT

Stress that the ozone layer began to form as water vapor in the upper atmosphere was broken down by sunlight.
• **What elements make up water?** (Hydrogen and oxygen.)
• **Do you know the chemical formula for water?** (H_2O.)

• **If a molecule of water were broken down, what would you expect to obtain?** (Two atoms of hydrogen and one atom of oxygen.)

Point out that as water vapor in the atmosphere broke down, atoms of hydrogen and oxygen were released. The atoms of oxygen began combining to form molecules of ozone (O_3), which consist of three atoms of oxygen.

● ● ● ● **Integration** ● ● ● ●

Use the discussion of ultraviolet radiation and the ozone layer to integrate concepts of electromagnetism into your lesson.

Figure 1–7 *The ozone layer absorbs most of the sun's harmful ultraviolet radiation before it reaches the Earth's surface. Visible light is not absorbed by the ozone layer.*

organisms were protected from most of the ultraviolet radiation from the sun. After the formation of the ozone layer, certain types of microorganisms called blue-green bacteria started to appear on or near the water's surface. These bacteria used the energy in sunlight to combine carbon dioxide from the air with water to produce food.

A byproduct of this food-making process would change the planet forever. This byproduct was oxygen. Unlike ozone, which formed high in the atmosphere, oxygen remained near the surface of the Earth. It would be this oxygen that animals would later breathe.

In time, green plants began to grow on the land. And they, too, took in carbon dioxide and released oxygen during the food-making process. The oxygen content in the atmosphere increased greatly. Then, around 600 million years ago, the amounts of oxygen and carbon dioxide in the atmosphere began to level off. Since that time, the composition of the atmosphere has remained fairly constant.

Figure 1–8 *Billions of years ago, microscopic organisms such as blue-green bacteria helped to change the Earth's atmosphere by producing oxygen as a byproduct of their food-making process. This increase in the oxygen levels in the atmosphere permitted the evolution of green plants and eventually the animals that feed on green plants.*

The Present Atmosphere

The atmosphere that surrounds the Earth today contains the gases necessary for the survival of living things. The air you breathe is among the Earth's most important natural resources. What is the air made of?

The atmosphere is a mixture of gases. **The atmospheric gases include nitrogen, oxygen, carbon dioxide, water vapor, argon, and trace gases.** Nitrogen gas makes up about 78 percent of the atmosphere. Another 21 percent of the atmosphere is oxygen. The remaining 1 percent is a combination of carbon dioxide, water vapor, argon, and trace gases. Among the trace gases, which are present in only very small amounts, are neon, helium, krypton, and xenon.

NITROGEN The most abundant gas in the atmosphere is nitrogen. Living things need nitrogen to make proteins. Proteins are complex compounds that contain nitrogen. These compounds are required for the growth and repair of body parts. The muscles of your body are made mostly of protein, as are parts of the skin and internal organs.

atmosphere. Other bacteria, called nitrifying bacteria, convert ammonia directly into nitrates to be used again in protein synthesis.

● ● ● ● **Integration** ● ● ● ●

Use the discussion of the role of nitrogen in the human body to integrate concepts of human physiology into your lesson.

GUIDED PRACTICE

Skills Development

Skill: Interpreting diagrams

Have students observe the diagram of the nitrogen cycle in Figure 1–9.
● **According to the diagram, what natural processes renew the supply of nitrogen in the atmosphere?** (Volcanic eruptions and thunderstorms.)

ENRICHMENT

▶ *Activity Book*

Students can apply their understanding of the concepts in this section with skills in graphing and percentage in the Chapter 1 activity called Composition of the Atmosphere: A Graphic Model.

about the atmospheres that surround other planets. Have students find out what gases make up these atmospheres and how the environment of each planet is affected by the type of atmosphere it has.

CONTENT DEVELOPMENT

The process by which nitrogen is changed into nitrates and used by living things is called the nitrogen cycle. In the nitrogen cycle, bacteria that live in the soil and in water absorb free nitrogen from the air and convert it into nitrates. These bacteria are called nitrogen-fixing bacteria. Plants use the nitrates to make proteins; then animals get the proteins they need by eating plants.

When plants and animals die and decay, the compound ammonia is produced. Ammonia also results from animal wastes. Bacteria called denitrifying bacteria change the ammonia into free nitrogen, thus restoring the supply in the

GREENHOUSE GASES

Some of the gases in the atmosphere are considered to be "greenhouse gases" because they are opaque to the heat radiation that rises from the Earth. Three of the greenhouse gases are carbon dioxide (CO_2), ozone (O_3), and water vapor (H_2O)—each composed of molecules with three atoms.

In contrast, oxygen (O_2) and nitrogen (N_2) are not greenhouse gases. The molecules in these gases are composed of just two atoms so that oxygen and nitrogen allow the heat radiation from the Earth to pass through them.

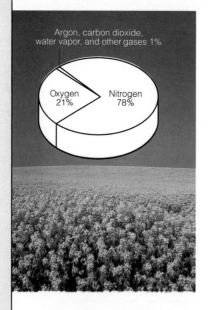

Argon, carbon dioxide, water vapor, and other gases 1%

Oxygen 21%

Nitrogen 78%

Figure 1–10 *The atmosphere is a mixture of many gases. Which two gases make up most of the Earth's atmosphere?* ❶

Figure 1–11 *Bacteria and other decay organisms play an important role, as they remove nitrogen and other substances from dead organisms and return these chemicals to the environment.*

20 ■ I

However, plants and animals are not able to use the nitrogen in the air directly to make proteins. Certain kinds of bacteria that live in the soil are able to combine the nitrogen from the atmosphere with other chemicals to make compounds called nitrates. These bacteria are called nitrogen-fixing bacteria. Plants are able to use the nitrates formed by the nitrogen-fixing bacteria to make plant proteins. In turn, animals get the proteins they need by eating plants.

Nitrogen is returned to the atmosphere when dead animals and plants decay. Decay is the breaking down of dead organisms, usually by bacteria, into simple chemical substances. Thus the organisms that bring about decay return the nitrogen to the atmosphere. The movement of nitrogen from the atmosphere to the soil then to living things and finally back to the atmosphere makes up the nitrogen cycle.

OXYGEN Oxygen is the second most abundant gas in the atmosphere. Oxygen is used directly from the atmosphere by most plants and animals. It is essential for respiration (rehs-puh-RAY-shuhn). During respiration, living things chemically combine oxygen with food. This breaks down the food and releases the energy needed by living things. Why do you think all living things need energy? ❷

Oxygen is also necessary for the combustion, or burning, of fuels such as oil, coal, and wood. Combustion will not take place without oxygen. This is why fire fighters use water or special chemicals to fight fires. Water or special chemicals prevent oxygen from reaching the burning material and supporting any further combustion. Without oxygen, the fire goes out.

CARBON DIOXIDE The amount of carbon dioxide in the atmosphere is very small. However, carbon dioxide is one of the important raw materials used by green plants to make food.

Carbon dioxide is removed from the atmosphere by plants during the food-making process. It is returned to the atmosphere by the respiration of

---

1–2 (continued)

REINFORCEMENT/RETEACHING

Have students work in small groups. Provide each group with a set of five index cards, each labeled with one of the following terms: free nitrogen, nitrogen-fixing bacteria, nitrates, protein synthesis, decay. Ask each group to use the terms on the cards to describe the nitrogen cycle.

CONTENT DEVELOPMENT

Emphasize to students that the oxygen in the Earth's atmosphere formed in two ways: first, by the breakdown of water vapor and second, by the release of oxygen by plants. Point out that the oxygen reacted to form ozone after the first formation of oxygen.

Have students observe the graph in Figure 1–10.
• **Is it possible to determine from this graph how much oxygen would be present in 1 liter of air?** (Yes, 21 percent of 1 liter, or 210 mL.)
• **Is it possible to determine how much argon would be present in 1 liter of air?** (No.)
• **Why not?** (The exact percentage of argon in air is not given. One can only tell that it would be less than 1 percent.)

GUIDED PRACTICE

▶ *Laboratory Manual*

Skills Development

Skills: Applying concepts, making observations, making calculations, calculator

At this point you may want to have students complete the Chapter 1 Laboratory Investigation in the *Laboratory Manual* called Finding the Percentage of Oxygen in the Atmosphere. In the inves-

tigation students will detemine how much air is consumed by combustion and then use their results to estimate the percentage of oxygen in the air.

CONTENT DEVELOPMENT

Have students observe Figure 1–12.
• **Does the oxygen–carbon dioxide cycle take place only on land?** (No.)
• **How is the cycle carried out in water?** (Aquatic plants use carbon dioxide and give off oxygen, while fish and other

Carbon dioxide used by plants

Carbon dioxide given off by animals

Carbon dioxide given off by decaying leaves

Oxygen given off by plants

Oxygen used by animals

Oxygen from food-making process available to animals

Carbon dioxide from respiration available to plants

Figure 1–12 *Carbon dioxide and oxygen are continuously exchanged among plants and animals. How is oxygen returned to the atmosphere?* ❸

plants and animals. The decay of dead plants and animals also returns carbon dioxide to the air.

Scientists believe that the amount of carbon dioxide used by plants equals the amount returned to the atmosphere by respiration, decay, and other natural processes. But the burning of fossil fuels such as oil and coal is adding even more carbon dioxide to the atmosphere. Scientists are concerned that the amount of carbon dioxide in the atmosphere is increasing to a level that may become dangerous. Studies have shown that the increased level of carbon dioxide traps more of the sun's heat energy in the Earth's atmosphere. Thus an increase in the level of carbon dioxide in the air could significantly increase the overall temperature of the Earth.

WATER VAPOR Water vapor in the atmosphere plays an important role in the Earth's weather. Clouds, fog, and dew are weather conditions caused by water vapor in the air. Rain and other forms of precipitation (snow, sleet, and hail) occur when water vapor forms droplets that are heavy enough to fall. Water vapor is also involved in the heating of the atmosphere. Water vapor absorbs heat energy given off by the sun. The amount of water vapor in

Answers

❶ Oxygen and nitrogen. (Interpreting graphs)

❷ To live, grow, and reproduce. (Making inferences)

❸ Oxygen is given off by plants during the food-making process. (Interpreting diagrams)

Integration

❶ Life Science: Ecology. See *Ecology: Earth's Living Resources,* Chapter 5.

❷ Earth Science: Meteorology. See *Exploring Earth's Weather,* Chapter 1.

ECOLOGY NOTE

THE GREENHOUSE EFFECT

Scientists have been aware of the buildup of carbon dioxide in the atmosphere for more than three quarters of a century. The effect of the carbon dioxide has been compared to the effect of the glass in a greenhouse. The glass panes let in sunlight so that the greenhouse is warmed by solar radiation. The glass, however, acts to decrease the rate of heat radiation out of the greenhouse at night or when the outside temperature decreases. In the same way, an increased amount of carbon dioxide in the atmosphere would slow up the radiation of heat away from the Earth.

aquatic animals use oxygen and give off carbon dioxide.)

• **How is it possible for these gases to be present in water?** (Both gases are soluble—able to dissolve—in water.)

● ● ● ● **Integration** ● ● ● ●

Use the discussion of carbon-dioxide increase in the atmosphere to integrate concepts of ecology into your lesson.

ENRICHMENT

Some students might enjoy drawing large posters of the nitrogen and carbon-dioxide cycles for display in the classroom.

CONTENT DEVELOPMENT

• **Name some gases that make up the Earth's atmosphere.** (Students will probably mention oxygen, nitrogen, and carbon dioxide.)

Explain that water vapor is also a gas that is an important component of the atmosphere. Most people do not think to mention water vapor because water normally exists in a liquid state on Earth rather than as a gas.

● ● ● ● **Integration** ● ● ● ●

Use the discussion of the role water vapor plays in Earth's weather to integrate concepts of meteorology into your lesson.

Discovery Learning

Skills: Applying concepts, making observations, making comparisons, making inferences

Materials: glass microscope slides, petroleum jelly, microscope

This activity allows students to make an estimate of particular air-pollution levels by means of microscopic examination.

Before students do the activity, have them predict which of the locations chosen will have the greatest and least number of particles. Then they can compare the results of the experiments with their predictions.

Have students repeat the activity under different weather conditions (such as during temperature inversions) and during different seasons. They may also wish to take and compare corresponding samples in urban/industrialized and rural/nonindustrialized areas.

1-2 (continued)

CONTENT DEVELOPMENT

Have students look at the photographs of the volcano and the smokestacks in Figure 1–14.

• **What effect do you think volcanoes and factories have on the Earth's atmosphere?** (Accept all logical responses.)

Explain that the gases in the atmosphere are mixed with many tiny particles of dust, smoke, dirt, and salt. Although many of these particles result from natural causes, many others are caused by human activities.

• **What are some ways that people increase the quantity of solid particles in the atmosphere?** (Accept all logical responses. Students may suggest driving automobiles and burning fossil fuels for manufacturing.)

Activity Bank

A Model of Acid Rain, p.166

ACTIVITY
DISCOVERING

Clean Air Anyone?

1. Spread a thin layer of petroleum jelly on each of three clean microscope slides. With your teacher's permission, place the slides in different locations in and around your school building. Leave the slides in place for several days.

2. Collect the slides and examine each one under a microscope. Count the particles you find. Draw what you observe.

Where was the slide with the fewest particles placed? Where was the slide with the most particles placed?

■ How can you account for the differences?

22 ■ I

Figure 1–13 *Where would you find more water vapor in the atmosphere—in a rain forest in Hawaii or the sand dunes of the Sahara?* ❶

the atmosphere varies from place to place. In desert regions, the amount of water vapor in the air is usually very small, although most deserts have rainy seasons that last for short periods of time. In tropical regions, the amount of water vapor in the air may be as high as 4 percent. Where else on Earth would you expect to find a great deal of water vapor in the atmosphere? ❷

SOLID PARTICLES   Many tiny particles of solid material are mixed with the air's gases. These particles are so small that they can float on even the slightest movements of the air. You may have noticed these particles if you have observed a flashlight beam in a darkened room. These particles in the air are dust, smoke, dirt, and even tiny bits of salt. Where do these particles come from? ❸

Every time a wave breaks, tiny particles of salt from ocean water enter the atmosphere and remain suspended in the air. Much of the dust in the air comes from the eruption of volcanoes. In 1883, the massive eruption of Krakatoa, a volcano in the East Indies, spewed huge amounts of volcanic dust and other materials into the air. As a result of this eruption, skies as far away as London became dark. The average temperature of the Earth fell 1.5°C as volcanic dust from this single eruption filled the air, preventing sunlight from warming the atmosphere. Dirt and smoke particles are also added to the air by

---

● ● ● ●   **Integration**   ● ● ● ●

Use the discussion of volcanic eruption to integrate concepts of geology into your lesson.

REINFORCEMENT/RETEACHING

🎧 **Media and Technology**

You may wish to have students review the concepts of this section by using the videodisc called Earth's Atmosphere.

After students have used the videodisc,

have them construct concept maps illustrating the ideas in the section.

ENRICHMENT

Ask students to design two posters depicting the atmosphere and conditions on the Earth in the past and today. Students may also want to draw a third poster showing what they think the conditions on Earth, including atmospheric conditions, will be like in the future. For example, some students may predict that

Figure 1–14 *Volcanoes and factories that burn fossil fuels add solid particles to the atmosphere. How are these bikers in Holland helping to keep the Earth's atmosphere a bit cleaner?* ④

the actions of people as they burn fuels, and as they drive cars and other vehicles. Factories and power plants that burn fossil fuels also add particles to the air. However, new kinds of smoke stacks reduce the amount of particles being added to the air by actually "scrubbing" the smoke before it is released into the air. Do you have any suggestions about what you and your family and friends can do to reduce the amounts of these particles that affect the quality of the air? ⑤

1–2 Section Review

1. What two gases were present in the greatest amounts in the atmosphere of Earth 4 billion years ago?
2. What four gases are present in the greatest amounts in the Earth's atmosphere today?
3. Describe the nitrogen cycle and the water cycle. Why is it important that certain substances in the atmosphere are used over and over again?
4. Why are scientists concerned that the level of carbon dioxide in the air is increasing?

Critical Thinking—*Relating Cause and Effect*
5. How have living organisms changed the composition of the atmosphere over time?

Figure 1–15 *Some pollutants found in the atmosphere include asbestos particles (top) and ash from burning coal (bottom).*

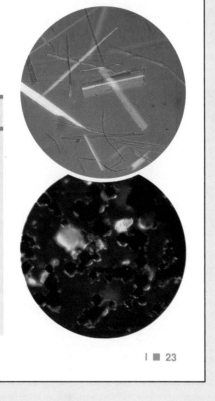

I ■ 23

4. An increase in the level of atmospheric carbon dioxide could cause the temperature of the Earth to rise to dangerous levels.

5. Answers will vary. One important example is the effect of early bacteria. These microorganisms used the energy in sunlight and carbon dioxide in the air to make food. In the process, they gave off oxygen. The oxygen allowed other forms of life to develop.

Students might also mention the effect on the atmosphere of green plants (release of oxygen), the nitrogen-fixing bacteria that are part of the nitrogen cycle, and the role of human activities in atmospheric change.

REINFORCEMENT/RETEACHING

Review students' responses to the Section Review questions. Reteach any material that is still unclear, based on students' responses.

CLOSURE

▶ *Review and Reinforcement Guide*

Have students complete Section 1–2 in the *Review and Reinforcement Guide.*

---

pollution will be so severe that people will be living in domed cities to protect them from the noxious atmosphere.

INDEPENDENT PRACTICE

Section Review 1–2

1. Methane and ammonia.

2. Nitrogen, oxygen, carbon dioxide, and water vapor.

3. Nitrogen cycle: Bacteria in the soil combine the nitrogen in the atmosphere with other chemicals to make nitrates. The nitrates are used by plants to make food. Animals eat the plants. When the plants and animals decay, nitrogen is returned to the atmosphere through decay.

Water cycle: Water evaporates from the Earth's surface to become water vapor in the air, then condenses, and falls back to Earth as precipitation.

If important substances such as oxygen could not be used over and over, the Earth's environment might run out of life-supporting substances.

ANNOTATION KEY

Answers

① Under water or on a tall mountain. (Making inferences)

② It decreases. (Applying concepts)

Integration

① Life Science: Ecology. See *Ecology: Earth's Living Resources*, Chapter 3.

② Earth Science: Meteorology. See *Exploring Earth's Weather*, Chapter 1.

PROBLEM SOLVING

PROTECTION FROM THE SUN

In this activity students use their skills in interpreting graphs.

1. The quantity had gone up from fewer than 2 parts per billion to about 2.3 parts per billion.

2. A bit more than 3 parts per billion.

3. Answers will vary.

4. If countries adhere to the London agreement, the amounts are predicted to start decreasing in the year 2005. If the Montreal agreement is used, the amounts will continue to increase.

According to the graph, the London agreement will help to protect the ozone layer.

5. Answers will vary.

Integration: Use the Problem Solving feature to integrate ecology into your science lesson.

PROBLEM Solving

Protection From the Sun ①

All life on Earth depends upon the sun. But the sun also poses certain dangers. You learned that the ozone layer acts like a shield that protects organisms on Earth from some of the dangerous radiation given off by the sun. Newspaper and magazine articles, television and radio programs issue warnings—on an almost daily basis—of the dangers posed to the ozone layer by certain chemicals. This graph shows the effects of limiting the release of ozone-damaging chemicals into the atmosphere.

Interpreting Graphs

1. How has the amount of ozone-damaging chemicals changed from 1975 to 1985?

2. What amount of ozone-damaging chemicals is projected to be in the atmosphere in 1995?

3. How does this amount compare with the amount in the atmosphere today?

4. Two meetings proposed controls on the amount of ozone-damaging chemicals that could be released into the atmosphere. What would happen to the amounts of ozone-damaging chemicals released in the air in 2005 according to the London agreement? According to the Montreal agreement?

■ Which agreement offers some protection for the ozone layer?

5. **On Your Own** Find out what you can do to limit the amounts of ozone-damaging chemicals that are released into the air.

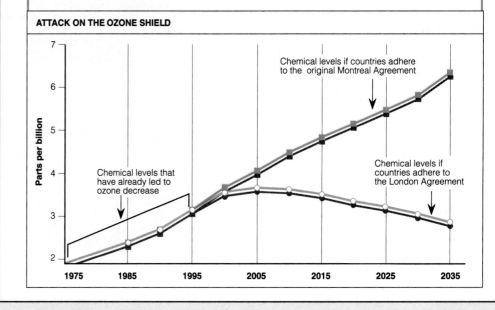

ATTACK ON THE OZONE SHIELD

Chemical levels if countries adhere to the original Montreal Agreement

Chemical levels that have already led to ozone decrease

Chemical levels if countries adhere to the London Agreement

TEACHING STRATEGY 1–3

FOCUS/MOTIVATION

Bring in a barometer and show it to the class. (If you cannot obtain a barometer, display a picture of one.)

• **Do you know what a barometer measures?** (Air pressure.)

• **What is air pressure?** (The downward push of air on the Earth's surface.)

Explain that a barometer is sensitive to changes in air pressure. An increase or decrease in the "push" of the air causes the barometer to register a higher or lower reading.

CONTENT DEVELOPMENT

Have students observe the photograph in Figure 1–16.

• **How is the person in this photograph dressed?** (In very warm clothing and oxygen mask.)

• **What do you notice about the surface of the mountain in the background?** (It is snow covered.)

1-3 Layers of the Atmosphere

If you were able to soar up from the surface of the Earth to the high edge of outer space, you would notice many changes in the atmosphere. The mixture of gases, the temperature, and the electrical and magnetic forces of the atmosphere change as the distance from the Earth's surface increases. For example, there is less oxygen in the upper atmosphere than in the lower atmosphere. You may have seen pictures of mountain climbers wearing oxygen masks when they were climbing very high mountains. They do this because there is only half as much oxygen available 5.5 kilometers above the Earth's surface as there is at the Earth's surface.

If you ever climb a high mountain yourself, you will notice that as you climb upward the air gets colder. At an altitude (height above sea level) of 3 kilometers, you will probably need a heavy jacket to keep warm! The temperature of the air decreases as the altitude increases because the air becomes less dense. That is, there are fewer and fewer particles of air in a given amount of space. The thin, less dense air cannot hold as much heat.

The atmosphere is divided into layers according to major changes in its temperature. The layers of air that surround the Earth are held close to it by the force of gravity. Gravity is a force of attraction by which objects are pulled toward each other. Because of gravity, the layers of air surrounding the Earth push down on the Earth's surface. This push is called **air pressure.**

The upper layers of air push down on the lower layers. So the air pressure near the surface of the Earth is greater than the air pressure further from the surface. If you have ever flown in an airplane, you may have felt your ears "pop." This popping was caused by a change in air pressure. Where else might you experience a change in air pressure? ①

It is interesting to note that 99 percent of the total mass of the atmosphere of the Earth is below an altitude of 32 kilometers. The remaining 1 percent of the atmosphere's mass is in the hundreds of kilometers above an altitude of 32 kilometers.

Guide for Reading

Focus on this question as you read.

▶ How are the layers in the atmosphere related to temperature?

AIR PRESSURE AND ALTITUDE

Altitude (meters)	Air Pressure (g/cm²)
Sea level	1034
3000	717
6000	450
9000	302
12,000	190
15,000	112

Figure 1–16 *Climbers need warm clothing and oxygen masks on a high mountain because the air is colder and thinner (less dense). How does air pressure change as altitude increases?* ②

I ■ 25

1-3 Layers of the Atmosphere

MULTICULTURAL OPPORTUNITY 1-3

Have students build a model of the atmosphere. They can use a Styrofoam ball cut in half and decorated to represent the Earth. This can be glued on a piece of poster board with the layers of the atmosphere drawn around the sphere.

Ask students to research examples of areas where high altitude may affect people's life. For instance, people who visit Mexico City, which is 2195 meters above sea level, need a few days to get used to the high altitude. People traveling by railroad from Lima, the Peruvian capital, to Huancayo in the Andes may take oxygen masks along on the trip: The railroad is one of the highest in the world—with Ticilio Tunnel at 4758 meters above sea level!

ESL STRATEGY 1-3

Have students copy the following chart. Point out that each term has the same suffix, *-sphere*. The meaning of each prefix is given. Ask students to use their textbooks to find the definition of each term. Then have them add a fourth column to the right side of the chart to show the definitions.

Term	Prefix	Meaning
troposphere	*tropo-*	a change
stratosphere	*strato-*	spreading out
mesosphere	*meso-*	middle
thermosphere	*thermo-*	hot
ionosphere	*iono-*	going
exosphere	*exo-*	outside

Give each student ten small cards. Have students write a term with the suffix *-sphere* on the front of the card and a list of clues on the back. Pair English-speaking students with ESL students to check the cards and practice reading them aloud. Later, the cards will be useful individual study tools.

• **Would you believe it if someone told you that this scene is taking place in the middle of July?** (Answers may vary, but students should be guided to recognize that at high elevations, the temperature can be below freezing even if the temperature at the foot of the mountain is very warm.)

● ● ● ● **Integration** ● ● ● ●

Use the discussion of air pressure to integrate concepts of meteorology into your lesson.

REINFORCEMENT/RETEACHING

▶ *Activity Book*

The Chapter 1 activity called It's Getting Colder can be used to introduce students to the relationship between temperature and distance above the Earth's surface.

ACTIVITY
DISCOVERING
THE TEMPERATURE PLOT

Discovery Learning

Skills: Making observations, recording measurements, making graphs, making inferences, making calculations, calculator

Materials: Celsius thermometer, graph paper

Students should find that the temperature at the 1.25-m mark changes more rapidly and by a greater amount over time.

There are many reasons for this, but the one students will most likely point to is that land absorbs and retains heat longer than air does. During the day, the land absorbs heat and is warmer than the air above it. During the night, the land releases heat, but the air above the land does not retain this heat, and the temperature changes in the air at 1.25 m will be greater.

Another fact students may point out is that the winds are stronger farther above the land. If students have trouble with this concept, ask them where the temperature stays most stable on a sunny day at the beach.

Integration: Use this Activity to integrate mathematics into your science lesson.

ACTIVITY
DISCOVERING

The Temperature Plot

1. At three times during both the day and evening, use an outdoor thermometer to measure air temperature 1 centimeter above the ground and 1.25 meters above the ground. Record the time of day and the temperature for both locations.

❶ **2.** On graph paper, plot time (X axis) versus temperature (Y axis) for each thermometer location. Label both graphs.

In which area did the temperature change most rapidly? In which area did the temperature change a greater amount over the entire time period?

■ Why do you think the temperatures changed as they did?

Now let's pretend that you are able to soar upward from the Earth's surface through the levels of the atmosphere. What will each layer look and feel like? Read on to find out.

The Troposphere

The layer of the atmosphere closest to Earth is the **troposphere** (TRO-po-sfeer). It is the layer in which you live. Almost all of the Earth's weather occurs in the troposphere.

The height of the troposphere varies from the equator to the poles. Around the equator, the height of the troposphere is about 17 kilometers. In areas north and south of the equator, the height is about 12 kilometers. At the poles, the troposphere extends upward between 6 and 8 kilometers.

As the heat energy from sunlight travels through the atmosphere, only a small amount of the heat energy is trapped by the atmosphere. Most of the heat energy is absorbed by the ground. The ground then warms the air above it. Warm air is less dense than cool air. The warm, less dense air rises and is replaced by cooler, denser air. Currents of air that carry heat up into the atmosphere are produced.

1–3 (continued)

REINFORCEMENT/RETEACHING

Use a diagram to reinforce the changes in temperature, pressure, and density that occur as one moves farther away from the Earth's surface. You might draw an outline of a mountain on the chalkboard and then use arrows to show that as altitude increases, temperature, pressure, and density all decrease.

CONTENT DEVELOPMENT

Point out to students that because air is invisible, we often are unaware of the pressure that it produces.

Explain that because there are more air particles close to the Earth's surface, air pressure is greatest at sea level. As altitude increases, the air thins out, so there are fewer particles to exert pressure on the Earth.

• **What other factor besides the number of air particles causes air pressure to change with altitude?** (Gravity. The force of gravity decreases as the distance between an object—in this case, an air particle—and the center of the Earth decreases.)

INDEPENDENT PRACTICE

▶ *Activity Book*

Students can learn more about planetary wind and pressure systems in the Chapter 1 activity called Global Wind Patterns.

CONTENT DEVELOPMENT

Discuss with students the formation of convection currents as warm air rises and is replaced by cooler air.

• **Why do you often feel a draft in a**

These air movements are called **convection** (kuhn-VEHK-shuhn) **currents.** You might be familiar with convection currents if you have observed a convection oven in use. This kind of oven contains a fan that continuously moves the hot oven air over the food. Food cooks more quickly and evenly in a convection oven than in a conventional oven.

Remember that temperature decreases with increasing altitude because the air becomes less dense. The temperature of the troposphere drops about 6.5°C for every kilometer above the Earth's surface. However, at an altitude of about 12 kilometers, the temperature seems to stop dropping. The zone of the troposphere where the temperature remains fairly constant is called the tropopause (TRO-po-pawz). The tropopause divides the troposphere from the next layer of the atmosphere.

The Stratosphere

The **stratosphere** (STRAT-uh-sfeer) extends from the tropopause to an altitude of about 50 kilometers. In the lower stratosphere, the temperature of the air remains constant and extremely cold—around −60°C. This temperature equals the coldest temperature ever recorded in a location other than Antarctica. It was recorded in Snag, in the Yukon Territory, Canada. The world's coldest recorded temperature, −90°C, occurred in Vostok, Antarctica.

The air in the lower stratosphere is not still. Here very strong eastward winds blow horizontally around the Earth. These winds, called the **jet stream,** reach speeds of more than 320 kilometers per hour. What effect do you think jet streams have on weather patterns in the United States? ②

A special form of oxygen called ozone is present in the stratosphere. Ozone has a clean sharp smell. You have probably smelled ozone after a thunderstorm or when you are near an electric motor that is running. In both cases ozone forms when electricity passes through the atmosphere. In the case of a thunderstorm, the electricity is in the form of lightning.

Most of the ozone in the atmosphere is found in the ozone layer located between 16 kilometers and

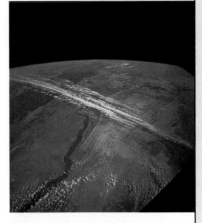

Figure 1-18 *A jet stream forms where cold air from the poles meets warmer air from the equator. This high-altitude jet stream is moving over the Nile Valley and the Red Sea.*

I ■ 27

BACKGROUND INFORMATION
JET STREAMS

Jet streams were discovered in the stratosphere in the 1940s when military aircraft were developed that could fly at altitudes higher than 10 km.

Jet streams are high-velocity streams of air that are hundreds of kilometers wide and several kilometers thick. They gain much of their energy from the difference in temperature between cold polar air and warm tropical air. Because jet streams blow from west to east, they enable eastbound airplanes to shorten their travel time.

Each hemisphere has, on the average, two jet streams. These are the subtropical jets, which are associated with subtropical highs, and the polar-front jets, which are usually located above polar fronts.

room where there is an open fire? (Convection currents are set up as warm air from the fire rises and is replaced by cooler air.)

● ● ● ● **Integration** ● ● ● ●

Use the discussion of convection currents to integrate concepts of heat into your lesson.

ENRICHMENT

▶ *Activity Book*
Students who understand the concepts in this section will be challenged by the Chapter 1 activity called Temperature and Pressure Patterns in the Troposphere.

INDEPENDENT PRACTICE

⚙ Media and Technology

Students can explore the lower layers of the atmosphere in the videodisc called Wind and Air Currents.

After students have used the videodisc, have them work in small groups to prepare weather reports similar to the ones shown on television. Each group should make charts showing the movement of air masses as a part of its presentation.

ECOLOGY NOTE
FAST FOOD, TRASH, AND THE OZONE LAYER

Every time we drive through a fast-food restaurant and pick up a hamburger in a plastic foam container, we are increasing our chances of getting a severe sunburn and, possibly, skin cancer!

As they slowly break down, the plastic foam packages used by fast-food restaurants give off chlorofluorocarbons (CFC). CFCs are chemicals that attack the ozone layer. Bombardment of CFCs by ultraviolet radiation releases chlorine. Each chlorine atom then goes on to attack and destroy 100,000 ozone molecules. Our fast-food, fast-paced society is upsetting an atmospheric balance that has protected us from ultraviolet radiation for millions of years.

Figure 1–19 *The ozone layer forms a protective umbrella in the stratosphere. Ozone, a molecule made up of three oxygen atoms, is formed when lightning passes through the atmosphere.*

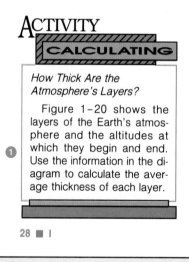

ACTIVITY
CALCULATING

How Thick Are the Atmosphere's Layers?

Figure 1–20 shows the layers of the Earth's atmosphere and the altitudes at which they begin and end. Use the information in the diagram to calculate the average thickness of each layer.

28 ■ I

60 kilometers above the surface of the Earth. Below and above these altitudes, there is little or no ozone. Although the total amount of ozone in the stratosphere is actually very small, ozone is extremely important to life on Earth. Ozone acts as a shield for the Earth's surface. As you learned in the previous section, ozone absorbs most of the ultraviolet radiation from the sun. Ultraviolet radiation is harmful to living things. Overexposure of the skin to ultraviolet radiation (often in the form of a bad sunburn) has been linked to skin cancer.

You may already know that you can get a bad sunburn on a cloudy day, even when it seems as if little sunlight is reaching the Earth. Ultraviolet rays are able to pass through cloud layers. In some ways, the ozone layer acts like a sunblock. Without it, more of the sun's harmful ultraviolet radiation would reach the Earth's surface, and you would always be in great danger of being badly burned by the sun's rays.

Ozone is also responsible for the increase in temperature that occurs in the upper stratosphere. Heat is given off as ozone reacts with ultraviolet radiation. This heat warms the upper stratosphere to temperatures around 18°C. The zone in which the temperature is at its highest is called the stratopause (STRAT-uh-pawz). The stratopause separates the stratosphere from the next layer of the atmosphere.

The Mesosphere

Above the stratopause, the temperature begins to decrease. This drop in temperature marks the beginning of the **mesosphere** (MEHS-oh-sfeer). The mesosphere extends from about 50 kilometers to about 80 kilometers above the Earth's surface. The temperature in the mesosphere drops to about −100°C. The upper region of the mesosphere is the coldest region of the atmosphere. If water vapor is present, thin clouds of ice form. You can see these feathery clouds if sunlight strikes them after sunset.

The mesosphere helps protect the Earth from large rocklike objects in space known as meteoroids (MEET-ee-uh-roidz). When meteoroids enter the atmosphere, they burn up in the mesosphere. The heat caused by the friction, or rubbing, between the meteoroid and the atmosphere causes this burning.

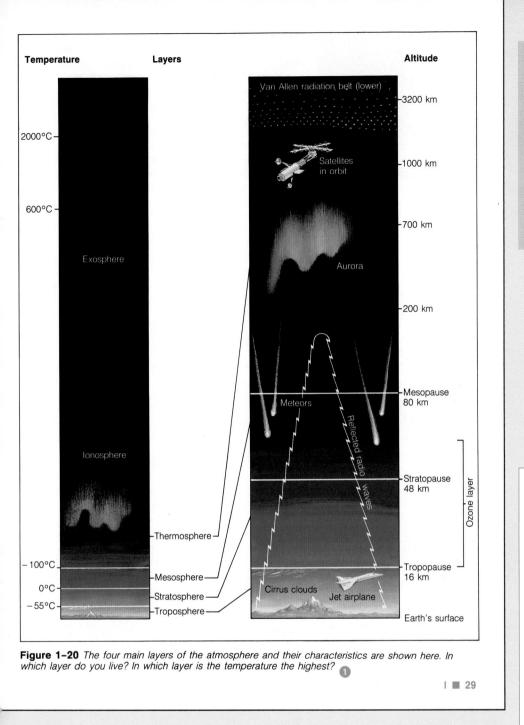

Temperature	Layers	Altitude

Van Allen radiation belt (lower)

3200 km

Satellites in orbit — 1000 km

2000°C

Exosphere

Aurora — 700 km

600°C

200 km

Ionosphere

Mesopause 80 km

Meters

Thermosphere

Stratopause 48 km

Ozone layer

−100°C

0°C — Mesosphere

Stratosphere — Tropopause 16 km

−55°C — Troposphere

Cirrus clouds   Jet airplane

Earth's surface

Figure 1–20 *The four main layers of the atmosphere and their characteristics are shown here. In which layer do you live? In which layer is the temperature the highest?* ❶

● ● ● ●   **Integration**   ● ● ● ●

Use the discussion of meteoroids burning up in the mesosphere to integrate concepts of astronomy into your lesson.

GUIDED PRACTICE

▶ *Laboratory Manual*

Skills Development

Skills: Applying concepts, making observations, making graphs, making inferences

At this point you may want to have students complete the Chapter 1 Laboratory Investigation in the *Laboratory Manual* called Effect of the Atmosphere on Cooling Rates of the Earth's Surface. In the investigation students will investigate the effect of the atmosphere on the rate of surface cooling.

CONTENT DEVELOPMENT

Have students use the data in Figure 1–20 to make a graph of temperature vs. altitude for the Earth's atmosphere. Have them plot altitude on the x-axis and temperature on the y-axis. Discuss the patterns of change that are evident from the graph.

air. Temperature changes are affected by the reaction of ozone gas and radiant energy in the stratosphere and by reactions between nitrogen and oxygen and radiant energy in the thermosphere.

Ask students to consider the following question.

• **If the mesosphere is the coldest part of the atmosphere, why do meteoroids burn up as they pass through the mesosphere?** (The friction between a meteoroid and the gas particles in the atmosphere creates enough heat to burn up the meteoroid.)

• **Can you think of an everyday situation in which heat is generated by friction?** (Answers may vary, but an excellent example is the way the blade of a skate cuts a figure on ice. The ice is very cold, but the friction of the blade creates enough heat to melt the ice under the blade and make a cut.)

BACKGROUND INFORMATION
SHOOTING STARS

Meteors are extremely common. Five or more per hour can be seen from any point on Earth if the sky is clear. The number of fainter meteors that can be seen with a telescope is estimated at between 5 and 10 thousand million per night.

BACKGROUND INFORMATION
TEMPERATURE

Temperature is a measure of the average kinetic energy of molecules. The liquid in a thermometer must be bombarded by high-energy molecules in order to gain enough heat to expand. When few air molecules are present, little energy is transferred to the thermometer—even if each individual molecule is very hot and possesses a great deal of energy. That is why an ordinary thermometer does not register high temperatures in the upper portion of the atmosphere.

FACTS AND FIGURES
LOWEST TEMPERATURE

The lowest temperature ever recorded in the atmosphere is −107.4°C at a height of about 80 to 96 km above Sweden in 1963.

1–3 (continued)

CONTENT DEVELOPMENT

Point out to students that the atmosphere of the Earth has no clearly defined upper limit. Thus, the thermosphere—unlike the lower three layers—has no definite depth.

Studies of meteors have demonstrated the presence of air up to 150 km, whereas studies of the auroras (northern and southern lights) indicate air at least 650 km above sea level. The auroras will be discussed in Section 1–4. They result from the solar wind interacting with the outlying gases of the atmosphere.

Figure 1–21 *A meteorite crater in Arizona formed when a meteorite struck the Earth around 20,000 years ago.*

At night, you may see a streak of light, or "shooting star," in the sky. What you are actually seeing is a bright trail of hot, glowing gases known as a meteor.

Most meteoroids burn up completely as they pass through the Earth's atmosphere. But some are large enough to survive the passage and actually strike the Earth. These pieces are called meteorites (MEET-ee-er-rights). A few large meteorites have produced huge craters on the Earth. The most famous is the Barringer meteorite crater in Arizona. It is 1.2 kilometers wide. Scientists estimate that the meteorite that caused this crater fell to the Earth within the last 20,000 years.

When artificial satellites fall from orbit, they also burn up as they pass through the atmosphere. However, pieces of the United States's *Skylab* and the Soviet Union's *Cosmos* satellite have fallen out of orbit and reached the Earth's surface. Why do you think some meteoroids and satellites do not burn up completely as they pass through the layers of the atmosphere? ❶

The Thermosphere

The **thermosphere** (THER-moh-sfeer) begins above the mesosphere at a height of about 80 kilometers. The thermosphere has no well-defined upper limit. The air in the thermosphere is very thin. The density of the atmosphere and the air pressure are only about one ten-millionth of what they are at the Earth's surface.

The word *thermosphere* means "heat sphere," or "warm layer." The temperature is very high in this layer of the atmosphere. In fact, the temperature of the thermosphere may reach 2000°C or more! To give you some idea of how hot this is, the temperature at the bottom of a furnace used to make steel reaches 1900°C. At this temperature, the steel mixture is a liquid! You may wonder why the temperature of the thermosphere is so high. (After all, for most of the atmosphere, temperature decreases as altitude increases.) The nitrogen and oxygen in the thermosphere absorb a great deal of the ultraviolet radiation from space and convert it into heat.

The temperature in the thermosphere is measured with special instruments, not with a thermometer.

Figure 1–22 *Temperatures in the thermosphere reach 2000°C, which is higher than the temperatures in a steel furnace.*

● ● ● ● **Integration** ● ● ● ●

Use the discussion of the temperature in the thermosphere to integrate concepts of heat energy into your lesson.

GUIDED PRACTICE

Skills Development
Skill: Making a model

Have students make scale drawings showing the relative size of the Earth compared with the thickness of the atmosphere surrounding the Earth. Have students use 6450 km as the radius of the Earth and 480 km as the height of the upper atmosphere above the Earth's surface. Once students have made their drawings, ask this question.

• **How does the thickness of the atmosphere compare with the thickness of the whole Earth?** (The thickness of the atmosphere is about one-sixteenth the radius of the Earth.)

Tell students that if they think of the thickness of the Earth's crust as the peel

If a thermometer were placed in the thermosphere, it would register far below 0°C! This may seem strange since the thermosphere is so hot. How can this be explained? Temperature is a measurement of how fast ❶ particles in the air move. The faster the air particles move, the higher the temperature. And the particles present in the thermosphere are moving very fast. Therefore the particles themselves are very hot.

But these particles are very few and very far apart. There are not enough of them present to bombard a thermometer and warm it. So the thermometer would record a temperature far below 0°C.

THE IONOSPHERE The lower thermosphere is called the **ionosphere** (igh-AHN-uh-sfeer). The ionosphere extends from 80 kilometers to 550 kilometers above the Earth's surface. The size of the ionosphere varies with the amount of ultraviolet and X-ray radiation, two types of invisible energy given off by the sun.

Nitrogen oxides, oxygen, and other gas particles in the ionosphere absorb the ultraviolet radiation and X-rays given off by the sun. The particles of gas become electrically charged. Electrically charged particles are called **ions.** Hence the name ionosphere.

The ions in the ionosphere are important to ❷ radio communication. AM radio waves are bounced

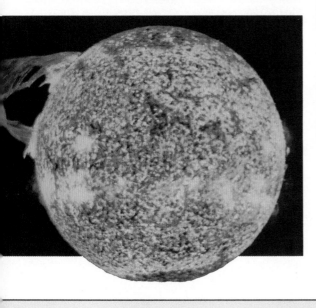

Figure 1–23 *Radio waves are bounced off the ionosphere to transmit radio messages overseas or across continents. There are three types of waves, and each travels to a different height in the ionosphere. Why do storms on the sun interfere with the transmission of radio waves in the ionosphere?* ❷

I ■ 31

Transmitter in Florida

Receiver in Paris

Ionosphere

KEY

Short waves

Medium waves

Long waves

---

which the wave returns to Earth? (The angles are equal. If students have difficulty seeing this, display the diagram on an overhead projector.)

Point out that the ionosphere reflects radio waves back to the Earth. Explain that for any type of wave, the angle of incidence will always equal the angle of reflection.

● ● ● ● **Integration** ● ● ● ●

Use the discussion of radio waves to integrate concepts of electromagnetism into your lesson.

REINFORCEMENT/RETEACHING

Have students work in pairs. Provide each pair with four index cards, each labeled with one of the following words: troposphere, stratosphere, mesosphere, and thermosphere. Have each pair arrange the cards vertically in the correct order. Then have the two students take turns describing the characteristics of each atmospheric layer.

ENRICHMENT

Two popular songs that students might know are "Up, Up, and Away" and "On a Clear Day, You Can See Forever." These songs use imagery of the atmosphere to express feelings of freedom and vision. Try to obtain records or tapes of these songs and play them for the class. Then have students use words or drawings to express their reactions to the music.

---

of an apple, the relative thickness of the atmosphere is somewhat greater, rather like the skin on a very thick-skinned orange.

INDEPENDENT PRACTICE

▶ *Activity Book*

Students who need further practice with the concepts of this section should be provided with the Chapter 1 activity called Examining Temperature Patterns in the Atmosphere.

CONTENT DEVELOPMENT

Have students observe the diagram in Figure 1–23. Encourage students to look carefully at the arrows that represent the radio waves.

• **Describe the path of the radio waves.** (First they travel into the ionosphere; then they travel to places all over the Earth.)

• **What do you notice about the angle with which a wave reaches the ionosphere compared with the angle with**

THE SOLAR CONSTANT

The rate at which the sun's rays strike the top of the Earth's atmosphere is known as the solar constant. The average value for the solar constant is 1.94 calories per square cm per min. During a year, the solar constant fluctuates least near the equator and most near the poles. On the average, locations at or near the equator receive two and a half times more solar radiation per year than do locations near the poles.

Figure 1–24 *Weather satellites orbiting the Earth transmit information used by scientists to track weather patterns. What type of weather do you think the southeastern United States is having?* ●

off the ions in the ionosphere and back to the Earth's surface. As a result, AM radio messages can be sent over great distances.

Sometimes large disturbances on the sun's surface, known as solar flares, cause the number of ions in the ionosphere to increase. This increase in ions can interfere with the transmission of some radio waves.

THE EXOSPHERE The upper thermosphere is called the **exosphere** (EHKS-oh-sfeer). The exosphere extends from about 550 kilometers above the Earth's surface for thousands of kilometers. The air is so thin in the exosphere that one particle can travel great distances without hitting another particle.

It is in the exosphere that artificial satellites orbit the Earth. Satellites play an important role in television transmission and in telephone communication. Does it surprise you to learn how great a distance a long distance call actually travels if the signal bounces off a satellite in the exosphere before it returns to the Earth? Satellites are also used to keep a 24-hour watch on the world's weather. And because the very thin air in the exosphere makes seeing objects in space easier, telescopes are often carried aboard satellites.

1–3 (continued)

REINFORCEMENT/RETEACHING

Emphasize to students the idea that each layer of the atmosphere has a temperature boundary. Also stress that many temperature changes occur as one moves from the Earth's surface to the upper atmosphere.

• **Is it correct to say that temperature always decreases as one travels higher in the Earth's atmosphere?** (No.)

• **Why did scientists once believe this to be true?** (Accept all logical answers. Scientists based this belief on the experiences of mountain climbers and early balloonists, who did not go very far above the Earth's surface.)

• **What caused scientists to revise their ideas about temperature changes and altitude?** (Accept all logical answers. Evidence from high-altitude balloons and rockets showed that temperature decreases steadily up to about 10 km. After that, temperature levels off, increases, levels off again, decreases, levels off, then finally increases.)

CONTENT DEVELOPMENT

Explain that there are several ways in which disturbances on the sun affect the atmosphere. The most intense of these are solar flares. These radio emissions cause the number of ions in the ionosphere to increase.

1–3 Section Review

1. How are the layers of the atmosphere divided? What are the four main layers?
2. Identify one significant characteristic of each layer of the atmosphere. How is that characteristic important to you on Earth?
3. Why is ozone important to life on Earth?
4. Why is the temperature in the thermosphere not measured with a thermometer?

Connection—*Ecology*

5. Scientists are concerned that "holes" are being created in the ozone layer. In such a hole, the amount of ozone is reduced. Predict what would happen to life on Earth if the amount of ozone in the ozone layer were depleted.

● ● ● ● **Integration** ● ● ● ●

Use the discussion of solar flares to integrate concepts of astronomy into your lesson.

GUIDED PRACTICE

Skill Development

Skills: Making observations, recording data, making comparisons, making inferences

At this point have students complete the in-text Chapter 1 Laboratory Investigation: Radiant Energy and Surface Temperature. In the investigation students will explore the heat-absorption characteristics of various types of surfaces.

INDEPENDENT PRACTICE

Section Review 1–3

1. The layers of the atmosphere are determined by major changes in temperature. The four layers are the troposphere, the stratosphere, the mesosphere, and the thermosphere.

CONNECTIONS

Sneezing and Wheezing— ❷ It's Allergy Time

It's spring again. The days get longer. The sun seems warmer and friendlier. Plants once again begin to grow. After the short, cold days of winter, most people look forward to spring as a promise of the season to come. But for many others, spring brings the misery of allergies. An allergy is a reaction caused by an increased sensitivity to a certain substance. With every breath they take, allergy sufferers are reminded of the many natural sources of air pollution.

Pollen grains are one kind of particle normally found in the air. Pollen grains are male plant reproductive cells. During certain times of the year, different kinds of pollen are released into the air. For example, maple and oak trees flower in the early spring, releasing millions upon millions of pollen grains into the air. These pollen grains are light-weight and float on air currents. If a person with an allergy to maple and oak tree pollen breathes in these pollen grains, certain cells in the respiratory system overreact, producing a chemical called histamine. This chemical causes the nose to run, the throat to tickle, and the eyes to water and itch.

You have probably heard of the condition called hay fever. Hay fever is neither a fever nor is it caused by hay. Hay fever is another example of an allergy. In this case, the culprit is ragweed pollen. Ragweed pollen also causes histamine to be produced.

There is no complete cure for allergies. If the particular pollen cannot be avoided, sufferers can take allergy-relief medicines prescribed by their physicians. As you can see, for some people, there are dangers hidden in the beauty of the natural world.

Ragweed pollen (left), ragweed plant (right)

I ■ 33

1-4 The Magnetosphere

TEACHING STRATEGY 1-4

FOCUS/MOTIVATION

Show students a compass.
- **Do you know in which direction the needle of the compass is pointing?** (North.)
- **Do you know why it points north?** (Answers may vary; correct answer is that the magnetized needle is attracted to the north magnetic pole of the Earth.)

CONTENT DEVELOPMENT

Use the Motivation demonstration to introduce the concept of the Earth's magnetic field. Point out that although the magnetic force of the Earth operates thousands of kilometers above the Earth's surface, the force can still be felt by a tiny needle here on the Earth.
- **Can you describe the pattern of force lines that surround a bar magnet?** (The lines of force spread outward from the

north and south poles of the magnet, then form two large semicircles between the north and south poles.)
- **Look at Figure 1–25. How do the lines of force around the bar magnet compare with the lines of magnetic force around the Earth?** (They are very similar.)
- **What does this tell you about the Earth?** (The Earth acts like a magnet; therefore, the Earth must have magnetic properties.)

1-4 The Magnetosphere

The area around the Earth that extends beyond the atmosphere is called the **magnetosphere** (mag-NEET-oh-sfeer). The Earth's magnetic force operates in the magnetosphere. The magnetosphere begins at an altitude of about 1000 kilometers. On the side of the Earth that faces the sun, the magnetosphere extends out into space about 4000 kilometers. It extends even farther into space on the other side of the Earth. See Figure 1–25. The difference in size of the magnetosphere is caused by the solar wind, which is a stream of fast-moving ions given off by the outermost layer of the sun's atmosphere. (Ions, recall, are electrically charged particles common to the ionosphere.) The solar wind pushes the magnetosphere farther into space on the side of the Earth away from the sun.

The magnetosphere is made up of positively charged protons and negatively charged electrons. Protons and electrons are two of the most important particles that make up atoms. An atom is considered the basic building block of matter, or the smallest unit from which all substances are made. Protons and electrons are given off by the sun and captured by the Earth's magnetic field. The charged particles

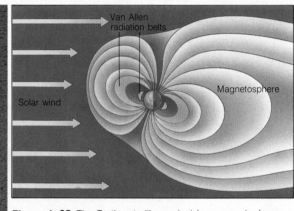

Figure 1–25 *The Earth acts like a giant bar magnet whose lines of force produce the same pattern as a small bar magnet. Why does the magnetosphere formed by the Earth extend farther on one side than on the other?* ❶

34 ■ I

● ● ● ●   **Integration**   ● ● ● ●

Use the discussion of the protons and electrons in the magnetosphere to integrate the physical science concepts of matter into your lesson.

CONTENT DEVELOPMENT

Explain that the magnetosphere can be affected by disturbances on the sun. Charged particles emitted by the sun can collide with particles in the upper atmosphere. One result of this can be the mul-

Figure 1–26 *Electrically charged particles from the sun collide with particles in the upper atmosphere and produce the multicolored lights called an aurora. Here you see the aurora borealis, or northern lights.*

are concentrated into belts, or layers, of high radiation. These belts are called the **Van Allen radiation belts.** They were discovered by satellites in 1958 and named after James Van Allen, the scientist whose work led to their discovery.

The Van Allen radiation belts pose a problem for space travelers. Space flights have to be programmed to avoid the radiation or suitable protection must be provided for astronauts who travel through the belts. However, the Van Allen belts are important to life on the Earth. They provide protection by trapping other deadly radiation.

When there is a solar flare, the magnetosphere is bombarded by large quantities of electrically charged particles from the sun. These charged particles get trapped in the magnetosphere. Here they collide with other particles in the upper atmosphere. The collisions cause the atmospheric particles to give off light. The multicolored lights are called the aurora borealis, or northern lights, and the aurora australis, or southern lights.

After a heavy bombardment of solar particles, sometimes called a magnetic storm, the magnetic field of the Earth may change temporarily. A compass needle may not point north. Radio signals may be interrupted. Telephone and telegraph communications may also be affected.

1–4 Section Review

1. What is the magnetosphere made of?
2. Why are the Van Allen radiation belts important to life on Earth?
3. How can scientists predict when an aurora will be visible?

Critical Thinking—*Relating Concepts*
4. How did technology contribute to the discovery of the Van Allen radiation belts?

I ■ 35

HISTORICAL NOTE
MAGNETISM

The magnetic properties of the Earth were first observed by the ancient Greeks. The Greeks discovered that if a piece of lodestone, which is a natural magnet, were suspended from a string, the lodestone would always align itself in a north-south direction.

The earliest compasses consisted of magnetized needles that floated in water on a piece of cork. Later on, the needles were mounted on a card, and the various directions were marked off about the rim of a circle. Because the directions encompassed the rim of the card, the magnetized needle came to be called a compass.

ticolored lights called the auroras (singular: aurora).

● ● ● ● **Integration** ● ● ● ●

Use the discussion of the auroras to integrate concepts of light into your lesson.

INDEPENDENT PRACTICE

▶ *Activity Book*

Further practice with the concepts of this section may be provided with the Chapter 1 activity called Plotting Radio Reception.

INDEPENDENT PRACTICE
Section Review 1–4

1. Protons and electrons.
2. They trap other deadly radiation.
3. By watching for solar flares on the sun.
4. Information collected by satellites led to the discovery of the belts.

REINFORCEMENT/RETEACHING

Review students' responses to the Section Review questions. Reteach any material that is still unclear, based on students' responses.

CLOSURE

▶ *Review and Reinforcement Guide*

Have students complete Section 1–4 in the *Review and Reinforcement Guide*.

Laboratory Investigation

RADIANT ENERGY AND SURFACE TEMPERATURE

BEFORE THE LAB

1. At least one day prior to the investigation, gather enough materials for your class, assuming six students per group.
2. Check thermometers to make sure all are in good condition.

PRE-LAB DISCUSSION

Discuss how radiant energy heats the Earth. Remind students that the atmosphere plays an important role in this process because it keeps our planet from being too hot or too cold. Point out to students that the heating of the Earth involves an energy change, as radiant energy from the sun is changed into heat energy.

Have students read the complete laboratory procedure. Discuss the procedure by asking questions similar to the following.

• **What is being explored in this investigation?** (Whether different types of surfaces gain different amounts of heat in and out of direct sunlight.)

Emphasize to students that time is also a factor in this investigation—they will observe whether certain surfaces absorb radiant energy more quickly than others do.

• **What factors will be the variables?** (Whether the surface is or is not exposed to direct sunlight; what the nature of the surface is.)

• **What measurement will you use to determine how much radiant energy a surface has absorbed?** (Temperature.)

Point out that temperature is a measure of the average kinetic energy of molecules. As molecules absorb the sun's radiant energy, they gain kinetic energy, and temperature increases.

• **How would the results change if it were a very cloudy day?** (The readings in the sun would be lower; those in the shade would not be much different—making inferences.)

Laboratory Investigation

Radiant Energy and Surface Temperature

Problem

Does the type of surface affect the amount of heat absorbed both in and out of direct sunlight?

Materials   (per group)

10 thermometers
stopwatch or clock with sweep second hand
2 shallow containers of water

Procedure 🔥

1. Place a thermometer on the grass in the sun. Place a second thermometer on the grass in the shade.
2. Place the remaining thermometers—one in the sun and one in the shade—on bare soil, on concrete, on a blacktop surface, and in water.
3. After 2 minutes, record the temperature of each surface.
4. Continue recording the temperature of each surface every 2 minutes for a period of 10 minutes.
5. Record your results in a data table similar to the one shown here.

Surface	Temperature in the Sun					Temperature in the Shade				
	2 min	4 min	6 min	8 min	10 min	2 min	4 min	6 min	8 min	10 min
Grass										
Soil										
Concrete										
Blacktop										
Water										

Observations

1. Which surface was the warmest? Which surface was the coolest?
2. By how many degrees did the temperature of each surface in direct sunlight change during the 10-minute time period?
3. By how many degrees did the temperature of each surface in the shade change during the 10-minute period?

Analysis and Conclusions

1. Why do you think the warmest surface was the warmest?
2. How do you explain the temperature change that occurred in water?
3. What conclusions can you reach about the amount of heat energy different surfaces absorb from the sun?
4. **On Your Own**   How can you apply your observations to the kinds of clothing that should be worn in a warm climate? In a cold climate? In what other ways do the results of this investigation affect people's lives?

SAFETY TIPS

Remind students to be careful when handling thermometers. Encourage students to consider safety when deciding where to place their thermometers.

TEACHING STRATEGY

1. Have teams follow the directions carefully as they work in the laboratory.
2. Remind students that when observing the "warmest" and "coolest" surfaces, they must consider the change in temperature, not just the final temperature.

Study Guide

Summarizing Key Concepts

1–1 A View of Planet Earth: Spheres Within a Sphere

▲ The solid parts of planet Earth make up the lithosphere.

▲ Parts of the Earth that are made up of water compose the hydrosphere.

▲ The envelope of gases that surrounds the Earth is the atmosphere.

1–2 Development of the Atmosphere

▲ About 3.8 billion years ago, chemical reactions triggered by sunlight produced new substances in the atmosphere.

▲ The ozone layer is sometimes referred to as an "umbrella" for life on Earth. The ozone layer absorbs much of the harmful radiation from the sun.

▲ The present atmosphere consists mainly of nitrogen, oxygen, carbon dioxide, water vapor, argon, and several other gases present in trace amounts.

1–3 Layers of the Atmosphere

▲ The four main layers of the atmosphere are the troposphere, stratosphere, mesosphere, and the thermosphere.

▲ Almost all of the Earth's weather occurs in the troposphere.

▲ Temperature decreases with increasing altitude in the troposphere. The zone of the troposphere where the temperature remains fairly constant is called the tropopause.

▲ Most of the ozone in the atmosphere is located in a layer of the stratosphere.

▲ The upper mesosphere is the coldest region of the atmosphere.

▲ The thermosphere is made up of the ionosphere and the exosphere.

1–4 The Magnetosphere

▲ The magnetosphere extends from an altitude of about 1000 kilometers far into space.

▲ The Van Allen radiation belts are layers of high radiation that form as a result of the concentration of charged particles.

Reviewing Key Terms

Define each term in a complete sentence.

1–1 A View of Planet Earth: Spheres Within a Sphere

equator
hemisphere
lithosphere
hydrosphere
atmosphere

1–2 Development of the Atmosphere

ozone

1–3 Layers of the Atmosphere

air pressure
troposphere
convection current
stratosphere
jet stream
mesosphere
thermosphere
ionosphere
ion
exosphere

1–4 The Magnetosphere

magnetosphere
Van Allen radiation belt

I ■ 37

---

3. Students should observe that all surfaces had similar temperature changes.

ANALYSIS AND CONCLUSIONS

1. The blacktop absorbs more heat energy from the sun because the color black is a poor reflector of heat energy.

2. The sun's heat energy is more slowly absorbed by the water than by the other surfaces.

3. Dark surfaces, such as blacktop and possibly soil, absorb more radiant energy than lighter surfaces do.

4. Light-colored clothing should be worn in warm climates and dark-colored clothing in cold climates.

One possible application of the investigation is in heating buildings. Homes that have a black roof would absorb more radiant energy from the sun than would homes with a light-colored roof. Therefore, energy consumption in these homes would be greater during the summer when air conditioning is used to cool the home.

GOING FURTHER: ENRICHMENT

Part 1

Have students do the same experiments at different times of day and compare the results. For example, they might carry out the investigation once at 9 AM and once at noon.

Part 2

Have students find out how the tilt of the Earth's axis affects the absorption of radiant energy in various locations on the Earth.

DISCOVERY STRATEGIES

Discuss how the investigation relates to the chapter ideas by asking open questions similar to the following:

• **How do you think the results of this experiment would change if you were doing it on top of a very high mountain?** (All the temperature readings would likely be lower—making inferences.)

OBSERVATIONS

1. Students should find that temperatures in the sun are higher than those in the shade. They should observe that the blacktop has the highest temperature, followed by the concrete, soil, grass, and water.

2. Students should observe that temperature change was rapid on the blacktop, concrete, and soil. The grass would also show a slight temperature change but not as great as the previous three surfaces. Very little temperature change will be noted in the shallow pan of water because the sun's heat energy is more slowly absorbed by the water than by the other surfaces.

Chapter Review

ALTERNATIVE ASSESSMENT

The *Prentice Hall Science* program includes a variety of testing components and methodologies. Aside from the Chapter Review questions, you may opt to use the Chapter Test or the Computer Test Bank Test in your *Test Book* for assessment of important facts and concepts. In addition, Performance-Based Tests are included in your *Test Book*. These Performance-Based Tests are designed to test science process skills, rather than factual content recall. Since they are not content dependent, Performance-Based Tests can be distributed after students complete a chapter or after they complete the entire textbook.

CONTENT REVIEW

Multiple Choice

1. b
2. d
3. b
4. d
5. c
6. b
7. c
8. d

True or False

1. T
2. F, atmosphere
3. F, ozone
4. T
5. F, ions
6. F, decreases
7. T

Concept Mapping

Row 1: Northern Hemisphere
Row 2: Hydrosphere, Atmosphere

CONCEPT MASTERY

1. Microscopic organisms living on or near the surface of the oceans used sunlight and carbon dioxide to produce food. In the process, they gave off oxygen, allowing other living things to develop.

2. Accept all logical answers. Oxygen is necessary because people cannot breathe the atmosphere on Mars; a spacesuit would provide protection against extremes of temperature; radiation protection might be necessary because Mars does not have the ozone layer that Earth does.

Content Review

Multiple Choice

Choose the letter of the answer that best completes each statement.

1. The envelope of gases that surrounds the Earth is called the
   a. lithosphere.   c. hydrosphere.
   b. atmosphere.   d. equator.
2. Oceans, lakes, and the polar ice caps are part of the Earth's
   a. crust.   c. fresh water.
   b. argons.   d. hydrosphere.
3. Four billion years ago the Earth's atmosphere contained the deadly gases
   a. nitrogen and oxygen.
   b. methane and ammonia.
   c. methane and oxygen.
   d. nitrogen and ozone.
4. The most abundant gas in the atmosphere is
   a. oxygen.   c. argon.
   b. carbon dioxide   d. nitrogen.

5. The layer of the atmosphere where the temperature may reach 2000°C is called the
   a. stratosphere.   c. thermosphere.
   b. mesosphere.   d. troposphere.
6. Ultraviolet radiation from the sun is absorbed by ozone in the
   a. troposphere.   c. thermosphere.
   b. stratosphere.   d. ionosphere.
7. Artificial satellites orbit the Earth in the part of the thermosphere called the
   a. ionosphere.   c. exosphere.
   b. mesosphere.   d. troposphere.
8. The lowest layer of the atmosphere is called the
   a. stratosphere.   c. thermosphere.
   b. mesosphere.   d. troposphere.

True or False

If the statement is true, write "true." If it is false, change the underlined word or words to make the statement true.

1. Almost <u>85 percent</u> of the fresh water on Earth is trapped in ice.
2. The envelope of gases that surrounds the Earth is called the <u>hydrosphere</u>.
3. Few living things could survive on Earth without the presence of <u>methane</u>, the gas that absorbs ultraviolet radiation.
4. The <u>magnetosphere</u> is the area that extends beyond the atmosphere.
5. Electrically charged particles are called <u>molecules</u>.
6. As altitude increases, the temperature of the air <u>increases</u>.
7. Because of the increased burning of fossil fuels, the level of <u>carbon dioxide</u> in the air is increasing.

Concept Mapping

Complete the following concept map for Section 1–1. Refer to pages I6–I7 to construct a concept map for the entire chapter.

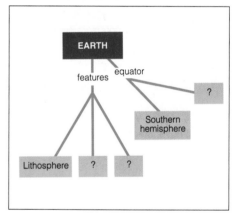

---

3. Nitrogen makes up 78 percent of the atmosphere, oxygen makes up 21 percent, and the remaining 1 percent is composed of carbon dioxide, water vapor, argon, and trace gases.

4. The layers of air that surround the Earth are held close to it by gravity. The layers of air push down on the Earth's surface. This is called air pressure. The upper layers of air also push down on the lower layers. Because of this, air pressure is greater near the surface of the Earth than it is farther away from it.

5. Ultraviolet radiation has a wavelength shorter than that of visible light. It helps to produce vitamin D in the human body. Too much ultraviolet radiation, however, can cause sunburn and, possibly, skin cancer.

6. Satellites have helped to gather a variety of information about the temperature and composition of the layers of the atmosphere. Also, the use of satellites led to the discovery of the Van Allen radiation belts in the magnetosphere.

Concept Mastery

Discuss each of the following in a brief paragraph.

1. How did living organisms change the atmosphere of ancient Earth?
2. Tell how each of the following items would be useful for an astronaut on a trip to Mars: a supply of oxygen, a space suit, radiation protection.
3. What are the four most common gases in the troposphere? In what percentages do these gases occur?
4. Explain why air pressure decreases as altitude increases.
5. What is ultraviolet radiation? What effect does this type of radiation have on living things?
6. How have satellites contributed to our knowledge of the atmosphere?

Critical Thinking and Problem Solving

Use the skills you have developed in this chapter to answer each of the following.

1. **Applying concepts** Could animals have lived on ancient Earth before green plants? Explain your answer.
2. **Applying concepts** Traveling from New York to San Francisco, California takes about 5 hours and 30 minutes. The return trip from San Francisco to New York, however, takes about 5 hours. Use your knowledge of the jet stream to explain the difference in travel time.

3. **Relating cause and effect** Scientists are concerned that certain chemicals, when released into the atmosphere, cause the level of ozone to decrease. Predict what might happen to living things on Earth if the ozone layer continues to decrease.
4. **Sequencing events** Make a series of drawings or small dioramas to show how the atmosphere of Earth has changed over time.
5. **Making diagrams** The diagrams on pages 19 and 21 show the nitrogen and the oxygen-carbon dioxide cycles. Use these diagrams as a guide to draw pictures of each cycle as it occurs in your surroundings. Include plants and animals found in your area.
6. **Using the writing process** People have walked on the moon during your parents' or your teachers' lifetime. Conduct an interview with your parents or a teacher. Ask them if they saw the first step onto the moon. Have them describe their feelings at the time of the first moon walk. Organize the information from the interview into a short essay.

5. Students' drawings will vary, depending on location. Students, however, should correctly label the parts of their diagrams and the arrows indicating the cycle of events. Drawings might include school, home, local landmarks, farm animals, vegetable gardens, plants, and trees.
6. Students' essays might include information on the observed characteristics of the moon's atmosphere.

KEEPING A PORTFOLIO

You might want to assign some of the Concept Mastery and Critical Thinking and Problem Solving questions as homework and have students include their responses to unassigned questions in their portfolio. Students should be encouraged to include both the question and the answer in their portfolio.

ISSUES IN SCIENCE

The following issues can be used as springboards for discussion or given as writing assignments.

Air pollution is changing our present atmosphere in many ways. Get together with several classmates and research two or three of the most serious problems caused by air pollution. Then present a round-table discussion in which each problem is described and possible solutions are presented.

CRITICAL THINKING AND PROBLEM SOLVING

1. No. Animals require oxygen to breathe. Before green plants, there was very little, if any, oxygen on Earth.
2. Jets flying in the same direction as the jet stream, west to east, make better time because they meet less wind resistance and move with the jet stream's "push." Jets flying against the jet stream are slowed because of wind resistance.

3. A thinning of the ozone layer will permit more of the dangerous rays of the sun, primarily ultraviolet rays, to reach Earth. The protective functions of the ozone layer may be diminished, causing harm to life on Earth.
4. Students' drawings should depict all the changes discussed in this chapter. For example, drawings should show the sunlight breaking water vapor into hydrogen and oxygen.

SECTION	HANDS-ON ACTIVITIES
2–1 The World's Oceans pages I42–I43 Multicultural Opportunity 2–1, p. I42 ESL Strategy 2–1, p. I42	**Activity Book** CHAPTER DISCOVERY: Help! I'm Drowning, p. I37 **Teacher Edition** Relating Evaporation and Salinity, p. I40d
2–2 Properties of Ocean Water pages I44–I48 Multicultural Opportunity 2–2, p. I44 ESL Strategy 2–2, p. I44	**Student Edition** ACTIVITY (Doing): Temperature and Salinity, p. I45 ACTIVITY (Discovering): A Drink of Water, p. I47 LABORATORY INVESTIGATION: The Effect of Water Depth on Sediments, p. I74 ACTIVITY BANK: Sink or Swim—Is It Easier to Float in Cold Water or Hot? p. I167 **Laboratory Manual** Relating Salinity and Density, p. I15 **Activity Book** ACTIVITY: The Salty Ocean, p. I47
2–3 The Ocean Floor pages I49–I56 Multicultural Opportunity 2–3, p. I49 ESL Strategy 2–3, p. I49	**Student Edition** ACTIVITY (Doing): Ocean-Floor Model, p. I55
2–4 Ocean Life Zones pages I57–I63 Multicultural Opportunity 2–4, p. I57 ESL Strategy 2–4, p. I57	**Student Edition** ACTIVITY (Doing): Fish for the Table, p. I62 **Laboratory Manual** Culturing and Observing Brine Shrimp. p. I19
2–5 Mapping the Ocean Floor pages I63–I64 Multicultural Opportunity 2–5, p. I63 ESL Strategy 2–5, p. I63	
2–6 Motions of the Oceans pages I65–I73 Multicultural Opportunity 2–6, p. I65 ESL Strategy 2–6, p. I65	**Student Edition** ACTIVITY (Discovering): Currently Current, p. I68 ACTIVITY: (DOING): The Moon's Attraction, p.173 **Laboratory Manual** Investigating Density Currents, p. I25
Chapter Review pages I74–I77	

OTHER ACTIVITIES	MEDIA AND TECHNOLOGY
Student Edition ACTIVITY (Writing): A Salty Tale, p. I43 **Review and Reinforcement Guide** Section 2–1, p. I17	Video Introduction to Oceanography (Supplemental) English/Spanish Audiotapes Section 2–1
Activity Book ACTIVITY: Composition of Sea Water: Constructing a Graphic Model, p. I59 ACTIVITY: Profile of a Tropical Ocean, p. I63 **Review and Reinforcement Guide** Section 2–2, p. I19	English/Spanish Audiotapes Section 2–2
Student Edition ACTIVITY (Reading): The Great Whale, p. I50 ACTIVITY (Thinking): Strolling Under the Seas, p. I52 **Activity Book** ACTIVITY: Ocean and Continental Profiles, p. I45 **Review and Reinforcement Guide** Section 2–3, p. I21	Interactive Videodisc Investigating Science: Treasures From the Deep Video Ocean Floor (Supplemental) Courseware Ocean Floor (Supplemental) Transparency Binder Ocean-Floor Features English/Spanish Audiotapes Section 2–3
Student Edition ACTIVITY (Writing): Sea Turtles, p. I67 **Activity Book** ACTIVITY: Physical Properties of the Ocean's Life Zones, p. I49 **Review and Reinforcement Guide** Section 2–4, p. I25	Video Troubled Sea (Supplemental) Estuaries (Supplemental) Marine (Supplemental) Videodisc Aquatic Ecosystems: Estuaries Aquatic Ecosystems: Marine Courseware Life Zones in the Ocean English/Spanish Audiotapes Section 2–4
Activity Book ACTIVITY: Determining Ocean Depth, p. I53 ACTIVITY: Major Features of the Earth's Solid Surface, p. I69 **Review and Reinforcement Guide** Section 2–5, p. I27	English/Spanish Audiotapes Section 2–5
Activity Book ACTIVITY: Characteristics of Ocean Waves, p. I41 ACTIVITY: Temperature Effects and Surface Currents, p. I55 **Review and Reinforcement Guide** Section 2–6, p. I29	Video Waves (Supplemental) Transparency Binder Ocean Wave Characteristics Long-Distance Surface Currents Rip Currents English/Spanish Audiotapes Section 2–6
Test Book Chapter Test, p. I31 Performance-Based Tests, p. I119	Test Book Computer Test Bank Test, p. I37

*All materials in the Chapter Planning Guide Grid are available as part of the Prentice Hall Science Learning System.

Chapter 2 EARTH'S OCEANS

CHAPTER OVERVIEW

Approximately 71 percent of the Earth is covered by ocean water. To an alien observer, the oceans of Earth might appear lifeless. The oceans, however, contain a tremendous variety of plant and animal life and physical features.

The Earth is covered by three major oceans—the Atlantic, Indian, and Pacific. Water in any ocean is a mixture of gases and solids dissolved in pure water. Though oceans can be thought of as being salt water, they also contain other dissolved substances, notably the gases carbon dioxide and oxygen. These gases are essential for the life functions of all ocean organisms.

Ocean floors also display major features, both near the edges of continents and on the deep ocean floor. Near continents, features of the ocean floor generally include a continental shelf, a continental slope, and a continental rise. Farther away from continents, features of the ocean floor include abyssal plains, seamounts, guyots, trenches, ridges, and reefs.

2-1 THE WORLD'S OCEANS
THEMATIC FOCUS

The purpose of this section is to introduce students to the world's oceans. Although about 71 percent of the Earth's surface is covered by oceans, the three major oceans are the Atlantic, Indian, and Pacific. The ocean and the water cycle combine to provide a source of fresh water for all living things.

The theme that can be focused on in this section is systems and interactions.

*Systems and interactions: Water in the atmosphere is cycled through Earth's oceans. Pure water in the form of precipitation falls to land, returning to the oceans as runoff in rivers and streams. The sun completes the cycle by powering evaporation of ocean water into the atmosphere.

PERFORMANCE OBJECTIVES 2-1

1. Name the three major oceans of Earth.
2. Relate the role of the oceans to the water cycle.

2-2 PROPERTIES OF OCEAN WATER
THEMATIC FOCUS

The purpose of this section is to introduce students to the properties of ocean water. Students will discover that materials other than salts are dissolved in ocean water, including but not limited to various gases. The dissolved gases in ocean water relied on most by living organisms are oxygen and carbon dioxide. These gases allow plants and animals to survive in the ocean.

The sun is the major source of heat for ocean water, and the temperature of ocean water helps to determine the types of organisms that can live in any location. The surface zone has a relatively constant temperature except for seasonal changes. The thermocline zone is characterized by rapid temperature changes. The deep zone has cold, quite constant water temperatures.

The themes that can be focused on in this section are stability and unity and diversity.

*Stability: The salinity of ocean water remains within a relatively narrow range, varying from 33 to 37 parts per thousand and averaging 35 parts per thousand.

Unity and diversity: Different water temperatures and density areas in the ocean contain varying amounts of certain gases and other dissolved materials.

PERFORMANCE OBJECTIVES 2-2

1. Describe the composition and characteristics of ocean water.
2. Explain what is meant by salinity.
3. Describe the three temperature zones of the oceans.

SCIENCE TERMS 2-2

oceanographer p. I44
salinity p. I44
surface zone p. I47
thermocline p. I47
deep zone p. I47

2-3 THE OCEAN FLOOR
THEMATIC FOCUS

The purpose of this section is to introduce students to the characteristics and major features of the ocean floor. Near the edges of continents, the ocean floor generally consists of a continental shelf, a continental slope, and a continental rise. The continental shelves and slopes are sometimes cut by submarine canyons.

The ocean floor, or ocean basin, contains features such as flat abyssal plains, mountains such as guyots and seamounts, long and narrow trenches, rugged ridges of mountains, and several varieties of reefs.

The theme that can be focused on in this section is unity and diversity.

Unity and diversity: The Earth's crust that lies under the ocean has higher mountains and deeper valleys than the crust on land has.

PERFORMANCE OBJECTIVES 2-3

1. Compare the topography of the ocean floor to the topography of the land.
2. Describe the components of the continental margin.
3. Describe the major features of the ocean floor.

SCIENCE TERMS 2-3

shoreline p. I49
continental margin p. I49
continental shelf p. I49
continental slope p. I50
continental rise p. I50
turbidity current p. I50
submarine canyon p. I51
abyssal plain p. I51
seamounts p. I52
guyot p. I53
trench p. I53
midocean ridge p. I54
coral reef p. I55

fringing reef p. I55
barrier reef p. I56
atoll p. I56

bathyal zone p. I62
abyssal zone p. I62

2-4 OCEAN LIFE ZONES
THEMATIC FOCUS

The purpose of this section is to describe the great variety of life that exists in the ocean. Ocean life has been classified into three major groups according to their habits and the depth of water in which they live. The largest group of plants and animals is called plankton, which are very small, often microscopic organisms living near the surface or on the surface of an ocean. Forms of ocean life that swim are called nekton. They can move to search for food or to avoid predators. Organisms that live on the ocean floor are called benthos. These three groups of ocean life exist in three major environments, or life zones—intertidal, neritic, and bathyal.

The themes that can be focused on in this section are scale and structure and evolution.

*Scale and structure: The Earth's oceans are divided into three life zones: intertidal, neritic, and bathyal. These life-zone classifications are based on the conditions in the ocean.

Evolution: Over time, ocean life has changed. Today the life zones in the oceans support organisms that are adapted to the environmental conditions that exist there.

PERFORMANCE OBJECTIVES 2-4

1. **Describe the factors that affect ocean life.**
2. **Describe the three major groups of ocean organisms.**
3. **Identify the three major life zones of the ocean.**

SCIENCE TERMS 2-4

plankton p. I57
nekton p. I57
benthos p. I58
intertidal zone p. I59
neritic zone p. I61

2-5 MAPPING THE OCEAN FLOOR
THEMATIC FOCUS

The oceans have been called the last great unexplored places on Earth. In this section students will learn that mapping the ocean floor can only be done by indirect methods, such as echo sounding, radar, sonar, and seismographic surveys.

The theme that can be focused on in this section is patterns of change.

*Patterns of change: The shallower regions of oceans are changed by the action of waves and currents. The deep regions of the ocean are changed by earthquakes and volcanic actions. Features of the oceans are changing over time in our dynamic oceans.

PERFORMANCE OBJECTIVES 2-5

1. **Describe early efforts to map the ocean floor.**
2. **Discuss the methods available today to map the ocean floor.**
3. **Explain how satellite technology has provided an accurate map of the ocean floor.**

2-6 MOTIONS OF THE OCEANS
THEMATIC FOCUS

The purpose of this section is to introduce the three basic motions of the ocean: the up-and-down movement of waves, the steady movement of ocean currents, and the rise and fall of ocean water in tides.

The theme that can be focused on in this section is energy.

*Energy: The energy of the wind causes the formation of waves. The energy of an earthquake can produce a tsunami—a very large wave that carries much destructive energy with it.

PERFORMANCE OBJECTIVES 2-6

1. **Describe the characteristics and causes of waves.**
2. **Distinguish between the causes of surface currents and deep currents.**
3. **Describe the characteristics and causes of tides.**

SCIENCE TERMS 2-6

crest p. I66
trough p. I66
wavelength p. I66
tsunami p. I67
surface current p. I68
deep current p. I70
upwelling p. I71

Discovery *Learning*

TEACHER DEMONSTRATIONS MODELING
Relating Evaporation and Salinity

This demonstration will emphasize the concept of salinity. For the demonstration, you will need table salt, water, a hot plate, a balance scale, and a container large enough to hold 1 kilogram of solution. It would be ideal if ocean salts could be purchased and used in place of the table salt or if a sample of ocean water could be used in place of the solution.

Prepare a 1-kilogram solution containing 35 to 37 grams of salt. Heat the solution until all of the water evaporates. Carefully collect the residue and have a volunteer determine its mass. Record the mass on the chalkboard and ask students to calculate the salinity of the water sample.

Stress the idea that when water evaporates, the salt is left behind.
• **What do you think happens to the salinity of ocean water when water evaporates from the Earth's surface?** (It increases.)
• **Why?** (The total amount of water is less, but the amount of salt remains the same.)
• **How do you think unusually hot, dry weather affects salinity?** (It causes salinity to increase because more water tends to evaporate.)

CHAPTER 2
Earth's Oceans

INTEGRATING SCIENCE

This earth science chapter provides you with numerous opportunities to integrate other areas of science, as well as other disciplines, into your curriculum. Blue numbered annotations on the student page and integration notes on the teacher wraparound pages alert you to areas of possible integration.

In this chapter you can integrate social studies (pp. 42, 63, 68), earth science and meteorology (pp. 42, 69), physical science and solutions (p. 44), earth science and erosion (p. 45), life science and photosynthesis (p. 46), physical science and convection (p. 47), earth science and energy resources (p. 49), language arts (pp. 50, 52, 73), earth science and earthquakes and volcanoes (p. 55), life science and zoology (pp. 55, 57), earth science and satellite technology (p. 63), physical science and sonar (p. 64), physical science and waves (p. 67), earth science and oceanography (p. 71), earth science and tides (p. 72), and physical science and sound (p. 73).

SCIENCE, TECHNOLOGY, AND SOCIETY/COOPERATIVE LEARNING

About 71 percent of the Earth's surface is covered by water. In the future, underwater cities may provide space for increasing populations; mining the ocean may provide many natural resources; and aquaculture—farming of the ocean—may produce the food that society will one day need.

Another promising benefit that society might derive from the ocean is new generations of drugs and other useful chemicals. More than one half of the drugs in use today are derived from land-dwelling plants. Considering that 80 percent of all life on Earth lives in the ocean, the potential for useful chemicals and drugs from ocean materials is large. Already, promising substances from the ocean include tetrodotoxin, a possible anesthetic; pseudoptersin, an anti-inflammatory painkiller that might be used to treat arthritis; an adhesive protein produced by mussels that might be used as a dental ad-

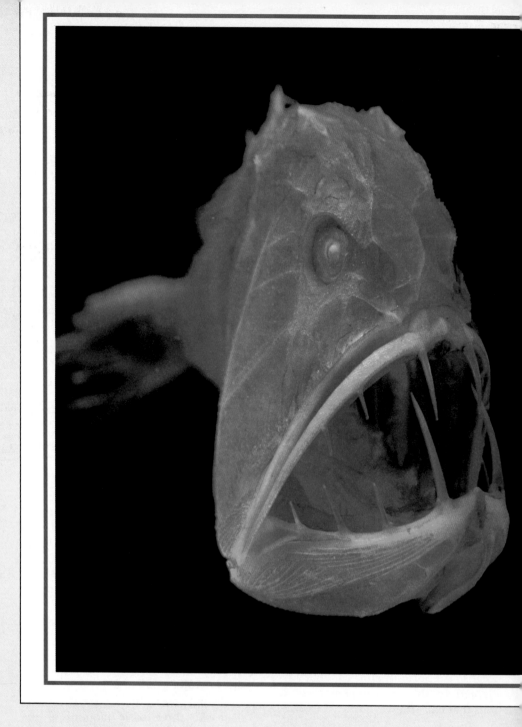

INTRODUCING CHAPTER 2

DISCOVERY LEARNING

▶ *Activity Book*

Begin teaching the chapter by using the Chapter 2 Discovery Activity from the *Activity Book*. Using this activity, students will explore the relationship between salt water and buoyancy.

USING THE TEXTBOOK

Have students observe the photograph on page I40 and encourage them to share their impressions of the anoplogaster.

• **What characteristic of the anoplogaster is most obvious in this photograph?** (Most students will probably say the teeth.)
• **What do the teeth tell you about the anoplogaster?** (It preys upon other animals for food.)

Earth's Oceans

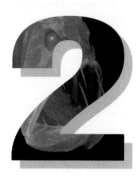

Many bizarre living things make their home deep beneath the ocean waves. Indeed, some fish look as if they recently swam out of the pages of the strangest science fiction novel. The anoplogaster on the opposite page is but one example. With its needlelike teeth bared, the 15-centimeter fish stalks its prey. Food, however, is scarce in the 6000-meter-deep water this fish calls home.

At this profound depth, the water temperature is near freezing, the pressure tremendous. But in this blue-black ocean water where no sunlight penetrates, the anoplogaster is a fearsome predator.

The oceans are rich in many forms of life. Tiny single-celled plants share the salt waters of the Earth with mammoth whales. A wide variety of organisms obtain the gases and foods they need from ocean water. The ocean plays an important role in your survival, as well. It is a direct source of food and an indirect source of fresh water for all living things.

In this chapter, you will learn more about the oceans—their properties, motions, and the land beneath them. And you will become more familiar with the variety of living things that make the oceans their home.

Journal *Activity*

You and Your World In 1492, it took Christopher Columbus weeks to reach the New World by sailing across the Atlantic in ships powered by winds. Would you have liked to be a member of Columbus's crew? What do you think that long voyage was like? In your journal, keep a diary for a week in which you are a member of Columbus's crew.

Tiny but terrifying, an anoplogaster patrols the ocean depths in search of food.

hesive; and an immune-system stimulant extracted from blue-green bacteria.

The ocean contains hundreds of thousands of species of plants and animals. Even if only 10 percent of these species yield biologically active substances, the ocean will quickly become the Earth's medicine chest.

Cooperative learning: Using preassigned groups or randomly selected teams, have groups complete the following assignment.

- Design a magazine cover that highlights a magazine issue that will devote its entire contents to articles about the ocean. Groups should review the material in this chapter, the Futures in Science gazette article "Cities Under the Sea," and the material in this column to help prepare a table of contents for their magazine. The final product of each group should include a drawing of the magazine cover and a table of contents detailing the articles that the magazine will contain.
- See Cooperative Learning in the *Teacher's Desk Reference.*

JOURNAL ACTIVITY

You may want to use the Journal Activity as the basis of a class discussion. Have students volunteer to describe what a day might have been like as a crew member of sailing ships such as Columbus's. Have students consider the dangers that weather and diseases posed to the ship and crew. Would the risks be worth the possible reward? Students should be instructed to keep their Journal Activity in their portfolio.

- **In this photograph, does the anoplogaster look large or small?** (It appears rather large.)
- **What is the actual size of the anoplogaster?** (Only 15 centimeters long.)

Have students use metric rulers to illustrate the size of the anoplogaster.

Point out that until a little more than 100 years ago, scientists thought that no significant life existed in deep ocean water. In 1841, the British survey ship *Beacon* lowered a fishing line several me-

ters below the ocean's surface. When they reeled the line back into the ship, it yielded nothing much in terms of life. The naturalists aboard the *Beacon* concluded that they had "proven" that no life existed beneath the surface of the ocean.

The real breakthrough in deep-sea exploration came with the launch of the British ship *Challenger* in 1872. From the *Challenger*, probes were sent down several kilometers below the ocean's sur-

face. Scientists discovered strange and beautiful life forms that they never thought existed.

2-1 The World's Oceans

MULTICULTURAL OPPORTUNITY 2-1

Have students research some ancient ship voyages. These might be of particular interest: the ancient Egyptians who sailed on the Nile River in northern Africa, on the Red Sea, and off the eastern Mediterranean coast; the early sea journeys of the Chinese; the travels of the Vikings; the sea voyages of the fleet of the great African King Abubakari II; or the later travels of Columbus.

ESL STRATEGY 2-1

Prepare a worksheet that contains a blank map of the world and space to answer questions. Ask students to work in pairs or small groups as they perform the following activities.

1. Locate each of the world's three major oceans by writing their names in the proper area.

2. List the three major oceans in order of greatest area, volume, and depth.

3. Explain how the oceans' salt water becomes fresh water, while the salt remains in the ocean.

Selectively check students' work by having volunteers read their answers to the class.

TEACHING STRATEGY 2-1

FOCUS/MOTIVATION

Point out that from the vantage point of space, the oceans are the Earth's most dominant feature. Explain that space technology has greatly aided scientists in exploring the ocean. Many of the things students will learn about and explore in this chapter have been discovered or made much clearer as a result of satellite photographs.

CONTENT DEVELOPMENT

Students may not realize that the oceans are all connected to one another as one continuous body of water. Point out that the continents are really islands in one great ocean.

2-1 The World's Oceans

Suppose a contest was held in which you were asked to rename the Earth? What would you call it? If you looked at the Earth's surface features from space, you might call it Oceanus. This would probably be a good name to choose because about 71 percent of the Earth's surface is covered by ocean water. In fact, the oceans contain most of the Earth's water—about 97 percent. And although each ocean and sea has a separate name, all of the oceans and seas are actually one continuous body of water. **The Atlantic, Indian, and Pacific oceans are the three major oceans.** Smaller bodies of ocean water, such as the Mediterranean Sea, the Black Sea, and the Arctic Ocean, are considered part of the Atlantic Ocean. A sea is a part of an ocean that is nearly surrounded by land. Can you name any other seas?

The Pacific Ocean is the largest ocean on Earth. Its area and volume are greater than those of the Atlantic and Indian oceans combined. The Pacific Ocean is also the deepest ocean. Its average depth is 3940 meters. The Atlantic Ocean is the second largest ocean. The average depth of the Atlantic Ocean is 3350 meters. Although the Indian Ocean is much smaller than the Atlantic, its average depth is greater.

The ocean, which you may already know is made of salt water, plays an important role in the water cycle. During this cycle, the sun's rays heat the surface of the ocean. The heat causes the water to evaporate, or change from the liquid phase to the gas phase. The evaporating water—pure, fresh water—enters the atmosphere as water vapor. The salts remain in the ocean.

Winds carry much of the water vapor over land areas. Some of the water vapor in the atmosphere condenses to form clouds. Under the right conditions, the water in clouds falls as precipitation (rain, snow, sleet, and hail). Some of this water runs into

Figure 2-1 *Notice the sea stacks that have been carved by ocean waves off Big Sur in California. What percent of the Earth's surface is covered by water?*

42 ■ I

● ● ● ● **Integration** ● ● ● ●

Use the discussion of the smaller bodies of water on Earth to integrate social studies concepts into your science lesson.

GUIDED PRACTICE

Skills Development

Skill: Interpreting maps

Display a political world map or make atlases or geography books available to students. Divide the class into three

groups. Ask one group to name as many countries as they can that border the Atlantic Ocean; ask a second group to do the same for the Indian Ocean; ask a third group to do the same for the Pacific Ocean. Upon completion of the activity, have volunteers from each group discuss their findings with the class.

CONTENT DEVELOPMENT

Review the concept of the water cycle with students. Point out that this cycle is also called the hydrologic cycle.

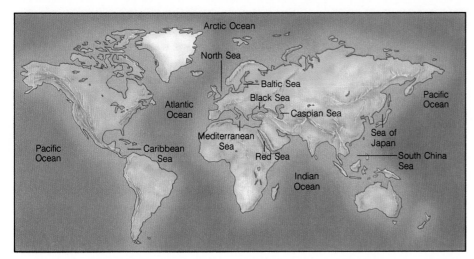

Figure 2–2 *The major oceans and seas of the world are actually part of one continuous body of water. What are the three major oceans?* ③

rivers and streams that flow directly back into the ocean. Some of it seeps deep into the soil and rocks of the Earth to become part of the groundwater beneath the Earth's surface. As you can see, the ocean is a source of fresh water for all living things.

2–1 Section Review

1. What are the three main oceans of the world?
2. What is a sea?
3. What part does the ocean play as a source of fresh water for all living things?

Critical Thinking—*Relating Cause and Effect*

4. The state of Washington lies on the Pacific Ocean. Certain parts of this state receive large amounts of rain throughout the year. Predict which parts receive the most rain. Explain why.

ACTIVITY WRITING

A Salty Tale

In the past, many people who did not eat seafood experienced an enlargement of the thyroid gland. The thyroid is a gland located in the neck that regulates how food is used by the body. This enlargement, called a goiter, results from a lack of a chemical in the body, a chemical commonly found in seafoods. You might like to look up this disease in a library to find out the name of this chemical. Find out what other food this chemical is commonly added to. Report on your findings to the class.

I ▪ 43

ANNOTATION KEY

Answers

① Answers might include the Caspian, Arabian, Red, South China, Caribbean, North, Baltic, or Sea of Japan. (Applying facts)

② About 71 percent. (Relating facts)

③ Atlantic, Indian, and Pacific. (Relating facts)

Integration

① Social Studies

② Earth Science: Meteorology. See *Exploring Earth's Weather*, Chapter 1.

ACTIVITY WRITING
A SALTY TALE

Check students' findings for scientific accuracy. Students should find that goiter results from a lack of iodine in the body and that iodine is commonly added to table salt.

4. Predictions may include the windward areas of land nearest the coast or the windward areas of land having the highest elevation. Windward coastal areas and windward elevated regions tend to receive large amounts of precipitation when compared to other inland or less-elevated regions.

REINFORCEMENT/RETEACHING

Monitor students' responses to the Section Review questions. If students appear to have difficulty with any of the questions, review the appropriate material in the section.

CLOSURE

▶ *Review and Reinforcement Guide*

At this point have students complete Section 2–1 in the *Review and Reinforcement Guide*.

• **Why is the ocean the source of all fresh water?** (When ocean water evaporates, the salts are left behind in the ocean. When the water vapor condenses and falls as rain, it becomes fresh water. The rain (as well as snow and other forms of precipitation) forms ponds, lakes, rivers, underground water sources, and the like.)

● ● ● ● **Integration** ● ● ● ●

Use the discussion of the sun's relationship to the water cycle to integrate meteorology into your science lesson.

INDEPENDENT PRACTICE

Section Review 2–1

1. Pacific, Atlantic, Indian.
2. A sea is a part of an ocean that is nearly surrounded by land.
3. As a result of the water cycle, ocean water is returned to the Earth as fresh water.

2-2 Properties of Ocean Water

MULTICULTURAL OPPORTUNITY 2-2

The ancient Egyptians were among the first to make important advancements in shipbuilding. As early as 4000 BC, Egyptians used reeds to make boats and galleys. Some 1000 years later, they invented the sail and soon afterward built boats made of wood. Ask students to research the history of shipbuilding in ancient Egypt. How were the different kinds of vessels designed and made? How were they steered? How were they able to withstand huge waves and unfavorable winds? Have interested students build a model of a ship. Students may also visit a museum where ancient vessels are displayed.

ESL STRATEGY 2-2

Ask students to do the following.
1. Make an illustration that demonstrates the oceans' three temperature zones.
2. Make an illustration that shows the sun as the major heat source of oceans.
3. Make notations on the physical conditions of each ocean.

Suggest that students exchange papers and check each other's work.

TEACHING STRATEGY 2-2

FOCUS/MOTIVATION

Direct students' attention to the chart in Figure 2–3. Have students take turns choosing an element listed in the chart and telling what they know about the element. If certain elements are unfamiliar, have students research them in a physical science book or an encyclopedia.

CONTENT DEVELOPMENT

Continue the Focus/Motivation discussion by pointing out that the chart lists only the most abundant elements in the ocean (the total percentage is not exactly 100 percent). So far, 85 different elements have been discovered in the ocean.

Guide for Reading

Focus on these questions as you read.
▶ What is ocean water composed of?
▶ What are some characteristics of ocean water?

Figure 2–3 Ocean water is composed of hydrogen, oxygen, and about 85 other elements. Of those other elements, which two are the most abundant? ❶

MAJOR ELEMENTS IN OCEAN WATER	
Element	**Percent of Total (%)**
Oxygen Hydrogen	96.5
Chlorine	1.9
Sodium	1.1
Magnesium Sulfur Calcium Potassium Bromine Carbon Strontium Silicon Fluorine Aluminum Phosphorus Iodine	0.5
	100

44 ■ I

2–2 Properties of Ocean Water

Ocean water is a mixture of gases and solids dissolved in pure water. Scientists who study the ocean, or **oceanographers** (oh-shuh-NAHG-ruh-fuhrz), believe that ocean water contains all of the natural elements found on Earth. Ninety elements are known to exist in nature. So far, about 85 of these have been found in ocean water. Oceanographers are hopeful that with improved technology, they will find the remaining elements.

Ocean water is about 96 percent pure water, or H_2O. So the most abundant elements in ocean water are hydrogen (H) and oxygen (O). The other 4 percent consists of dissolved elements. Figure 2–3 lists the major elements in ocean water.

Salts in Ocean Water

Sodium chloride is the most abundant salt in ocean water. If you have ever accidentally swallowed a mouthful of ocean water, you have probably recognized the taste of sodium chloride. Sodium chloride is, in fact, common table salt. It is made of the elements sodium and chlorine.

Sodium chloride is only one of many salts dissolved in ocean water. Figure 2–4 shows the other salts. Oceanographers use the term **salinity** (suh-LIHN-uh-tee) to describe the amount of dissolved salts in ocean water. Salinity is the number of grams of dissolved salts in 1 kilogram of ocean water. When 1 kilogram of ocean water evaporates, 35 grams of salts remain. Of these 35 grams, 27.2 grams are sodium chloride. How many grams are magnesium chloride? ❷

The salinity of ocean water is expressed in parts per thousand. It ranges between 33 and 37 parts per thousand. The average salinity of ocean water is 35 parts per thousand.

Salts and other materials dissolved in ocean water come from several different sources. One important source is volcanic activity in the ocean. When volcanoes erupt, rock materials and gases spew forth. These substances dissolve in ocean water. Chlorine

---

• **What must be true about the amounts of the elements not listed in the chart?** (They total a very small number.)

Stress that it is water's unique property as a solvent that makes it possible for so many elements to dissolve in it.

GUIDED PRACTICE

Skills Development

Skill: Making computations

Have students solve the following exercises involving salinity.

1. A 2-kilogram sample of ocean water contains 72 grams of dissolved salts. What is the salinity of the water? (36 parts per thousand.)
2. The salinity of ocean water in a particular region is 37 parts per thousand. How many grams of dissolved salts would you expect to find in a 500-gram sample of the water? (18.5 grams.)

CONTENT DEVELOPMENT

Emphasize that the salinity of ocean water increases or decreases depending

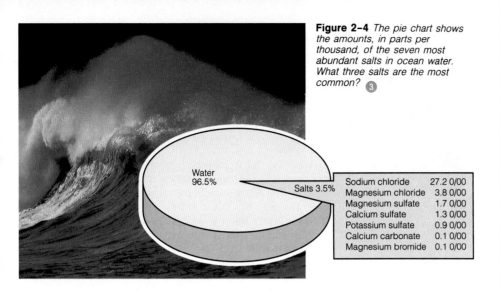

Figure 2–4 *The pie chart shows the amounts, in parts per thousand, of the seven most abundant salts in ocean water. What three salts are the most common?* ❸

Water 96.5%	Salts 3.5%

Sodium chloride	27.2 0/00
Magnesium chloride	3.8 0/00
Magnesium sulfate	1.7 0/00
Calcium sulfate	1.3 0/00
Potassium sulfate	0.9 0/00
Calcium carbonate	0.1 0/00
Magnesium bromide	0.1 0/00

gas is one substance that is added to ocean water as a result of volcanic activity.

❷ Another source of dissolved materials is the erosion of the land by rivers, streams, and glaciers. As rivers, streams, and glaciers move over rocks and soil, they dissolve salts in them. Sodium, magnesium, and potassium reach the ocean in this way.

The action of waves breaking along the shore is also a source of salts and other dissolved materials. As waves pound the shoreline, they dissolve the salts contained in the rocks along the coast.

In most areas of the ocean, the salinity is about the same. But in some areas, greater or lesser amounts of dissolved salts cause differences in the salinity. Several reasons explain these differences. The salinity is much lower in areas where freshwater rivers run into the ocean. This is especially true where major rivers such as the Mississippi, Amazon, and Congo flow into the ocean. Can you suggest a reason for the lower salinity? At these points, huge amounts of fresh water pour into the ocean, diluting the normal amount of salts in the ocean water.

In warm ocean areas where there is little rainfall and much evaporation, the amount of dissolved salts in the water is greater than average. Thus, the salinity is higher. The salinity is higher in the polar regions also. Here temperatures are cold enough for

ACTIVITY
DOING

Temperature and Salinity

1. Pour 100 mL of hot tap water into a glass.

2. Add salt, one teaspoonful at a time, to the water. Stir the water after each addition. Stop adding salt when no more can be dissolved. Record the number of teaspoons of salt added. Empty the contents of the glass. Wash the glass.

3. Now pour 100 mL of cold water into the same glass. Repeat steps 1 and 2.

In which glass did more salt dissolve?

What relationship have you illustrated by doing this investigation?

I ▪ 45

ACTIVITY
DOING

TEMPERATURE AND SALINITY

Skills: Identifying relationships, relating concepts

Materials: 100 mL hot water, glass, salt, teaspoon, 100 mL cold water

This activity will help students understand the relationship between temperature and salinity. Students should observe that more salt (solute) dissolves in hot water than in cold water. As the temperature of a solvent increases, the solubility of the solute (salt) increases.

on various conditions. These conditions include the deposition of fresh water into the ocean by a river (decreases), the freezing of water in polar regions (increases), and unusually warm temperatures or below-normal rainfall (increases).

● ● ● ● **Integration** ● ● ● ●

Use the discussion of the salinity of ocean water to integrate concepts about solutions into your science lesson.

Use the discussion of dissolved materials in ocean water in integrate concepts about erosion into your earth science lesson.

REINFORCEMENT/RETEACHING

▶ *Activity Book*

Students who need practice on the concept of dissolved materials in ocean water should complete the chapter activity The Salty Ocean. In this activity students will explore the residue left behind after water turns to water vapor.

I ▪ 45

TEMPERATURE AND WATER

The heat capacity of ocean water is two to three times greater than the heat capacity of land and more than ten times greater than the heat capacity of air. Consequently, the ocean serves as a stabilizer of the Earth's temperature.

Temperature changes occur very gradually in the ocean, and this factor is important in terms of world climate. If it were not for the stabilizing effect of the ocean, drastic shifts in land and air temperatures would cause such radical changes in weather that the Earth would probably be uninhabitable.

Even small variations in normal ocean temperatures can cause drastic changes in weather. Oceanographers have discovered that sometimes pools of water form in the ocean that have temperatures one to two degrees Celsius higher or lower than the surrounding water. One such pool of warm water caused a hurricane along the east coast of the United States. A pool of cool water off the Pacific coast caused a severe drought in the West.

2-2 (continued)

CONTENT DEVELOPMENT

Point out that the flow of oxygen and carbon dioxide between plants and animals is the same in the ocean as it is on land.

• **Why is it important that oxygen and carbon dioxide are soluble in water?** (If these gases could not dissolve in water, ocean plants and animals could not live.)

• **What happens to a fish that is left on land?** (The fish will quickly die.)

Mention that plants and animals that live in the ocean have the ability to take in oxygen and carbon dioxide from water but that they do not have this ability in the atmosphere of gases over land.

● ● ● ● **Integration** ● ● ● ●

Use the discussion of gases in ocean water to integrate the concept of photosynthesis into your earth science lesson.

Figure 2–5 *One source of minerals in ocean water is the erosion of cliffs by ocean waves.*

Figure 2–6 *The salinity of the ocean is fairly constant. However, in areas where rivers dump sediment-laden fresh water into the ocean, the salinity is reduced. Ocean animals such as flame scallops also reduce salinity.*

ocean water to freeze. When ocean water freezes, pure water is removed and the salts are left behind.

Scientists believe that the salinity of ocean water is also affected by animal life. Animals such as clams and oysters use calcium salts to build their shells. They remove these salts from ocean water, thus lowering the salinity of the water.

Gases in Ocean Water

The most abundant gases dissolved in ocean water are nitrogen, carbon dioxide, and oxygen. Two of these gases, carbon dioxide and oxygen, are vital to ocean life. Most plants take carbon dioxide from the water and use it to make food. In the presence of sunlight, the plants combine carbon dioxide with water to make sugars. During this process, oxygen is released into the water. Plants and animals use oxygen to break down food and provide energy for all life functions.

The amount of nitrogen, carbon dioxide, oxygen, and other gases in ocean water varies with depth. Nitrogen, carbon dioxide, and oxygen are more abundant at the ocean's surface. Here sunlight easily penetrates and plant growth abounds. The abundant plant growth ensures a large supply of oxygen—certainly a great deal more than is found in the depths of the oceans. Can you explain why?

The amount of dissolved gases is also affected by the temperature of ocean water. Warm water holds less dissolved gas than cold water. When ocean water cools, as in the polar regions, it sinks. (Cold water is

---

ENRICHMENT

▶ *Activity Book*

Students will be challenged to make a hands-on representation by the Chapter 2 activity called Composition of Sea Water: Constructing a Graphic Model.

CONTENT DEVELOPMENT

Point out that the ocean gains and loses heat much more slowly than land does. This is why ocean water will feel chilly in June even though land temper-

atures may be warm, and ocean water will feel warm in October even though land temperatures may be cool.

The major source of heat for the ocean is the sun. Solar radiation is absorbed by the water and converted into heat, effectively raising the temperature of the water. Almost all of the solar radiation is absorbed in the surface zone of ocean water, although some of the radiation in the blue-green wavelengths penetrates much deeper. This penetration enables

denser, or heavier, than warm water.) It carries oxygen-rich water to the ocean depths. As a result, fish and other animals can live in deep parts of the ocean.

Temperature of Ocean Water

The sun is the major source of heat for the ocean. Because solar energy enters the ocean at the surface, the temperature of the water is highest there. Motions of the ocean, such as waves and currents, mix the surface water and transfer the heat downward. The zone where the water is mixed by waves and currents is called the **surface zone.** The surface zone extends to a depth of at least 100 meters. Sometimes it extends as deep as 400 meters.

The temperature of the water remains fairly constant within a surface zone. It does not change much with depth. But the temperature in a surface zone does change with location and with season. Water near the equator is warmer than water in regions farther north and south. Summer water temperatures are warmer than winter water temperatures. For example, the summer water temperature near the surface of the Caribbean Sea may be 26°C. Farther north, off the coast of England, the temperature near the surface may be 15°C. What do you think happens to the water temperature at these two places during the winter? ②

Below the surface zone the temperature of the water drops very rapidly. This zone of rapid temperature change is called the **thermocline** (THER-moh-klighn). The thermocline does not occur at a specific depth. The season and the flow of ocean currents alter the depth of the thermocline.

The thermocline exists because warm surface water does not easily mix with cold deep water. The difference in the densities of the warm water and the cold water keeps them from mixing. The less dense warm water floats on top of the denser cold water.

The thermocline forms a transition zone between the surface zone and the **deep zone.** The deep zone is an area of extremely cold water that extends from the bottom of the thermocline to depths of 4000 meters or more. Within the deep zone, the temperature decreases only slightly. At depths greater than

A Drink of Water

■ Use your knowledge of the properties of salt water to devise a procedure for obtaining fresh water from ocean water by freezing. Describe the steps to your teacher. With permission, try your procedure using the following: Dissolve 3 grams of table salt in 100 mL of water. Report your results to your class.

Figure 2–7 *There are three temperature zones in the ocean.*

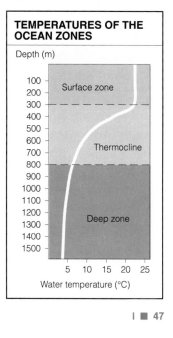

TEMPERATURES OF THE OCEAN ZONES

Depth (m)

Surface zone
Thermocline
Deep zone

Water temperature (°C)

I ■ 47

plants to carry on photosynthesis at depths of more than 300 meters.

During daylight hours, and also during summer when the sun is directly overhead, the amount of radiation absorbed will exceed the radiation that is lost. This will cause a rise in the temperature of the water. The opposite effect occurs at night and during the winter.

Most of the ocean's waters are not heated directly by incoming solar radiation. Ocean water beneath the surface zone is warmed by conduction and by mixing caused by waves and ocean currents.

● ● ● ● **Integration** ● ● ● ●

Use the discussion of the warming of ocean water by solar radiation to integrate concepts of heat energy and convection into your earth science lesson.

BACKGROUND INFORMATION

THE CONTINENTAL SHELF

The continental shelf can be up to 1600 kilometers wide. It is narrowest where it borders on steep land and widest where it borders on gently sloping land. Along the western coast of the United States, the continental shelf is narrow because the land is mountainous. Along the eastern coast of the United States, the continental shelf is wider because the land slopes gently.

2–2 (continued)

ENRICHMENT

▶ *Activity Book*

Students will be challenged by the Chapter 2 activity called Profile of a Tropical Ocean. In this activity students will explore the variables that influence the physical characteristics of ocean water.

INDEPENDENT PRACTICE

Section Review 2–2
1. Ocean water is a mixture of gases and solids dissolved in pure water.
2. Salinity is the amount of dissolved salts, in parts per thousand, in ocean water.
3. Nitrogen, carbon dioxide, and oxygen.
4. Surface zone, thermocline, and deep zone; temperature.
5. Greater numbers of fish would be found away from the equator; as the temperature of water increases, the amount of dissolved gases that water can hold decreases.

Figure 2–8 *Ocean temperatures vary from the Caribbean Sea to the White Cliffs of Dover to the polar regions. Notice the blue-green bacteria below the frozen surface of Lake Hoare in Antarctica.*

1500 meters, the temperature is about 4°C. So the temperature of most ocean water is just above freezing (0°C)!

The three ocean zones are not found in the polar regions. In the Arctic and Antarctic oceans, the surface waters are always very cold. The temperature changes only slightly as the depth increases.

Ⓐctivity Bank

Sink or Swim—Is It Easier to Float in Cold Water or Hot?, p.167

2–2 Section Review

1. What does ocean water consist of?
2. What is salinity?
3. What three gases are most abundant in ocean water?
4. What are the three zones of the ocean? On what property of ocean water are these zones based?

Critical Thinking—*Applying Concepts*
5. Fish get the oxygen they need by removing it from water. Would you expect to find greater numbers of fish near the equator or in ocean areas farther north and south of the equator? Explain your answer. (*Hint:* Consider the effect of temperature on the amount of gases that can dissolve in water.)

REINFORCEMENT/RETEACHING

Review students' responses to the Section Review questions. Reteach any material that is still unclear, based on students' responses.

CLOSURE

▶ *Review and Reinforcement Guide*
Students may now complete Section 2–2 in the *Review and Reinforcement Guide*.

TEACHING STRATEGY 2-3

FOCUS/MOTIVATION

Before students read this section, ask this question.
● **How do you picture the bottom of the ocean floor?** (Answers will vary.)
Discuss the various student responses. Point out that although the topography of the ocean floor is different from that of the continents, both are part of the Earth's surface and both have similar fea-

2–3 The Ocean Floor

A description of the shape of the ocean floor—its characteristics and major features—is known as its topography. The topography of the ocean floor is different from the topography of the continents. The ocean floor has higher mountains, deeper canyons, and larger, flatter plains than the continents. The ocean floor also has more volcanoes than the continents. Earthquakes occur with greater frequency under the ocean than on the land. The rocks that form the ocean floor are very different from the rocks that form the crust of the continents. The crust of the Earth is much thinner under the ocean than under the continents.

Edges of the Continents

On a continent, there is a boundary where the land and the ocean meet. This boundary is called a **shoreline.** A shoreline marks the average position of sea level. It does not mark the end of the continent.

The edge of a continent extends into the ocean. The area where the underwater edge of a continent meets the ocean floor is called a **continental margin.** Although a continental margin forms part of the ocean floor, it is more a part of the land than it is a part of the ocean.

A continental margin generally consists of a continental shelf, a continental slope, and a continental rise. Sediments worn away from the land are deposited in these parts of a continental margin.

The relatively flat part of a continental margin that is covered by shallow ocean water is called a **continental shelf.** A continental shelf usually slopes very gently downward from the shoreline. In fact, it usually slopes less than 1.2 meters for every 100 meters from the shoreline.

The width of a continental shelf varies. Off the Atlantic coast, the continental shelf extends more than 200 kilometers into the ocean. Off the Arctic shore of Siberia, the continental shelf extends over 1200 kilometers into the ocean. Off the coast of southeastern Florida, there is almost no continental shelf.

Guide for Reading

Focus on these questions as you read.

▶ What are the parts of a continental margin?

▶ What are some major features of the ocean floor?

Figure 2–9 *An offshore oil rig drills for oil trapped beneath the ocean floor in the continental shelf.*

I ■ 49

MULTICULTURAL OPPORTUNITY 2-3

Seashells are used throughout the world as decorations and jewelry. Boxes, chests, musical instruments, frames, and trays are frequently decorated with seashells. Since ancient times, people have traded with seashells, using them as money in exchange for food, clothing, tools, or gifts. Suggest that students find out about the use of shells as money in different lands such as China, African countries such as Zaire and Nigeria, the Philippines, Papua New Guinea and the Trobriand Islands in the South Pacific, as well as by native peoples in North and South America.

ESL STRATEGY 2-3

To reinforce some of the terms in this section, have students match the terms in Column A with their definitions in Column B. Then have volunteers read their answers aloud.

Column A	Column B
continental shelf	area where continent's underwater edge meets the ocean floor
continental rise	
submarine canyons	boundary between continent's crust and ocean floor's crust
continental margin	water that carries large amounts of sediments
turbidity currents	
continental slope	relatively flat part of continental margin covered by shallow ocean water
	sediments separating continental slope from the ocean floor
	deep, V-shaped valleys cut through continental shelf and continental slope

tures. Also, point out that millions of years ago, parts of the Earth that are now landmasses were once underwater.

CONTENT DEVELOPMENT

Students may have a misconception that the boundary between an ocean and a continent is a single line, like the line on a drawing. Point out that this type of line usually represents the shoreline, which is simply the place where land and ocean meet. Emphasize that a continent meets the ocean floor in an extended area called the continental margin. The continental margin consists of the continental shelf, the continental slope, and the continental rise.

● ● ● ● **Integration** ● ● ● ●

Use the picture of an offshore oil rig to integrate concepts of energy resources into your earth science lesson.

THE GREAT WHALE

Skill: Reading comprehension

You may want to have volunteers give a brief synopsis of *Moby Dick* or read their favorite excerpts aloud to the class.

Integration: Use this Activity to integrate language arts skills into your science lesson.

FACTS AND FIGURES

WATER PRESSURE

Pressure increases dramatically from the surface of the ocean to the ocean floor. In the deep zone, pressure is greater than 1 ton per 8 cm².

2-3 (continued)

GUIDED PRACTICE

Skills Development

Skill: Making models

Have students work in small groups. Challenge each group to make a model of the continental margin. Students may wish to use such materials as modeling clay, papier-mâché, or soil for their models. In each model, the continental shelf, the continental slope, and the continental rise should be clearly labeled.

CONTENT DEVELOPMENT

Remind students that a continental margin usually consists of features known as a continental shelf, a continental slope, and a continental rise.

In recent years, scientists have conducted extensive studies of the ocean and its unique features. The Earth's continental shelves were formed in the past when materials carried by rivers, winds, and glaciers were deposited on the shelves when they were above the water level of the ocean.

At the edge of the continental shelves,

A C T I V I T Y
READING

The Great Whale

Moby Dick is one of the greatest stories ever written in the English language. This tale of the sea and the whalers who sailed it describes a time when people made a living by hunting the great whales. You might enjoy reading this book written by Herman Melville and reporting on it to your class.

Figure 2-10 *In this illustration, you can see the major features of the ocean floor. What are some of these features?* ❶

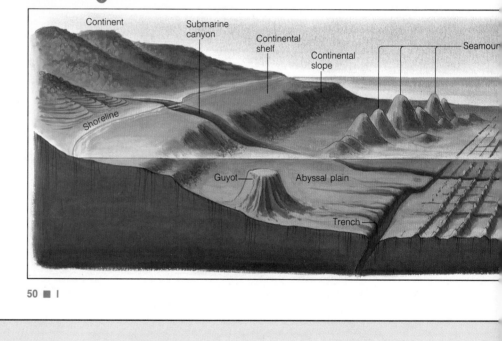

The best fishing areas of the ocean are found in waters over a continental shelf. Large mineral deposits, as well as large deposits of oil and natural gas are also found on a continental shelf. Because of the presence of these precious resources, many countries have extended their natural boundaries to include the continental shelf that lies off their shores.

At the edge of a continental shelf, the ocean floor plunges steeply 4 to 5 kilometers. This part of the continental margin is called a **continental slope.** A continental slope marks the boundary between the crust of the continent and the crust of the ocean floor. Separating a continental slope from the ocean floor is a **continental rise.** You can see the parts of a continental margin and other features of the ocean floor in Figure 2-10.

A continental rise is made of large amounts of sediments. These sediments include small pieces of rocks and the remains of plants and animals washed down from the continent and the continental slope. Sometimes the sediments are carried down the slope in masses of flowing water called **turbidity** (ter-BIHD-uh-tee) **currents.** A turbidity current is a flow of water that carries large amounts of sediments. A turbidity current is like an underwater avalanche.

the continental slopes begin. Here the ocean bottom drops about 70 meters for every kilometer in distance away from the continental shelves. The actual slope, however, is not as dramatic as is indicated on most diagrams depicting features of the ocean floor because such diagrams are seldom drawn to scale.

Separating a continental slope from the ocean floor is a continental rise. A continental rise is made of large amounts of sediments that have been washed down from the continent and the continental slope. Turbidity currents, which resemble underwater avalanches, occur when these sediments are carried down the continental slope.

To reinforce these concepts, ask the following questions.

• **Describe a continental margin.** (The edge of a continent extends into the ocean. A continental margin is the area where the underwater edge of a continent meets the ocean floor.)

In many areas, **submarine canyons** cut through a continental shelf and slope. Submarine canyons are deep, V-shaped valleys that have been cut in rock. Some of the canyons are very deep indeed. For example, the Monterey Submarine Canyon off the coast of central California reaches depths of more than 2000 meters. It is actually deeper than the Grand Canyon!

Many scientists believe that submarine canyons are formed by powerful turbidity currents. Submarine canyons may also be caused by earthquakes or other movements that occur on a continental slope. Scientists still have much to learn about the origin and nature of submarine canyons.

Features of the Ocean Floor

Scientists have identified several major features of the ocean floor. (The ocean floor is also called the ocean basin.) Refer back to Figure 2–10 as you read about these features.

ABYSSAL PLAINS Large flat areas on the ocean floor are called **abyssal** (uh-BIHS-uhl) **plains.** The abyssal plains are larger in the Atlantic and Indian oceans than in the Pacific Ocean. Scientists believe

Figure 2–11 *These divers are exploring a submarine canyon in the continental shelf. How are submarine canyons formed?* ②

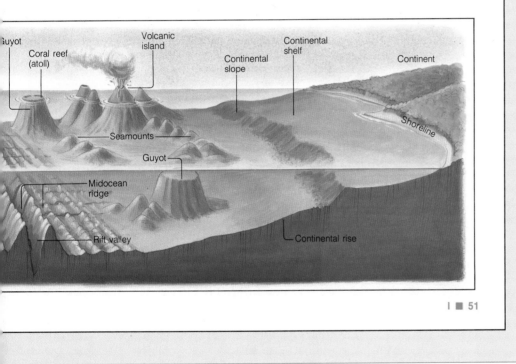

I ■ 51

ECOLOGY NOTE
POLAR ICECAPS

Interested students should research the effect that global warming may have on polar ice. If the Earth becomes warm enough to melt all of the polar ice, will the levels of the Earth's oceans increase, decrease, or remain the same? Have students share their findings with the class.

on the ocean floor. Have interested students find out more about manganese nodules and the efforts being made to mine them. Volunteers should report their findings to the class.

CONTENT DEVELOPMENT

The continental-shelf areas are commercially important to many countries. A wealth of resources usually lies in and under the waters of the continental shelf. The best fishing areas of an ocean are usually found in these waters, along with large mineral, oil, and natural gas deposits. Because of the potential economic value of the many resources in and under the waters of the continental shelf, many countries that border oceans have extended their natural boundaries to include the continental shelf that lies off their shores.

• **Is a continental margin best described as a land feature or an ocean feature?** (A land feature.)
• **Describe a continental shelf.** (A continental shelf is the relatively flat portion of a continental margin that is covered by shallow ocean water.)
• **Is a continental-shelf area of an ocean usually important to the economies of neighboring countries?** (Yes.)
• **What kinds of resources can be found in a continental-shelf area?** (Fish, minerals, oil, natural gas.)

• **At the edge of a continental shelf, the ocean floor plunges steeply. What is this feature of an ocean called?** (A continental slope.)
• **What is the name given to the currents that flow down a continental slope carrying sediments and remains of plants and animals?** (Turbidity currents.)

ENRICHMENT

Many valuable minerals are contained in manganese nodules, which are found

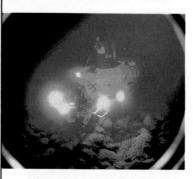
2-3 (continued)

CONTENT DEVELOPMENT

Review with students the technique of echo sounding. This process, also called sonar, is used to explore the depths of the ocean. Point out that when sound waves of echo sounding are sent out, they reflect off a solid surface, bouncing back toward the source of the waves. By measuring the time it takes for the sound waves to reach a solid surface and echo back, scientists can determine the distance to the solid object.

• **Why do you think scientists can "see" better with sound waves than with their eyes beneath the ocean's surface?** (There is little light as one descends below the ocean's surface, and the water can be murky. Visibility also can be very much like a thick fog—solid objects may not be visible, at least not from a safe distance. Sound waves, however, travel through water and darkness, indicating the presence and position of solid objects.)

Figure 2-12 *The submersible Alvin searches for unusual organisms in the sediments covering the abyssal plains.*

ACTIVITY
THINKING

Strolling Under the Seas

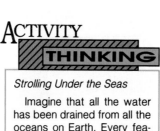

Imagine that all the water has been drained from all the oceans on Earth. Every feature once hidden under the waves is now seen easily. You and a friend decide to take a hike across the dry ocean floor. Choose a starting point and a destination. In a report, describe the features of the ocean floor you observe on your trip.

REINFORCEMENT/RETEACHING

▶ *Activity Book*

Students who need help on the concept of mapping the features of the ocean floor should complete the chapter activity Ocean and Continental Profiles. In this activity students will explore cross-sectional views of underwater-surface features and land-surface features.

ENRICHMENT

• **What do you think the Earth's surface would look like if all the water were**

that two reasons account for the difference in the size of these abyssal plains.

First, the world's greatest rivers flow directly or indirectly into the Atlantic and Indian oceans. These rivers include the Mississippi, Congo, Nile, and Amazon, which flow into the Atlantic Ocean, and the Ganges and Indus rivers which flow directly into the Indian Ocean. These major rivers, and many smaller ones, deposit large amounts of sediments on the abyssal plains.

Second, the floor of the Pacific Ocean contains a number of deep cracks along the edges of the continents. These long, narrow cracks trap sediments that are carried down a continental slope.

Deep-sea drilling operations and sound-wave detection equipment have shown that the sediments of the abyssal plains close to continents consist of thick layers of mud, sand, and silt. Farther out on the abyssal plains, some of the sediments contain the remains of tiny organisms. These organisms are so small they can be seen only with the aid of a microscope. They form a sediment called ooze. Where ocean life is not abundant, the floor of the ocean is covered with a sediment called red clay. Red clay is made of sediments carried to the oceans by rivers.

SEAMOUNTS AND GUYOTS Scattered along the floor of the ocean are thousands of underwater mountains called **seamounts.** Seamounts are volcanic mountains that rise more than 1000 meters above the surrounding ocean floor. Seamounts have steep sides that lead to a narrow summit (or top). To date, oceanographers have located more than 1000 seamounts. They expect to find thousands more in the future as more ocean areas are explored. Many more seamounts have been found in the Pacific Ocean than in either the Atlantic or the Indian Ocean.

Some seamounts reach above the surface of the ocean to form islands. The Azores and the Ascension Islands in the Atlantic Ocean are examples of volcanic islands. Perhaps the most dramatic and familiar volcanic islands are the Hawaiian Islands in the Pacific Ocean. The island of Hawaii is the top of a great volcano that rises more than 9600 meters from the ocean floor. It is the highest mountain on Earth when measured from its base on the ocean floor to its peak high above the surface of the ocean.

drained out of the oceans? (Accept all logical answers. Some students may think that the Earth's surface above water will look the same as the Earth's surface below water; others may think that the greatest part of the ocean floor may be smooth and uniform; whereas others may have the idea that the ocean floor varies greatly in terms of contour and height.)

Using a volunteer to record students' responses on the chalkboard, have stu-

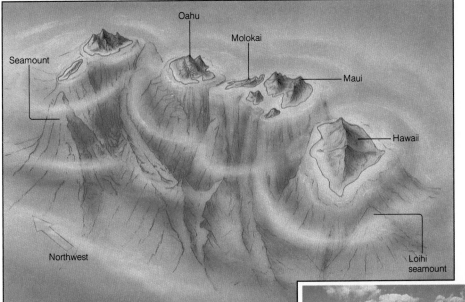

Figure 2–13 *The Hawaiian island of Kauai is the top of a seamount that extends above the ocean's surface (bottom). The age of the Hawaiian Islands increases as you travel toward the northwest. Loihi Seamount, off the coast of Hawaii, is slowly growing taller. Loihi will eventually become the newest Hawaiian island (top).*

During the mid-1940s, scientists discovered that many seamounts do not rise to a peak. Instead they have a flat top. These flat-topped seamounts are called **guyots** (gee-OHZ). Scientists believe that the flat tops are the result of wave erosion. Waves broke apart the tops of seamounts that once were at sea level. The flattened volcanic seamounts were later submerged.

TRENCHES The deepest parts of the ocean are not in the middle of the ocean floor. The greatest depths are found in **trenches** along the edges of the ocean floor. Trenches are long, narrow crevices (or cracks) that can be more than 11,000 meters deep.

The Pacific Ocean has more trenches than the other oceans. The Mariana Trench in the Pacific Ocean contains the deepest spot known on the Earth. This spot is called Challenger Deep. Challenger Deep is more than 11,000 meters deep. To

I ■ 53

FACTS AND FIGURES

THE MONTEREY SUBMARINE CANYON

The Monterey Submarine Canyon off the coast of central California reaches depths of more than 2000 meters. It is deeper than the Grand Canyon.

disturbed. Because of this, thick layers of sediment collect on the ocean floor.

Ocean-floor sediments can originate from three sources: the land, ocean plants and animals, and ocean water. Most sediments from the land are the result of weathering and erosion. They are carried into the ocean by rivers and by wind. Wind can also carry dust and ash from volcanic eruptions.

The type of sediment that comes from ocean plants and animals is called ooze. Ooze is made up of the shells and skeletons of dead ocean organisms.

The abyssal plains are the most level areas on the Earth's surface—flatter than any plain on land. Abyssal plains are formed as various sediments cover rough and uneven places on the ocean floor.

dents list as many features of land topography as possible (plains, mountains, valleys, and so forth).

• **How do you think the topography of the ocean floor compares with that of the continents?** (Accept all logical responses.)

Point out that although the topography of the ocean floor is different from that of land, both are part of the Earth's surface, and both have similar features.

INDEPENDENT PRACTICE

📖 **Media and Technology**

Use the transparency in the *Transparency Binder* called Ocean-Floor Features to help develop the concept of the variety of features on the ocean floor.

CONTENT DEVELOPMENT

Changes occur frequently and rapidly on the Earth's land surfaces, but the floor of the ocean remains relatively un-

OCEAN-FLOOR SPREADING

As molten rock rises up through rift valleys, new ocean floor is formed. This process is called ocean-floor spreading. As the molten rock cools and spreads out, colder ocean floor on either side of the rift valley is pushed away. Eventually, this older ocean floor is pushed to the trenches that run parallel to the coasts of the continents. At the trenches, older ocean floor is pushed back down into the mantle. This process is called subduction. Some of the older ocean floor is reheated in the mantle and eventually pushes up through rift valleys to become, once again, new ocean floor.

2-3 (continued)

GUIDED PRACTICE

Skills Development

Skill: Making comparisons

Have students find out how high the mountains are in the midocean ridges and compare these heights to the heights of major mountain ranges on land.

CONTENT DEVELOPMENT

Students may be surprised to learn that the depths of the deepest ocean trenches are greater than the heights of the highest mountains on land. The highest mountain on Earth, the island of Hawaii, is 9600 meters high—measured from the ocean floor, whereas the deepest ocean trench, Mindinao, extends 11,500 meters below the ocean surface.

● ● ● ● **Integration** ● ● ● ●

Use the discussion of rift valleys to integrate concepts about earthquakes and volcanoes into your lesson.

GUIDED PRACTICE

Skills Development

Skill: Making comparisons

Working in small groups, students can research the ten highest mountains on

MAJOR OCEAN TRENCHES	
Trench	**Depth (meters)**
Pacific Ocean	
Aleutian	8100
Kurile	10,542
Japan	9810
Mariana (Challenger Deep)	11,034
Philippine	10,497
Tonga	10,882
Kermadec	10,800
Peru-Chile	8055
Mindanao	10,030
Atlantic Ocean	
Puerto Rico	8648
South Sandwich	8400

Figure 2–14 *Ocean trenches are the deepest parts of the ocean floor. Which ocean, the Atlantic or Pacific, has the most trenches?* ❶

give you some idea of the depth of Challenger Deep, consider this: The Empire State Building in New York is about 430 meters tall. It would take a stack of 26 Empire State Buildings to break the ocean surface from the bottom of Challenger Deep!

MIDOCEAN RIDGES Some of the largest mountain ranges on Earth are located under the oceans. These mountain ranges are called **midocean ridges.** They form an almost continuous mountain belt that extends from the Arctic Ocean, down through the middle of the Atlantic Ocean, around Africa into the Indian Ocean, and then across the Pacific Ocean north to North America. In the Atlantic Ocean, the mountain belt is called the Mid-Atlantic Ridge. In the Pacific Ocean, the mountain belt is called the Pacific-Antarctic Ridge or East Pacific Rise or Ridge.

The midocean ridges are unlike any mountain ranges on land. Why? Mountain ranges on land are formed when the Earth's crust folds and is squeezed together. Midocean ridges are areas where molten (or hot liquid) material from deep within the Earth flows up to the surface. At the surface, the molten material cools and piles up to form new crust.

Figure 2–15 *This map shows the topography of the ocean floor.*

land and compare these heights to the depths of the eleven deepest ocean trenches, given in Figure 2–14. Graphs that show the comparisons should then be constructed and displayed.

INDEPENDENT PRACTICE

🔘 Media and Technology

Students can reinforce and broaden their understanding of the ocean by using the Interactive Videodisc called Treasures From the Deep. Using this vid-

eodisc, students will explore how scientists use modern technology to study ancient forms of life in and around the gold-laden wreck of the S.S. *Central America.*

ENRICHMENT

If possible, obtain a photograph of a map of the ocean floor made by satellite. Such photographs are available directly from NASA, or they can be found in various reference sources. (Excellent pho-

Figure 2–16 *This illustration shows a submarine above a rift valley surrounded by mountains that make up part of the oceanic ridge system. In the central part of the rift valley you can see molten rock that has cooled. This rock will eventually become new ocean floor (inset).*

Running along the middle of the midocean ridges between the rows of almost parallel mountains are deep crevices, or rift valleys. Rift valleys are about 25 to 50 kilometers wide and 1 to 2 kilometers below the bases of the surrounding midocean ridges. ❶ Rift valleys are regions of great earthquake and volcanic activity. In fact, rift valleys may mark the center of the areas where new crust is formed. Scientists have learned about changes in the Earth's crust by studying the rocks in and around the midocean ridges. Why do you think this is so? ❷

REEFS Sometimes unusual-looking volcanic islands can be seen in tropical waters near a continental shelf. Surrounding these islands offshore are large masses and ridges of limestone rocks. The limestone structures contain the shells of animals ❷ and are called **coral reefs.** Because the reef-building organisms cannot survive in waters colder than 18°C, reefs are found only in tropical waters. Reefs are found in the warmer parts of the Pacific Ocean and in the Caribbean Sea. The organisms that build reefs also cannot live in deep water. They need sunlight to make their hard limestone skeletons. Not enough sunlight for these organisms to survive penetrates water deeper than 55 meters.

There are three types of coral reefs. One type is called **fringing reefs.** Fringing reefs are coral reefs that touch the shoreline of a volcanic island. Fringing reefs are generally less than 30 meters; however, some may be several hundred meters wide.

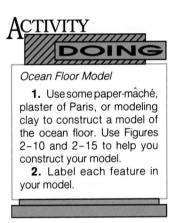

ACTIVITY
DOING

Ocean Floor Model

1. Use some paper-mâché, plaster of Paris, or modeling clay to construct a model of the ocean floor. Use Figures 2–10 and 2–15 to help you construct your model.

2. Label each feature in your model.

I ■ 55

ACTIVITY
DOING

OCEAN-FLOOR MODEL

Skills: Making models, applying concepts
Materials: modeling clay, plaster, or papier-mâché

Students' models should represent all the major features shown in Figure 2–10. Have students check one another's model features and labels.

tos can be found in *Planet Earth,* the companion book to the PBS television series.) Display the photograph and encourage students to comment on the characteristics of the map.
• **How is this map different from maps not made by satellite?** (Answers may vary, but have students note the unusual colors on the map.)

Explain that the unusual colors on satellite maps occur because satellite photographs are made using infrared light.

Infrared light makes it possible for the satellite to "see" things that cannot be seen with visible light.

CONTENT DEVELOPMENT

Emphasize to students that reefs are ridges of limestone that surround volcanic islands. Point out that although these structures are called coral reefs, they really contain only a small amount of coral. A more accurate name would be limestone reef or carbonate reef because

limestone is made up of calcium carbonate.
• **What is the source of the limestone that makes up a coral reef?** (It comes from the shells of certain types of sea organisms.)
• **Why are coral reefs found only in tropical waters?** (The animals whose remains make up the reef can live only in water that is at least 18°C.)

● ● ● ● **Integration** ● ● ● ●

Use the discussion of coral-reef organisms to integrate zoology into your earth science lesson.

I ■ 55

Figure 2–17 *The development of the three types of coral reefs is shown in the illustration. A barrier reef is separated from the shore by a lagoon (top photograph). An atoll surrounds only a lagoon because the island has been worn away and is no longer above the ocean surface (bottom photograph).*

56 ■ I

2–3 (continued)

GUIDED PRACTICE

Skills Development

Skill: Making models

Have students use clay or other water-proof materials to make a model of a fringing reef, a barrier reef, or an atoll. Students can build their models in baking pans or similar containers and then add water to show how the relationship of the reef to the volcanic island changes as the reef changes from fringing to barrier to atoll.

INDEPENDENT PRACTICE

Section Review 2–3

1. It is an area where the underwater edge of a continent meets the ocean floor. Continental shelf—flat part of a continental margin covered by shallow water; continental slope—part of a continental margin where the ocean floor plunges steeply; continental rise—part of a continental margin that separates a continental slope from the ocean floor.
2. Abyssal plains, seamounts, guyots, trenches, midocean ridges, rift valleys, and/or reefs.
3. Fringing reefs, barrier reefs, and atolls.
4. Students should suggest that the plot is not realistic because the temperature of the waters off the coast of Maine would be too cold to sustain coral-reef growth.

Barrier reefs are another type of coral reef. Barrier reefs are separated from the shore by an area of shallow water called a lagoon. Barrier reefs are generally larger than fringing reefs. And the islands that barrier reefs surround usually have sunk farther into the ocean than the islands that fringing reefs surround. The largest barrier reef on Earth is the Great Barrier Reef of Australia. It is about 2300 kilometers long and ranges from 40 to 320 kilometers wide. The Great Barrier Reef is rich in many kinds of animal and plant life.

The third type of coral reef can be found farther out in the ocean. It is a ring of coral reefs called an **atoll.** An atoll surrounds an island that has been worn away and has sunk beneath the surface of the ocean. Figure 2–17 shows the three types of coral reefs.

2–3 Section Review

1. What is the continental margin? Describe the parts of a continental margin.
2. Identify five major features of the ocean floor.
3. What are three types of coral reefs?

Connection—*Literature*

4. A famous science fiction writer once said that "... good science fiction must also be good science." In a new science fiction movie, a giant sea monster lives in a coral reef off the coast of Maine near the Canadian border. During the day, the monster terrorizes the local population, devouring pets and people. At night it returns to the safety of its reef. Is this plot good science fiction? Explain your answer.

REINFORCEMENT/RETEACHING

Monitor students' responses to the Section Review questions. If students appear to have difficulty with any of the questions, review the appropriate material in the section.

CLOSURE

▶ *Review and Reinforcement Guide*

At this point have students complete Section 2–3 in the *Review and Reinforcement Guide.*

TEACHING STRATEGY 2-4

FOCUS/MOTIVATION

Prepare a display of pictures from magazines or other sources of familiar sea organisms. Try to include some plants and animals from each of the three major groups. Have students respond to the display by discussing the varied characteristics of these organisms.

2-4 Ocean Life Zones

A visit to a public aquarium will convince you that a great variety of life exists in the ocean. But even the most well-stocked aquarium is home to relatively few kinds of fishes and plants. People who visit a real coral reef, for example, swim away amazed at the colors, shapes, and variety of the fishes that inhabit the reef.

The animal and plant life found in the ocean is affected by several factors. One factor is the amount of sunlight that penetrates the ocean. Another factor is the temperature of the water. Because there is less sunlight deep in the ocean, the temperature is much lower. So more plants and animals are found in the upper layers of the ocean and near the shoreline than in the deeper layers. Another factor that affects ocean life is water pressure. Water pressure increases as depth increases. Do you know why? With increasing depth, the amount of water pushing down from above increases. This increases the pressure. Organisms that live deep in the ocean must be able to withstand great pressure.

The animals and plants in the ocean can be classified into three major groups according to their habits and the depth of the water in which they live. The largest group of animals and plants is called **plankton** (PLANGK-tuhn). Plankton float at or near the surface of the ocean where sunlight penetrates. Near the shore, they live at depths of about 1 meter. In the open ocean, they can be found at depths of up to 200 meters.

Most plankton are very small. In fact, many forms are microscopic. These organisms drift with the currents and tides of the ocean. Tiny shrimplike organisms and various forms of algae are all plankton. Plankton are the main food for many larger organisms, including the largest organisms on Earth— whales. Certain kinds of whales strain plankton from the water. It is interesting to note that the throat of some of the largest whales is so small that they cannot swallow food larger than a fifty-cent piece!

Forms of ocean life that swim are called **nekton** (NEHK-ton). Whales, seals, dolphins, squid, octopuses, barracudas, and other fishes are all nekton.

Guide for Reading

Focus on these questions as you read.

▶ *What are the three major groups of animals and plants in the ocean?*

▶ *What are the three major life zones in the ocean?*

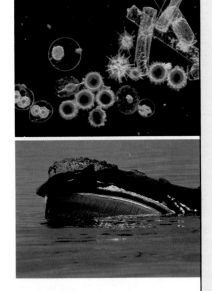

Figure 2–18 *Microscopic plankton (top) are the main source of food for many large sea creatures. The Southern right whale uses its strainerlike mouth to filter plankton from ocean water. Can you imagine how many plankton it must take to satisfy this whale's appetite?* ❶

I ■ 57

• **What kind of conditions do you think each of these organisms needs in order to survive?** (Accept all answers.)

• **In what part of the ocean do you think each of these organisms lives?** (Accept all answers.)

• **Do you think all sea organisms can live anywhere in the ocean?** (Accept all answers.)

● ● ● ● **Integration** ● ● ● ●

Use the discussion of the variety of life that inhabits coral reefs to integrate zoology into your earth science lesson.

▶◀ **Media and Technology**

Use the Videodisc called Aquatic Ecosystems: Marine to introduce the class to ways different communities of organisms occupy regions of the ocean. This Videodisc also explores the interrelationships that link different communities.

2-4 Ocean Life Zones

MULTICULTURAL OPPORTUNITY 2-4

Seaweed is especially rich in vitamins and minerals such as iodine. It is eaten in many regions of the world and is available in the United States in Japanese markets as well as in ethnic sections of various supermarkets. Students may be familiar with sushi, which includes seaweed, as a Japanese dish popular in the United States. Ask students what the ingredients and presentation of sushi might indicate about the Japanese people, their sense of aesthetics, and their reverence for nature and tradition.

Students may also be interested in researching the diet of native inhabitants of the Hawaiian Islands. They obtained food and earned their livelihood from the ocean. Suggest that students investigate how this way of life is changing as a result of commercial development.

ESL STRATEGY 2-4

Have students make a study chart for the three major groups of ocean plants and animals, including the ocean life zones of the organisms. Given the following headings and information, students can work in pairs to supply the remaining data.

Group	Method of Movement	Life Zone(s)	Location
_____	_____	intertidal	_____
_____	_____	neritic	_____
_____	_____	neritic, bathyal	_____
_____	_____	neritic	_____
_____	_____	abyssal	_____

The chart may also be used to stimulate discussion about species in each group and conditions in zone locations.

2-4 (continued)

CONTENT DEVELOPMENT

Discuss with students the general characteristics of ocean organisms. Remind students that ocean plants and animals must be able to obtain the gases they need for vital life processes from gases that are dissolved in water.

Point out that some ocean organisms can swim, whereas others cannot. Ask this question.

• **What advantages do organisms that can swim have over those that cannot?** (They are free to move around in search of food and to escape from predators.

Figure 2–19 *Among the most-feared nekton, or forms of life that swim, are the sharks. Here you see the dangerous great white shark (left), the huge and harmless whale shark (top right), and the bottom-dwelling leopard shark (bottom right).*

Figure 2–20 *The sea anemone's "tentacles" carry stinging cells that enable it to capture unsuspecting fish. The clownfish swimming between the tentacles is immune to the anemone's poison. It helps attract other fish to the anemone. How does this unusual behavior help the clownfish survive?* ❶

58 ■ I

Because they can swim, nekton are able to actively search for food and avoid predators. Predators are organisms that eat other organisms. The organisms that get eaten are called prey. Some types of sharks are feared predators in the ocean; other fish are their prey.

Nekton can be found at all levels of the ocean. Some swim near the ocean surface, others along the bottom. Some are found in the deepest parts of the ocean. Because they can swim, nekton can move from one part of the ocean to another. But they remain in areas where conditions are most favorable.

Organisms that live on the ocean floor are called **benthos** (BEHN-thahs). Some benthos are plants that grow on the ocean floor in shallow waters. Plants are able to survive in water only where sunlight penetrates. Other benthos are animals such as barnacles, oysters, crabs, and starfish. Many benthos, such as sea anemones, attach themselves to the ocean floor. Others live in shore areas. A few kinds live on the ocean floor in the deepest parts of the ocean.

Intertidal Zone

As you just read, there are three major groups of ocean life. There are also three major environments, or life zones, in the ocean. **The classification of the ocean into life zones is based on the conditions in the ocean—conditions that vary widely.** There are

They also can move around to find water that is a comfortable temperature.)

CONTENT DEVELOPMENT

Emphasize to students that the three major factors that affect the kinds of plant and animal life found in the ocean are available sunlight, temperature, and pressure.

• **How do you think available sunlight affects ocean organisms?** (Answers may vary. Guide students to recognize that

most ocean plants need sunlight to make food and that these plants are in turn used as food by sea animals. As a result, neither the plants nor the animals that feed on the plants can survive without a certain amount of sunlight.)

• **How do you think temperature affects ocean plants and animals?** (Many plants and animals can live only at certain temperatures. In particular, many sea organisms would not be able to live in cold temperatures. Remind students that most

Figure 2–21 *The intertidal zone lies between the low- and high-tide lines. Organisms that live in the intertidal zone include starfish (inset), giant limpets (inset), clams (top right), barnacles (center), and sea anemones (bottom right).*

shallow beach areas that dry out twice a day and then become wet again. There are ocean depths where no ray of sunlight ever reaches and where the temperature stays a few degrees above freezing all year round. And in between these extremes is the open ocean with a range of environments at different depths. Scientists know a great deal about these areas, but much of the ocean still remains an unexplored frontier.

The region that lies between the low– and high–tide lines is the **intertidal zone.** This region is the most changeable zone in the ocean. Sometimes it is ocean. Sometimes it is dry land. These changes occur

FACTS AND FIGURES

PRESSURE

Pressure increases below the surface of the ocean at a rate of 1 atmosphere per 10 meters. The pressure at any given depth is constant. This is important to ocean organisms because each type of organism is adapted to live at a certain pressure.

CONTENT DEVELOPMENT

Abundant and tremendously varied ocean life exists at all ocean depths. The animals and plants of the ocean have been classified into three major groups—plankton, nekton, and benthos. These groups of plants and animals are separated or grouped according to their habits and the depth of the water in which they live.

Planktonic organisms account for most of the organisms found in the world's oceans. These organisms include zooplankton and phytoplankton, in addition to the eggs and larvae of larger marine life. Plankton is capable of existing at a depth of approximately 200 meters because sunlight can penetrate the surface of the ocean to this depth.

Nekton are free-swimming organisms. They feed on other nekton as well as on plankton and may have adaptations enabling them to function at depths that have great pressure and no light.

Benthos are bottom-dwelling organisms. The forms of these animals include crustaceans and shellfish. The deep-bottom environments, however, are sparsely populated with benthos.

living things in an ocean would be expected to be found in the warmer regions of that ocean.)

• **How do you think pressure affects ocean organisms?** (The cells and bodies of many plants and animals cannot survive high pressures. Although some organisms live at depths having relatively high pressures, most organisms live fairly near the surface of the ocean.)

Have students note that as ocean depth increases, available sunlight and

temperature decrease while pressure increases.

ENRICHMENT

Just as crops and animals can be raised on land, plants and animals can be farmed in the ocean. Farming of the ocean is called aquaculture. Some products that are currently being farmed are algae, shrimp, and fish. Have interested students find out more about aquaculture, including pictures of ocean farms, to share with the class.

One of the oldest human occupations is fishing. Some fishing methods used have been in existence for thousands of years. More and more, however, people who fish are relying on modern technology to help them increase their catches. They use radar, sonar, electronic devices, and information from satellites.

Fishing is an important industry because it provides food for the world's people, particularly in heavily populated areas where land for raising animals is scarce.

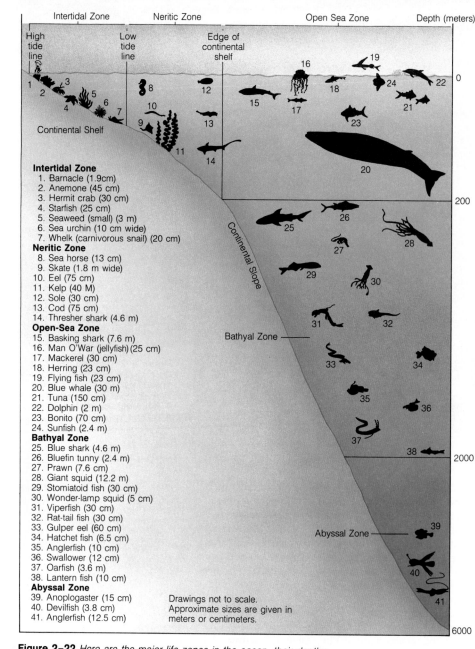

Intertidal Zone
1. Barnacle (1.9cm)
2. Anemone (45 cm)
3. Hermit crab (30 cm)
4. Starfish (25 cm)
5. Seaweed (small) (3 m)
6. Sea urchin (10 cm wide)
7. Whelk (carnivorous snail) (20 cm)

Neritic Zone
8. Sea horse (13 cm)
9. Skate (1.8 m wide)
10. Eel (75 cm)
11. Kelp (40 M)
12. Sole (30 cm)
13. Cod (75 cm)
14. Thresher shark (4.6 m)

Open-Sea Zone
15. Basking shark (7.6 m)
16. Man O'War (jellyfish)(25 cm)
17. Mackerel (30 cm)
18. Herring (23 cm)
19. Flying fish (23 cm)
20. Blue whale (30 m)
21. Tuna (150 cm)
22. Dolphin (2 m)
23. Bonito (70 cm)
24. Sunfish (2.4 m)

Bathyal Zone
25. Blue shark (4.6 m)
26. Bluefin tunny (2.4 m)
27. Prawn (7.6 m)
28. Giant squid (12.2 m)
29. Stomiatoid fish (30 cm)
30. Wonder-lamp squid (5 cm)
31. Viperfish (30 cm)
32. Rat-tail fish (30 cm)
33. Gulper eel (60 cm)
34. Hatchet fish (6.5 cm)
35. Anglerfish (10 cm)
36. Swallower (12 cm)
37. Oarfish (3.6 m)
38. Lantern fish (10 cm)

Abyssal Zone
39. Anoplogaster (15 cm)
40. Devilfish (3.8 cm)
41. Anglerfish (12.5 cm)

Drawings not to scale.
Approximate sizes are given in meters or centimeters.

Figure 2–22 *Here are the major life zones in the ocean, their depths, and some of the living things usually found in these zones. Above what depth is most ocean life found?* ❶

2–4 (continued)

CONTENT DEVELOPMENT

Point out that there are three major zones in the ocean that support ocean life. The intertidal zone is the area that lies between the low-tide and high-tide line. This zone supports a variety of organisms with special adaptations that allow them to exist without water for short periods of time and to withstand the force of waves breaking on the shore. The neritic zone includes the water and ocean bottom between the shoreline and the edge of the continental shelf. This zone contains the richest fishing grounds. The open-ocean zone can be subdivided into the bathyal and abyssal zones.

INDEPENDENT PRACTICE

▶ *Activity Book*

Students can learn more about the life zones of the ocean by completing the chapter activity Physical Properties of the Ocean's Life Zones. In this activity students will explore the characteristics of the various life zones of the ocean.

GUIDED PRACTICE

Skills Development
Skill: Interpreting charts

Have students observe Figure 2–22.
• **Which life zones include the waters above the continental shelf?** (The intertidal zone and the neritic zone.)
• **Which life zones lie along the continental slope?** (The bathyal subzone and the abyssal subzone.)
• **Which life zones include the surface waters of the ocean?** (The intertidal zone, the neritic zone, and the open-sea zone.)
• **Which life zones lie along the ocean floor?** (The abyssal subzone.)
• **The diagram shows three different**

Figure 2–23 *Mandarin, or psychedelic, fish (left) and the highly venomous lion fish (right) are but two of the many types of fishes that inhabit Earth's oceans.*

twice a day as the ocean surges up the shore at high tide and retreats at low tide. It is difficult for living things to survive in the intertidal zone. The tides and the waves breaking along the shore constantly move materials in this zone. Because the tide rises and falls, organisms must be able to live without water some of the time.

Some of the organisms that live in the intertidal zone are anemones, crabs, clams, mussels, and plants such as certain kinds of seaweeds. To keep from being washed out to sea, many of these organisms attach themselves to sand and rocks. Others, such as certain worms and some kinds of shellfish, burrow into the wet sand for protection.

Neritic Zone

The **neritic** (nee-RIHT-ihk) **zone** extends from the low-tide line to the edge of a continental shelf. This zone extends to a depth of about 200 meters.

The neritic zone receives plenty of sunlight. The water pressure is low and the temperature remains fairly constant. Here the ocean floor is covered with seaweed. Many different animals and plants live in this zone, including plankton, nekton, and benthos. In fact, the neritic zone is richer in life than any other ocean zone. Most of the world's great fishing areas are within this zone. Fish, clams, snails, some types of whales, and lobsters are but a few of the kinds of organisms that live in the neritic zone. This

Figure 2–24 *This California spiny lobster searching for food at night is among the many interesting creatures in the neritic zone.*

I ■ 61

FACTS AND FIGURES

OCEAN LIFE

Ninety percent of all ocean life is found in the waters above the continental shelf.

tory Investigation in the *Laboratory Manual* called Culturing and Observing Brine Shrimp. In this investigation students will culture brine shrimp and then examine them with a homemade water-drop microscope.

ENRICHMENT

Students may be interested to learn that the fishing industry takes more than 60 million tons of food from the ocean each year. Approximately 90 percent of this food is fish such as herring, cod, and salmon. The other 10 percent is shellfish such as clams, lobster, and shrimp. In some areas, there is increasing concern about the environmental consequences of overfishing. For example, in the early 1980s, Alaska banned fishing for the Alaskan king crab because the population of this species was becoming too small.

CONTENT DEVELOPMENT

🎧 **Media and Technology**

Use the Videodisc called Aquatic Ecosystems: Estuaries to explore organisms that exist in areas where salt and fresh waters meet and mix. This Videodisc will also show ways organisms are adapted to life in water with changing salinity.

shades of blue. What do you think these color changes represent? (Changes in temperature and/or available sunlight.)

REINFORCEMENT/RETEACHING

Students will better understand the location of the intertidal zone if you show them a picture of an area at high tide and a picture of the same area at low tide. Ideal photos of this type can be found of Mont-St-Michel in France.

Point out that when the tide is high,

much more of the beach is covered by water than when the tide is low. This portion of the ocean floor—the part that is first covered, then uncovered as the tides change—constitutes the intertidal zone.

GUIDED PRACTICE

▶ *Laboratory Manual*

Skills Development

Skill: Making observations

At this point you may want to have students complete the Chapter 2 Labora-

A C T I V I T Y
DOING

FISH FOR THE TABLE

Skills: Relating concepts, applying definitions

By completing this activity, students will gain firsthand knowledge in field application of information from the textbook. This activity will reinforce students' knowledge of the oceans' life zones, characteristics, and the food uses of various sea organisms. Have volunteers share their findings with the class.

2–4 (continued)

INDEPENDENT PRACTICE

Section Review 2–4

1. Plankton, nekton, and benthos.
2. Sunlight, temperature, and water pressure.
3. Intertidal zone—variable conditions, difficult for living things to survive; neritic zone—sunny, relatively constant temperature, low pressure, wide array of organisms; open-ocean zones—little sunlight, high pressure, harsh conditions, relatively few organisms.
4. Neritic zone; plenty of sunlight, low water pressure, fairly constant temperature, seaweed.
5. The cost of catching fish from deep water would outweigh the economic value of the fish that could be caught.

ACTIVITY
DOING

Fish for the Table

Visit a supermarket or a fish market. List the different foods available that come from the ocean. Answer the following questions about the foods you listed:

1. Which foods are plankton? Nekton? Benthos?

2. From which ocean-life zone did each food come?

3. Where did the store obtain each food?

4. Which foods are sold fresh? Which are sold frozen?

5. Which foods have you eaten?

zone is the source of much of the seafood people eat. The neritic zone ends where there is too little sunlight for seaweed to grow.

Open-Ocean Zones

There are two open-ocean zones. The first is the **bathyal** (BAHTH-ee-uhl) **zone.** It begins at a continental slope and extends down about 2000 meters. Sunlight is not able to penetrate to the bottom of this zone. Many forms of nekton live in the bathyal zone, including squid, octopus, and large whales. Because there is little sunlight in the lower parts, plants do not grow near the bottom of this zone.

At a depth of about 2000 meters, the **abyssal zone** begins. This is the second open-ocean zone. The abyssal zone extends to an average depth of 6000 meters. This zone covers the large, flat plains of the ocean. No sunlight is able to penetrate to this zone. Thus little food is available. The water pressure is very great. What do you think the temperatures are like in the abyssal zone? ①

Even with extremely harsh conditions, life exists in the abyssal zone. Most of the animals that live here are small. Many are quite strange looking. Look again at the anoplogaster shown in the chapter opener. Some of the animals that live in this zone are able to make their own light.

Figure 2–25 *Organisms that live in the open-ocean zone include deep-sea anglerfish (top left), hatchet fish (bottom left), and krill (right).*

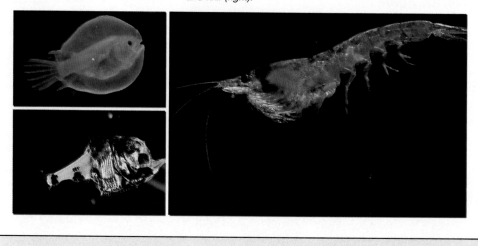

REINFORCEMENT/RETEACHING

Monitor students' responses to the Section Review questions. If students appear to have difficulty with any of the questions, review the appropriate material in the section.

CLOSURE

▶ *Review and Reinforcement Guide*

At this point have students complete Section 2–4 in the *Review and Reinforcement Guide.*

TEACHING STRATEGY 2–5

FOCUS/MOTIVATION

Display a world map and have students locate the Galapagos Islands in the Pacific Ocean. (The islands are located off the western coast of South America, near the equator.) Point out that about 2600 meters below the ocean's surface near these islands, scientists made a discovery that added a new feature to maps of the Pacific Ocean floor.

2-4 Section Review

1. What are the three major groups of ocean life?
2. What are some factors that affect ocean life?
3. Describe the three major ocean life zones.
4. Which zone contains the greatest variety of ocean life? Why?

Critical Thinking—*Applying Concepts*
5. Most commercial fishing occurs near the ocean surface. Why would fishing in extremely deep water prove to be unsuccessful?

2-5 Mapping the Ocean Floor

The oceans have been called the last great unexplored places on Earth. In fact, we probably know more about some of our neighbors in outer space than we do about the waters that make up almost 71 percent of our planet.

In 1872, the first expedition to explore the ocean began when the *Challenger* sailed from England. Equipped for ocean exploration, the *Challenger* remained at sea for $3\frac{1}{2}$ years. Scientists aboard the *Challenger* used wire to measure ocean depth. They used nets attached to heavy ropes to collect animals and plants from the ocean floor. Organisms that had

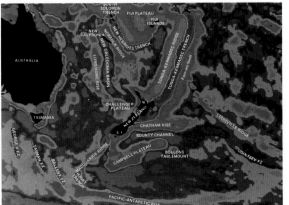

Figure 2-26 *This computerized geologic map of the southwest Pacific sea floor was constructed from data collected by a NASA satellite orbiting the Earth.*

I ■ 63

2-5 Mapping the Ocean Floor

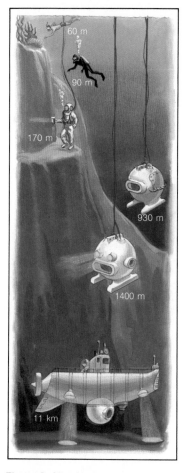

Figure 2-27 *Different instruments are used to explore the ocean. The type of instrument used is determined by the ocean depth. To what depth can a person descend without special breathing equipment?* ●

2-5 (continued)

CONTENT DEVELOPMENT

Remind students that the ocean floor must be mapped by indirect methods.

• **Why is it nearly impossible to map the ocean floor using direct methods?** (The tremendous pressure at the ocean floor makes it very difficult for humans to explore the ocean floor directly, even in special submersible devices.)

Explain that the earliest type of indirect method used to map the ocean floor was the use of wires that were lowered from ships. Some of the indirect methods used to explore the ocean floor today include radar, sonar, echo sounding, seismographs, and satellites.

● ● ● ● **Integration** ● ● ● ●

Use the discussion of indirect methods of mapping the ocean floor to integrate concepts about sonar into your earth science lesson.

INDEPENDENT PRACTICE

▶ *Activity Book*

Students can practice with indirect measurement methods by completing the chapter activity Determining Ocean Depth. In this activity students will use data to find the depth of the ocean bottom.

INDEPENDENT PRACTICE

Section Review 2-5

1. Underwater cameras, corers, diving vehicles, radar, sonar, and/or satel-

lites. These instruments are much more complex, sophisticated, and accurate than instruments used in the earliest expeditions.

2. Speed of sound in water and length of time for sound waves to make one complete round trip.

3. Answers will vary. Reasons might include the high cost of doing research and the vast area and depth of our oceans.

---

long remained undisturbed—free from the probing eyes of humans—were brought to the surface. Special thermometers enabled the scientists to record deep-ocean temperatures. And samples of ocean water were collected in special bottles.

Today oceanographers have many modern instruments to aid them in the exploration of the oceans. Underwater cameras provide pictures of the ocean floor. Devices called corers bring up samples of mud and sand from the ocean bottom. And a variety of vehicles, including bathyspheres, bathyscaphs, and other submersibles, are able to dive deep under the surface to explore the ocean depths.

One of the most important goals of oceanographers is to map the ocean floor. **Mapping the ocean floor can only be done by indirect methods, such as echo sounding, radar, sonar, and seismographic surveys.** All of these methods are based on the same principle: Energy waves, such as sound waves, sent down to the ocean surface are reflected from (bounce off) the ocean floor and return to the surface, where they are recorded. Knowing the speed of sound in water, which is about 1500 meters per second, and the time it takes sound waves to make a round trip, oceanographers can determine the ocean depth at any location along the ocean floor.

The most complete picture of the ocean floor has been pieced together from information gathered by *Seasat*, a scientific satellite launched in 1978. From the 8 billion readings radioed back by *Seasat*, scientists have created the most accurate map yet.

2-5 Section Review

1. Name three instruments used by oceanographers today to explore the ocean. How do these instruments compare with ones used in the earliest expeditions?
2. What two pieces of information are needed to map the ocean depth using sonar?

Connection—*You and Your World*

3. Even though the oceans are one of the grandest features of Planet Earth, we know relatively little about them. What are some reasons to explain this lack of knowledge?

REINFORCEMENT/RETEACHING

Monitor students' responses to the Section Review questions. If students appear to have difficulty with any of the questions, review the appropriate material in the section.

CLOSURE

▶ *Review and Reinforcement Guide*

At this point have students complete Section 2-5 in the *Review and Reinforcement Guide.*

2-6 Motions of the Ocean

Ocean water never stops moving. **There are three basic motions of ocean water: the up and down movement of waves, the steady movement of ocean currents, and the rise and fall of ocean water in tides.** In this section you will read more about each of these ocean movements.

Waves

Waves are pulses of energy that move through the ocean. Waves are set in motion by winds, earthquakes, and the gravitational pull of the moon. The most common source of energy for waves, however, is wind blowing across the surface of the ocean.

Have you ever observed ocean waves—first far out at sea and then closer to shore? If not, perhaps you have seen pictures of them. Ocean waves begin as wind-stirred ripples on the surface of the water. As more energy is transferred from wind to water, the waves formed look like great forward surges of rapidly moving water. But the water is not moving forward at all! Only energy moves forward through the water, producing one wave after another. The energy is passed from one particle of water to another. But the particles of water themselves remain in relatively the same positions.

Wave energy is not only passed forward from one water particle to another, it is also passed downward from particle to particle. With increasing depth, the motion of the particles decreases. At a certain depth, motion stops. In deep water, there are no waves except for those caused by tides and earthquakes.

The height of surface waves depends upon three different factors. Do you know what they are? These factors are the wind's speed, the length of time the wind blows, and the distance the wind blows over the water. As each of these factors increases, the height of a wave increases. And some waves can become really huge. The largest surface wave ever measured in the middle of any ocean occurred in the North Pacific on February 7, 1933. At that time, a wind storm was sweeping over a stretch of water thousands of kilometers long. A ship in the United States Navy, the *U.S.S. Ramapo*, was plowing through

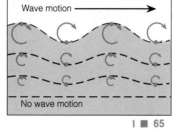

Figure 2-28 *Waves are set in motion as energy is transferred from wind to water. The wave pulses of energy are passed forward from particle to particle, as well as downward from particle to particle. Notice that it is not the water that is moving forward, but the pulse of energy.*

Wave motion ⟶

No wave motion

I ■ 65

2-6 Motions of the Ocean

MULTICULTURAL OPPORTUNITY 2-6

Suggest that students research tidal waves, particularly the destructive force of tsunamis (Japanese word for "storm waves"). Students will discover that most tsunamis are not caused by storms but by submarine earthquakes and that they are capable of great destruction. An example of their power is a tsunami that hit Awa, Japan, in 1703, killing 100,000 people.

ESL STRATEGY 2-6

Ask students to describe the three basic motions of the oceans, the most common source of energy for waves, and the cause of currents. Then have students circle the word that does not belong in each of the following groups and write the definitions for the words not circled.

1. crest, wavelength, waver, trough
2. wave height, wave set, wave period, wave frequency
3. swells, undertows, surf, underground

Have students describe the difference between surface, longshore, and deep currents.

Finally, students should explain why *tsunamis, upwelling, spring tides,* and *neap tides* are important terms in the study of oceanography.

TEACHING STRATEGY 2-6

FOCUS/MOTIVATION

On the chalkboard, draw several waves of different heights and wavelengths. Ask these questions.

• **How would you describe the shapes that have been drawn on the chalkboard?** (Answers may vary. Students will probably point out that the shapes are all curved, with a regular pattern of rising and falling.)

• **How do the shapes differ from one another?** (Do not introduce the terms *wave height* or *wavelength* at this time. Have students point out such differences as these: Some waves are steeper or higher, whereas others are flatter; some appear more spread out than others; some repeat a similar up-down pattern many times, whereas others may repeat it only once.)

CONTENT DEVELOPMENT

Emphasize the definition of waves as pulses of energy that move through the ocean. Some students may have the misconception that waves are moving water. Refer students to Figure 2-28 and point out that water moves up and down as the pulses of energy pass through water, but the water particles themselves stay essentially in the same place.

THE RISING OCEANS

Over the past 100 years, the level of the ocean has risen faster than ever before. Even though sea-level changes are natural, scientists believe that humans have increased the rate of change by burning coal, gas, and oil. Since the Industrial Revolution, human dependence on fossil fuels has increased the level of carbon dioxide in the atmosphere. Carbon dioxide traps infrared light radiating from the Earth. This trapped energy heats the atmosphere, causing the icecaps at the poles to melt and the sea level to rise.

Continued reliance on fossil fuels may place many coastal communities in danger. As the sea level rises, damage created by ocean waves will affect larger numbers of structures. Homes, shops, offices, and hotels originally built away from the destruction of waves may one day become oceanfront property.

CAREERS

Biological Oceanographer

Biological oceanographers study ocean life that ranges from tiny, one-celled plankton to huge blue whales, the largest of all living organisms.

Biological oceanographers are employed by universities, governments, and industry. To become a biological oceanographer, a person should have an interest in science and in the sea. For more information, write to the International Oceanographers Foundation, 3979 Rickenbacker Causeway, Virginia Key, Miami, FL 33149.

FACTORS THAT AFFECT THE HEIGHT OF SURFACE WAVES

Wind Speed (m/sec)	Length of Time Wind Blows (hr)	Distance Wind Blows Over Water (km)	Average Height of Wave (m)
5.1	2.4	18.5	0.27
10.2	10.0	140.0	1.5
15.3	23.0	520.0	4.1
20.4	42.0	1320.0	8.5
25.5	69.0	2570.0	14.8

Figure 2–29 The factors that affect the height of surface waves are shown in this chart. What happens to the height of a wave as the wind speed increases? ❶

the sea when its officers spotted and measured a gigantic wave. It was at least 34 meters high! Such a wave would rise above a ten-story apartment house.

WAVE CHARACTERISTICS Ocean waves, like all other waves, have several characteristics. The highest point of a wave is called the **crest.** The lowest point of a wave is called the **trough** (TRAWF). The horizontal distance between two consecutive (one after the other) crests or two consecutive troughs is called the **wavelength.** The vertical distance between a crest and a trough is called the wave height. Waves have various wavelengths and wave heights. The basic characteristics of waves are shown in Figure 2–30.

Figure 2–30 Characteristics of ocean waves are shown in this diagram. What is the distance between two consecutive crests called? What is the lowest point of a wave called? ❷

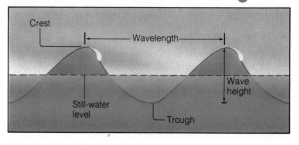

2–6 (continued)

CONTENT DEVELOPMENT

Review the characteristics of waves described in the textbook. Refer to the waves you drew on the chalkboard and ask these questions.
• **Can you identify the crests in each wave?** (Have a volunteer indicate the highest point of each wave.)
• **Can you identify the troughs?** (Have a volunteer indicate the lowest point of each wave.)
• **Which of the waves has the greatest wave height?** (Answers will vary.)
• **Which of these waves has the greatest wavelength?** (Answers will vary.)

GUIDED PRACTICE

Skills Development

Skill: Interpreting diagrams

Sketch the wave-motion diagram from Figure 2–28 on the chalkboard. Ask these questions.
• **How would you describe the motion of each water particle as the wave passes through the water?** (Each particle moves in a small circle.)
• **How does this circular motion relate**

to the water moving up and down? (When a particle is at the top of the circle, the water wave is at its highest point. When the particle is at the bottom of the circle, the water wave is at its lowest point.)

INDEPENDENT PRACTICE

📖 Media and Technology

Use the transparency in the *Transparency Binder* called Ocean Wave Characteristics to help students develop an

The amount of time it takes consecutive crests or troughs to pass a given point is called the wave period. The number of crests or troughs passing a given point in a certain wave period is called the wave frequency. What is the relationship between wavelength and wave frequency? ❸

Out in the open ocean, waves stay about the same distance apart for thousands of kilometers. So wavelength is usually constant. These waves are called swells. Swells are long, wide waves that are not very high.

But waves change as they approach the shore. They slow down, and they get closer and closer together. Their wavelength decreases and their wave height increases. They finally crash forward as breakers and surge onto the shore. This surging water is called the surf.

The water then flows back toward the ocean. Bits of seaweed, sand, and pebbles are pulled back by the retreating water. This retreating water is called an undertow. Undertows can be quite strong. Occasionally, they can be strong enough to pose danger to swimmers, pulling them farther out into the ocean and under the water. Undertows can also extend for several kilometers offshore.

TSUNAMIS Some ocean waves are caused by earthquakes. These waves are called **tsunamis** (tsoo-NAH-meez). Tsunami is a Japanese word meaning "large wave in a harbor." Tsunamis are the highest ocean waves.

Sea Turtles

Sea turtles lay their eggs on sandy coastal beaches. On shore the female turtle digs a hole and begins to deposit her eggs. In time, the eggs hatch. The tiny turtles will scurry to the sea. They will spend years in the open sea. If they survive, female turtles will return years later to the same beach on which they hatched.

See if you can find information that explains this remarkable navigational ability. How are female sea turtles able to find their way without maps to guide them?

Figure 2–31 *The pattern of a swell as it reaches a sloping beach is shown in this diagram. What happens to the wavelength and the wave height as the wave nears the beach?* ❹

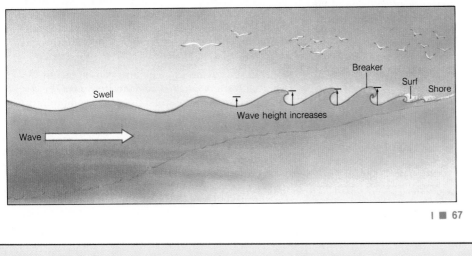

Swell · Breaker · Surf · Shore · Wave height increases · Wave

I ■ 67

ACTIVITY
WRITING

SEA TURTLES

Check student's writing for scientific accuracy. Students should be able to supply a list of the references they used to write their reports. Many scientists think sea turtles find their way home by using the Earth's magnetic fields as navigational aids.

ENRICHMENT

On the chalkboard, write this formula: Frequency = Speed/Wavelength.
• **How does this formula compare with the formula for the period of a wave?** (One is the reciprocal of the other.)

Show a sample computation for finding the frequency of a wave. For example, if a wave has a wavelength of 10 meters and travels at a speed of 60 meters per second,

Frequency = 60 m per sec/10 m
= 6 cycles/sec

Provide students with several exercises that ask them to use this formula to compute the frequency, speed, or wavelength of a wave.

understanding of the different characteristics of ocean waves.

CONTENT DEVELOPMENT

Point out that another characteristic of waves is frequency. Frequency is equal to the number of cycles per unit of time.
• **What is a cycle?** (Answers may vary. Guide students to recognize that a cycle is a complete wave, one that includes one crest and one trough.)

Draw several cycles of a wave on the chalkboard and mark the divisions for each cycle. Explain that if, for example, three complete waves pass by a given point in one second, the frequency of the wave would be three cycles per second.

● ● ● ● **Integration** ● ● ● ●

Use the discussion of the relationship of wave frequency and wavelength to integrate the physical science concepts of waves into your lesson.

CURRENTLY CURRENT

Discovery Learning

Skills: Making observations, making inferences

Materials: glass, ice-cold water, food coloring, glass bowl, warm water

By completing this activity, students can observe the motions of a current in a bowl and then relate their observations to the Earth's ocean currents. Students should conclude that the food coloring is used to make the currents more visible, and they should infer that because the cold water is more dense than the warm water, the cold water moves downward under the less dense warm water. This forms a current of water closer to the bottom of the glass bowl. This current is most like the deep current that develops in the world's polar regions.

2–6 (continued)

REINFORCEMENT/RETEACHING

▶ *Activity Book*

Students who need help on the concept of waves should complete the chapter activity Characteristics of Ocean Waves. In this activity students will use diagrams to explore the various characteristics of ocean waves.

CONTENT DEVELOPMENT

Obtain a photograph of a coastal area that has been battered by a hurricane or other severe tropical storm. Display the photograph and ask the following questions.

• **What has caused the damage shown in the photograph?** (The breaking of heavy waves against the shore, along with heavy wind and rain.)

• **Why are waves able to cause so much damage?** (Waves break with a great deal of force.)

Figure 2–32 *The power of a tsunami left this boat high and dry on the dock.*

ACTIVITY
DISCOVERING

Currently Current

1. Fill a glass half-full with ice-cold water. Add several drops of food coloring to the water.

2. Fill a clear glass bowl a little more than half-full with warm water.

3. Carefully pour the cold water down the side of the bowl. Observe what happens.

What is the purpose of the food coloring? Explain why the current forms. What type of ocean current does the current in the bowl most resemble?

■ Plan an investigation to see what kind of current, if any, forms when you add a glass of warm water with food coloring to a bowl of ice-cold water.

Tsunamis have very long wavelengths and are very deep. They carry a huge amount of energy. As tsunamis slow down in shallow water, they pile closer and closer together. Their wave heights increase. The energy that was once spread throughout a great depth of water is now concentrated in much less water. This energy produces the tsunamis, which can reach heights of 35 meters or more when they strike the shore. To give you some idea of the imposing height of a tsunami, consider this: The average height of a building story is between 3 and 4 meters. So a 35-meter wave is about the height of a ten-story building!

As you might suspect, tsunamis can cause great damage and loss of life along coastal areas. One of the most famous groups of tsunamis was caused by the volcanic eruption of Krakatoa between Java and Sumatra in 1883. Nine tsunamis that rose up to 40 meters high hit along the Java coast. Nothing was left of the coastal towns and about 36,000 people died.

Currents

You can easily see water moving on the surface of the ocean in the form of waves. But it is not only water on the surface that moves. Water below the surface also has motion. This water moves in streams called currents. Some currents are so large—up to several thousand kilometers long—that they are better described as "rivers" in the ocean. In fact, the mighty Mississippi River can be considered a mere brook when compared with the largest of the ocean currents. But long or short, all ocean currents are caused by the same two factors: wind patterns and differences in water density.

SURFACE CURRENTS Currents caused mainly by wind patterns are called **surface currents.** These currents usually have a depth of several hundred meters. Some surface currents are warm-water currents, others are cold-water currents. The temperature of a current depends upon where the current originates. A warm current begins in a warm area. A cold current begins in a cold area.

Surface currents that travel thousands of kilometers are called long-distance surface currents. The

• **Which waves do you think would break with the greatest amount of force—those produced on a calm day or those produced on a stormy day?** (Stormy day.)

• **Why?** (The energy of a wave originates from the wind. When wind is strong, more energy is transferred to the water. Eventually, this energy travels to the shoreline and produces a force. The greater the amount of energy carried by the wave, the stronger the force.)

● ● ● ● **Integration** ● ● ● ●

Use the discussion of the eruption of Krakatoa to integrate social studies concepts into your earth science lesson.

REINFORCEMENT/RETEACHING

Review the basic definitions of a current, reminding students that surface currents are caused mainly by wind.

• **Where does a warm-water current originate?** (In an area that contains warm waters, such as tropical areas.)

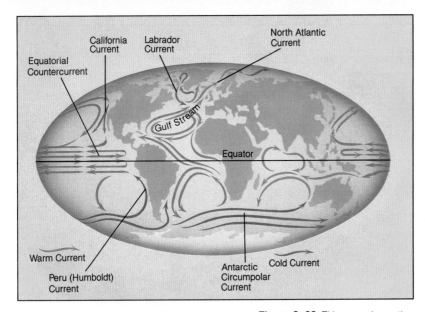

Equatorial Countercurrent · California Current · Labrador Current · North Atlantic Current · Gulf Stream · Equator · Warm Current · Peru (Humboldt) Current · Antarctic Circumpolar Current · Cold Current

Gulf Stream is a well-known long-distance surface current. It is about 150 kilometers wide and may reach a depth of about 1000 meters. It carries warm water from the southern tip of Florida north along the eastern coast of the United States. It moves along at speeds greater than 1.5 meters per second. And more than 150 million cubic meters of water may pass a given point each second!

Figure 2–33 shows the major warm and cold surface currents of the world and the general directions in which they flow. Because all the oceans are connected, these ocean currents form a continuous worldwide pattern of water circulation.

You will notice from Figure 2–33 that the water in each ocean moves in a large, almost circular pattern. In the Northern Hemisphere, the currents move clockwise, or the same way the hands of a clock move. In the Southern Hemisphere, the currents move counterclockwise, or in the opposite direction. These motions correspond to the direction of wind circulation in each hemisphere.

As you might expect, surface currents that move over short distances are called short-distance surface currents. These currents usually are found near a shoreline where waves hit at an angle. When the

Figure 2–33 *This map shows the directions of flow of the major long-distance surface currents. Is the Gulf Stream a warm or a cold current?* ❶

Figure 2–34 *Two surface currents converge, or come together, in the Atlantic Ocean near Bermuda.*

I ■ 69

BACKGROUND INFORMATION

NORTH AMERICAN CURRENTS

In the Atlantic Ocean, there are two major ocean currents that have an effect on North American weather, especially weather on the eastern coast—the Labrador Current and the Gulf Stream. The Labrador Current is a cold current; the Gulf Stream is a warm current.

In the Pacific Ocean, there are two major ocean currents that have an effect on North American weather, especially weather on the western coast—the California Current and the Equatorial Countercurrent. The California Current is a cold current; the Equatorial Countercurrent is a warm current.

effect, named after the nineteenth-century French physicist Gaspard de Coriolis, who first explained the phenomenon.

● ● ● ● **Integration** ● ● ● ●

Use the discussion of surface currents of the world to integrate concepts of meteorology into your science lesson.

INDEPENDENT PRACTICE

📖 **Media and Technology**

Use the transparency in the *Transparency Binder* called Long-Distance Surface Currents to help students understand the patterns of ocean currents.

● **Where does a cold-water current originate?** (In an area that contains cold waters, such as the polar regions.)

CONTENT DEVELOPMENT

Explain to students that when wind blows across the surface of the ocean, it sets a current moving in the same direction as the wind. Once the current is moving, however, two additional factors affect its path. These factors are the position of landmasses and the rotation of the Earth. Ask this question.

● **How do you think the position of a landmass affects the path of a current?** (The current must bend when it reaches a landmass.)

Point out that as a current is bent, it begins to flow along the coast of the landmass. Stress that it is the rotation of the Earth that causes currents to flow clockwise in the Northern Hemisphere and counterclockwise in the Southern Hemisphere. Students may be interested to know that this bending of the currents by the Earth's rotation is caled the Coriolis

Upwellings occur when wind along a coast pushes warm surface water out to sea. Cold water from below the surface rises to replace the warm water.

Sometimes the winds that cause upwellings die down, and the upwellings cease to occur. Cold waters from below the surface no longer replace warm surface waters. The result is a dramatic rise in ocean temperature that is called El Niño.

Although El Niño has no regular pattern of occurrence, it tends to strike at two- to ten-year intervals. The damage from El Niño can be very great. In 1982 in Peru, a spell of El Niño caused tons of fish and other sea creatures to die. The fishing industry in that country was all but devastated.

El Niño can also cause strange weather patterns. While creatures in the ocean were dying, Peru and its neighboring countries were experiencing floods and torrential rains. The island of Tahiti, which is usually known for its serene weather, was struck by an endless series of typhoons. Even as far away as Africa, the weather patterns went berserk—bringing about the worst drought the region had ever had.

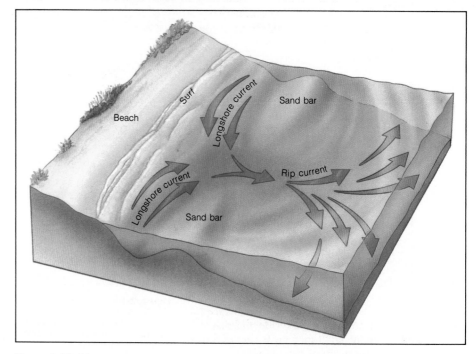

Figure 2–35 *When longshore currents cut through a sand bar, a rip current is formed.*

waves hit the shoreline, the water turns and produces currents that move parallel to the shoreline. These streams of water are called longshore currents.

As longshore currents move parallel to the shoreline, they pick up large quantities of material, such as sand from the beach. The sand is deposited in water close to the shoreline. A long, underwater pile of sand called a sand bar builds up.

Longshore currents can become trapped on the shoreline side of a sand bar. These currents may eventually cut an opening in the sandbar. The currents then return to the ocean in a powerful narrow flow called a rip current. A rip current is a type of undertow.

DEEP CURRENTS Some currents are caused mainly by differences in the density of water deep in the ocean. Such currents are called **deep currents.** The density, which you can think of as the heaviness of

---

2–6 (continued)

GUIDED PRACTICE

Skills Development

Skill: Making models

Students can make a model to illustrate the Coriolis effect by using a globe and a piece of chalk. Have one student spin the globe while another student attempts to draw a vertical line from the North Pole to the South Pole with the piece of chalk. Students will observe that no matter how hard they try, the line will never be straight; it will always be skewed diagonally to some degree. Point out that this same effect is essentially what happens to ocean currents; they would tend

to flow in straight lines, but their paths are bent by the rotation of the Earth.

INDEPENDENT PRACTICE

▶ *Activity Book*

Students who need practice on the concept of ocean currents should complete the chapter activity Temperature Effects and Surface Currents. In this activity students will explore climatic effects caused by the Earth's surface ocean currents.

CONTENT DEVELOPMENT

Explain that when the waves of longshore currents hit the shoreline, the water turns and produces currents that move parallel to the shoreline.

• **Why would the effects of a longshore current be much more obvious along a sandy shoreline than along a rocky shoreline?** (The longshore current picks up sand and other materials as it moves along a sandy shoreline. These materials are then deposited in the water. Along a

water, is affected by temperature and salinity. (Density is actually defined as mass per unit volume of a substance.) Cold water is more dense than warm water. And the saltier water is, the more dense it is. For example, cold dense water flowing from the polar regions moves downward under less dense warm water found in areas away from the poles.

Cameras lowered to the ocean floor have photographed evidence of powerful deep currents. The photograph in Figure 2–36 shows ripples carved into the sand of the ocean floor. In places on the floor, heavy clay has been piled into small dunes, as if shaped by winds. These "winds," scientists conclude, must be very strong ocean currents.

Most deep currents flow in the opposite direction from surface currents. For example, in the summer the Mediterranean Sea loses more water by evaporation than it gets back as rain. The salinity and density of the Mediterranean Sea increase. As a result, deep currents of dense water flow from the Mediterranean into the Atlantic Ocean. At the same time, the less salty and thus less dense water of the Atlantic Ocean flows into the Mediterranean at the water's surface.

The densest ocean water on Earth lies off the coast of Antarctica. This dense, cold Antarctic water sinks to the ocean floor and tends to flow north through the world's oceans. These deep Antarctic currents travel for thousands of kilometers. At the same time, warm surface currents near the equator tend to flow south toward Antarctica.

As the deep Antarctic currents come close to land, the ocean floor rises, forcing these cold currents upward. The rising of deep cold currents to the ocean surface is called **upwelling.** Upwelling is very important because the rising currents carry with them rich foodstuffs that have drifted down to the ocean floor. The foodstuffs are usually the remains of dead animals and plants. Wherever these deep currents rise, they turn the ocean into an area of plentiful ocean life. For example, deep currents move upward off the coasts of Peru and Chile. The nutrients they carry to the surface produce rich fishing grounds and important fishing industries in these areas.

Figure 2–36 *In this photograph you can see ripples carved into the ocean floor by a slow-moving deep current.*

Figure 2–37 *Areas of upwelling are important fishing areas because ocean life is plentiful. What factors cause upwelling?* ❶

I ■ 71

FACTS AND FIGURES

DEEP CURRENTS

Deep water currents move much more slowly than surface currents do. For example, cold water from the poles usually takes at least 300 years to reach the equator.

ocean water to integrate concepts of oceanography into your science lesson.

GUIDED PRACTICE

▶ *Laboratory Manual*

Skills Development

Skills: Recording data, plotting graphs, making comparisons, making inferences

Students may now complete the Chapter 2 Laboratory Investigation in the *Laboratory Manual* called Investigating Density Currents. In this investigation students will create a model of a density current and explore some factors that affect its behavior.

ENRICHMENT

Because the Gulf Stream is so important to sailors, the National Oceanic and Atmosphere Administration publishes the Gulf Stream Mailing List three times a week. This publication gives detailed information about the Gulf Stream based on satellite photographs. Have interested students find out more about the Gulf Stream Mailing List and the type of information it contains. Also, have them find out about the techniques used by satellites to map the current and then report their findings to the class.

rocky coastline, there would be little sand or other loose materials for the current to pick up and deposit elsewhere.)

INDEPENDENT PRACTICE

▤ **Media and Technology**

Use the transparency in the *Transparency Binder* called Rip Currents to help develop the concept of surface ocean currents.

CONTENT DEVELOPMENT

Point out to students that the rising of cold ocean waters from the Antarctic is called an upwelling. Upwellings are deep currents, occurring when wind along a coast pushes warm surface water out to sea. Cold water from below the surface rises to replace the warm water.

● ● ● ● **Integration** ● ● ● ●

Use the discussion of the effect of temperature and salinity on the density of

Figure 2–38 *The daily rise and fall of tides is magnificently evident at the Bay of Fundy in Canada.*

Figure 2–39 *Spring tides occur when the sun and the moon are in line with the Earth. Neap tides occur when the sun and the moon are at right angles to the Earth.*

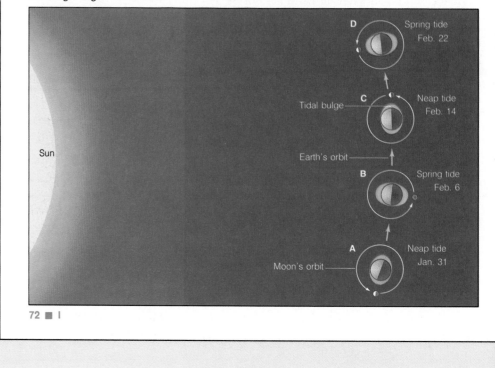

Tides

Tides are the regular rise and fall of ocean water caused by the gravitational attraction among the Earth, moon, and sun. The Earth's gravity pulls on the moon. But the moon's gravity also pulls on the Earth, producing a bulging of the ocean. The ocean bulges in two places: on the side of the Earth that faces the moon, and on the side of the Earth that faces away from the moon. Both bulges cause a high tide, or rising of ocean water, on nearby shorelines.

At the same time that the high tides occur, low tides occur between the two bulges. Observations show that at most places on Earth there are two high tides and two low tides every 24 hours.

Some high tides are higher than other high tides. For example, when the moon is at its full- and new-moon phases, the Earth has higher tides than at other times. These higher tides are called spring tides. Spring tides occur when the sun and the moon are in line with the Earth (which is the arrangement of the sun, moon, and Earth during full-moon and new moon phases). The increased gravitational effect due to the sun's gravity causes the ocean bulges to become even larger than usual.

72 ■ I

land and the water rotate together. The side of the Earth nearest the moon experiences the greatest gravitational pull from the moon. The moon's gravity pulls the water slightly away from the Earth on the moon side and pulls Earth slightly away from the water on the other side. This causes two "bulges" in the oceans.

When the moon is in its full and new phases, Earth has tides higher than normal. These tides are called spring tides. Spring tides occur when the moon and

sun are pulling at Earth together. When the moon is in its first- and last-quarter phases, there are lower tides than normal. These lower tides are called neap tides. Neap tides occur when the sun and moon are pulling at right angles to each other.

● ● ● ● **Integration** ● ● ● ●

Use the discussion of the influence of gravity on the ocean to integrate concepts of tides into your lesson.

When the moon is at its first- and last-quarter phases, its gravitational pull on the oceans is partially canceled by the gravitational pull of the sun. High tides that are lower than usual result. These minimum high tides are called neap tides. What is the position of the sun and moon with respect to each other during neap tides? ❶

2–6 Section Review

1. What are the three basic motions of the ocean?
2. What are four characteristics of a wave?
3. What are currents? What is the difference between surface currents and deep currents?
4. What are tides? What causes them?

Critical Thinking—*Relating Cause and Effect*
5. For maximum excitement, a surfer wants to find the highest waves possible. In what ocean would the surfer have the best chance of finding enormous waves? Why?

The Moon's Attraction

Tide forecasts for each month are usually given in the newspaper on the first day of the month. You can also find tide forecasts in the *Farmer's Almanac.*

Use the information to plot a graph of daily high- and low-tide heights for the month. There are two high and two low tides given for each day. Plot only the heights that occur earlier in the day.

What is the relationship of the phases of the moon to the tide heights? ❷

CONNECTIONS

The Sound of the Surf ❸

Waves are beautiful to watch and thrilling to listen to. Even the smallest waves do not creep silently onto a beach. Instead they break with a gentle sigh. And when large waves break on shore, the crashing sounds are quite impressive. Did you ever wonder why waves make noise when they roll onto shore? The explanation may surprise you.

The answer to this question is as near as the bubble gum in your mouth. When you blow a bubble, you trap air in the gum. When the bubble breaks, it makes a popping sound. Breaking bubbles of trapped air also cause a sound when waves break. Ocean water picks up tiny

bubbles of air, bubbles that become trapped within the water. When waves crash on the shore, the tiny air bubbles in the waves break. The characteristic sound of waves is produced. Keep this in mind, however. Even though there is a sound scientific reason that explains the *physics* of the noise, waves are still beautiful to look at and still wonderful to listen to.

Laboratory Investigation

THE EFFECT OF WATER DEPTH ON SEDIMENTS

BEFORE THE LAB

1. This activity requires approximately 15 minutes out of two class periods, preferably at least an hour apart or on successive days.

2. At least one day prior to the investigation, gather enough materials assuming six students per group.

3. Sandy soil can serve as the source of sediments. The columns should vary considerably in length, from less than 10 centimeters to as long as 1 meter, if possible.

PRE-LAB DISCUSSION

Have students read the complete laboratory procedure.

• **How do sediments settle on the ocean floor?** (The largest particles will generally settle first.)

• **Why are the abyssal plains so flat?** (Sediments are constantly filling in uneven places.)

• **What is the origin of ocean sediments?** (Much of the sediment comes from land.)

• **What is the name given to ocean currents that carry sediments from the continental shelf down the slopes and onto the abyssal plains?** (Turbidity currents.)

Laboratory Investigation

The Effect of Water Depth on Sediments

Problem

To determine the effects that differences in water depth have on the settling of sediments.

Materials   *(per group)*

> plastic tubes of different lengths that contain sediment samples and salt water

Procedure

1. Obtain a plastic tube from your teacher.

2. Make sure that both ends of the tube are securely capped.

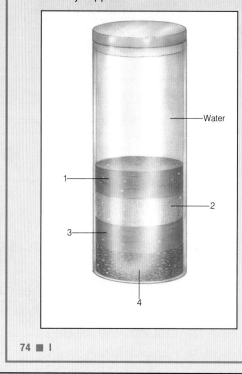

3. Hold the tube by both ends and gently tip it back and forth until the sediments in the tube are thoroughly mixed throughout the water.

4. Set the tube in an upright position in a place where it will not be disturbed.

5. Repeat steps 1 through 4 for each of the remaining tubes.

6. Carefully observe the sediments in each tube.

Observations

1. Make a detailed sketch to illustrate the heights of the different layers formed when the sediments in each tube settled.

2. What general statement can you make about the size of the sediment particles and the order in which each type of sediment settled in the tube?

Analysis and Conclusions

1. What effect does the length of the water column have on the number and types of sediment layers formed in each tube?

2. How are these tubes accurate models of what happens to sediments carried to the ocean?

3. What is the variable present in this investigation? What variables that may be present in the ocean are not tested in this investigation?

4. On Your Own   Design an investigation to determine the effect of different amounts of salinity on the formation of sediment layers.

TEACHING STRATEGY

1. Tell students to gently tip the tubes back and forth until the sediment is thoroughly mixed. Caution them not to shake the tubes.

2. As students work, ask them to think about other factors that might influence the settling of sediments on the ocean floor.

DISCOVERY STRATEGIES

Discuss how the investigation relates to the chapter by asking open questions similar to the following.

• **Do you think surface weather patterns influence sediments settling on the bottom of the ocean?** (Most students will say no—relating, predicting.)

• **In what parts of the ocean might surface weather patterns influence sediments settling on the ocean bottom?** (Shallow regions—relating, applying.)

• **Explain how water temperature and wind speed, both separately and together, might influence the settling of sediments in an ocean.** (Explanations will vary. Students might suggest that

Study Guide

Summarizing Key Concepts

2–1 The World's Oceans
▲ The Atlantic, Pacific, and Indian oceans are the three major oceans.

2–2 Properties of Ocean Water
▲ Ocean water is a mixture of gases and solids dissolved in pure water.

▲ Ocean water is classified into three zones based on water temperature: surface zone, thermocline, and deep zone.

2–3 The Ocean Floor
▲ A continental margin consists of a continental shelf, a continental slope, and a continental rise.

▲ Major features of the ocean floor include, abyssal plains, seamounts, guyots, trenches, midocean ridges, rift valleys, and reefs.

2–4 Ocean Life Zones
▲ Ocean life forms are classified by habits and depth in which they live.

▲ The three major ocean life zones are the intertidal, neritic and open-ocean zones.

2–5 Mapping the Ocean Floor
▲ The ocean floor is mapped by echo sounding, radar, sonar, and seismographic surveys.

2–6 Motions of the Ocean
▲ Motions of the ocean include waves, currents, and tides.

▲ Waves have the following characteristics: crests, troughs, wavelength, wave height, wave period, and wave frequency.

▲ Surface currents are caused mainly by wind patterns; deep currents by differences in the density of ocean water.

▲ Tides are the regular rise and fall of ocean water caused by the gravitational attraction among the Earth, moon, and sun.

Reviewing Key Terms

Define each term in a complete sentence.

2–2 Properties of Ocean Water
oceanographer
salinity
surface zone
thermocline
deep zone

2–3 The Ocean Floor
shoreline
continental margin
continental shelf
continental slope

continental rise
turbidity current
submarine canyon
abyssal plain
seamounts
guyot
trench
midocean ridge
coral reef
fringing reef
barrier reef
atoll

2–4 Ocean Life Zones
plankton
nekton
benthos
intertidal zone
neritic zone
bathyal zone
abyssal zone

2–6 Motions of the Ocean
crest
trough
wavelength
tsunami
surface current
deep current
upwelling

---

effect of different amounts of salinity on the formation of sediment layers.

Part 1

Have students conduct a similar investigation using different soil types. To save time, you may wish to give each group a different soil type. Then have students compare their sketches to see how the patterns for each soil type may differ.

Part 2

Have students do library research or, if possible, visit an oceanographic facility to obtain information on the study of core samples that have been taken from ocean-floor sediments.

---

these factors, both individually and collectively, might influence the rate, or speed, of settling—relating, inferring.)

OBSERVATIONS

1. Sketches will vary, depending on the contents of each tube, but they should accurately display the arrangement of the contents of each tube.

2. The largest particles will generally settle first and will be found at the bottom of the tube.

ANALYSIS AND CONCLUSIONS

1. The greatest degree of sorting occurs in the longest tube. That is, the most clearly differentiated layers are formed in that tube.

2. The ocean contains varying depths, similar to the varying depths of water in the tubes.

3. The depth of the water; ocean currents, water temperature, water density, salinity, and so on.

4. Investigations will vary. Check each design to ensure that it will determine the

Chapter Review

ALTERNATIVE ASSESSMENT

The *Prentice Hall Science* program includes a variety of testing components and methodologies. Aside from the Chapter Review questions, you may opt to use the Chapter Test or the Computer Test Bank Test in your *Test Book* for assessment of important facts and concepts. In addition, Performance-Based Tests are included in your *Test Book*. These Performance-Based Tests are designed to test science process skills, rather than factual content recall. Since they are not content dependent, Performance-Based Tests can be distributed after students complete a chapter or after they complete the entire textbook.

CONTENT REVIEW

Multiple Choice

1. b
2. a
3. d
4. d
5. c
6. a
7. d
8. d
9. b
10. c

True or False

1. F, sodium chloride
2. F, trough
3. T
4. F, the moon
5. F, continental shelf
6. F, Neap tides

Concept Mapping

Row 1: Atlantic, Indian, Pacific

Content Review

Multiple Choice

Choose the letter of the answer that best completes each statement.

1. The three major oceans of the world are the Atlantic, Pacific, and
   a. Arctic.
   b. Indian.
   c. Mediterranean.
   d. Caribbean.

2. The amount of dissolved salts in ocean water is called
   a. salinity.
   b. turbidity.
   c. upwelling.
   d. current.

3. The zone in the ocean where the temperature changes rapidly is called the
   a. surface zone.
   b. benthos.
   c. tide zone.
   d. thermocline.

4. The amount of time it takes consecutive wave crests or troughs to pass a given point is called the
   a. wavelength.
   b. tsunami.
   c. wave height.
   d. frequency.

5. All ocean currents are caused by
   a. winds and earthquakes.
   b. volcanoes and tides.
   c. winds and water density.
   d. tides and water density.

6. The most common source of energy for surface waves is
   a. wind.
   b. earthquakes.
   c. tides.
   d. volcanoes.

7. The deepest parts of the ocean are found in long, narrow crevices called
   a. guyots.
   b. seamounts.
   c. reefs.
   d. trenches.

8. Organisms that live on the ocean floor are called
   a. nekton.
   b. plankton.
   c. diatoms.
   d. benthos.

9. The rising of deep cold currents to the ocean surface is called
   a. surfing.
   b. upwelling.
   c. mapping.
   d. reefing.

10. High tides that are higher than other high tides are called
    a. tsunamis.
    b. neap tides.
    c. spring tides.
    d. ebb tides.

True or False

If the statement is true, write "true." If it is false, change the underlined word or words to make the statement true.

1. The most abundant salt in the ocean is <u>magnesium bromide</u>.
2. The lowest point of a wave is called the <u>crest</u>.
3. The Gulf Stream is a <u>long-distance</u> surface current.
4. Tides are caused mainly by the gravitational attraction of <u>Jupiter</u>.
5. The relatively flat part of a continental margin covered by shallow water is called a <u>continental slope</u>.
6. <u>Spring tides</u> occur during the first- and last-quarter phases of the moon.

Concept Mapping

Complete the following concept map for Section 2–1. Refer to pages I6–I7 to construct a concept map for the entire chapter.

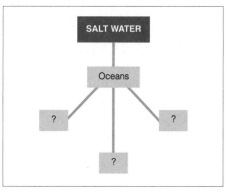

CONCEPT MASTERY

1. Surface waves depend on wind speed, the length of time the wind blows, and the distance the wind blows over water. Deep waves do not exist except for those caused by tides and earthquakes.

2. The greater the temperature, the greater the potential for salinity.

3. Generally speaking, ocean organisms depend on other organisms smaller than themselves for food. The largest ocean organisms depend on smaller organisms, which feed on even smaller organisms, with the "cycle" or "chain" continuing through the smallest organisms.

4. Surface zone—greatest temperatures, water mixed by waves and currents; thermocline zone—surface zone with rapid temperature changes; deep zone—cold water, relatively constant temperature.

5. Abyssal plains—large, flat areas; seamounts—volcanic mountains; guyots—flat-topped seamounts; trenches—long, narrow crevices; midocean ridges—mountain ranges; reefs—masses and

Concept Mastery

Discuss each of the following in a brief paragraph.

1. How do surface waves and deep waves differ?
2. How does the salinity of ocean water change with temperature?
3. Some of the largest animals in the oceans, (certain whales, for example) depend upon some of the smallest living organisms in the sea. Explain this statement.
4. List the three temperature zones of the ocean. Describe the physical conditions present in each zone.
5. Describe the topography of the ocean floor.
6. What are the three types of coral reefs? How are they alike? How are they different?

Critical Thinking and Problem Solving

Use the skills you have developed in this chapter to answer each of the following.

1. **Applying concepts** Many countries in the world extend their borders to a "two hundred mile limit" from shore. What are several reasons countries might impose this limit?
2. **Making inferences** Suppose conditions in the ocean changed and a major upwelling occurred off the coast of New York City. How would this change the life in the ocean in this area?
3. **Drawing conclusions** Suppose you were asked to design a special suit that would allow people to explore areas deep under the surface of the ocean. What are some important features the suit would need in order to help a diver survive?
4. **Applying concepts** Many legends tell of the appearance and disappearance of islands. Explain why such legends may be fact rather than fiction.
5. **Making calculations** Sound travels about 1500 meters per second in water. How deep would the ocean be if it took twenty seconds for a sound wave to return to the surface from the ocean bottom?
6. **Relating concepts** How do nekton organisms differ from benthos organisms?
7. **Identifying parts** The accompanying illustration shows a typical wave. Provide labels for the parts shown.
8. **Using the writing process** Suppose you and your family and friends lived in a huge glass bubble deep beneath the ocean waves. Write several pages in a diary to explain what life is like over a week's time.

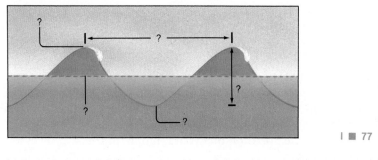

I ■ 77

---

tect against the great pressure of deep ocean water.

4. Some islands are the tops of volcanic seamounts rising up from the ocean floor. An island can suddenly appear as a volcano spews out more material, raising the height of the seamount. Islands can also disappear as the tops of seamounts are eroded away by the action of wind and waves.

5. 30,000 meters.

6. Nekton—organisms that swim, actively search for food, have the potential to avoid predators, found in all levels of the ocean; benthos—plants and animals that live only on the ocean floor.

7. Check to make sure students have correctly identified the parts of the wave.

8. Explanations will vary but should contain descriptions of life during a one-week stay in an underwater bubble.

KEEPING A PORTFOLIO

You might want to assign some of the Concept Mastery and Critical Thinking and Problem Solving questions as homework and have students include their responses to unassigned questions in their portfolio. Students should be encouraged to include both the question and the answer in their portfolio.

ISSUES IN SCIENCE

The following issues can be used as springboards for discussion or given as writing assignments.

1. Environmentalists are concerned that the use of continental shelves by the fishing industry is causing the areas to become overfished. Find out more about the environmental problems caused by overfishing. Then propose actions that might be taken to alleviate this problem.

2. What country owns or has rights to the resources of the sea? Some nations feel that whoever explores an area first should have a right to that area's riches. Other nations claim that the oceans' resources should be regulated by an international agreement. Find out what efforts have been made to regulate the oceans' resources and how successful these efforts have been. Then give your own opinion on this issue.

---

ridges of limestone rocks built by organisms.

6. Fringing reefs—small reefs that touch the shoreline of a volcanic island; barrier reefs—generally large reefs separated from shore by a lagoon; atoll reefs—ring of reefs surrounding an underwater island.

CRITICAL THINKING AND PROBLEM SOLVING

1. This limit serves to protect and monopolize the natural resources of the off-shore areas and to help provide defense of the country's shores.

2. An upwelling can distort regular weather patterns, potentially causing drought, floods, and great wind speeds, which would affect the ocean activity and the ocean life in the area, possibly causing an increase in number of some species populations and a decrease in others, eventually leading to an ecological imbalance.

3. The suit would need to regulate body temperature, provide oxygen, and pro-

Chapter 3   EARTH'S FRESH WATER

SECTION	HANDS-ON ACTIVITIES
3–1 Fresh Water on the Surface of the Earth pages I80–I92 Multicultural Opportunity 3–1, p. I80 ESL Strategy 3–1, p. I80	**Student Edition** ACTIVITY (Discovering): Making a Model of the Water Cycle, p. I83 ACTIVITY BANK: How Does a Fish Move? p. I168 **Activity Book** CHAPTER DISCOVERY: Hard Water/Soft Water, p. I79 ACTIVITY: Icebergs, p. I87 **Teacher Edition** Observing the Water Cycle, p. I78d
3–2 Fresh Water Beneath the Surface of the Earth pages I93–I99 Multicultural Opportunity 3–2, p. I93 ESL Strategy 3–2, p. I93	**Student Edition** ACTIVITY (Discovering): Drought and the Water Table, p. I97 LABORATORY INVESTIGATION: Porosity of Various Soils, p. I104 **Laboratory Manual** Investigating Porosity and Permeability, p. I31 **Activity Book** ACTIVITY: Stalactite and Stalagmite Formation, p. I85 ACTIVITY: Water Pressure: A Hidden Community Worker, p. I91 **Product Testing Activity** Bottled Water **Teacher Edition** Water Traveling Underground, p. I78d
3–3 Water as a Solvent pages I100–I103 Multicultural Opportunity 3–3, p. I100 ESL Strategy 3–3, p. I100	**Student Edition** ACTIVITY (Discovering): Water as a Solvent, p. I102 ACTIVITY BANK: What Is the Effect of Phosphates on Plant Growth? p. I169 **Laboratory Manual** Examining the Pollution of a Water Supply, p. I35 **Activity Book** ACTIVITY: Distillation and Desalination, p. I95
Chapter Review pages I104–I107	

OUTSIDE TEACHER RESOURCES

Books

Bisque, R. E., H. Pratt, and J. F. Thompson, *Earth Science: Patterns in Our Environment*, Prentice Hall.

Crickmay, C. H. *The Work of the River*, Elsevier.

Gilfond, Henry. *Water: A Scarce Source*, Watts.

Leopold, Luna B. *Water: A Primer*, W. H. Freeman.

OTHER ACTIVITIES	MEDIA AND TECHNOLOGY
Student Edition ACTIVITY (Writing): The Water Cycle, p. I84 ACTIVITY (Calculating): I Am Thirsty, p. I87 ACTIVITY (Calculating): A Water Bill, p. I88 ACTIVITY (Calculating): Hydroelectric Power, p. I91 **Activity Book** ACTIVITY: The Water Cycle, p. I81 ACTIVITY: Studying the Water Cycle, p. I83 ACTIVITY: Water Budget, p. I89 **Review and Reinforcement Guide** Section 3–1, p. I31	**Transparency Binder** The Water Cycle **Video** What's on Tap (Supplemental) Lakes and Streams (Supplemental) Freshwater Wetlands (Supplemental) Freshwater (Supplemental) **Videodisc** Aquatic Ecosystems: Freshwater Wetlands Aquatic Ecosystems: Freshwater **English/Spanish Audiotapes** Section 3–1
Review and Reinforcement Guide Section 3–2, p. I35	**English/Spanish Audiotapes** Section 3–2
Activity Book ACTIVITY: Wise Use of Fresh Water, p. I99 **Review and Reinforcement Guide** Section 3–3, p. I37	**English/Spanish Audiotapes** Section 3–3
Test Book Chapter Test, p. I55 Performance-Based Tests, p. I119	**Test Book** Computer Test Bank Test, p. I61

*All materials in the Chapter Planning Guide Grid are available as part of the Prentice Hall Science Learning System.

Audiovisuals

Clouds and Precipitation, film or video, Coronet Film and Video
The Earth and Its Wonders (The Story of Rivers, The Story of Underground Water), video, Encyclopaedia Britannica
Geyser Valley, video, Encyclopaedia Britannica
Groundwater, film or video, Encyclopaedia Britannica
Rivers: The Work of Running Water, video, Encyclopaedia Britannica

Chapter 3 EARTH'S FRESH WATER

CHAPTER OVERVIEW

One of the Earth's most precious resources is fresh water. Only about 3 percent of the Earth's water is made up of fresh water, and most of this is unusable because it is frozen, mainly in continental glaciers. The Earth's supply of fresh water is constantly being replenished by the water cycle through the processes of evaporation, condensation, and precipitation.

The major sources of the Earth's freshwater supply on the surface are frozen water, in the forms of glaciers and icebergs; running water, including surface runoff and water in rivers and streams; and standing water, in the form of lakes, ponds, and res-ervoirs. Groundwater is another important source of fresh water. More water is contained in the ground than in all the Earth's lakes and reservoirs. Groundwater is obtained for use by digging wells into the Earth at least to the water table.

Water is a solvent because of the polarity of its molecules. Because it is a solvent, water can be easily polluted. Safeguards must be instituted to protect freshwater sources from pollution because of the hazards the pollution presents to people, animals, and the environment. The conservation and preservation of the limited freshwater supply is the responsibility of everyone.

3-1 FRESH WATER ON THE SURFACE OF THE EARTH

THEMATIC FOCUS

The purpose of this section is to introduce the water cycles. Students learn that through the processes of evaporation, condensation, and precipitation, water is constantly moving from the ocean and freshwater sources to the air and the land and back to the ocean. The major emphasis of the section is on the sources of fresh water on Earth's surface and the fact that most of Earth's fresh water cannot be used because it is frozen in glaciers. These sources include frozen water in glaciers and icebergs, runoff water in rivers and streams, and standing water in ponds, lakes, and reservoirs.

The themes that can be focused on in this section are energy, patterns of change, systems and interactions, and stability.

*Energy: The energy of the sun provides the energy that drives the water cycle, which replenishes Earth's supply of fresh water.

*Patterns of change: During the water cycle, water passes through the processes of evaporation, condensation, and precipitation. Within the water cycle, water changes form from gas into liquid and sometimes into a solid and back again.

*Systems and interactions: Water evaporates from the ocean, leaving salts behind. This water becomes part of the atmosphere. Eventually, the water forms precipitation. There is constant movement of water from the ocean to the air and the land and back again.

*Stability: The amount of water and salts in the ocean remains constant because fresh water is constantly returning to the oceans through the water cycle. Water that evaporates from the ocean is returned to the ocean by rivers and streams as runoff.

PERFORMANCE OBJECTIVES 3-1

1. Describe the water cycle.
2. Compare the types of glaciers and explain that they hold most of the world's freshwater supply.
3. Identify the surface sources of fresh water.
4. Define watershed.

SCIENCE TERMS 3-1

water cycle p. I81
evaporation p. I81
condensation p. I82
precipitation p. I82
groundwater p. I83
glacier p. I83
valley glacier p. I84
continental glacier p. I85
iceberg p. I86
surface runoff p. I87
pore space p. I88
watershed p. I88
reservoir p. I91

3-2 FRESH WATER BENEATH THE SURFACE OF THE EARTH

THEMATIC FOCUS

The purpose of this section is to introduce students to the underground sources of water and to discuss the permeability of rock. Students learn that these sources can be tapped by digging or drilling wells. They identify aquifers as an important source of fresh water and distinguish between wells that must pump water and artesian wells. They also learn about how water can form caverns and the structures within them such as stalactites and stalagmites.

The themes that can be focused on in this section are unity and diversity and scale and structure.

Unity and diversity: All living things need water to survive. Because groundwater is more abundant than surface fresh water, plants and humans depend heavily on it as a source of fresh water.

*Scale and structure: More fresh water is below the surface of the land than is found in all the lakes and reservoirs on Earth. The porosity and permeability of rocks are among the factors that determine the level of the water table and the amount of groundwater available in an area.

PERFORMANCE OBJECTIVES 3-2

1. Identify the sources of fresh water under the surface of the Earth.
2. Explain the differences between artesian wells and other wells.
3. Define permeability.
4. Explain how fresh water forms caverns, stalactites, and stalagmites.

SCIENCE TERMS 3-2

permeable p. I93
impermeable p. I93

3–3 WATER AS A SOLVENT

THEMATIC FOCUS

The purpose of this section is to introduce water as a solvent. Because water is a solvent, it can be easily contaminated by chemicals and other pollutants. Students identify characteristics of hard and soft water, and they learn about the need to protect and conserve limited water sources.

The themes that can be focused on in this section are scale and structure and systems and interactions.

*Scale and structure: Water molecules have polarity. This property enables water to act as a solvent for many different substances. Because water can dissolve so many different substances, it is called the universal solvent.

*Systems and interactions: The pollution of freshwater sources, including groundwater sources, affects all life. It limits the amounts and kinds of wildlife that can live in water. It affects drinking water and destroys recreational areas.

PERFORMANCE OBJECTIVES 3–3

1. Describe how the polarity of water makes it a good solvent.
2. Relate water's ability to serve as a solvent to water pollution.
3. List ways of protecting freshwater sources.

SCIENCE TERMS 3–3

polarity p. I100
solvent p. I100
solution P. I100
hard water p. I102
soft water p. I102

Discovery *Learning*

TEACHER DEMONSTRATIONS MODELING

Observing the Water Cycle

This demonstration simulates the processes of the water cycle—evaporation, condensation, and precipitation. For this demonstration, you will need a quart-sized glass jar, a pie tin, hot water, a hot pad, a hot plate, a pot, a spoon, and a few ice cubes. Boil water in the pot on the hot plate. Add enough hot water to the jar so that it is one-fourth full. When pouring the water into the jar, place a spoon in the jar to help prevent the jar from cracking. Place a few ice cubes in the pie tin and then place it on top of the jar. Have students observe the setup.

• **What is forming on the underside of the pie tin?** (Water)
• **Which action in the demonstration is similar to evaporation?** (The rising hot-water vapor.)
• **Which action is similar to condensation?** (The formation of water on the bottom of the pie tin.)
• **Why is condensation occurring?** (As the moisture-ladened hot air nears the cold pie tin, the air is cooled. Cool air cannot hold as much water vapor as hot air can, so some of the water vapor is changed into liquid.)
• **Which action is similar to precipitation?** (Falling water droplets from the bottom of the pie tin.)

Water Traveling Underground

This demonstration will illustrate how water travels underground. For the demonstration, you will need two medium-sized beakers, some soil, water, and a piece of limestone or sandstone about the same diameter as that of the beaker.

Fill each beaker about two-thirds full with soil. Cover the soil in one beaker with a piece of limestone or sandstone. Explain to the class that you are about to pour "rain" on the soil in each beaker.
• **What do you think will happen to the water as it is poured into each beaker?**

(Answers will vary, but many students may think the soil in the uncovered beaker will absorb the water, whereas the soil in the other beaker will be prevented by the rock layer from absorbing water.)

Pour water into each beaker and have students observe what happens. (The water will be absorbed immediately by the uncovered beaker, whereas it will temporarily puddle on top of the rock layer of the covered soil.) Leave the soil with the rock layer standing for the rest of the class period. Then have students observe what has happened. (Some of the water will have penetrated the rock layer and flowed into the soil.) Point out that this is one of the ways in which water is absorbed by the Earth—through permeable rock, which allows water to flow through it.
• **Why was water able to seep through the rock?** (The rock is porous, and the water seeps through the pores of the rock.)
• **Do you think the water would seep through clay? Why or why not?** (Clay is not very porous, so it is unlikely that the water would seep through the clay by the end of the class period.)

CHAPTER 3
Earth's Fresh Water

INTEGRATING SCIENCE

This earth science chapter provides you with numerous opportunities to integrate other areas of science, as well as other disciplines, into your curriculum. Blue numbered annotations on the student page and integration notes on the teacher wraparound pages alert you to areas of possible integration.

In this chapter you can integrate earth science and meteorology (p. 81), life science and botany (p. 81), physical science and heat transfer (p. 82), language arts (p. 84), earth science and erosion (p. 84), social studies (p. 86), mathematics (pp. 87, 88, 91), earth science and ecology (pp. 89, 103), water management (pp. 91, 92, 97), earth science and geology (p. 93), life science and biomes (p. 95), earth science and climate (p. 95), physical science and acids and bases (p. 98), physical science and atoms (p. 100), physical science and magnetism (p. 100), and physical science and solutions (p. 100).

SCIENCE, TECHNOLOGY, AND SOCIETY/COOPERATIVE LEARNING

Incidents involving contamination of water supplies have caused many consumers to avoid using municipal water supplies. Many people (one in sixteen households) now use bottled water or have installed home water-treatment systems to protect themselves from contaminated and polluted water supplies.

Bottled water is big business! In the United States alone, there is a 2.2-billion-dollar market for bottled water, and competitors are aggressively pursuing new customers.

Water purification in the form of home treatment systems is also a growing industry—there are already 50 million purifying devices in use today! Purification devices range from inexpensive drinking jugs with filters to elaborate and expensive systems. Activated charcoal filters work by absorbing pollutants, but they are not effective against heavy metals and bacteria. Reverse osmosis systems use membranes to separate pure from

INTRODUCING CHAPTER 3

DISCOVERY LEARNING

▶ *Activity Book*

Begin teaching the chapter by using the Chapter 1 Discovery Activity from the *Activity Book*. Using this activity, students will discover the differences between hard and soft water.

USING THE TEXTBOOK

Because so much of Earth's surface is covered by water, many people erroneously think that water is an unlimited resource. As you teach this chapter, it is important to emphasize the value of water as a resource and the importance of maintaining pollution-free sources of fresh water.

Begin by having students observe the chapter-opener photograph. Ask these questions.

Earth's Fresh Water

The newspaper headlines said it all. Water, a substance most people take for granted, was creating problems all over the country. In some places there was too little water, in other places too much.

A severe drought in the West had left hundreds of square kilometers of forest dry. Forest fires raged in these areas, causing heavy damage. Firefighters battled in vain to stem the fire's destructive path.

Meanwhile, heavy rains in some southern states had flooded rivers, lakes, and streams. Dams could no longer hold the huge quantities of water building up behind them. In several places, dams collapsed. Water and thick streams of mud buried land and homes under a heavy sheet of wet, brown dirt.

Perhaps you have never thought of water as the cause of such problems. To you, water is a natural resource you use every day to stay alive. In fact, more than 500 billion liters of water are used every day in the United States alone. Within the next 20 years, this staggering volume will probably double! Where does our supply of fresh water come from? Will there always be enough? In this chapter you will learn about the Earth's supply of fresh water, as well as the answers to these questions.

Journal *Activity*

You and Your World The average American family uses 760 liters of water a day. In some parts of the world, however, the average family uses 7 to 10 liters of water a day! Suppose your family's supply of water were limited to 10 liters a day. In your journal, make a list of the things you would use this water for. Make a list of the things you couldn't do.

◀ *Fresh water is one of the Earth's most important natural resources.*

I ■ 79

---

impure water. These systems do eliminate heavy metals like lead but waste up to 3 gallons of water to generate each gallon of pure water. Distillation systems turn water into steam and then recondense it in a cleaner state. Used with a charcoal filter, distillation provides the purest water attainable. Nevertheless, distillation systems can pass along some harmful chemicals. Ultraviolet systems eliminate microbes but are ineffective against other contaminants. Experts caution that consumers should have their water analyzed to find out what contaminants need to be removed and then purchase the type of system appropriate for their needs.

Cooperative learning: Using preassigned groups or randomly selected teams, have groups complete one of the following assignments.
- **Prepare a list of questions to be used in an interview with the head of the water department in your community. Questions should include inquiries about the water source, methods of purification, testing procedures, possible sources of contamination, amount of water used by the community, and so on.**
- **Have groups design an experiment/taste test to compare tap water and various types of bottled water. You may want to share with the class these guidelines: Water should be clean tasting, colorless, odorless, refreshing (not stale or heavy), and thirst quenching and should not leave a residual aftertaste.**

See Cooperative Learning in the *Teacher's Desk Reference.*

JOURNAL ACTIVITY

You may want to use the Journal Activity as the basis of a class discussion. As students discuss the ramifications of severe water-usage restriction, encourage them to consider multiple uses of water; for example, water used for washing dishes or for personal hygiene could be used to water indoor and outdoor plants. Point out that 10 liters is little more than 1 percent of the water presently used by the average American family. Instruct students to include their Journal Activity in their portfolio.

- **What do you see in this picture?** (A waterfall emptying into a body of water below.)
- **What words would you use to describe the water in this picture?** (Clean, sparkling, cool, rapidly moving.)
- **Does this water appeal to you as a source of water that you might drink or bathe in?** (Most will probably say yes.)

After students have read the chapter-opener text, ask these questions.
- **What two problems regarding water are described in the text?** (Having too little water and having too much water.)
- **What does this suggest about the distribution of Earth's water supply?** (It is not evenly distributed.)

Explain that part of this uneven distribution results from droughts or heavy rains in certain areas, but that some areas of the world have many more natural water sources than do other areas.

3-1 Fresh Water on the Surface of the Earth

Guide for Reading

Focus on this question as you read.

▶ What are the major sources of fresh water on the Earth's surface?

3-1 Fresh Water on the Surface of the Earth

When you look at a photograph of Planet Earth taken from space, you can observe that water is one of the most abundant substances on Earth's surface. In fact, astronauts—whose views of Earth differ from those of most people—have described the Earth as the blue planet!

A casual glance at a world map might make you think that the Earth has an unending supply of fresh water—a supply that can meet the needs of living things forever. After all, the oceans cover more than 70 percent of the Earth's surface. Actually, about 97 percent of all the water on Earth is found in the oceans. But most of the ocean water cannot be used by living things because it contains salt. The salt would have to be removed before ocean water could be used.

Figure 3-1 *Most water on Earth is salt water found in the oceans. Only a small percent is fresh water, most of which is trapped as ice in the polar icecaps. That leaves only a small portion of fresh water available for use by living things.*

Fresh water makes up only about 3 percent of the Earth's water. However, most of this fresh water cannot be used because it is frozen, mainly in the icecaps near the North and South poles and in glaciers. In fact, only about 15 percent of the Earth's fresh water can be used by living things. This extremely small percent represents the Earth's total supply of fresh water. With such a limited supply, you might wonder why the Earth does not run out of fresh water. Fortunately, the Earth's supply of fresh water is continuously being renewed.

The Water Cycle

Most of the fresh water on the Earth's surface is found in moving water and in standing water. Rivers, streams, and springs are moving water. Ponds, lakes, and swampy wetlands are standing water.

Water moves among these sources of fresh water, the salty oceans, the air, and the land in a cycle. A cycle has no beginning and no end. It is a continuous chain of events. The **water cycle** is the movement of water from the oceans and freshwater sources to the air and land and finally back to the oceans. The water cycle, also called the hydrologic cycle, constantly renews the Earth's supply of fresh water.

Three main steps make up the water cycle. The first step involves the heat energy given off by the sun. This energy causes water on the surface of the Earth to change to water vapor, the gas phase of water. This process is called **evaporation** (ih-vap-uh-RAY-shuhn). Enormous amounts of water evaporate from the oceans. Water also evaporates from freshwater sources and from the soil. Animals and plants release water vapor into the air as well. You might be surprised to learn just how much water actually evaporates into the air from a single plant. (As you might suspect, a scientist has measured it!) In one day, a single large tree can move more than 1800 liters of water from the ground, through its stems and branches, to its leaves, and finally into the air! Other organisms do not move quite the same amount of water as this single large tree. But if you consider the vast number of plants, animals, and other living things that are part of the water cycle, you can see that the total amount of water given off by living things is very large indeed.

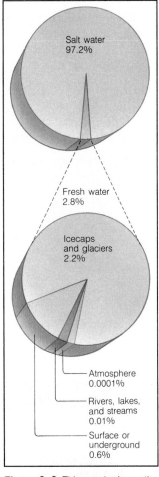

Figure 3–2 *This graph shows the distribution of Earth's water. What percent is fresh water? Is all this water available for use? Explain.* ❶

I ■ 81

FACTS AND FIGURES

SALT IN WATER

The maximum amount of dissolved salts that can be present in drinking water is 500 parts per million; in water used for irrigation, the maximum is 700 parts per million. Sea water normally contains about 35,000 parts per million dissolved salts.

CONTENT DEVELOPMENT

When explaining the water cycle, it is important to point out that when water evaporates from Earth's surface, precipitation does not necessarily return it to exactly the same place. In fact, scientists have concluded that more water evaporates from the oceans than is returned to the oceans, and more water is returned to the land than evaporates from land. The balance of loss and gain is maintained by the flow of water from rivers, streams, and groundwater sources into the oceans. The following equation sums up the balance of the water cycle:

Precipitation = Evaporation
+ Riverflow + Groundwater outflow

● ● ● ● **Integration** ● ● ● ●

Use the discussion of the water cycle to integrate earth science concepts of meteorology into your lesson.

Use the text information about water evaporation from plants to integrate life science concepts of botany into your lesson.

MAKING A MODEL
OF THE WATER CYCLE

Discovery Learning

Skills: Manipulative, observing, inferring, relating, applying

Materials: small jar, salt, wide-mouthed jar, paper cup, sand, plastic wrap, rubber band, small rock

In this activity students observe the evaporation and then the condensation of salt water. They should note that the purpose of sealing the jar is twofold. First, the seal allows students to collect and taste the water that condenses on the plastic wrap. Second, the seal simulates the atmosphere of the Earth. Students should note that the water on the wrap is not salty. They should infer that the salt has been left behind when the water evaporated, as is the case in the water cycle. Evaporation and condensation are processes involved in the model.

Students' models will vary. They may choose to lower temperatures after exposing water to high temperatures so that they can observe condensation and precipitation.

3–1 (continued)

GUIDED PRACTICE

 **Media and Technology**

Skills Development

Skill: Interpreting diagrams

Use the transparency The Water Cycle to reinforce students' understanding of the water cycle.
• **From what sources does water evaporate into the atmosphere?** (From the oceans, from lakes and streams, and from vegetation and soil.)
• **According to the diagram, what happens to surface runoff?** (It flows into rivers and streams, which eventually flow into the ocean.)

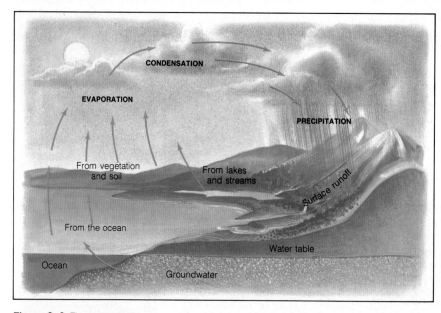

Figure 3–3 *The water cycle constantly renews the Earth's supply of fresh water. What three processes make up the water cycle?* ❶

Figure 3–4 *A large tree can release up to 1800 liters of water a day into the atmosphere. By what process does liquid water in a tree become water vapor in the atmosphere?* ❷

82 ■ I

The second step of the water cycle involves a process called **condensation** (kahn-dehn-SAY-shuhn). Condensation is the process by which water vapor changes back into a liquid. For condensation to occur, the air containing the water vapor must be cooled. And this is exactly what happens as the warm air close to the Earth's surface rises. As it moves farther from the Earth's surface, the warm air cools. Cool air cannot hold as much water vapor as warm air. In the cooler air, most of the water vapor condenses into droplets of water that form clouds. But these clouds are not "salty" clouds. Do you know why? When water evaporates from the oceans, the salt is left behind. Water vapor is made of fresh water only.

During the third step of the cycle, water returns to the Earth in the form of rain, snow, sleet, or hail. This process is called **precipitation** (prih-sihp-uh-TAY-shuhn). Precipitation occurs when the water droplets that form in clouds become too numerous and too heavy to remain afloat in the air. The water that falls as rain, snow, sleet, or hail is fresh water. After the water falls, some of it returns to the

---

• **What eventually happens to groundwater?** (It flows into the ocean.)

Point out that the water cycle includes the movement of water from the land to the oceans, then back to the land.

CONTENT DEVELOPMENT

Explain that the evaporation of water from plant leaves is called transpiration. The water lost through transpiration is replaced by water moving up through the roots.

One way to illustrate transpiration and thus begin a discussion of transpiration pull is to take a houseplant, water it normally, put a clear plastic bag over the plant, and set it in a well-lighted area to observe for a few days. As the moisture accumulates on the inside of the bag, you can discuss transpiration and the fact that the water is coming up through the plant from the roots. This should help students understand that as each drop evaporates from the leaves, another

Figure 3-5 *The third step of the water cycle is precipitation, which may occur as rain, snow, sleet, or hail.*

atmosphere through evaporation. The cycle of water movement continues. The Earth's supply of fresh water is continuously renewed.

Some of the water that falls as precipitation may run off into ponds, lakes, streams, rivers, or oceans. Some may soak into the ground and become **groundwater.** Groundwater is the water that remains in the ground. At some point, the groundwater flows underground to the oceans. You will learn more about groundwater in the next section.

Frozen Water

If you make a snowball out of freshly fallen snow and hold it tightly in your hands for awhile, the warmth of your body will cause the snow to melt. Snow is actually a solid form of water. You may also notice that some of the snow pressed together by your hands forms ice. The same thing happens when new snow falls on top of old snow. The pressure of the piled-up snow causes some of the snow to change into ice. In time, a **glacier** forms. A glacier is a huge mass of moving ice and snow.

ACTIVITY

DISCOVERING

Making a Model of the Water Cycle

1. Stir salt into a small jar filled with water until no more will dissolve. Pour a 1-cm deep layer of the salt water into a large, wide-mouthed jar.

2. Place a paper cup half filled with sand in the center of the jar.

3. Loosely cover the jar's mouth with plastic wrap. Seal the wrap around the jar's sides with a rubber band.

4. Place a small rock or weight on the plastic wrap directly over the paper cup.

5. Place the jar in direct sunlight. After several hours, observe the setup. Carefully remove the plastic wrap and try to collect a few drops of the water that cling to the undersurface. Taste this water.

What is the purpose of sealing the jar? What did you notice about the taste of the water? What processes of the water cycle are in this model?

■ Develop another model to show the effect of temperature on the water cycle.

I ■ 83

FACTS AND FIGURES

CLOUD DROPLETS

The average cloud droplet has a diameter of about 10 micrometers. It takes approximately 1 million cloud droplets to make a rain droplet.

BACKGROUND INFORMATION

THE PHASES OF WATER

Water is the only common chemical compound that can occur as a solid, liquid, or gas under natural conditions. The unique conditions of Earth provide just the right temperatures for all three phases to occur. The water cycle would not be possible if it were not for this important property of water.

FACTS AND FIGURES

PRECIPITATION IN THE UNITED STATES

Fifteen trillion liters of fresh water fall on the United States every day in the form of rain or snow. But the distribution of this precipitation is not even. The East receives about 65 percent of the rainfall; the West, 35 percent.

moves up from the roots in a continuous column.

● ● ● ● **Integration** ● ● ● ●

Use the discussion of the water cycle to integrate physical science concepts of heat transfer into your lesson.

INDEPENDENT PRACTICE

▶ *Activity Book*

Students can gain practice in identifying the processes involved in the water cycle through the chapter activity Studying the Water Cycle. In the activity students interpret a diagram and complete a circular chart of the water cycle.

REINFORCEMENT/RETEACHING

Have students work in groups of three. Challenge each group to present in a creative way the three main steps of the water cycle. Students should include in their demonstrations how the first step follows the last step to begin the cycle again.

ACTIVITY
WRITING

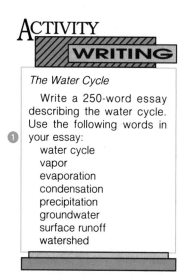

The Water Cycle

Write a 250-word essay describing the water cycle. Use the following words in your essay:
- water cycle
- vapor
- evaporation
- condensation
- precipitation
- groundwater
- surface runoff
- watershed

Glaciers form in very cold areas, such as high in mountains and near the North and the South poles. Because of the extremely cold temperatures in these areas, the snow that falls does not melt completely. As more snow falls, it covers the older snow. As the snow builds up, the pressure on the older snow squeezes the snow crystals together. Eventually ice forms. When the layers of ice become very thick and heavy, the ice begins to move.

Glaciers contain about 2 percent of the available fresh water on the Earth. As sources of fresh water become more scarce, scientists are trying to develop ways to use this frozen supply of fresh water.

VALLEY GLACIERS Long, narrow glaciers that move downhill between the steep sides of mountain valleys are called **valley glaciers.** Usually, valley glaciers follow channels formed in the past by running water. As a valley glacier moves downhill, it bends and twists to fit the shape of the surrounding land. The valley walls and the weight of the ice itself keep the glacier from breaking apart. But on its surface, the ice cracks. Cracks on the surface of glaciers are called crevasses (krih-VAS-sehz).

As a valley glacier slides downward, it tears rock fragments from the mountainside. The rock fragments become frozen in the glacier. They cut deep grooves in the valley walls. Finer bits of rock smooth the surfaces of the valley walls in much the same way

Figure 3–6 *Valley glaciers are long, narrow glaciers that move downhill between mountain valleys. Here you see valley glaciers in the Alps (left) and in Alaska (right).*

3–1 (continued)

CONTENT DEVELOPMENT

Emphasize to students that the most important factor in the formation of a glacier is pressure. Glaciers form from snow, which is normally light and fluffy with considerable air space between crystals. As new snow piles on top of old snow, however, individual snowflakes on the bottom layer are pushed together.

The amount of air space between crystals decreases, and a dense, closely packed form of snow called firn results. This process usually takes about one year. Then, as decades or even centuries pass, pressure causes the air spaces in the firn to disappear. The result is true glacial ice.

● ● ● ● **Integration** ● ● ● ●

Use the discussion of valley glaciers to integrate earth science concepts of erosion into your lesson.

Figure 3-7 *A crevasse, or crack in a glacier, can make mountain climbing a difficult sport indeed.*

as a carpenter's sandpaper smooths the surface of a piece of wooden furniture.

Mountains located anywhere from the equator to the poles can contain glaciers. Many glaciers are found in the United States. Mount Rainier in Washington State and Mount Washington in New Hampshire contain small glaciers. Glaciers can also be found in many mountains of Alaska.

As a valley glacier moves, some of the ice begins to melt, forming a stream of water. This water is called meltwater. Meltwater is usually nearly pure water. Some cities use meltwater as a source of their drinking water. Boulder, Colorado, uses meltwater from the nearby Arapaho Glacier. Meltwater is also used in some places to generate electricity in hydroelectric plants. But some problems arise in the use of meltwater in these ways. Building channels or pipelines to transport meltwater from glaciers to cities can be costly. And the construction of hydroelectric plants in the underdeveloped areas where glaciers are located could alter the surrounding environment.

CONTINENTAL GLACIERS   In the polar regions, snow and ice have built up to form thick sheets. These thick sheets of ice are called **continental glaciers,** or polar ice sheets. Continental glaciers cover millions of square kilometers of the Earth's surface and may be several thousand meters thick. Continental glaciers move slowly in all directions.

Figure 3-8 *Continental glaciers such as Mertz Glacier in Antarctica cover millions of square kilometers.*

I ■ 85

FACTS AND FIGURES

FRESH WATER IN GLACIERS

The amount of fresh water locked up in glaciers is equal to 60 years' worth of rainfall and snowfall over the entire Earth.

CONTENT DEVELOPMENT

Point out to students that during the last ice age, continental glaciers covered much of North America. As the glaciers melted, masses of gravel and rocks dropped out of the ice masses. Debris blocked valleys and created lake sites. Piles of debris were dumped and created hills. Bunker Hill, of American Revolution fame, is one such hill known as a drumlin. Lakes formed in depressions, or kettles, gouged by ice chunks. Walden Pond, made famous by naturalist and writer Henry David Thoreau, is one such kettle lake. Erratics, boulders moved by glaciers from one place to another, dropped from the melting ice masses. Plymouth Rock, traditionally considered the place where the Pilgrims stepped off the *Mayflower* to settle in America, is an example of an erratic.

ENRICHMENT

Have students choose a mountainous area of the United States and research the annual snow line for the region. Have them find out what factors cause the snow line to vary from place to place or from year to year.

GUIDED PRACTICE

Skills Development

Skills: Inferring, predicting

• **What danger could result if a glacier or an iceberg were to begin to melt?** (The release of large amounts of water could cause flooding.)

• **What would happen to valley glaciers if the snow lines were lowered by 1000 to 2000 meters?** (The valley glaciers would increase significantly in size.)

3–1 (continued)

CONTENT DEVELOPMENT

Every year, more than 15,000 icebergs break away from glaciers in Greenland. They melt as they float southward in the North Atlantic Ocean. Parts of icebergs break off as well, and these smaller chunks may be as large as a house.

● ● ● ● **Integration** ● ● ● ●

Use the information about the *Titanic* to integrate social studies into your science lesson.

INDEPENDENT PRACTICE

▶ *Activity Book*

Students can gather more information about icebergs by completing the chapter activity called Icebergs. In the activity students research and organize information about icebergs.

CONTENT DEVELOPMENT

When precipitation falls to the Earth, some of it is intercepted by plants and trees. The water is held in temporary

---

Continental glaciers are found in Greenland and Antarctica. Nearly 80 percent of Greenland is covered by ice. More than 90 percent of Antarctica is covered by ice. These huge glaciers are more than 3200 meters thick at the center. In the future, continental glaciers could be another source of fresh water.

ICEBERGS At the edge of the sea, continental glaciers form overhanging cliffs. Large chunks of ice, called **icebergs,** often break off from these cliffs and drift into the sea. Some icebergs are as large as the state of Rhode Island! The continental glaciers of Greenland and Antarctica are the major sources of icebergs in ocean waters.

Icebergs can pose a major hazard to ships. In 1912, the ocean liner *Titanic* sank after smashing into an iceberg in the North Atlantic Ocean. Many lives were lost as this ship, thought to be unsinkable, plunged to the ocean bottom on her first voyage. Today, sea lanes are patrolled constantly by ships and planes on the lookout for icebergs.

Much fresh water is frozen in icebergs. Attempts have been made to develop ways of towing icebergs to areas that need supplies of fresh water, such as deserts. But transporting icebergs from Greenland and Antarctica poses several problems. First, the effects of an iceberg on local weather conditions must be evaluated. Second, the cost and time involved in moving the iceberg must be considered.

Figure 3–9 *Icebergs, which often have spectacular shapes, are large chunks of ice that break off glaciers and drift into the sea. Only a small part of an iceberg rises above the water's surface. Can you explain the meaning of the phrase "tip of the iceberg"?* ❶

86 ■ I

---

storage by the leaves, then returned to the atmosphere by evaporation. This water never reaches the soil, nor does it flow into running or standing water sources.

INDEPENDENT PRACTICE

▶ *Activity Book*

Students can draw conclusions about the rate of precipitation and evaporation by completing the chapter activity called Water Budget. In the activity students

graph data and make comparisons based on the data.

GUIDED PRACTICE

Skills Development

Skill: Relating cause and effect

Discuss with students various factors that can affect the amount of surface runoff.

• **Which do you think would produce more surface runoff—a heavy down-**

Third, scientists would have to find a way of preventing the iceberg from melting during the ocean journey. Can you think of ways to use icebergs? ②

Running Water

Rivers and streams are important sources of fresh water. Many cities and towns were built near rivers and streams. The water is used for irrigating crops, generating electricity, drinking, and other household uses. Rivers and streams are also used for recreational purposes, such as fishing, swimming, and boating. Industry and commerce depend on rivers for transporting supplies and equipment and for shipping finished products. River and stream water is also used to cool certain industrial processes. In the past, industries and towns used rivers and streams as natural sewers to carry away waste products. Today, although pollution is still a problem, strict controls regulate the kinds and amounts of wastes that can be dumped into rivers and streams.

Rain and melted snow that do not evaporate or soak into the soil flow into rivers and streams. The water that enters a river or stream after a heavy rain or during a spring thaw of snow or ice is called **surface runoff.**

The amount of surface runoff is affected by several factors. One factor is the type of soil the precipitation falls on. Some soils soak up more water

ACTIVITY
CALCULATING

I Am Thirsty

An average person needs about 2.5 L of water a day to live.

Use this amount to calculate how much water an average person needs in a year. How much water is needed by your class to live in a day? In a year? ②

Figure 3–10 *Running water from rivers and streams is an important resource used for crop irrigation and for generating electricity in hydroelectric plants.*

I ■ 87

INTEGRATION
PHYSICAL SCIENCE

In the water cycle, water acts as an "energy converter." Radiant energy from the sun is converted into heat energy as it strikes the water molecules. Some water molecules then gain enough kinetic energy to leave the liquid phase and enter the gas phase. When the water vapor condenses and falls back to the Earth as precipitation, some of the water eventually flows into rivers. This rushing, or flowing, water has kinetic energy that can be changed into mechanical energy, such as at a hydroelectric power plant; or the water can also once again absorb radiant energy and evaporate.

pour lasting several hours or intermittent light showers occurring throughout the day? (Heavy downpour.)
• Why? (Much of the rain from a heavy downpour would not be absorbed quickly enough by plants or soil. Rain from light showers would be much more easily absorbed by plants and soil, and some of it would evaporate rapidly back into the atmosphere.)
• Suppose the same amount of rain were to fall on two areas: Area A is parched

from a long period of dryness, whereas area B is muddy from frequent rain and melting snow. In which area would there be a greater amount of runoff? Why? (Area B. The soil in area A is dry, so it will soak up a great deal of moisture. Little of the rain will be left as runoff. The soil in area B is already saturated with water, so much of the rain will be left as runoff.)

Media and Technology

The Videodisc called Aquatic Ecosystems: Freshwater examines the major types of freshwater communities. It allows students to explore organisms that live in lakes, ponds, streams, and rivers.

ACTIVITY
CALCULATING

A WATER BILL

Skills: Computational, calculator

This activity reinforces students' computational skills. It also illustrates the household costs of water and how conserving water can be a financial boon as well as a water-saving measure. Students should find that the cost of water is $19.00. To compute the first problem, students should have found that if 1000 L costs $0.50, then 38,000 L would be 38 times $0.50, or $19.00. To determine the amount of increase, students should subtract the original cost by the new cost for 1000 L. The increase is $0.15 per 1000 L. This amount is then multiplied by 38 and is equal to an annual increase of $5.70.

Integration: Use this Activity to integrate mathematics into your science lesson.

Figure 3–11 *Over the course of millions of years, the Colorado River has carved the Grand Canyon out of the Earth's rocky crust.*

ACTIVITY

A Water Bill

In some areas, water is supplied by a government agency or by a private water company. In these areas, people are charged for the amount of water they use. If an average household uses 38,000 L of water a month and the cost of water is $0.50 per 1000 L, how much is the water bill at the end of a month? What is the increase in the bill for an average household if the cost of water is increased to $0.65 per 1000 L?

than others. These soils have more spaces between their particles. The space between particles of soil is called **pore space.** The more pore space a soil has, the more water it will hold. The condition of the soil also affects the amount of runoff. If the soil is dry, it will soak up a great deal of water and reduce the surface runoff. If the soil is wet, it will not soak up much water. Surface runoff will increase.

The number of plants growing in an area also affects the amount of surface runoff. Plant roots absorb water from the soil. In areas where there are many plants, large amounts of water are absorbed. There is less surface runoff. The season of the year is another factor that affects the amount of surface runoff. There will be more runoff during rainy seasons and during the spring in areas where large amounts of snow are melting.

A land area in which surface runoff drains into a river or a system of rivers and streams is called a **watershed.** Watersheds vary in size. Especially large watersheds can cover millions of acres and drain their water into the oceans. Watersheds prevent floods and water shortages by controlling the amount of water that flows into streams and rivers. Watersheds also help to provide a steady flow of fresh water into the oceans. How do you think the construction of roads in a watershed area might affect nearby rivers and streams? ❶

3-1 (continued)

REINFORCEMENT/RETEACHING

Review with students the different things that can happen to precipitation once it falls to the Earth. Point out that it can evaporate directly back into the atmosphere; it can be absorbed and temporarily stored by plants; it can soak into the soil; or it can flow into rivers and streams as surface runoff.

CONTENT DEVELOPMENT

Refer students to the diagram of the water cycle in Figure 3–3 on page 82. Review the idea that surface runoff flows into rivers and streams. Point out that the land area in which this takes place is called a watershed. Emphasize to students that a watershed is a natural flow of water, not something made or controlled by human beings. Therefore, it is important that the environmental conditions that created a watershed be preserved.

Point out that pollutants in surface water can pollute rivers and streams.

● ● ● ● **Integration** ● ● ● ●

Use the discussion of river pollution to integrate concepts of ecology into your lesson.

GUIDED PRACTICE
Skills Development
Skill: Drawing conclusions
• **Why would factories find it advantageous to locate near a river?** (The river

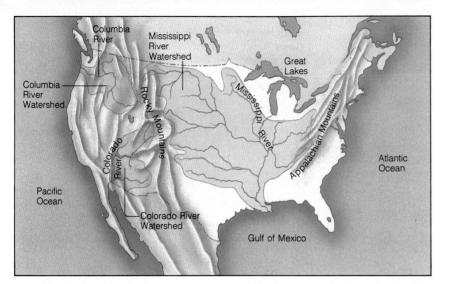

Many rivers are sources of fresh water. The amount of water in a river and the speed at which the water flows affect the usefulness of a river as a source of fresh water. Rivers that move quickly carry a lot of water. But because the water is moving rapidly, fast-moving rivers also carry a large amount of soil, pebbles, and other sediments. The water in these rivers often looks cloudy. Slow-moving rivers do not churn up as much sediment. Their water is clearer. These rivers are better sources of fresh water.

In recent years, pollution has had an effect on the usefulness of rivers and streams as sources of fresh water. If a river or stream has many factories along its banks that discharge wastes into the water, the water becomes polluted. Water in a polluted river or stream must be cleaned before it can be used. Some rivers are so heavily polluted that they cannot be used as a source of fresh water.

Standing Water

Within a watershed, some of the surface runoff gets caught in low places. Standing bodies of fresh water are formed there. Depending on their size, these standing bodies of water are called lakes or ponds.

Figure 3–12 *The major watersheds of the United States are shown in this map. Which watershed is the largest?* ②

Figure 3–13 *Our supply of fresh water is reduced every year by dangerous wastes released into the water. In what ways can you personally reduce water pollution?* ③

I ■ 89

provides a source of water, a possible source of electric power, and a means of travel and commerce.)

• **In what ways is a factory hazardous to the river environment?** (If a factory discharges waste into the river, the water will become polluted. Also air pollution from factories can result in acid rain, which will eventually pollute the water supply.)

📺 Media and Technology

Use the Videodisc entitled Aquatic Ecosystems: Freshwater Wetlands to explore bogs, marshes, and swamps. Students will examine the kinds of organisms that live in these environments.

ECOLOGY NOTE

THE DEATH OF A RIVER

In 1991, a disastrous chemical spill into the Sacramento River in California killed most of the water life there. The spill occurred when a derailed train car carrying a herbicide was punctured and its contents were spilled. For kilometers downriver of the spill, insects, fish, and water plants died. Many residents feared that the reservoir fed by the river would also become polluted. Fortunately, the amount of herbicide spilled was diluted enough so that it did not affect people adversely. Ask students to consider what might be done to prevent such a disaster in the future.

Activity Bank

How Does a Fish Move?, p.168

Like rivers and streams, lakes and ponds receive their water from the land. Surface runoff keeps lakes and ponds from drying up. In many areas, these standing bodies of water are important sources of fresh water. Moosehead Lake, in Maine, is a natural source of fresh water. It is 56 kilometers long and varies from 3 to 16 kilometers wide. The pine-forested shores of the lake hold huge amounts of water from rains and melting snow. The water is released slowly to the lake, so flooding is not likely. During times of drought (long periods with little rainfall), the lake holds water in reserve.

LAKES AND PONDS Lakes are usually large, deep depressions in the Earth's crust that have filled with fresh water. Rain, melting snow, water from springs and rivers, and surface runoffs fill these depressions. A lake is sometimes formed when there is a natural obstruction, or blockage, of a river or stream. Lakes can be found in many places on the Earth. They are found most frequently at relatively high altitudes and in areas where glaciers were once present.

Ponds are shallow depressions in the Earth's crust that have filled with fresh water. They are usually smaller and not as deep as lakes. Because the water is shallow, sunlight can penetrate to the bottom of a pond. Plants need light to make food, so plants can be found throughout a pond. Lakes, however, often have very deep parts where sunlight cannot reach. Will you find plants at the bottom of a deep lake? ❷

Figure 3–14 *Standing water is found in lakes and ponds throughout the world. What is the difference between a lake and a pond?* ❶

ter-opener text. Remind them that the main problems discussed were lack of water and too much water.

• **How can a reservoir help to alleviate these problems?** (By absorbing excess water in times of heavy rain and by storing water for use in times of drought.)

● ● ● ● **Integration** ● ● ● ●

Use the information about reservoirs to integrate water management concepts into your lesson.

RESERVOIRS The most frequently used sources of fresh water are artificial lakes known as **reservoirs** (REHZ-uhr-vwahrz). A reservoir is built by damming a stream or river that runs through a low-lying area. When the stream or river is dammed, water backs up behind the dam, forming a reservoir. Reservoirs have been built near cities and towns and in mountainous regions throughout the country.

Reservoirs serve several purposes. They help to prevent flooding by controlling water during periods of heavy rain and runoff. Reservoirs store water. During periods when rainfall and runoff are scarce, reservoirs serve as sources of drinking water for nearby towns and cities. In certain areas, reservoirs provide irrigation water for farms. The water held in reservoirs can also be used to generate electricity. Hydroelectric generators are built in the walls of a dam. The water stored in the reservoir can generate electricity when it moves through turbines, which are connected to the dams. Hydroelectric plants convert the energy of moving water into electrical power.

A reservoir, however, cannot be used for all purposes at the same time. Why is this so? Suppose a reservoir is used to store water. To use the water to generate electricity, the water would have to be drawn from the reservoir. The reservoir would no longer be storing water.

Figure 3–15 *The effects of a drought in California in 1991 can be seen in the low water level in the San Luis Reservoir.*

3–1 Section Review

1. What are the major sources of fresh water on the Earth's surface?
2. How much of the Earth's supply of fresh water is available for use? Where is the bulk of fresh water on Earth found?
3. Briefly outline the water cycle.

Critical Thinking—*Applying Concepts*

4. A builder wants to level all the trees in a water-shed area to construct homes. What would be some effects of the builder's actions on the watershed and on nearby rivers and streams?

ACTIVITY

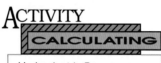

CALCULATING

Hydroelectric Power

The total potential hydroelectric power of the world is 2.25 billion kilowatts. Only 363 million kilowatts of this is actually being utilized, however. The United States uses one sixth of the world's hydroelectric power. Calculate the percent of the world's hydroelectric power that is actually being used. What percent of the world's hydroelectric power is used in the United States?

plete the chapter activity called The Water Cycle. The activity will help them review the major processes involved in the cycle.

INDEPENDENT PRACTICE

Section Review 3–1

1. Reservoirs, lakes, ponds, rivers, and glaciers.

2. Less than 3 percent; frozen in glaciers mainly near the poles.

3. Through evaporation, condensa-tion, and precipitation, water moves from the ocean and freshwater sources to the air and land and then back to the oceans in a continuous cycle.

4. Runoff would probably increase and could cause flooding of the land and nearby streams and rivers.

REINFORCEMENT/RETEACHING

Monitor students' responses to the Section Review questions. If students appear to have difficulty understanding any of the concepts, review this material with them.

CLOSURE

▶ *Review and Reinforcement Guide*

At this point have students complete Section 3–1 in the *Review and Reinforcement Guide.*

CONNECTIONS

WATER, WATER EVERYWHERE— AND EVERYONE WANTS TO USE IT

Water, Water Everywhere— And Everyone Wants to Use It ❶

There is nothing more soothing than the sound of raindrops hitting a windowpane. Most outdoor activities are postponed during a heavy rain. But you can be sure that the rain will eventually stop, and the sun will shine once again. You might not be happy when it rains, but you should be thankful. For rain replenishes the Earth's supply of fresh water.

Water is needed by all forms of life on Earth. Without water, Earth would be a dry and lifeless planet. Visit a desert after a heavy rain and you will see plants appear in the once dry, blowing sands. These plants take advantage of the rain to flower and make seeds before the soil again becomes too dry to support life.

People make great demands on the Earth's supply of fresh water. The average American family uses 760 liters of water a day—and not just to satisfy their thirsts. About half of that total is used to flush away wastes and for showers and baths. Seventy-five liters or more is used each time a dishwasher or a clothes washer cleans up after us.

The *technology* to manufacture the many products that contribute to our way of life takes water—often a great deal of water. For example, about 3.8 million liters of water are used to produce a ton of copper—the metal used to make electric wires and the pennies jingling in your pocket. Almost 1.1 million liters of water are used to make a ton of aluminum—a metal used to make cooking utensils and food containers. It even takes about 3.7 liters of water to make a single page in this textbook. We hope you feel that this was water well used!

CONNECTIONS

WATER, WATER EVERYWHERE— AND EVERYONE WANTS TO USE IT

Students will see the extent of our dependence on our water supplies as they read the Connections feature. Point out that each day industries use about 50 percent of our water supplies, agriculture uses about 40 percent, and homes use about 10 percent. The 1990–1991 drought in California dramatized our dependence on water. In many communities, water usage was restricted, and people adapted to the restrictions. They made multiple use of water, for example, by taking bath water and using it to water indoor and outdoor plants. As you discuss the limitations of the water supply, emphasize the ways that individuals can help to conserve one of the most needed resources—water.

If you are teaching thematically, you may want to use the Connections feature to reinforce the themes of unity and diversity and patterns of change.

Integration: Use the Connections feature to integrate concepts of water management into your science lesson.

TEACHING STRATEGY 3–2

FOCUS/MOTIVATION

Direct students' attention to the photograph of a well in Figure 3–16.
• **Do you know how a well works?** (A well is dug or drilled; then water is pumped up from the underground source.)
• **Do any of you receive your home water supply from a well?** (Answers will vary.)

• **What advantages do you think there are to using a well as a water source?** (Answers will vary; possible answers include purer water or a water supply less affected by changing weather conditions.)
• **Can you think of any disadvantages of using water from a well?** (Because the water supply is not visible, it may be possible to overpump the well and run out of water; also, it may take too much energy and too many wells to supply water to a large area.)

3-2 Fresh Water Beneath the Surface of the Earth

Not all of the water that falls to the Earth as rain, snow, sleet, or hail runs off into lakes, ponds, rivers, and streams. Some of the water soaks into the ground. Water contained in the ground is one of the Earth's most important natural resources. There is more fresh water below the surface of the land than in all the lakes and reservoirs on the Earth's surface.

Groundwater

If you live in a rural, or country, area, you probably do not get your water from a reservoir or river. More likely, your water is pumped from a well in the ground. As you learned in the previous section, the water stored in the ground is known as groundwater. In many areas, groundwater provides a continuous supply of fresh water.

Groundwater is present because the various forms of precipitation—rain, snow, sleet, and hail—do not stop traveling when they hit the ground. Instead, the precipitation continues to move slowly downward through pores, or spaces, in the rocks and soil. If the rocks and soil have many pores between their particles, they can hold large quantities of groundwater. Sand and gravel are two types of soil that contain many pores.

As the water seeps down, it passes through layers of rocks and soil that allow it to move quickly. Material through which water can move quickly is described as **permeable** (PER-mee-uh-buhl). Sandstone is a rock that is very permeable. But clay, which has small pores between its particles, is not as permeable. Clay is sometimes described as **impermeable.**

UNDERGROUND ZONES Groundwater continues to move downward through permeable rock and soil until it reaches an impermeable layer of rock. When it reaches an impermeable layer, it can go no farther. So the groundwater begins to fill up all the pores above the impermeable layer. This underground region in which all the pores are

Figure 3–16 *Some of the water that falls to Earth as rain, snow, sleet, or hail soaks into the ground. In some places this water is very close to the Earth's surface. So a well such as this can be used to obtain water.*

I ■ 93

3-2 Fresh Water Beneath the Surface of the Earth

MULTICULTURAL OPPORTUNITY 3-2

Many ancient cultures used caves as part of their religious ceremonies as well as for storage and safety. Ask students to investigate how the Mayans used caves. Suggest that they investigate information on the Balankanche Caves of the Yucatan Peninsula.

ESL STRATEGY 3-2

When discussing permeable and impermeable materials, explain that the word *permeable* is taken from the Latin word meaning "to pass through"; therefore, the prefix *im-* (meaning "not") creates the opposite, or antonym, of *permeable*. This concept should be easily understood by Spanish-speaking LEP students because *impermeable* is one of the words used for "raincoat" in Spanish. This graphic explanation may also be helpful to speakers of other languages in learning the English usage of both words.

Have students classify the following materials as permeable or impermeable with regard to fresh water: sand, gravel, clay.

Ask students to use complete sentences to answer this question: Which would require more water in order for the plants to grow—a garden whose soil is mixed with clay and sand or one with sand only?

CONTENT DEVELOPMENT

Explain that groundwater is water that seeps into porous soil or rocks underground. Gravity causes the water to move from higher to lower elevations. The water continues to seep through the soil and rocks until it reaches an impermeable layer of rock. An impermeable layer is made up of materials that have very few pores for absorbing water. This is the impermeable level. At this point, water no longer sinks but rather fills the pores of layers above this level to form a zone of saturation, or a level in which all pores are filled with water.

● ● ● ● **Integration** ● ● ● ●

Use the discussion of rock permeability to integrate earth science concepts of geology into your lesson.

GUIDED PRACTICE

Skills Development

Skills: Manipulative, observing, relating, recording

At this point you may want to assign the in-text Laboratory Investigation called Porosity of Various Soils. In this investigation students will identify and compare the porosity of various soil types.

CALIFORNIA DROUGHT

In the late 1980s and the early 1990s, California experienced a severe drought. Many communities in the state relied heavily on groundwater as their source of fresh water. As the drought continued, the water table began to drop, and the water level in reservoirs was seriously low. Throughout the state, restrictions on water usage were set up and enforced. Industries, farmers, and consumers all were affected by the water shortage and began conserving water. Even the American space program could have been affected by the water shortage in California. As more and more water was drained from the aquifer below Edwards Air Force Base north of Los Angeles, cracks began appearing near the runways on the base. Most of the Space Shuttle flights land at Edwards Air Force Base and concern was expressed about the safety of the runways. Fortunately, the Space Shuttles were able to continue landing at the base.

filled with water is called the **zone of saturation** (sach-uh-RAY-shuhn).

An example from the kitchen may help you to understand what happens when spaces in the ground become filled with water. You may never have looked closely at the sponge on a kitchen sink. When a sponge is barely moist, only some of the spaces in the sponge are filled with water. Most of the spaces hold air. When you place the sponge in water, it swells. Eventually, all the spaces are filled and the sponge cannot take up any more water. The ground acts in much the same way as the sponge. Once the spaces in the ground are filled, the ground is saturated. It cannot hold any more water.

Above the water-filled zone, the ground is not as wet. Pores in the soil and rocks are filled mostly with air. This drier region in which the pores are filled mostly with air is called the **zone of aeration.**

The surface between the zone of saturation and the zone of aeration is an important boundary. It

Figure 3–17 *A cross section of the zones of underground water is shown here. What separates the zone of aeration from the zone of saturation?* ❶

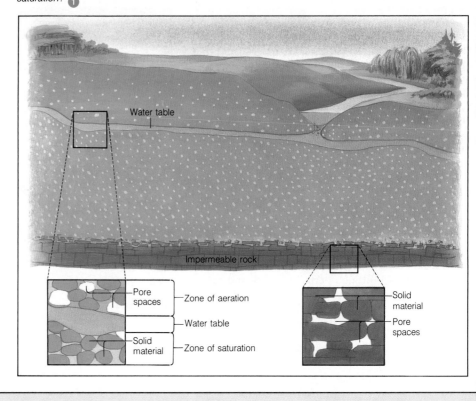

3–2 (continued)

CONTENT DEVELOPMENT

Point out that groundwater is formed when water that strikes the surface of the Earth in the form of precipitation moves downward through porous soil and rock.
• **What eventually stops the downward flow of water?** (The water reaches an impermeable rock layer.)

Emphasize that the water stored underground is not just sitting in a kind of underwater lake. Rather, it is stored in the pore spaces of soil and rock in the zone of saturation.

REINFORCEMENT/RETEACHING

Make sure students understand the meaning of the terms *zone of saturation, zone of aeration,* and *water table.* Point out that the water table is the minimum depth to which a well must be drilled in order to reach a reliable water supply.

CONTENT DEVELOPMENT

The water table generally follows the shape of the land. Where the water table meets the land's surface, swamps, ponds, and springs can form.

● ● ● ● **Integration** ● ● ● ●

Use the photographs in Figure 3–18 and the caption to integrate life science concepts of biomes into your earth science lesson.

Figure 3-18 *What factors influence the levels of the water table in this marsh (left) and at this Saharan oasis (right)?* ②

marks the level below which the ground is saturated, or soaked, with water. This level is called the **water table.** See Figure 3–17.

At the seashore, the water table is easy to find. After you dig down 10 or 20 centimeters, you may notice that the hole you are digging fills with water. At this point, you have located the water table. In general, the water table is not very deep near a large body of water.

In areas near hills or mountains, the water table may be deep within the ground. In low-lying areas such as valleys with swamps and marshes, the water table may be close to or at the surface. The depth of ② the water table also varies with the climate of an area. It may be deep in very dry areas, such as deserts. It may be close to the surface in wet, low-lying forest areas. In very moist climate regions, the water table may come right to the surface and form a swamp, lake, or spring. Why do you think low-lying areas have a water table that is close to the surface? ③

Even in the same area, the depth of the water table may change. Heavy rains and melting snows will make the water table rise. If there is a long, dry period, the water table will fall. The depth of the water table will also change if wells are overused or if many wells are located in a small area. Wells are

I ■ 95

FACTS AND FIGURES
USABLE WATER

Groundwater makes up more than 90 percent of the world's usable fresh water.

Use the information about water tables to integrate concepts of climate into your lesson.

GUIDED PRACTICE
Skills Development
Skill: Defining concepts

On the left side of the chalkboard, list in a column the terms *water table, zone of aeration, zone of saturation,* and *aquifer.* On the right side, list in random order the definitions of these terms. Call on students to draw a line from the term to its matching definition. If students have difficulty with any of the definitions, refer them to the appropriate student pages.

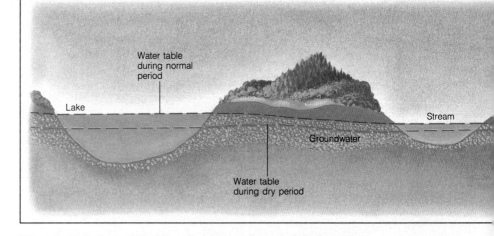

Figure 3–19 *The water table follows the shape of the land. Springs, swamps, and ponds sometimes form where the water table meets the land's surface. What happens to the water table during a dry period?* ①

BACKGROUND INFORMATION

TYPES OF AQUIFERS

All the water stored in aquifers is the result of precipitation. The part of the Earth's surface from which water drains downward into an aquifer is called the recharge area.

Aquifers can be classified as unconfined or confined. In an unconfined aquifer, water is not under pressure; thus, the water will never rise above the level of the water table unless it is pumped to the surface. In a confined aquifer, a layer of impermeable material above the aquifer creates pressure, and this pressure is intensified if the confining layer slopes downward. In a confined aquifer where the pressure is high, water may rise to the Earth's surface. Such is the cause of artesian wells, which gush water without being pumped.

3–2 (continued)

CONTENT DEVELOPMENT

Point out that one potential problem with undergound water supplies is that water may be pumped out of an aquifer faster than it is replenished. When this happens, the water supply runs out, and wells must be deepened. In some areas, experiments are being conducted to determine whether it is possible to recharge aquifers artificially.

● ● ● ● **Integration** ● ● ● ●

Use the discussion of aquifers to integrate concepts of water management into your science lesson.

---

holes drilled or dug to the water table to bring water to the surface. The use of several wells in an area may draw so much water from the water table that only very deep wells are able to pump water to the surface. Figure 3–19 shows some characteristics of the water table.

The depth of the water table may have other effects. In order to provide a proper foundation for a tall building, a builder must dig a deep hole. In some places in New York City, the water table is very high, and water rapidly fills the foundation hole. This water must be pumped out in order for construction to proceed. This extra work adds to the cost of a building. In certain areas, wells are dug to provide a source of household water. It is relatively inexpensive to dig a well in areas where the water table is high. In areas where the water table is deep, however, it can be very expensive to dig a well. Remember—a water table is always present, no matter where you live. And you will always reach it if you dig deep enough!

AQUIFERS As groundwater moves through a permeable rock layer, it often reaches an impermeable rock layer or the water table. At this point, the groundwater may move sideways through a layer of rock or sediment that allows it to pass freely. Such a layer is called an **aquifer** (AK-wuh-fer). Aquifers are

96 ■ I

GUIDED PRACTICE

▶ *Laboratory Manual*

Skills Development

Skills: Manipulative, observation, drawing conclusions, making inferences

At this point you may want to assign the Laboratory Investigation entitled Investigating Porosity and Permeability in the *Laboratory Manual*. In the investigation students will measure the rate at

which groundwater filters through different materials.

INDEPENDENT PRACTICE

▶ *Activity Book*

Students can increase their understanding of the role water pressure plays in their lives by completing the chapter activity called Water Pressure: A Hidden Community Worker. In the activity students demonstrate water-pressure principles and apply them to their own environments.

usually layers of sandstone, gravel, sand, or cracked limestone.

Because rocks form in layers, a layer of permeable rock may become trapped between two layers of impermeable rock. Sandstone (permeable rock) trapped between two layers of shale (impermeable rock) is an example. If the layer of sandstone contains water, an aquifer forms. An aquifer may also form when soil saturated with groundwater is located above an impermeable rock layer.

An aquifer is a source of groundwater. To reach this water, a well is often dug or drilled into the aquifer. Groundwater moves into the well hole and forms a pool. Each time water is pumped from the well, more water moves through the aquifer into the well hole. Nassau and Suffolk counties in New York State pump much of the water used by their inhabitants from huge aquifers.

Because water often moves great distances through aquifers, these underground water sources are extremely vulnerable to pollution. Any pollutants added to an aquifer may spread through the aquifer, endangering water sources far from the pollutants' point of origin.

In some places where the underground rock layers slope, an aquifer carries water from a higher altitude to a lower altitude. If the aquifer is trapped between two layers of impermeable rock, pressure may build up at the lower altitude. A well

ACTIVITY
DISCOVERING

Drought and the Water Table

1. Fill a deep clear-glass baking dish about halfway with sand. Make sure that the sand covers the bottom.

2. Slowly add enough water so that 1 cm of water is visible above the surface of the sand.

3. Add more sand above the water in only one half of the baking dish.

4. Observe the water level during the next few days.

What changes do you notice in the water level?

■ What different conditions of the water table does your model represent?

■ Design an experiment to show the effect of drought on the water table in an area with a clay soil.

I ■ 97

ENRICHMENT

Have students interview local construction workers or architects about whether the water table affects the work they do. You may wish to help students develop a list of questions for the interview, such as these: Is the water table level high in our area? Do you have to adjust your architectural designs or blueprints to accommodate the level of the water table? Encourage students to tape-record the interviews and to prepare a written report based on the interviews. As an alternative activity, you might invite a construction worker or an architect to speak to the class and to field prepared questions from the students.

INDEPENDENT PRACTICE

▶ *Product Testing Activity*

Have students perform the product test on bottled water from the Product Testing Activity Worksheets. Ask students to relate their findings of various bottled waters to what they have learned about water underground. They can also relate their findings to the information about water as a solvent that they will study in the next section.

Mammoth Cave is a limestone cavern in Kentucky. The cave area is about 16 kilometers in diameter, but it has about 240 kilometers of passageways winding around at various levels below ground. The temperature of the cave is a fairly constant 12 degrees Celsius.

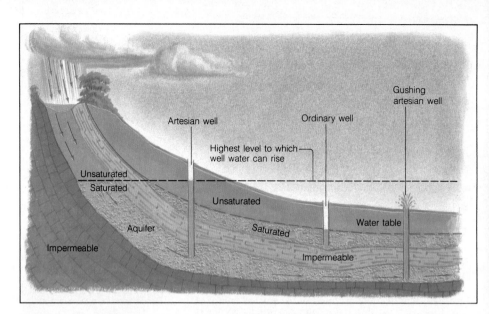

Figure 3–20 *Groundwater can be obtained from an aquifer by means of an ordinary well or an artesian well. The amount of water pressure in an artesian well depends on how close the well is to the water table.*

Figure 3–21 *This giant sinkhole in Winter Park, Florida, was caused when groundwater dissolved the limestone base on which part of the town was constructed.*

drilled into the aquifer at this point will provide water without pumping. A well from which water flows on its own without pumping is called an artesian (ahr-TEE-zhuhn) well. See Figure 3–20.

Groundwater Formations

In some areas, the underlying rock is limestone. Because limestone is affected by groundwater in a particular way, underground **caverns** (KAV-ernz) often form in these areas. As water moves down through the soil, it combines with carbon dioxide to form a weak acid that can dissolve limestone. This acid, called carbonic acid, is the weak acid found in seltzer water and other carbonated beverages. You are probably familiar with this weak acid as the "fizz" in a carbonated beverage.

When groundwater enters cracks in limestone, the carbonic acid it contains causes the cracks to become wider. If this process continues long enough, underground passages large enough to walk through may be formed.

Sometimes large underground caverns with many passages are formed. If you walk through these caverns, you will see what looks like long stone icicles

---

3–2 (continued)

CONTENT DEVELOPMENT

It can take thousands of years for water to erode limestone caverns. Some of the caverns are very beautiful, and some are relatively small and unimpressive except for the fact that they were created by water power.

● ● ● ● **Integration** ● ● ● ●

Use the information about carbonic acid to integrate the physical science concepts of acids and bases into your lesson.

GUIDED PRACTICE

Skills Development

Skill: Predicting

Display a diagram of a water molecule. Then explain that carbon dioxide when mixed with water produces positively charged carbon (C+) and negatively charged oxygen (O−).

● **Can you predict how the carbon and oxygen ions will arrange themselves with respect to the water molecule?** (The positively charged carbon will be attracted to the negatively charged oxygen

atoms, and the negatively charged oxygen will be attracted to the positively charged hydrogen atom.)

ENRICHMENT

Although permeable rock and soil tend to act as natural filters, certain pollutants can seep into aquifers. Have students find out what pollution problems exist with regard to groundwater and what is being done to alleviate these problems.

INDEPENDENT ACTIVITY

▶ *Activity Book*

Students can gain understanding about the formation of stalactites and stalagmites by completing the chapter activity called Stalactite and Stalagmite Formation. In the activity students compare the hands-on investigation of salt buildup to the formation of stalactites and stalagmites.

hanging from the ceilings. These icicles are called stalactites (stuh-LAK-tights). Stalagmites (stuh-LAG-mights) look like stone icicles built up from the floors of the caverns. Stalactites and stalagmites are formed when dissolved substances in groundwater are deposited. You will learn more about the dissolving properties of water in the next section.

Figure 3–22 *In many caverns, underground lakes are formed as groundwater moves through limestone. This lake is found in Hams Caves, Spain. What are the cavern formations hanging from the ceiling and rising from the ground called?* ❶

3–2 Section Review

1. How does groundwater form?
2. What are the three underground zones through which groundwater moves?
3. What causes differences in the depth of the water table?
4. Describe the formation of the following: aquifer, artesian well, cavern.

Connection—*Ecology*
5. Because it is too expensive to truck dangerous pollutants away from the plant, the factory manager proposes that a hole be dug deep in the ground on the side of the factory building and that wastes be dumped into this hole. Predict the effects of this action on the water pumped from wells a short distance from this factory.

I ■ 99

mate of the region, and amount of vegetation in the region.
4. An aquifer is formed when groundwater reaches an impermeable layer of rock and moves sideways through a layer of rock or sediment that allows it to pass freely. An artesian well is a well drilled into an aquifer in which the water flows on its own and does not need to be pumped. A cavern is formed when groundwater absorbs carbon dioxide to form a weak acid that cuts into underlying limestone.
5. The pollutants are likely to spread through permeable rock and pollute underground water in aquifers. The water from nearby wells is likely to be contaminated by the pollutants and will have to be purified before it is used.

REINFORCEMENT/RETEACHING

Monitor students' responses to the Section Review questions. If students appear to have difficulty with any of the concepts, review the appropriate material.

CLOSURE

▶ *Review and Reinforcement Guide*
At this point have students complete Section 3–2 in the *Review and Reinforcement Guide.*

GUIDED PRACTICE

Skills Development

Skills: Manipulative, modeling, interpreting diagrams

Challenge students to work in groups to build models of a cavern with stalactites and stalagmites. Encourage students to use materials such as clay or papier-mâché for their models. Students can base their models on illustrations in the textbook or on information and illustrations from reference sources.

INDEPENDENT ACTIVITY

Section Review 3–2
1. Groundwater is formed when precipitation moves slowly downward into the Earth through pores in the rocks and soil.
2. From top to bottom: the zone of aeration, the water table, the zone of saturation.
3. Differences in the amount of rainfall, type of soil, permeability of soil, cli-

3-3 Water as a Solvent

MULTICULTURAL OPPORTUNITY 3-3

Have students research the procedures used by their community to purify water and compare them with procedures used in other parts of the world. You might plan a field trip to the local water treatment plant.

ESL STRATEGY 3-3

Have students give an oral answer to this problem or explain it by means of an illustration with labels:

You have a package of powdered soft-drink mix. You and your friends are thirsty. You make a pitcher of the powdered soft drink and pour yourself and your friends a refreshing drink. Name the substance and the solvent used and the solution that resulted.

Ask students to try to remember what the water was like in their native land or in the place they lived last. Did it taste different from the water they now drink? Do they think it was "harder" or "softer"? Why? Did they have more, less, or as much water there?

Guide for Reading

Focus on this question as you read.

▶ *How does the structure of a water molecule relate to its ability to dissolve substances?*

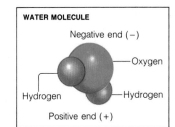

WATER MOLECULE

Negative end (−)

Oxygen

Hydrogen

Hydrogen

Positive end (+)

Figure 3-23 *A molecule of water exhibits the property of polarity. Why is this property important?* ❶

100 ■ I

3-3 Water as a Solvent

Water is the most common substance on Earth. It exists as a solid, a liquid, or a gas. Water moves in a cycle among the oceans, the air, and the land. Water changes form as it moves through this cycle. In this section, you will take a look at the chemical makeup of water and some of its important properties.

Composition of Water

A water molecule (MAHL-uh-kyool) is the smallest particle of water that has all the properties of water. A water molecule forms when two atoms of hydrogen and one atom of oxygen combine. (Atoms are the basic building blocks of all materials on Earth.) The chemical formula for water is H_2O. As you can see, this formula describes the number of atoms of hydrogen (2) and oxygen (1) that combine to form a water molecule.

In a water molecule, the atom of oxygen has a slight negative charge (−). Each atom of hydrogen has a slight positive charge (+). So a molecule of water has oppositely charged ends. See Figure 3–23. These charged ends give a water molecule the property known as **polarity** (poh-LAR-uh-tee). You might be familiar with the property of polarity as it applies to a magnet. A magnet has two poles—a positive pole and a negative pole. Each pole attracts the oppositely charged pole of another magnet.

It is the polarity of water molecules that makes water a **solvent** (SAHL-vuhnt). A solvent is a substance in which another substance dissolves. The dissolving process produces a **solution.** A solution contains two or more substances mixed on the molecular level.

For example, if you pour a small quantity of salt into a container of water, the salt will dissolve in the water. Although you will not be able to see the dissolved salt, you will know that it is there if you taste the water. The water molecules, having oppositely charged ends, attract the charged particles that make up the salt. It is as if the water molecules "pull" the charged particles out of the solid salt, dissolving the salt.

TEACHING STRATEGY 3-3

FOCUS/MOTIVATION

Begin by asking this question.
• **Do you think the water you drink is pure?** (Answers will vary; allow students to speculate and encourage them to define what they mean by "pure.")

Point out that when we refer to "pure" drinking water, we usually mean free of bacteria and other harmful substances. Chemically pure (or nearly pure) water can be obtained by distillation. Normal drinking water is far from chemically pure, although the substances dissolved in the water are not harmful, and, in the case of some minerals, are actually beneficial.

CONTENT DEVELOPMENT

Use a ball-and-stick model to illustrate a water molecule. Point out to students that the angle between the hydrogen atoms would be smaller if it were not for the slight positive charge on the hydrogen atoms and the slight negative charge on the oxygen atom. Guide students to understand that this is because the hydrogen atoms of like charge repel each other, making the angle between them larger.

● ● ● ● **Integration** ● ● ● ●

Use the discussion of the structure of a water molecule to integrate physical science concepts of atoms into your lesson.

INDEPENDENT PRACTICE

▶ *Activity Book*

Remind students that distillation can make water nearly chemically pure. Students can gain experience with one process of distillation—desalination—

Because of its polarity, water is able to dissolve many different substances. Water can dissolve so many different substances, in fact, that it is called the universal solvent. You probably use water as a solvent every day without realizing it. For example, flavoring and carbon dioxide gas are dissolved in water to make soft drinks. In fact, all the beverages you drink contain substances dissolved in water. What other products can you name that are made with water? ❷

Farmers use water to dissolve fertilizers for crops. Many medicines use water to dissolve the medication. Certain minerals and chemicals are dissolved in water in water-treatment plants to remove harmful minerals, chemicals, and wastes. For example, chlorine, a chemical that kills bacteria, is added to drinking water. In some cities and towns, fluorides are also added to water. The dissolved fluorides help to prevent tooth decay.

Figure 3–24 *In this sewage-treatment plant in California, water hyacinths are used to help purify "dirty" water.*

PROBLEM ??? Solving

How Sweet It Is

Several factors affect the rate at which a substance dissolves in water.

Making inferences Use the photographs to determine these factors.

I ■ 101

through the chapter activity called Distillation and Desalination: Fresh Water From Salt Water. In the activity students will use laboratory equipment to demonstrate the process of distillation.

CONTENT DEVELOPMENT

Review the properties of solutions, noting that the substance being dissolved is called the solute and the substance doing the dissolving is called the solvent. Explain to students that although a solution is the "best mixed" of all mixtures,

it is still a physical, not a chemical, combination. Explain that the charged ends of a water molecule attract the positive and negative ions of the solute.

● ● ● ● **Integration** ● ● ● ●

Use the discussion about water's polarity to integrate physical science concepts of magnetism into your lesson.

Use the information about water as a solvent to integrate physical science concepts of solutions into your lesson.

ECOLOGY NOTE

SAFE DRINKING WATER

In 1990, only about 54 of the countries around the world could claim safe drinking water. Most of these countries were in Europe and North America. Even within the United States, some areas have unsafe drinking water. The vacation site of the Grand Canyon has been cited by the Environmental Protection Agency for not adequately monitoring its water quality. Ask students to consider what precautions they should take when traveling. Guide students' suggestions by reminding them that fruits and vegetables are often washed in tap water and that ice is made from tap water.

ACTIVITY
DISCOVERING

Water as a Solvent

1. Chalk is composed of calcium carbonate, a substance found in many rocks. Add a piece of chalk to a glass of water. To another glass of water, add some quartz sand.

2. Allow both to soak for 30 minutes and then feel each sample.

What happened to the chalk? What happened to the sand? Why do you think certain substances dissolve in water more quickly than others? Why is most beach sand made of quartz?

■ Plan investigations to determine the ability of water to dissolve other substances.

102 ■ I

Hardness of Water

The taste, odor, and appearance of water vary from area to area. The differences depend on the amounts and types of materials dissolved in the water.

The water that you drink may come from a surface source or from a groundwater source. This water may be "hard" or "soft." The hardness or softness of water depends on the source of the water and the types of rocks and soils the water comes in contact with. **Hard water** contains large amounts of dissolved minerals, especially calcium and magnesium. Soap will not lather easily in hard water. Also, hard water causes deposits of minerals to build up in water heaters and plumbing systems. **Soft water** does not contain these minerals. Soap lathers easily in soft water, and mineral deposits do not build up when soft water is used.

Some water is softened naturally as it passes through and reacts with rock formations that contain certain minerals. These minerals remove the calcium and magnesium from the water, making it soft. Many homes with hard water have water softeners that remove the minerals that make the water hard. Do you know what type of water you have in your home? How could you experiment to find out? ❷

Quality of Water

Water is necessary to all life on Earth. So it is important to maintain the quality of our water.

3-3 (continued)

ENRICHMENT

▶ *Activity Book*

Students will be challenged by the chapter activity called Wise Use of Fresh Water. In the activity students will examine uses of water by their own families and relate their water use to the demand for fresh water.

CONTENT DEVELOPMENT

Explain to students that one pollutant of water is phosphates and that phosphates can be found in many laundry detergents. If possible, obtain samples of pond water with algae. Have students pour the water into four different jars. In one jar, they should place a tablespoon of laundry detergent without phosphates; in another, a low-phosphate laundry detergent; in still another, a high-phosphate laundry detergent. They should

Unfortunately, many of Earth's freshwater sources are becoming polluted. In nature, water is usually filtered as it passes through soil and sand. This filtering removes impurities. But the careless dumping of sewage, silt, industrial wastes, and pesticides into water has produced many serious problems. Because so many different substances can be dissolved in water, water is becoming more and more polluted.

Water pollution limits the amount and kinds of wildlife that can live in water. Water pollution also affects supplies of drinking water and destroys recreational areas. Among the chemicals that cause water pollution are nitrates and phosphates. These chemicals are used on farms to improve the growth of plants or to kill harmful insects. Nitrates and phosphates have entered the groundwater in many areas and must be removed before water can be used for drinking or swimming.

Federal laws have been passed to prevent industries from dumping certain chemical wastes into the Earth's waters. Waste-water treatment systems are being built to remove pollution from water before it enters rivers and lakes. Although Earth is called the water planet (and the supply of water seems unending), the truth is that we have a limited supply of fresh water. This water must be protected from sources of pollution. Can you think of some other steps that might be taken to do just this? ③

Figure 3–26 *One of the most serious problems facing society is the pollution of its water supply. Here you see an oil spill in Galveston Bay, Texas.*

Activity Bank

What Is the Effect of Phosphates on Plant Growth?, p.169

3–3 Section Review

1. Describe the structure of a molecule of water. How is this structure related to its ability to act as a solvent?
2. What is hard water? Soft water?
3. What are three sources of water pollution? Why must the water supply be protected from pollutants?

Critical Thinking—*Designing an Experiment*

4. Design an experiment to compare the hardness of two sources of water using only common, everyday substances. You can use tap water from your home, bottled water, or water from your school or the home of a friend or relative.

I ■ 103

use the fourth glass of pond water as a control. Have students record any changes they observe in the jars.

● ● ● ● **Integration** ● ● ● ●

Use the discussion of water pollution to integrate concepts of ecology into your lesson.

GUIDED PRACTICE

▶ *Laboratory Manual*

Skills Development

Skills: Manipulative, making and interpreting a data chart, making observations, making comparisons, drawing conclusions

At this point you may want to have students complete the Laboratory Investigation in the *Laboratory Manual* called Examining the Pollution of a Water Supply. In the investigation students add a pollutant to a model of a well system so that they can observe the spread of the pollutant.

Laboratory Investigation

POROSITY OF VARIOUS SOILS

BEFORE THE LAB

At least one day prior to the investigation, gather sufficient materials for your class, assuming six students per group.

PRE-LAB DISCUSSION

Have students read the complete laboratory procedure.
- **What is porosity?** (The amount of open pore space in a material.)
- **What type of soil do you think will hold the most water? Why?** (Students' answers will vary, but they should explain that the soil with the greatest pore space will hold the most water.)
- **What is the variable in this investigation? Is there more than one variable?** (The only variable is the type of soil. The experimental conditions remain the same for each type of soil.)

SAFETY TIPS

Remind students to handle breakable glassware carefully.

Laboratory Investigation

Porosity of Various Soils

Problem

How can the water-holding capability, or porosity, of various soils be determined?

Materials (per group)

> 250 mL sand
> 250 mL clay
> 250 mL gravel
> 4 small paper cups
> 2 L water
> 500-mL graduated cylinder

Procedure 🔺

1. Fill the first paper cup about three-fourths full of sand. Fill the second paper cup about three-fourths full of clay. Fill the third paper cup about three-fourths full of gravel. Fill the fourth paper cup about three-fourths full of a mixture of sand, clay, and gravel.

2. Fill the graduated cylinder with water to the 500 mL mark. Slowly pour water into the first cup. Let the water seep through the sand. Slowly add more water until a small pool of water is visible on the surface of the sand. At this point, the sand can hold no more water.

3. Determine the amount of water you added to the sand by subtracting the amount of water left in the graduated cylinder from 500 mL. Record this figure in the appropriate place in a data table similar to the one shown here.

4. Repeat steps 2 and 3 for the cups of clay, gravel, and the mixture of sand, clay, and gravel.

Observations

1. Which soil sample holds the most water?
2. Which soil sample holds the least water?

Soil	Amount of Water Added to Soil
Sand	
Clay	
Gravel	
Sand, clay, gravel	

Analysis and Conclusions

1. Why can some soil samples hold more water than others?

2. What can you conclude about the porosity of the soil samples you used?

3. If you wished to test the porosity of the soil found on your school grounds, what procedure would you follow? Which tested soil sample do you think the soil of the grounds at your school would most resemble?

4. **On Your Own**   What effects, if any, do the roots of plants have on the porosity of soil? Design an experiment to test your hypothesis.

TEACHING STRATEGY

1. Emphasize that the mixture of the three soil types should consist of equal amounts of each type.

2. If necessary, demonstrate how to calculate how much water is used by pouring water from a graduated cylinder and showing students how to identify the new level of water and subtract it from the original level of water.

DISCOVERY STRATEGIES

Discuss how the investigation relates to the chapter ideas by asking open questions similar to the following.

- **Would you expect to find an aquifer below nonporous soil and rock? Explain.** (No. An aquifer may be found above the nonporous rock, but because water could not seep through the nonporous rock, an aquifer could not be found below it—applying, inferring.)

- **If you were going to drill a well, would**

Study Guide

Summarizing Key Concepts

3–1 Fresh Water on the Surface of the Earth

▲ Fresh water—one of the Earth's most precious resources—is found in lakes, ponds, rivers, streams, springs, and glaciers.

▲ The water cycle is the continuous movement of water from the oceans and sources of fresh water to the air and land and then back to the oceans.

▲ The three steps in the water cycle are evaporation, condensation, and precipitation.

▲ A land area in which surface runoff drains into a river or system of streams and rivers is called a watershed.

3–2 Fresh Water Beneath the Surface of the Earth

▲ Fresh water beneath the ground's surface is called groundwater.

▲ The water table is the underground level below which all the pore spaces are filled with water. The water table separates the zone of aeration from the zone of saturation.

▲ The depth of the water table depends on the location of groundwater, the climate of the area, the amount of rainfall, the type of soil, and the number of wells drawing water.

▲ Groundwater formations include caverns, stalactites, and stalagmites.

3–3 Water as a Solvent

▲ A molecule of water is made up of two atoms of hydrogen combined with one atom of oxygen.

▲ Because of the polarity of water molecules, water is a good solvent. It can dissolve many substances.

▲ Water may be hard or soft depending on the kinds and amounts of minerals in it.

▲ People must protect and conserve their sources of fresh water.

Reviewing Key Terms

Define each term in a complete sentence.

3–1 Fresh Water on the Surface of the Earth
water cycle
evaporation
condensation
precipitation
groundwater
glacier
valley glacier
continental glacier
iceberg
surface runoff
pore space
watershed
reservoir

3–2 Fresh Water Beneath the Surface of the Earth
permeable
impermeable
zone of saturation
zone of aeration
water table
aquifer
cavern

3–3 Water as a Solvent
polarity
solvent
solution
hard water
soft water

I ■ 105

---

3. To compare the soil samples in this investigation with soil found on the school grounds, students would obtain three soil samples from three different places on the school grounds. Using a small trowel, they would fill each of three cups about three-fourths full with the soil samples. They then would follow steps 2 and 3 for each of the soil types. In general, the type of soil on the school grounds varies from one location to another. Soil from eroded areas will contain more clay and sand, whereas areas near plants will be more porous.

4. Students should conclude that the roots of plants help to prevent erosion and, therefore, the soil near plants would be more porous than soil in eroded areas. Hypotheses and experimental designs will vary.

GOING FURTHER: ENRICHMENT

Part 1

Have students conduct a similar investigation in which they test for permeability—the rate at which water will pass through soil. For this investigation, students should punch a hole in each paper cup and time with a stopwatch how long it takes for water to pass from the surface of the soil to the bottom of the cup. Challenge students to determine whether a relationship exists between porosity and permeability.

Part 2

Hydroponics is the science of growing plants without soil. Some forms of hydroponics use sand and gravel as soil substitutes. Have students find out more about this science and determine whether the porosity of certain materials makes them useful in hydroponic plant growth.

---

you drill in an area with claylike soil or sandy soil? Why? (Sandy soil, because it is more porous and permeable than claylike soil—predicting, applying.)

• **Why do some wells dry up during periods of drought?** (Because of the lack of precipitation, the groundwater is not replaced as it is used up—relating, applying.)

OBSERVATIONS

1. Students will find that the gravel holds the most water.

2. Students will discover that the clay holds the least water.

ANALYSIS AND CONCLUSIONS

1. The amount of water that can be held in soil depends on how large each of the individual soil particles is.

2. Students should conclude that porosity is determined by the size of individual soil particles. Therefore, the gravel will hold the most water, sand the next, the mixture the next, and clay the least.

Chapter Review

Chapter Review

ALTERNATIVE ASSESSMENT

The *Prentice Hall Science* program includes a variety of testing components and methodologies. Aside from the Chapter Review questions, you may opt to use the Chapter Test of the Computer Test Bank Test in your *Test Book* for assessment of important facts and concepts. In addition, Performance-Based Tests are included in your *Test Book*. These Performance-Based Tests are designed to test science process skills, rather than factual content recall. Since they are not content dependent, Performance-Based Tests can be distributed after students complete a chapter or after they complete the entire textbook.

CONTENT REVIEW

Multiple Choice

1. b
2. c
3. d
4. a
5. a
6. a
7. b
8. c

True or False

1. F, evaporation
2. T
3. F, surface runoff
4. F, deep
5. F, permeable

Concept Mapping

Row 1: Frozen Water, Standing Water

Row 2: icebergs, lakes or ponds

CONCEPT MASTERY

1. The water cycle is the continuous movement of water from the ocean and freshwater sources to the air and land and then back to the ocean. Fresh water is renewed by the processes of evaporation, condensation, and precipitation.

2. Water is made up of one atom of slightly negatively charged oxygen and two atoms of slightly positively charged hydrogen. Water acts as a solvent because the charged atoms in a water molecule attract the ions of solid substances, thus dissolving the substance.

3. A watershed is the land area in which surface runoff drains into a river or a system of rivers or streams. Watersheds prevent floods and water shortages and provide a steady flow of fresh water into the oceans.

4. The pollutants in underground sources of water may spread, endangering water sources far from the point of origin of the pollution.

5. A lake is a natural, large, deep depression in the Earth's crust that has filled with water. A reservoir is an artificial lake built by damming a stream or river. Both can be used as sources of drinking water for nearby communities.

6. The supply of fresh water must be conserved because it is a limited supply. New sources are needed because of increased demand for water.

Content Review

Multiple Choice

Choose the letter of the answer that best completes each statement.

1. The continuous movement of water from the oceans and freshwater sources to the air and land and back to the oceans is called the
   a. nitrogen cycle. c. runoff.
   b. water cycle. d. oxygen cycle.

2. The process in which water vapor changes to a liquid is called
   a. precipitation. c. condensation.
   b. evaporation. d. runoff.

3. Very thick sheets of ice found mainly in polar regions are called
   a. aquifers.
   b. crevasses.
   c. valley glaciers.
   d. continental glaciers.

4. The space between soil particles is called
   a. pore space.
   b. zone of aeration.
   c. surface runoff.
   d. polarity.

5. The underground region where all the pores are filled with water is called the
   a. zone of saturation.
   b. aquifer.
   c. watershed.
   d. zone of aeration.

6. The level below which all of the pore spaces in the soil are filled with water is called the
   a. water table. c. meltwater.
   b. groundwater. d. watershed.

7. The property of water that enables it to dissolve many substances easily is called
   a. hardness. c. softness.
   b. polarity. d. permeability.

8. A substance in which another substance dissolves is called a
   a. solution.
   b. saturated substance.
   c. solvent.
   d. molecule.

True or False

If the statement is true, write "true." If it is false, change the underlined word or words to make the statement true.

1. The process by which water changes to a gas is <u>condensation</u>.
2. Rain, snow, sleet, and hail are all forms of <u>precipitation</u>.
3. Water that enters a river or a stream after a heavy rain or during thawing of snow or ice is called <u>groundwater</u>.
4. In dry desert areas, the water table is usually very <u>shallow</u>.
5. Materials through which water can move quickly are described as <u>saturated</u>.

Concept Mapping

Complete the following concept map for Section 3–1. Refer to pages I6–I7 to construct a concept map for the entire chapter.

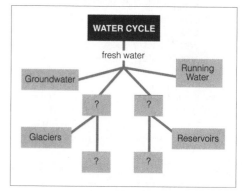

Concept Mastery

Discuss each of the following in a brief paragraph.

1. What is the water cycle? How does this cycle renew the Earth's supply of fresh water?
2. Describe the structure of a molecule of water. How does this structure affect its ability to dissolve substances?
3. What is a watershed? Why are watersheds important?
4. Why is it important to keep from polluting underground sources of water?
5. What is the difference between a lake and a reservoir? How could both bodies of water be used to supply a city with water?
6. Why is it important to protect our sources of fresh water? Why is it important to develop new sources?
7. What is hard water? How does hard water differ from soft water?
8. What is an aquifer? How can aquifers be used as a source of fresh water?

Critical Thinking and Problem Solving

Use the skills you have developed in this chapter to answer each of the following.

1. **Making diagrams** Two different areas of the United States receive the same amount of rainfall during a day. Area A has soil that contains many large pores and rocks made of sandstone. The soil in Area B is mainly heavy clay. Area A is a desert. Area B is a swamp. For each area draw two diagrams: one that shows the level of the water table before a day of rain and one that shows the level after a day of rain.
2. **Designing an experiment** Clouds are not salty. The salt from the oceans is left behind when the water evaporates. Devise an experiment to illustrate this fact. Describe the problem, materials, procedure, expected observations, and your conclusions.

3. **Applying concepts** Water molecules have polarity. Explain how water molecules can attract each other. Illustrate your explanation.
4. **Applying concepts** Pure water evaporates continuously from the oceans while salts are left behind. Explain why the salinity of ocean water does not increase over time.
5. **Relating concepts** A factory dumps harmful chemical wastes into a huge hole dug in the ground behind the building. Explain why and how these chemicals might affect a well located in a town several kilometers away from the factory site.
6. **Designing an experiment** Soap does not lather easily in hard water. It does so, however, in soft water. Devise a simple test to determine if water from a tap in your school is hard or soft.
7. **Using the writing process** Develop an advertising campaign to warn people about the dangers of polluting rivers and streams. You might want to design a poster campaign and/or write a letter to your neighbors to enlist their help.

the steam will readily condense into the beaker. When students taste the water from the beaker, they should note that it is no longer salty.

3. The positive H end of one water molecule is attracted to the negative O end of another water molecule. A weak bond, called a hydrogen bond, is formed between water molecules.

4. The salinity of the ocean does not increase over time because fresh water is continually added to the ocean through the water cycle.

5. The chemicals dumped into the hole seep into the groundwater, which may be the source of the well water, and thus the chemicals could pollute the well water in the community several kilometers away.

6. Experiments may include comparing the way the school's water lathers in comparison to water known to be soft or hard.

7. Students' campaigns should point out the dangers of pollution and the results of pollution in a dramatic display.

KEEPING A PORTFOLIO

You might want to assign some of the Concept Mastery and Critical Thinking and Problem Solving questions as homework and have students include their responses to unassigned questions in their portfolio. Students should be encouraged to include both the question and the answer in their portfolio.

ISSUES IN SCIENCE

The following issue can be used as a springboard for discussion or given as a writing assignment.

Some scientists advocate the use of cloud seeding to increase the amount of rainfall in a particular area. Other scientists question the wisdom of this technique. They claim that there is only a certain amount of rain available and that redistributing it will only upset a region's natural weather pattern. Based on your knowledge of the water cycle, decide whether or not you think cloud seeding would be effective in controlling rainfall.

7. Hard water contains large amounts of dissolved minerals; soft water does not.

8. An aquifer is a layer of rock or sediment through which water moves sideways and passes freely. Aquifers can be used as a source of fresh water by drilling a well.

CRITICAL THINKING AND PROBLEM SOLVING

1. Students' drawings should illustrate a water table fairly deep underground in Area A and close to the surface in Area B. This is due to the type of soil and rock and to climatic conditions. After a day of rain, the water table should be shown to have risen in both areas. Some flooding could be evident in Area B.

2. Basically, students' experiments should include that they first taste the salty water to determine that it is in fact salty. Then the water should be boiled, using a hot plate. The steam that rises from the water must be passed through a glass tubing of some sort and collected in a beaker. If the beaker sits in an ice bath,

Chapter 4 EARTH'S LANDMASSES

SECTION	HANDS-ON ACTIVITIES
4–1 The Continents pages I110–I112 Multicultural Opportunity 4–1, p. I110 ESL Strategy 4–1, p. I110	**Activity Book** CHAPTER DISCOVERY: Mapping an Outdoor Area, p. I109
4–2 Topography pages I112–I120 Multicultural Opportunity 4–2, p. I112 ESL Strategy 4–2, p. I112	**Student Edition** ACTIVITY BANK: Making Soil, p. I171
4–3 Mapping the Earth's Surface pages I121–I129 Multicultural Opportunity 4–3, p. I121 ESL Strategy 4–3, p. I121	**Student Edition** ACTIVITY (Doing): Mapping Your Neighborhood, p. I124 ACTIVITY (Doing): Latitude and Longitude, p. I125 **Teacher Edition** A Distorted View, p. I108d
4–4 Topographic Maps page I130–I135 Multicultural Opportunity 4–4, p. I130 ESL Strategy 4–4, p. I130	**Student Edition** LABORATORY INVESTIGATION: Making a Topographic Map, p. I136 **Laboratory Manual** Constructing a Topographic Map, p. I39 Using a Topographic Map, p. I43
Chapter Review pages I136–I139	

OTHER ACTIVITIES	MEDIA AND TECHNOLOGY
Student Edition ACTIVITY (Calculating): Comparing the Continents, p. I111 **Review and Reinforcement Guide** Section 4–1, p. I39	**Courseware** Plate Tectonics (Supplemental) Continental Drift (Supplemental) **Interactive Videodisc/CD ROM** Amazonia **English/Spanish Audiotapes** Section 4–1
Student Edition ACTIVITY (Calculating): Mountain Landscapes, p. I114 ACTIVITY (Reading): To the Roof of the World, p. I117 ACTIVITY (Writing): A Dream Vacation, p. I119 **Activity Book** ACTIVITY: Identifying Our Planet's Most Noticeable Features, p. I115 ACTIVITY: Mountain Ranges, p. I123 ACTIVITY: Identifying Landscape Regions of the United States, p. I125 **Review and Reinforcement Guide** Section 4–2, p. I41	**Transparency Binder** Landscape Regions **Interactive Videodisc** On Dry Land: The Desert Biome ScienceVision: EcoVision **English/Spanish Audiotapes** Section 4–2
Student Edition ACTIVITY (Writing): Technology and Mapmaking, p. I123 **Activity Book** ACTIVITY: Latitude, Longitude, and Time Zones, p. I113 ACTIVITY: An Island Trip, p. I117 **Review and Reinforcement Guide** Section 4–3, p. I43	**English/Spanish Audiotapes** Section 4–3
Student Edition ACTIVITY (Writing): The History of Mapmaking, p. I131 **Activity Book** ACTIVITY: Science Concentration, p. I119 ACTIVITY: Topographic Maps, p. I129 ACTIVITY: A Typical Topography, p. I131 **Review and Reinforcement Guide** Section 4–4, p. I45	**English/Spanish Audiotapes** Section 4–4
Test Book Chapter Test, p. I77 Performance-Based Tests, p. I119	**Test Book** Computer Test Bank Test, p. I83

*All materials in the Chapter Planning Guide Grid are available as part of the Prentice Hall Science Learning System.

Chapter 4 EARTH'S LANDMASSES

CHAPTER OVERVIEW

For thousands of years, most people thought that the Earth was flat. As people were able to explore more of the world, the theory that the Earth was flat became more suspect—Columbus's voyage to the New World finally proved that the Earth was round.

The landmasses of today's Earth consist of seven continents—Asia, Africa, Australia, Antarctica, North America, South America, and Europe. Though many people may tend to think of these continents as seven distinct continents, some of these continents combine to form giant landmasses. The continents of North America and South America are connected by Central America, forming a giant landmass, and the continents of Asia, Europe, and Africa are connected to form an even larger, single landmass.

Any landmass has characteristic features. These features include mountains, plains, and plateaus. These features are scattered throughout Earth's continents to varying degrees.

The Earth has been divided into a coordinate system of lines, which help people plan their travel routes over great distances in an efficient way. These lines are lines of latitude (measuring distance north and south of the equator) and lines of longitude (measuring distance east and west of the prime meridian).

A more precise system of mapping exists for local land areas. This system of maps, called topographic maps, depicts the elevations of selected regions or specific land features.

4-1 THE CONTINENTS
THEMATIC FOCUS

The purpose of this section is to introduce students to the term *landmass* and the seven continents of Earth. A landmass is a relatively large area of land that consists of one or more continents. The continents of Earth are Asia, Africa, Australia, Antarctica, North America, South America, and Europe. Though all these continents share similar features, the degree to which they share these features varies, and each continent is unique with respect to the others.

The theme that can be focused on in this section is patterns of change.

*Patterns of change: The Earth's landmasses have different characteristics, which are often caused by climatic conditions. The climate and characteristics of Antarctica, for example, are radically different from the climate and characteristics of the continent of Africa.

PERFORMANCE OBJECTIVES 4-1

1. Identify the Earth's major landmasses.
2. Name the seven continents.

SCIENCE TERMS 4-1

island p. I110
continent p. I110

4-2 TOPOGRAPHY
THEMATIC FOCUS

This section will introduce students to the topography, or the shape of the Earth's surface. Students will discover that a landscape comprises the physical features of the Earth's surface found in an area and that there are three main types of landscape regions. These landscape regions consist of mountains, plains, and plateaus. Mountains can be old or young and can be formed in several different ways. Plains, or flat areas, are divided into two groups: coastal plains, which occur where land touches an ocean, and interior plains, which occur on the inland areas of continents. Plateaus are like plains in that they are relatively flat areas of land. But unlike plains, plateaus are located high above sea level.

The themes that can be focused on in this section are scale and structure and systems and interactions.

*Scale and structure: The landscape of the Earth varies greatly. Mountains, plains, and plateaus exist on Earth. These landscape features are characterized in great part by their altitude above sea level.

*Systems and interactions: Mountains can form in several ways. Mountains form when magma (liquid rock) from within the Earth pushes its way to the surface. Mountains also form when parts of the Earth's crust are folded or broken. The continents of Earth display young, old, and middle-aged mountains.

PERFORMANCE OBJECTIVES 4-2

1. Define the term *topography*.
2. Describe the three major landscape regions.
3. Explain how mountains are grouped into ranges, systems, and belts.
4. Distinguish between coastal plains and interior plains.

SCIENCE TERMS 4-2

topography p. I113
landscape p. I113
elevation p. I113
relief p. I113
mountain p. I114
mountain range p. I116
mountain system p. I116
mountain belt p. I116
plain p. I117
coastal plain p. I117
interior plain p. I118
plateau p. I119

4-3 MAPPING THE EARTH'S SURFACE
THEMATIC FOCUS

The purpose of this section is to introduce students to the mapping system used to map the surface of the Earth. Because humans have the potential to travel to virtually any place on the planet, effective maps are essential to allow these travels to occur in an efficient manner. The entire Earth is divided into a coordinate, or grid, system of mapping. Lines of latitude, or parallels, are used to measure distance north and south of a specific reference line known as the equator. Lines of longitude, or meridians, are used to measure distance east and west of a specific reference line, also called the prime meridian. To find an exact location on the Earth, a person needs only a latitude and a longitude value.

Lines of longitude also divide the Earth into different time zones. The reference, or beginning line, for these zones is the international date line. Although lines of longitude appear as straight lines, the international date line is not a completely straight line. It forms angles around islands and other populated areas, effectively preventing one side of a street from having a different time and day than the other side of that street.

The theme that can be focused on in this section is stability.

*Stability: Because the Earth rotates appoximately 15 degrees per hour, and there are 360 degrees in a circle, the Earth has been divided into a series of 24 time zones of 15 degrees each. In the United States, movement to the west results in moving backward through time zones.

PERFORMANCE OBJECTIVES 4–3

1. Identify the features of maps and globes.
2. Discuss the use of meridians and parallels.
3. Describe the Earth's time zones.
4. Compare different map projections.

SCIENCE TERMS 4–3

map p. I121
globe p. I121
scale p. I121
meridian p. I121
prime meridian p. I121
longitude p. I122
time zone p. I123
international data line p. I124
parallel p. I125
equator p. I125

latitude p. I125
projection p. I126
Mercator projection p. I126
equal-area projection p. I127

4–4 TOPOGRAPHIC MAPS
THEMATIC FOCUS

Topographic maps, used to show the relief of the land, will be explored in this section. Like other maps, topographic maps use symbols to represent features. Symbols for buildings and roads are usually black. Symbols for bodies of water such as rivers, lakes, and streams are blue. Green represents woods and swamps. And contour lines are brown or red. Contour lines can be the most striking feature of a topographic map, depending on their concentration and interval, or scale.

The themes that can be focused on in this section are unity and diversity, and evolution.

Unity and diversity: There are ways to show the Earth's surface using maps and globes. A topographic map is a detailed, flat display of the different shapes and sizes of land and other surfaces in a specific area.

Evolution: Over time, the surface of the Earth has been altered by natural forces, as well as by the action of people. For this reason, topographic maps of the same region may change slightly as time passes. Though these changes seem gradual and small, they are substantial when compared against a much longer time period.

PERFORMANCE OBJECTIVES 4–4

1. Describe the use of topographic maps to show the relief of a land surface.
2. Explain how contour lines are used to show elevation on a topographic map.
3. Interpret the symbols and colors commonly used on topographic maps.

SCIENCE TERMS 4–4

topographic map p. I130
contour line p. I130

Discovery *Learning*

TEACHER DEMONSTRATIONS MODELING

A Distorted View

Students can participate in this demonstration, which shows some of the difficulties encountered in attempting to represent the round Earth on a flat map. For this demonstration you will need several round objects, pieces of paper large enough to cover each object, crayons, and tape.

Begin by giving each student a round object, a piece of paper, and a crayon. Ask students to draw a simple design or picture on the paper. Then challenge students to cover the round object tightly with the paper, using tape to fasten it. After they have attempted to do this, ask the following questions.

• **Are you encountering any difficulties in trying to cover the round object with the paper?** (Yes.)
• **What kinds of difficulties?** (The paper will not smooth out; the paper will not curve enough to fit the surface.)
• **What is happening to the design or picture that you drew on the paper?** (It is becoming distorted as the paper folds or sticks out; it is difficult to tell what the original design or picture was.)
• **Can you relate what you are experiencing to the problem of making a flat map of the Earth's surface?** (Round and flat surfaces cannot easily be superimposed on each other. Therefore, it is difficult to accurately represent a round surface on a flat map, and vice versa.)

CHAPTER 4
Earth's Landmasses

INTEGRATING SCIENCE

This earth science chapter provides you with numerous opportunities to integrate other areas of science, as well as other disciplines, into your curriculum. Blue numbered annotations on the student page and integration notes on the teacher wraparound pages alert you to issues of possible integration.

In this chapter you can integrate earth science and ecology (p. 111), earth science and volcanoes (p. 112), mathematics (p. 114), earth science and geology (p. 114), language arts (pp. 117, 119, 123, 131), agriculture (p. 118), earth science and erosion (p. 119), food science (p. 120), geography (pp. 121, 122, 125, 126, 131), and social studies (p. 129).

SCIENCE, TECHNOLOGY, AND SOCIETY/COOPERATIVE LEARNING

"Spring forward, fall back!" This expression reminds us about daylight saving time and the need to move our clocks one hour ahead in April and one hour back in October. Daylight saving time is a time system in which one or two hours of additional daylight are gained by lengthening the period of evening daylight. Daylight saving time is used most often in summer, but supporters of this time system are finding increased enthusiasm for its year-round use.

Daylight saving time has a long history. Benjamin Franklin unsuccessfully advocated its use to save on candles. During World War I, Germany was the first country to adopt the use of this time system in order to conserve fuel and power for the German war effort.

In the United States, daylight saving time received little interest until 1917, when legislation was enacted to advance clocks forward from the end of March until the end of October. Vigorously opposed by farmers, the legislation was appealed in 1919. During World War II, the United States (along with most countries involved in the war) went on year-round daylight saving time to assist the war effort. In 1966, Congress passed the

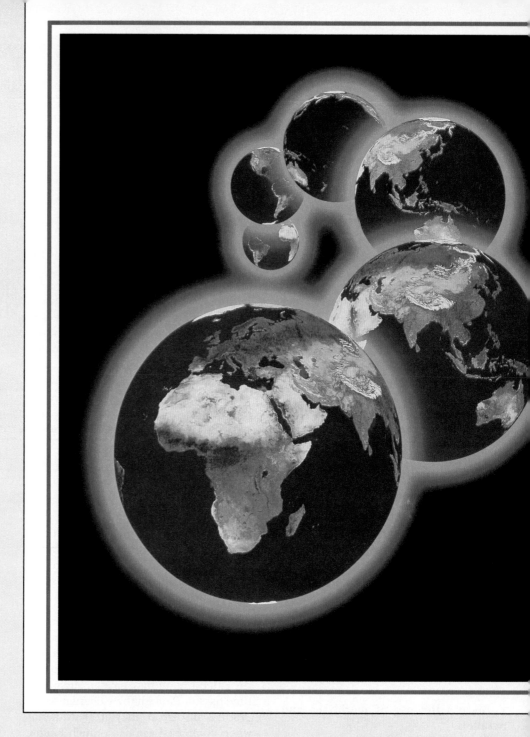

INTRODUCING CHAPTER 4

DISCOVERY LEARNING

▶ *Activity Book*

Begin teaching the chapter by using the Chapter 4 Discovery Activity from the *Activity Book*. Using this activity, students will explore procedures used to map an outdoor area.

Collect and display several examples of ancient and modern maps of the world. Allow these maps to circulate throughout the classroom; then display them in front of the classroom.

• **What features on the ancient map are also included on the modern map?** (Depending on the maps used, students might respond continents, countries, or bodies of water.)

Earth's Landmasses

Just imagine how hard it would be to visit a strange place for the first time without a map to guide you. Although someone might be able to give you accurate directions to this unfamiliar location, it is certainly easier and more helpful if you look at a map and visualize the trip before you begin.

The same idea holds true for the pilots of an airplane. Without maps, it would be very difficult for an airplane leaving Illinois to arrive in Germany. With accurate maps, however, you can enjoy a frankfurter at a baseball game in Chicago, and the next day eat a knockwurst at a soccer game in Berlin.

Throughout history, as people explored Planet Earth, maps became more and more accurate. By the middle of the eighteenth century, maps showed the Earth's land areas in the same shapes and sizes you see on maps today. Today, map-making is aided by photographs taken by high-flying satellites.

In this chapter, you will learn about different land features. You will also learn how these land features are represented on maps, and you will gain a better understanding of maps in general.

Journal *Activity*

You and Your World If you live in a city or town, make a map of your neighborhood. If you live in a rural area, make a map of the road you live along. Include places of interest and landmarks that would make it easy for a relative or friend to find your home if they wanted to visit you.

◄ *In centuries past, maps of Earth were drawn by the skilled hands of artists. Today a new type of Earth map—made from thousands of images relayed by satellite—shows just how remarkably beautiful Earth is.*

I ■ 109

Uniform Time Act, which mandated that beginning in 1967, states were to begin daylight saving time on the last Sunday in April and return to standard time on the last Sunday in October.

Many nations of the world have some period of daylight saving time—believing that it helps conserve energy and also allows people extra hours of daylight for recreation and relaxation.

Cooperative learning: Using preassigned groups or randomly selected teams, have groups complete one of the following assignments.
- Have groups answer these questions about daylight saving time: What? Why? When? Where? Who? How? After answering these questions, groups should compare the advantages and disadvantages of the year-round use of daylight saving time. What recommendation would they make to a congressional committee considering a law mandating year-round daylight saving time in the United States?
- Time is measured with many different devices. Randomly assign each group one of the following types of "clocks" used to measure time: quartz wristwatch, pendulum clock, radioactive dating, atomic clock, sundial, water clock, clepsydra. Following their research, groups should present a diagram or drawing of their assigned devices to the class. Groups should also include information on how the device or method works and how accurate it is.

See Cooperative Learning in the *Teacher's Desk Reference.*

JOURNAL ACTIVITY

You may want to use the Journal Activity as the basis of a class discussion. Have students describe the criteria they might use for including places of interest and landmarks on their map—there are many such places that could be included on any map that would be of interest to someone. Also, have students discuss whether they feel it is important to include a key or legend on their map and whether they think some attempt should be made to draw the map to scale. Students should be instructed to keep their Journal Activity in their portfolio.

- **What errors can you find on ancient maps?** (Answers might include omitted bodies of land and water and the general proportion, or scale, of the map.)
- **Why is it necessary to have accurate maps?** (Accept logical answers. Students might suggest that because we have the technology to travel almost anywhere on Earth, accurate maps are essential.)

Have students observe the picture on page I108. Ask these questions.
- **How is the satellite map different from ancient maps?** (Modern satellite maps are extremely accurate and detailed.)

Have students read the chapter introduction on page I109.
- **Around 300 BC, the Greeks theorized that the Earth was round. Believing this, why do you think they still drew maps of a flat Earth?** (Accept logical responses. Responses might include the Greeks had no practical way of testing their theory, or hypothesis.)

4-1 The Continents

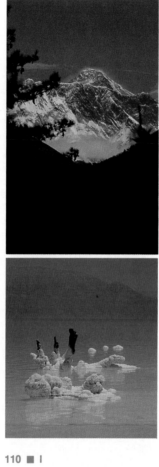

Figure 4–1 *Mount Everest is considered to be the highest point on Earth. The lowest point on Earth is the Dead Sea. The difference in altitude between these two points is 9200 meters!*

4-1 The Continents

All the land on Earth is surrounded by oceans. There are many **islands**, or small landmasses completely surrounded by water, scattered throughout the oceans. But there are only four major landmasses on Earth. Each major landmass consists of one or more **continents**. A continent is a landmass that measures millions of square kilometers and rises a considerable distance above sea level. Each continent has at least one large area of very old rock exposed at its surface. This area is called a shield. Shields form the cores of the continents. The shield of North America is located in Canada.

There are seven continents on the Earth: Asia, Africa, Europe, Australia, North America, South America, and Antarctica. Some of the continents are joined to form a single landmass. See Figure 4–2. For example, Asia and Europe are joined together as one landmass, called Eurasia. And Africa is connected to Asia by a small piece of land. These three continents—Asia, Africa, and Europe—make up one giant landmass, the largest landmass on Earth.

The second largest landmass consists of the continents of North America and South America. Central America is located just to the south of North America. Central America is part of the North American continent. At the point where Central America connects to South America, the continents of North America and South America are joined.

The third largest landmass is the continent of Antarctica. Antarctica is about twice the size of the United States. Antarctica has only recently been explored. In fact, the first known exploration of Antarctica occurred in 1901.

Antarctica is very different from the other continents. It is almost completely covered by a thick icecap. In fact, the Antarctic icecap is the largest in

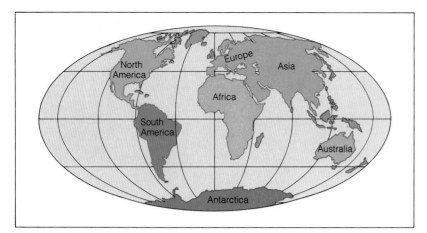

Figure 4–2 *This map shows the major islands and the seven continents of the world. Which continents make up the Earth's largest landmass?*

the world and covers an area of 34 million square kilometers! The Antarctic icecap is so large that it extends into the surrounding ocean. It contains almost 90 percent of the ice on the Earth's surface.

Antarctica is certainly the coldest area on Earth. In July 1983, the temperature in Vostok, Antarctica, dropped to nearly −89.2°C, the lowest temperature ever recorded on Earth. Many scientific stations have been built on Antarctica. Some scientific teams study life on the continent. Others study the land beneath the ice. Still others study conditions in the atmosphere over Antarctica. Today, one of the major areas of study is the depletion of the ozone layer over Antarctica. In the past several years, "holes" in the ozone layer have been observed there. Scientists study these areas in an attempt to determine the long-term effects of ozone depletion. Because of the extreme cold, however, the scientists who live and work in Antarctica are only temporary visitors to this continent.

Australia is the smallest landmass still considered a continent. It is the only continent that is a single country. Sometimes, Australia is referred to as the island continent. Why do you think this term is used to describe Australia? ②

ACTIVITY

CALCULATING

Comparing the Continents

1. From a globe, trace the outline of each of the seven continents. Cut out the outlines. Trace each outline on a piece of graph paper. Shade in the outlined continents.

2. Consider each square on the graph paper as an area unit of 1. Calculate the area units for each of the seven continents to the nearest whole unit. For example, suppose a continent covers all of 45 units, about one half of 20 units, and about one fourth of 16 units. The total area units this continent covers will be 45 + 10 + 4, or 59.

List the continents from the smallest to the largest.

I ■ 111

4-2 Topography

Figure 4-3 *Australia is a continent country completely surrounded by water. These steep cliffs border on the Indian Ocean.*

4-1 Section Review

1. Identify the seven continents.
2. What is a landmass? A continent? An island?
3. What makes the continent of Antarctica unusual? What makes Australia unusual?

Critical Thinking—*Applying Concepts*
4. Predict what would happen if the average temperature of Antarctica rose to 5°C.

Guide for Reading

Focus on this question as you read.

▶ *What are the three main types of landscape regions?*

4-2 Topography

Over billions of years, the surface of the Earth has changed many times. These changes are produced by several factors. Weather conditions such as wind and heat change the surface. Running water reshapes the land. Earthquakes and volcanoes cause major changes in the Earth's surface. Earthquakes can build up or level mountains, and volcanoes can produce new islands. Surtsey, an island off the coast of Iceland, was produced in 1963 by volcanic eruptions on the seabed. Even people alter the Earth's appearance. For example, they use huge earth-moving machinery to smooth the Earth's surface in order to construct the buildings that make up a large city. What other human activities can you think of that might change the shape of the land? ❶

Scientists refer to the shape of the Earth's surface as its **topography** (tuh-PAHG-ruh-fee). The Earth's topography is made up of different kinds of **landscapes**. A landscape is the physical features of the Earth's surface found in an area. Figure 4–5 shows landscape regions of the United States. In which landscape region do you live? ❷

There are three main types of landscape regions: mountains, plains, and plateaus. Each type has different characteristics. One characteristic of a landscape region is **elevation**, or height above sea level. Some landscape regions have high elevations; others have low elevations. Within a landscape region, the elevation can vary from place to place. The difference in a region's elevations is called its **relief**. If a landscape region has high relief, there are large differences in the elevations of different areas within the landscape region. What do you think is true of a landscape region with low relief? ❸

Figure 4–4 *Earth's landmasses are constantly undergoing changes. The island of Surtsey appeared in 1963 as a result of volcanic eruption on the ocean floor.*

Figure 4–5 *This map shows the major landscape regions of the continental United States. What type of landscape region covers most of the land shown? In what type of landscape region do you live?* ❹

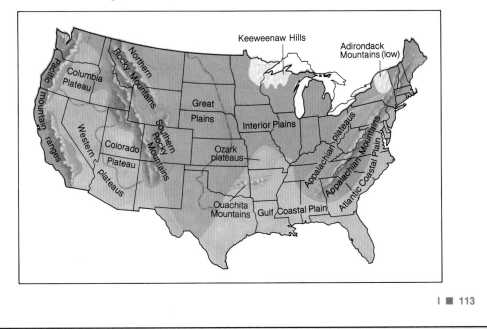

TEACHING STRATEGY 4–2

FOCUS/MOTIVATION

Collect and display photographs that show the various landscape regions in the United States. An excellent source of such photographs would be the tourist information centers of states in each region. Allow students time to examine the photographs; then have them discuss the characteristics of each different landscape.

CONTENT DEVELOPMENT

Explain that there are three main types of landscape regions: mountains, plains, and plateaus. One characteristic of any region is elevation, or height above sea level. Some students may have the mistaken impression that relief refers to the elevation of a region, rather than to the differences in elevation within a region. Emphasize the idea that both a plateau and a coastal plain have low relief, even though a plateau is high above sea level,

whereas a coastal plain is close to sea level.

● ● ● ● **Integration** ● ● ● ●

Use the discussion of how volcanic activity causes major changes in the Earth's surface to integrate concepts of volcanoes into your lesson.

Skills: Making computations, calculator

This activity will help to give students an idea about how much land on Earth is covered by mountains. Multiplying the total land area of 148,300,000 km² by ⅕ will give the correct answer of 29,660,000 km².

Integration: Use this Activity to integrate mathematics concepts into your science lesson.

4–2 (continued)

GUIDED PRACTICE

Skills Development

Skill: Interpreting maps

Have students observe the map in Figure 4–5. Ask these questions.

• **In which states are there plains, mountains, and plateaus?** (New York, Pennsylvania, New Mexico, Alabama, and Tennessee.)

• **What type of landscape is found in northern New England?** (Mountains.)

• **Where are major mountain ranges located?** (Along the west coast, through the interior western states, and slightly inland from the east coast.)

• **What landscape feature is located near plateaus?** (Mountains.)

• **What two types of mountains are shown on this map?** (High mountains and low mountains, or hills.)

• **What do you think the difference is between a hill or a low mountain and a mountain?** (Accept logical responses. Point out that a hilly or low mountainous area has an elevation above sea level of

---

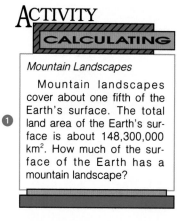

A C T I V I T Y
CALCULATING

Mountain Landscapes

❶ Mountain landscapes cover about one fifth of the Earth's surface. The total land area of the Earth's surface is about 148,300,000 km². How much of the surface of the Earth has a mountain landscape?

Figure 4–6 *Mountains may form when the Earth's crust breaks into great blocks that are then tilted or lifted (top). Folded mountains form when layers of the Earth's crust wrinkle into wavelike folds (bottom).*

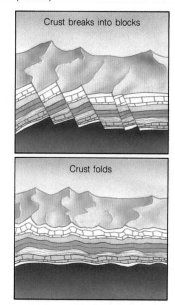

Crust breaks into blocks

Crust folds

114 ■ I

Mountains

Mountains make up one type of landscape region. Mountains are natural landforms that reach high elevations. Mountains have narrow summits, or tops, and steep slopes, or sides. Mountain landscapes have very high relief.

What do you think is the difference between a hill and a mountain? Most geologists agree that a mountainous area rises at least 600 meters above the surrounding land. But the actual height of a mountain is given as its height above sea level. For example, Pike's Peak in Colorado rises about 2700 meters above the surrounding land. But its actual height above sea level is 4301 meters.

The highest mountain in the world is Mount Everest. Mount Everest is part of the Himalayas, a great chain of mountains in Asia that extends from Tibet to Pakistan. The peak of Mount Everest soars more than 8 kilometers! The highest mountain in the United States is Mount McKinley in the state of Alaska. It is more than 6 kilometers high. What mountains are closest to your home? ❶

All mountains did not form at the same time. Some mountains are old; others are relatively young. Mountains are built very slowly. It is thought that the Rocky Mountains began to form about 65 million years ago. It took about 10 million years for these mountains to reach their maximum height. You might be surprised to learn that geologists consider the Rocky Mountains to be "young" mountains. In this case, "young" and "old" are relative terms compared to the age of the Earth.

Mountains can be formed in several ways. Some mountains result from the folding and breaking of the Earth's surface. Other mountains are created ❷ when hot magma (liquid rock) from the Earth's interior breaks through the Earth's surface. (You will learn more about the Earth's interior in Chapter 5.)

Streams and rivers in mountain areas move very quickly. The higher and steeper the mountain slopes, the faster the water flows. Mountain streams and rivers carry rocks of all sizes. When there is heavy rainfall or when snow melts, the streams and rivers become so swollen with water that they can even carry small boulders.

---

less than 600 meters, whereas a mountainous area has an elevation of at least 600 meters.)

• **Where are low mountains located?** (Near the Great Lakes and in northern New York State.)

• **What large section of the country consists only of mountains and plateaus?** (The western states.)

• **What major landscape regions are shown in your state?** (Answers will vary, depending on the state.)

INDEPENDENT PRACTICE

▶ *Activity Book*

Students who need practice on the concept of landscape types should complete the chapter activity Identifying Landscape Regions of the United States. In this activity students will use a map to locate some surface features of the United States.

CONTENT DEVELOPMENT

Mountains make up one of the three landscape regions (the others being

Figure 4–7 *Some of the world's mountains are described below. In what state is the highest mountain in North America located?* ❷

SOME OF THE WORLD'S MOST FAMOUS MOUNTAINS

Name	Height Above Sea Level (meters)	Location	Interesting Facts
Aconcagua	6959	Andes in Argentina	Highest mountain in the Western Hemisphere
Cotopaxi	5897	Andes in Ecuador	Highest active volcano in the world
Elbert	4399	Colorado	Highest mountain of Rockies
Everest	8848	Himalayas on Nepal-Tibet border	Highest mountain in the world
K2	8611	Kashmir	Second highest mountain in the world
Kanchenjunga	8598	Himalayas on Nepal-India border	Third highest mountain in the world
Kilimanjaro	5895	Tanzania	Highest mountain in Africa
Logan	5950	Yukon	Highest mountain in Canada
Mauna Kea	4205	On volcanic island in Hawaii	Highest island mountain in the world
Mauna Loa	4169	On volcanic island in Hawaii	Famous volcanic mountain
McKinley	6194	Alaska	Highest mountain in North America
Mitchell	2037	North Carolina	Highest mountain in the Appalachians
Mont Blanc	4807	France	Highest mountain in the Alps
Mount St. Helens	2549	Cascades in Washington	Recent active volcano in the United States
Pikes Peak	4301	Colorado	Most famous of the Rocky Mountains
Rainier	4392	Cascades in Washington	Highest mountain in Washington
Vesuvius	1277	Italy	Only active volcano on the mainland of Europe
Whitney	4418	Sierra Nevadas in California	Highest mountain in California

ANNOTATION KEY

Answers

❶ Answers will vary, depending on the state. (Relating facts)

❷ Alaska. (Interpreting charts)

Integration

❶ Mathematics

❷ Earth Science: Geology, See *Dynamic Earth,* Chapter 1.

FACTS AND FIGURES

THE HIMALAYAN MOUNTAINS

The greatest mountain range on land is the Himalayas. Of the world's 109 peaks more than 7200 meters high, 96 are located in the Himalayas.

plains and plateaus) that students will study in the section. Explain that mountains can be formed in several ways. Some mountains result from the folding and breaking of the Earth's surface. Other mountains are created when hot magma (liquid rock) from the Earth's interior breaks through the Earth's surface.

- **One way in which mountains are formed is through the breaking and folding of the Earth's surface. What do you think can cause the Earth's surface to fold and break?** (Lead students to infer seismic activity, or earthquakes.)
- **Another way mountains are formed is from magma, or liquid rock, reaching the Earth's surface. How can magma reach the surface of the Earth?** (Lead students to infer volcanoes.)

Point out that streams and rivers in mountain areas move very quickly. Ask volunteers to describe what these rivers and streams might be like.

- **Do you think mountain streams and rivers contain large amounts or small amounts of energy?** (Large amounts of energy.)
- **How might people use, or harness, this energy?** (Hydroelectric power.)

● ● ● ● Integration ● ● ● ●

Use the discussion of the forces that create mountains to integrate geology concepts into your lesson.

ENRICHMENT

For various reasons, people try to climb mountains. Occasionally, climbers are stranded on a mountain, and sometimes climbers die. What conditions exist at the top of a mountain that seldom exist at the bottom to help make climbing so dangerous? Have interested students research the answer to this question and report their findings to the class.

Figure 4–8 *The Rocky Mountains are considered "young" mountains because they formed a mere 65 million years ago (left). Mountains in the Appalachian Range are "old" mountains, having formed more than 300 million years ago (top right). Mount Kilimanjaro in Africa is an example of a mountain formed by volcanic activity (bottom right).*

Figure 4–9 *This stream, swollen with water from mountain snows, flows quickly.*

Streams and rivers often carve valleys in mountains. Valleys in older mountains are usually wide. Valleys in younger mountains are usually narrow. Why do you think this is so? ①

Individual mountains, which are mountains that are not part of a group, can be found in all parts of the world. These mountains are usually the products of volcanic activity during which magma broke through the Earth's surface. Examples of volcanic mountains are Fujiyama in Japan, Vesuvius in Italy, and Kilimanjaro in Tanzania.

Most mountains, however, are part of a group of mountains called a **mountain range**. A mountain range is a roughly parallel series of mountains that have the same general shape and structure. A group of mountain ranges in one area is called a **mountain system**. The Great Smoky, Blue Ridge, Cumberland, and Green mountain ranges are all in the Appalachian mountain system in the eastern United States.

Most mountain ranges and mountain systems are part of an even larger group of mountains called a **mountain belt.** The pattern of mountain belts on the Earth is shown in Figure 4–10.

There are two major mountain belts in the world. The Circum-Pacific belt rings the Pacific Ocean. The Eurasian-Melanesian belt runs across northern

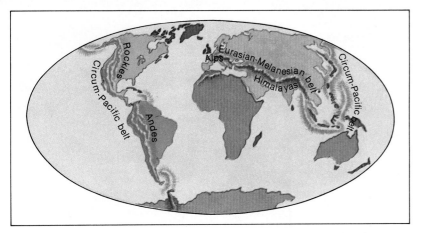

Africa, southern Europe, and Asia. The Eurasian-Melanesian belt and the Circum-Pacific belt meet in Indonesia, just north of Australia. These mountain belts may have been formed by movements of the Earth's crust.

Figure 4–10 *Most of the Earth's mountains are located within the two major mountain belts shown on this map: the Circum-Pacific belt and the Eurasian-Melanesian belt. Which major belt runs through the United States?* ❷

Plains

Another type of landscape region is made up of **plains**. Plains are flat land areas that do not rise far above sea level. Plains, then, have very small differences in elevation. They are areas of low relief. The difference between the highest and lowest elevations in a plain may be less than 100 meters. Plains areas are characterized by broad rivers and streams. Most of the plants that grow well here are grasses, related to the grass plants that are grown in a lawn or on a baseball field. Some plains are located at the edges of a continent. Others are located in the continent's interior.

COASTAL PLAINS A coast is a place where the land meets the ocean. Low, flat areas along the coasts are called **coastal plains.** The Atlantic and Gulf coastal plains of the United States are typical coastal plains. The change in elevation of the land from the Gulf of Mexico to southern Illinois is very small. Over a distance of more than 1000 kilometers, the land rises only about 150 meters above sea level.

The coastal plains of the United States were formed when soil and silt were deposited on the edge of the continent. In the past, shallow oceans

To the Roof of the World

Mount Everest is the highest mountain on Earth. Sir Edmund Hillary was the first person to reach the top of Mount Everest. Hillary described his exploits in a book entitled *High Adventure*. You might enjoy reading *High Adventure* (or any of several other books Hillary wrote describing his various exploits). ❶

| ■ 117

ACTIVITY
READING

TO THE ROOF OF THE WORLD

Ask students to describe the expedition of Hillary and Norgay to the top of Mount Everest.

Integration: Use this Activity to integrate language arts concepts into your science lesson.

ship between a mountain, a mountain range, a mountain system, and a mountain belt.

INDEPENDENT PRACTICE

▶ *Activity Book*

Students who need practice on the concept of mountains should complete the chapter activity Mountain Ranges. In this activity students will explore the physical characteristics of some mountain ranges of the world.

CONTENT DEVELOPMENT

Define the term *plains* by explaining that plains are flat land areas that do not rise far above sea level. These areas have very small differences in elevation and are areas of low relief.

Plains can be found in the interior of continents as well as at the edges of continents. Low, flat areas along the edges, or coasts, of continents are called coastal plains. Coastal plains were once covered by shallow water. As the oceans receded

or disappeared, large deposits of sand and silt were left behind. Through the years, more sediments were deposited into coastal-plain areas by rivers and streams, creating an abundance of fertile soil in a coastal-plain area. Because of this rich soil, farming is a major activity of great economic importance in coastal-plain areas.

ENRICHMENT

Many different crops are grown in coastal-plain regions. Have interested students choose different states that are all or partially covered by coastal plains and find out about the types of crops that are raised there. Students should explain to the class how crops vary according to the climate in their chosen state.

Figure 4–11 This area in Jacksonville Beach, Florida, is located within the Atlantic coastal plain. What characteristic of plains regions is visible in this photograph? ❶

Activity Bank

Making Soil, p.171

Figure 4–12 The land in interior plains regions has fertile soil. In the past, these lands supported huge herds of grazing animals, such as buffaloes. Today crops are grown in these areas.

covered these areas. As these oceans disappeared, large deposits of sand and silt were left behind. More sediments have been deposited onto coastal plains by rivers and streams. The soil in these areas has been enriched by these deposits.

Because of the abundance of fertile soil, farming is a major activity of great economic importance on coastal plains. In the United States, cotton, tobacco, vegetables, and citrus crops are grown in these areas.

INTERIOR PLAINS Some low flat areas are also found inland on a continent. These areas are called **interior plains**. Interior plains are somewhat higher above sea level than coastal plains. For example, the interior plains of the United States have an elevation of about 450 meters above sea level. This is considerably higher than the elevation of the Atlantic and Gulf coastal plains. But within an interior plain itself, the differences in elevation are small. So interior plains also have low relief.

The Great Plains of the United States are large interior plains. They were formed as mountains and hills that were later worn down by wind, streams, and glaciers. Large interior plains are found in the Soviet Union, central and eastern Europe, and parts of Africa and Australia.

Interior plains have good soil. The sediments deposited by rivers and streams make the soil suitable for farming. In the United States, grasses and grains such as wheat, barley, and oats are grown in the interior plains. Cattle and sheep are raised in these areas, too. ❶

4-2 (continued)

CONTENT DEVELOPMENT

Remind students that plains are flat land areas that are not far above sea level and that coastal plains are low, flat areas found along the coastline of a continent.

Explain that there is another type of plain called an interior plain. Interior plains and coastal plains are similar in that they are both low, flat areas. Interior plains, however, are different from coastal plains in that interior plains are

somewhere higher above sea level than coastal plains and are located within the interior region of a continent.

• **The soil of coastal-plain regions is fertile. Would you assume that the soil of an interior-plain region is also fertile? Why?** (Lead students to respond yes and to infer that flat areas are usually created by the settling of fine sediments.)

Remind students about their studies concerning physical features of the ocean floor.

• **What feature of the ocean floor is like the interior plain of a continent except that it is underwater?** (Lead students to infer the abyssal plain.)

• **What feature of the ocean floor is like the coastal plain of a continent except that it is underwater?** (Lead students to infer the continental shelf.)

• **How are the flat areas of continents and the flat areas of the ocean floor similar?** (They were both created to some degree by the deposits of sediments.)

Plateaus

A third type of landscape region consists of **plateaus**. Plateaus are broad, flat areas of land that rise more than 600 meters above sea level. Some plateaus reach elevations of more than 1500 meters. Plateaus are not considered mountains because their surfaces are fairly flat. Like plains, plateaus have low relief. But unlike plains, plateaus rise much higher above sea level.

Most plateaus are located inland. But a few plateaus are near oceans. The plateaus near oceans often end in a cliff at the edge of a coastal plain. If a plateau is directly next to an ocean, it ends in a cliff at the coast.

Plateaus often have the same landscape for thousands of kilometers. Some plateaus have been deeply cut by streams and rivers that form canyons. The Colorado River cuts through the Colorado Plateau to form the Grand Canyon in Arizona. The river flows 1.5 kilometers lower than the surface of the surrounding plateau. Have you ever visited the Grand Canyon or seen pictures of it? ❷

Many plateaus of the world are dry, nearly desert areas. They are often used for grazing cattle, sheep, and goats. Plateaus in the western United States are rich in coal and mineral deposits such as copper and lead.

Figure 4–13 *Plateaus are broad, flat areas of land with low relief. Some plateaus have been cut by streams and rivers that form canyons. Cut by the relentless action of the Colorado River, the Grand Canyon is among the most impressive on Earth.*

I ■ 119

Answers

① Scales help to relate accurate impressions of size or distance. (Applying concepts)

Integration
① Food Science
② Geography

CONNECTIONS

FROZEN FOODS—AN IDEA FROM FRIGID LANDS

Students may not have previously connected the idea that lifestyles are influenced by the landscape features of a region. Have interested students more thoroughly research the science involved in quick-frozen food and report their findings to the class. You also may wish to have students discuss other examples of how the landscape of a particular region influences the people that live there.

If you are teaching thematically, you may want to use the Connections feature to reinforce the themes of energy, patterns of change, scale and structure, systems and interactions, and stability.

Integration: Use the Connections feature to integrate food science into your lesson.

4–2 (continued)

REINFORCEMENT/RETEACHING

▶ *Activity Book*

Students who need practice on the concept of Earth's landmasses should complete the chapter activity Identifying Our Planet's Most Noticeable Features. In this activity students will explore the prominent features of the Earth's landscape.

ENRICHMENT

Have students use clay or plaster of Paris to make models of the three main

---

CONNECTIONS

Frozen Foods—An Idea ① From Frigid Lands

Near the North Pole—in climates almost as severe as those found in Antarctica—native peoples have lived for many thousands of years. They survive primarily by fishing and hunting. And a long time ago, they discovered that the extreme cold in which they live can have significant value—it can preserve food.

Clarence Birdseye was a businessman and inventor, who at his death owned more than 300 patents on his inventions. Early in his career, Birdseye traded in furs. In 1912 and 1916 he visited Labrador, a part of Canada. While there, he observed the people freezing food for use in the winter because it was difficult for them to get a fresh supply during the very cold months. Birdseye spent

years experimenting on ways to freeze food commercially. In 1929 he achieved success and began selling his quick-frozen foods. As a result of this technology, Birdseye became quite wealthy and famous. Today, his name is practically synonymous with frozen foods.

The idea seems a simple one. Extremely cold temperatures can protect foods from spoiling almost indefinitely. (Some Russian scientists claim that they have eaten the meat of a mammoth frozen 20,000 years ago and have found it edible!) But keep in mind that the original idea came from native peoples whose primary motive was to survive in a cold, hostile environment.

4–2 Section Review

1. What is a landscape? What are the three main landscape types found in the United States?
2. What do scientists mean by the Earth's topography?
3. Describe the following: mountain, mountain range, mountain system, mountain belt.
4. What is a coastal plain? An interior plain?

Connection—*Ecology*
5. Why are plains and plateaus good areas to grow crops, whereas the sides of mountains usually are not?

---

landscape regions discussed in this section of the text book. The models should be scaled to conform to the elevation and relief descriptions that students have learned for mountains, plains, and plateaus.

INDEPENDENT PRACTICE
Section Review 4–2
1. The physical features of the Earth's surface in a particular area; mountains, plains, plateaus.
2. Topography is the shape of the Earth's surface.
3. A mountain is a part of a mountain range. A mountain range is a part of a mountain system. A mountain system is a part of a mountain belt. (This progression is listed in order from least in size to greatest.)
4. Low, flat area along a coast; low, flat, inland area somewhat higher above sea level than a coastal plain.
5. Precipitation along the sides of

4-3 Mapping the Earth's Surface

A **map** is a drawing of the Earth, or a part of the Earth, on a flat surface. There are many ways to show the Earth's surface features on maps. Some maps show only a small area of the Earth. Others show the Earth's entire surface. Maps are often grouped together in a book called an atlas. Have you ever thumbed through an atlas and visited, if only in your imagination, distant and foreign places?

The most accurate representation of the entire surface of the Earth is a **globe**. A globe is a spherical, or round, model of the Earth. It shows the shapes, sizes, and locations of all the Earth's landmasses and bodies of water.

Both maps and globes are drawn to **scale**. A scale compares distances on a map or globe to actual distances on the Earth's surface. For example, 1 centimeter on a map might equal 10 kilometers on the Earth's surface. Different maps may have different scales. However, all maps and globes should have the scale used to represent the distances shown on that particular map or globe. Why is including a scale important? ❶

Meridians

When you look at a globe or a map, you see many straight lines on it. Some of the lines run between the points that represent the geographic North and South poles of the Earth. These lines are called **meridians** (muh-RIHD-ee-uhnz).

Each meridian is half of an imaginary circle around the Earth. Geographers have named the meridian that runs through Greenwich, England, the **prime meridian**. Because meridians run north and south, they measure distance east and west. The

Figure 4-14 Satellites that orbit the Earth provide information used to make maps. In the center of the photograph of Washington, DC, you can make out the mall that runs from the United States Capitol to the Washington Monument. Satellite images can also show evidence of living organisms. The yellow areas in the photograph represent great numbers of microscopic life in the oceans along the coasts of continents.

Guide for Reading

Focus on this question as you read.

▶ What are some features of the Earth shown on maps and globes?

mountains drains quickly, usually causing a great degree of soil erosion. The soil in flat areas such as plains and plateaus generally is not eroded to a great degree by precipitation.

REINFORCEMENT/RETEACHING

Monitor students' responses to the Section Review questions. Reteach any material that is still unclear, based on students' responses.

CLOSURE

▶ *Review and Reinforcement Guide*

Students may now complete Section 4–2 in the *Review and Reinforcement Guide.*

TEACHING STRATEGY 4-3

FOCUS/MOTIVATION

Collect as many different types of maps as you can find. Attempt to include high-

4-3 Mapping the Earth's Surface

MULTICULTURAL OPPORTUNITY 4-3

If you have students from different parts of the world, use a world map and pins to mark your students' homelands. Then identify the time zones in each area. If it is 12:00 noon at your school, what time would it be in the native lands of each of your students?

ESL STRATEGY 4-3

Help students understand the concept of time zones by having them answer the questions listed below. Provide them with a world map designating the international date line, the time zones of the continental United States, and the locations that are mentioned in the questions.

1. When it is 8:30 AM in Los Angeles, California, what time is it in Mexico City, Mexico?

2. When it is 6 PM in Phoenix, Arizona, what time is it in London, England?

3. When it is 8 PM in Madrid, Spain, what time is it in New Orleans, Louisiana?

way maps, world maps, state maps, relief maps, maps of recreational areas, and so on. Before displaying the maps, allow them to circulate through the classroom. Then ask these questions.

• **When is the last time you or your family members used a map?** (Accept all reponses. Students might respond during a vacation or when using a mass-transit system.)

• **What type of map did you use?** (Accept all answers. Students might suggest a road map or other travel-oriented map.)

• **Why did you choose this type of map?** (Students should suggest that the type of map they chose best suited their needs.)

● ● ● ● **Integration** ● ● ● ●

Use the references to globes and maps to integrate geography concepts into your earth science lesson.

The scale of a map is determined by the degree of detail that must be represented. For example, a study of erosion in an area might require a scale that accounts for every square meter of land. A detailed street map of a city would probably require a scale that accounts for every one hundred meters. A map of the entire United States, however, would require a scale that accounts only for every 100 or 1000 kilometers.

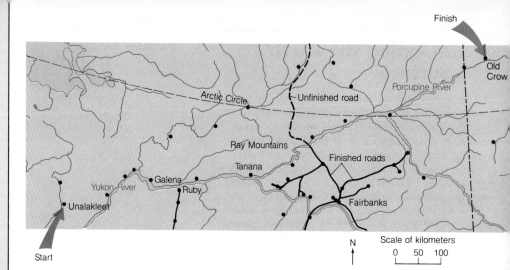

Figure 4–15 *The scale on this map is useful in finding the distance between two cities. If you took a plane ride from Unalakleet to Old Crow, how many kilometers would you fly?* ❶

measure of distance east and west of the prime meridian is called **longitude**. Meridians are used to measure longitude.

The distance around any circle, including the Earth, is measured in degrees. The symbol for degree is a small circle written at the upper right of a number. All circles contain 360°. Each meridian marks 1° of longitude around the Earth. But not all meridians are drawn on most globes or maps. (Just think how crowded a map would look if all 360 meridians were drawn.)

The prime meridian is labeled 0° longitude. Meridians to the east of the prime meridian are called east longitudes. Meridians to the west of the prime meridian are called west longitudes. Meridians ❶ of east longitude measure distances halfway around the Earth from the prime meridian. Meridians of west longitude measure distances around the other half of the Earth from the prime meridian. Because half the distance around a circle is 180°, meridians of east and west longitude go from 0° to 180°.

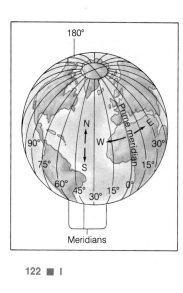

Figure 4–16 *Meridians are lines running north to south on a map or globe. What are meridians used to measure?* ❷

4–3 (continued)

CONTENT DEVELOPMENT

Discuss with students the different types of information that can be obtained from maps. Point out that some maps cover a large area and are very general—for example, a political map of the world. Other maps are very detailed and cover a much smaller area—for example, a street map of the New York City subway system or a map of the historic landmarks in Virginia. Emphasize that all maps strive to represent, as accurately as possible, the sizes and shapes of land areas and bodies of water, as well as the distances between various locations.

GUIDED PRACTICE

Skills Development

Skill: Interpreting maps

Have students observe the map in Figure 4–15. Ask the following questions:
• **Is the map a drawing of the entire Earth or a portion of it?** (A small portion of the Earth.)
• **What area of the world is represented in the map?** (A portion of Alaska.)

• **How can you tell that a portion of Alaska is represented in this map?** (The map shows the Yukon River, the city of Fairbanks, and the Arctic Circle.)
• **What features are shown on this map?** (Locations of cities and towns, finished and unfinished roads, and a scale to measure distance in kilometers.)
• **For what purposes might this map be useful?** (Accept all logical responses. Students might respond that the map is useful for determining the distance between

two cities or for planning a trip by air, land, or water.)

CONTENT DEVELOPMENT

Discuss the term *meridian* and point out that meridians are simply representations on a map or globe meant to help people find their way and to help divide the Earth into equal areas. Point out that the distance between each meridian is called longitude and that meridians are used to measure longitude.

Time Zones

On Earth, a day is 24 hours long. During these 24 hours, the Earth makes one complete rotation. You can think of this in another way. In one day, the Earth rotates 360°. If you divide 360° by the number of hours in a day (24), you will find that the Earth rotates 15° every hour. Thus the Earth has been divided into 24 zones of 15° of longitude each. These zones are called **time zones**. A time zone is a longitudinal belt of the Earth in which all areas have the same local time.

Suppose it is 6:00 AM in Miami, Florida. It is also 6:00 AM in Washington, DC, because Miami and Washington are in the same time zone. But it is not 6:00 AM in Dallas, Texas. Dallas is one time zone away from Miami and Washington. How can you tell whether it is earlier or later in Texas? ③

Figure 4–17 *The Earth has been divided into 24 time zones. All areas within a single time zone have the same local time.*

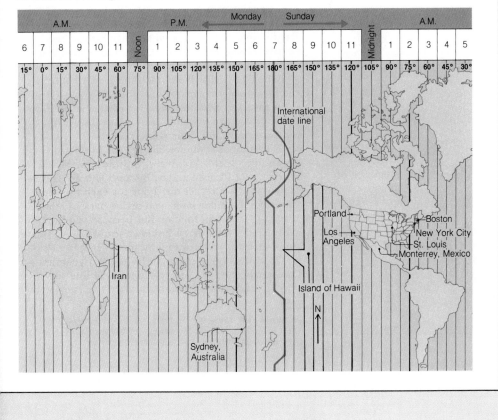

● ● ● ● **Integration** ● ● ● ●

Use the discussion of meridians to integrate geography concepts into your science lesson.

ENRICHMENT

Inform students that time zones were first developed and instituted by railroads. Before railroads opened up travel over great distances, there was no real need for standard time. Each town had its own system of time, and these systems would vary from one town to another. With the advent of railroads, however, schedules needed to be prepared for arrivals and departures in various cities. At this point, the United States was partitioned into the time zones we have today.

CONTENT DEVELOPMENT

Point out the difficulties involved in representing the curved surface of the Earth on a flat map. Explain that all maps have some distortions. The most common types of distortions involve the areas and shapes of landmasses. For example, in Figure 4–17, the island of Greenland looks considerably larger than it actually is. This distortion occurs because on this type of world map, landmasses far from the equator tend to be more distorted.

Help students understand that maps of very large areas, such as the entire world or an entire hemisphere, tend to show the most distortion. Maps of small areas, such as one state of the United States, tend to show little distortion because the curve over a small area of the Earth's surface is relatively slight.

MAPPING YOUR NEIGHBORHOOD

Skills: Making observations, relating concepts

This activity will provide students with hands-on development of an actual, useful map and will help to clarify the basic principles of mapmaking. Check to ensure that the scale drawn for each map is reasonable. You may also choose to have students make maps of smaller areas, such as their home or their room.

4–3 (continued)

REINFORCEMENT/RETEACHING

▶ *Activity Book*

Students who need practice understanding the divisions of Earth should complete the chapter activity Latitude, Longitude, and Time Zones. In this activity students will use coordinates to help determine the time and location of various places on Earth.

GUIDED PRACTICE

Skills Development

Skill: Making computations

Have students work in small groups. Challenge each group to use the maps in Figures 4–17 and 4–18 and write five exercises that involve determining changes in time. Encourage students to vary the subject matter of their exercises; for example, one situation might deal with placing a telephone call to Europe, whereas another might deal with arriving on time for a business meeting in Tokyo.

A C T I V I T Y
DOING

Mapping Your Neighborhood

1. Draw a detailed map of your neighborhood. Be sure to draw the map to scale.

2. Use different colors for buildings, industrial areas, crop fields, and bodies of water.

3. Make a legend that includes the symbols in the map and their meanings.

Monday ◄——I——► Sunday
150° 165° 180° 165° 150°

Arctic Ocean
Soviet Union
Alaska
Bering Sea
West longitude
International date line
East longitude
Hawaiian Islands
Australia
New Zealand

150° 165° 180° 165° 150°

124 ■ I

The Earth rotates on its axis from west to east. This direction of rotation makes the sun appear to rise in the east and travel toward the west. So the sun comes into view first in the east. Suppose the sun rises in New York City at 6:00 AM. After the Earth rotates 15°, the sun rises in Dallas. It is 6:00 AM in Dallas. But it is now 7:00 AM in New York City. Dallas is one time zone west of New York City.

After the Earth rotates another 15°, the sun rises in Denver. It is 6:00 AM in Denver. But by now it is 7:00 AM in Dallas and 8:00 AM in New York City. Denver is one time zone west of Dallas and two time zones west of New York City.

If it were not for time zones, the sun would rise in New York City at 6:00 AM, in Dallas at 7:00 AM, in Denver at 8:00 AM, and in Los Angeles at 9:00 AM. And the sun would not rise in Hawaii until 11:00 AM! Because of time zones, the sun rises at 6:00 AM in each city. Is this an advantage? Why? ❶

There are four time zones in the contiguous United States. From east to west they are: the Eastern, Central, Mountain, and Pacific time zones. The states of Alaska and Hawaii are further west than the Pacific time zone. Use a globe to find these two states. What is the time in Alaska and Hawaii if it is 9:00 AM in Los Angeles? ❷

When you cross from one time zone to another, the local time changes by one hour. If you are traveling east, you add one hour for each time zone you cross. If you are traveling west, you subtract one hour for each time zone you cross.

Now suppose you are taking a 24-hour trip around the world. You travel west, leaving Miami, Florida, at 1:00 PM Sunday. Because you are traveling west, you subtract one hour for each time zone you cross. One day later, you arrive back in Miami. It is now 1:00 PM Monday. But because you have subtracted a total of 24 hours as you traveled, you think that it is still 1:00 PM Sunday!

This situation is quite confusing. But geographers have established the **international date line** to simplify matters. The international date line is located

Figure 4–18 *Travelers going west across the international date line gain a day. Those going east across it lose a day. Why does the international date line zigzag?* ❸

Then have groups exchange exercise sets and find the answers.

CONTENT DEVELOPMENT

Define the term *parallel*. Point out that parallels are imaginary lines on a map or globe that run east to west, unlike meridians, which run north to south. Also, point out that a measure of the distance between parallels is called latitude. Make sure students realize that by knowing the longitude and latitude of a particular

place, they can identify the exact spot on the Earth of that location. To reinforce this concept, give students a series of latitude and longitude readings and have volunteers point out the locations on a globe. To reverse the exercise, choose several locations on a globe and then have volunteers determine the latitude and longitude of the locations.

● ● ● ● **Integration** ● ● ● ●

Use the discussion of the North and South poles and the equator to integrate

along the 180th meridian. When you cross this line going east, you subtract one day. When you cross this line going west, you add one day. So in your trip around the world, you should have added one day, or gone from Sunday to Monday, as you crossed the international date line traveling west. You would then have arrived back in Miami, as expected, at 1:00 PM Monday afternoon.

Parallels

There are also lines from east to west across a map or globe. These lines are called **parallels**. Parallels cross meridians at right angles. The parallel located halfway between the North and South poles is the **equator**. Because parallels run east and west, they measure distance north and south. So in relation to the equator, locations of other parallels are either north or south. The measure of distance north and south of the equator is called **latitude**. Parallels are used to measure latitude.

The equator is labeled 0° latitude. Parallels to the north of the equator are north latitudes. Parallels to the south of the equator are south latitudes. The distance from the equator to either the North or South pole is one quarter of the distance around the Earth.

ACTIVITY DOING

Latitude and Longitude

1. Select ten specific places on the Earth. Use a map or globe and determine the approximate latitude and longitude of each place. For example, if you select New Orleans, Louisiana, your answer will be 30°N, 90°W. If you select Tokyo, Japan, your answer will be 35°N, 140°E.

2. Write down ten random combinations of latitude and longitude. Refer to a map or globe to find the corresponding locations. For example, if you write down 50°S, 70°W, the corresponding location will be southern Argentina.

Why are latitude and longitude important?

Figure 4–19 *Parallels are lines running from east to west on a map or globe. Parallels and meridians form a grid used to determine exact locations. On what continent is 40° north latitude and 90° west longitude located?* 4

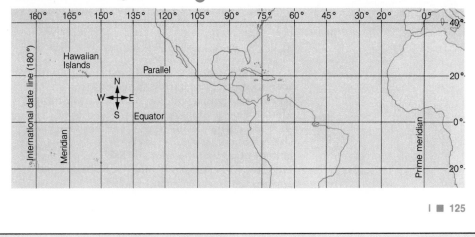

I ■ 125

ANNOTATION KEY

Answers

1 Answers will vary. Students might suggest that many people will be able to travel to and from work in daylight. (Relating concepts)

2 7 AM in Hawaii, 8 AM in Alaska. (Relating facts)

3 The line is crooked to compensate for country and state boundaries and to avoid heavily populated areas. (Interpreting maps)

4 North America. (Interpreting maps)

Integration

1 Geography

ACTIVITY DOING

LATITUDE AND LONGITUDE

Skills: Interpreting maps, applying concepts

This activity reinforces students' map-reading skills by specifically asking them to locate the latitude and longitude of various places on the Earth. The activity also helps students better understand and master the concept of global position.

Students should infer that divisions of latitude and longitude enable a person to locate precisely any place on Earth.

geography concepts into your earth science lesson.

GUIDED PRACTICE

Skills Development

Skill: Applying concepts

Have students work in small groups. Challenge each group to design "meridians" and "parallels" that define the area of a classroom. Then have each group make a map of the classroom, using these lines of "latitude" and "longitude" to determine the exact location of various objects or points of interest. (For example, a map might show that the location of the wastebasket is 40 degrees north and 80 degrees west.) Once they have finished their maps, groups may enjoy challenging each other to solve exercises created from the maps.

REINFORCEMENT/RETEACHING

Some students may need extra practice in learning to use the scale of a map.

Obtain a large map with an easy-to-use-scale. Point out that a scale is actually a ratio; for example, a map may have a scale that measures 100 kilometers for every 1 centimeter. Show students how to measure distances on the map accurately; then show them how to use a proportion to determine the number of kilometers represented. For instance, if 1 cm represents 100 km, then 5 cm would represent 500 km:

$$1 \text{ cm}/100 \text{ km} = 5 \text{ cm}/500 \text{ km}$$

The main challenge of mapmaking is to find a way of transferring the spherical surface of the Earth onto a flat sheet of paper. Any method of relating position on a globe to position on a flat map is called a projection. Many projections have been devised, each with its own advantages and distortions. Because no projection is free of distortion, a person using a map should choose the projection that is most suited to the intended use of the map.

Projections are classifed according to how the projection is made. The four basic types of projection are azimuthal—projection onto a plane; cylindric—projection onto a cylinder; conic—projection onto a cone; and geometrical—used to portray the entire globe. Figure 4–22 in the textbook shows one of the most common geometrical projections, in which the equator and prime meridian are shown as straight lines that intersect at right angles. Distortion in a geometrical projection is least near the center of the projection and greatest near the margins.

Because one quarter of the distance around a circle is 90°, north and south parallels are labeled from 0° to 90°. The North Pole is at 90° north latitude, or 90°N. The South Pole is at 90° south latitude, or 90°S. Just as there is a meridian for every degree of longitude, there is a parallel for every degree of latitude. But not all parallels are drawn on most globes or maps.

Meridians and parallels form a grid, or network of crossing lines, on a globe or map. They can be used to determine the exact locations east and west of the prime meridian and north and south of the equator. For example, if a ship reported its position as 30° south latitude and 165° east longitude, it would be off the coast of Australia. Why is this system of locating points helpful in shipping? ●

Types of Maps

Maps of the Earth are very useful. **Maps show locations and distances on the Earth's surface. They also show many different local features. Some maps show the soil types in an area. Some show currents in the ocean. Some maps show small, detailed areas of the Earth. Maps of cities may show every street in those cities.**

However, maps have one serious drawback. Because they are flat, maps cannot represent a round surface accurately. Like a photograph of a person, a map is only a **projection**, or a representation of a three-dimensional object on a flat surface. ● When the round surface of the Earth is represented on the flat surface of a map, changes occur in the shapes and sizes of landmasses and oceans. These changes are called distortion. Despite distortion, maps are still useful.

MERCATOR PROJECTIONS   There are many different ways to project the Earth's image onto a map. One type of map projection is a **Mercator projection**. Mercator projections are used for navigation. They show the correct shape of the coastlines. But the sizes of land and water areas become distorted in latitudes far from the equator. For example, on the Mercator projection in Figure 4–20, Greenland appears much larger than it really is.

4–3 (continued)

CONTENT DEVELOPMENT

Remind students that maps often distort the sizes of landmasses and oceans. This is especially true with larger maps, less true with smaller maps. Stress, however, that any kind of map contains some degree of distortion. Map distortions occur because a map (which is flat) cannot accurately represent the Earth (which is round and three-dimensional).

Introduce students to the mapping term *projection*. Point out that a projection is a representation of a three-dimensional object on a flat surface, very similar to a photograph, and that there are many different ways to project the Earth's image onto a map.

Use Figures 4–21 and 4–22, as well as the textbook discussion, to describe and compare the differences between Mercator projections and equal-area projections. Ask the following questions.
• **In which type of map would you be able to find a specific location, given latitude and longitude?** (Both maps would provide the location.)
• **Which projection would be more suitable for finding a specific location, given the latitude and longitude? Why?**

(The Mercator projection. The lines of latitude and longitude are straight on a Mercator projection and are very easy to read. On an equal-area projection, the lines of longitude are curved, making the longitude of a specific location extremely difficult to accurately determine.)
• **Which projection is more commonly used for navigation at sea? Why?** (Mercator. It shows the correct shape of coastlines.)

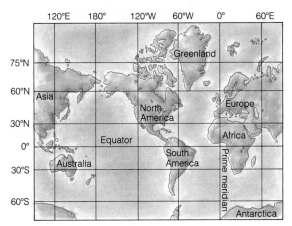

Figure 4–20 *This type of map is called a Mercator projection. What feature of this map is distorted?* ②

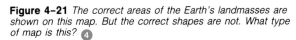

EQUAL-AREA PROJECTIONS Another type of map projection is called an **equal-area projection**. Equal-area projections show area correctly. The meridians and parallels are placed on the map in such a way that every part of the Earth is the same size on the map as it is on a globe. But the shapes of the areas are distorted on an equal-area projection. What areas in Figure 4–21 look distorted to you? ❸

Figure 4–21 *The correct areas of the Earth's landmasses are shown on this map. But the correct shapes are not. What type of map is this?* ❹

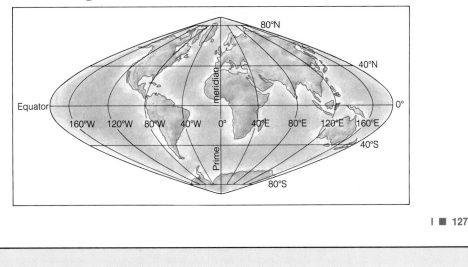

I ■ 127

• • • • **Integration** • • • •

Use the discussion of how maps distort the sizes and shapes of landmasses and oceans to integrate concepts of geography into your earth science lesson.

GUIDED PRACTICE

Skills Development

Skill: Applying concepts

Inform students that the type of projection used to make a map is usually noted in fine print in the corner of the map. (If possible, provide students with such a map and allow them time to examine the notation.) Challenge groups of students to use atlases and other sources to locate as many different map projections as they can find. Then have students compare the projections they discovered, noting the characteristics, accuracies, and distortions of each type of projection.

ENRICHMENT

The most recent advance in mapmaking has come about as a result of satellite technology. Remind students that they have previously studied how satellites have been used to map features of the ocean floor. Have interested students perform research to discover how land maps are made from information gathered by satellites. Also, have students describe the advantages of maps generated by satellites over maps created by other methods. Volunteers should share their results, including actual satellite maps or pictures of these maps, if possible, with the rest of the class.

Many types of specialized maps are important in the development of natural resources and in city and regional planning. For example, government agencies prepare maps of water and soil conditions, geologic phenomena, and timber and mineral resources. They also prepare maps based on economic and demographic statistics. Maps devoted to a single topic are called thematic maps.

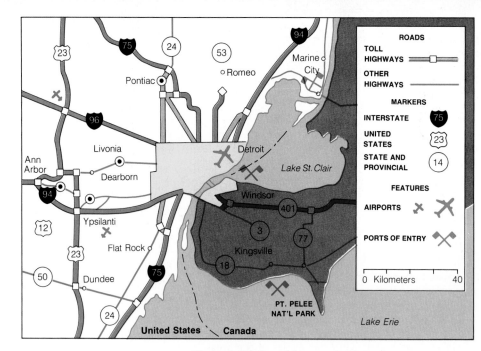

Figure 4–22 *One of the most familiar types of maps is a road map. What kinds of information are provided by the legend of this map?* ➊

4–3 (continued)

CONTENT DEVELOPMENT

Explain that maps show locations and distances on the Earth's surface. Maps also show many different local features, and these are the kinds of maps that students and their family members may be most familiar with.

Have students observe Figure 4–20. Discuss this map and its features with students. Then provide them with various starting points and have volunteers devise the best routes to specific locations. Make sure students can read and interpret the legend, pointing out that the best route is not always the shortest line between two places.

INDEPENDENT PRACTICE

▶ *Activity Book*

Students who need practice with mapping skills should complete the chapter activity An Island Trip. In this activity students will create a sketch of a small island.

4–3 Section Review

1. In what ways are maps useful?
2. Under what circumstances would a globe be more useful than a map?
3. What is a scale? Why is it important?
4. What is longitude? Latitude?
5. What is the international date line? How is this meridian used?
6. What is a time zone? Explain why the Earth has been divided into 24 time zones.
7. What is a projection? What are the two kinds?

Critical Thinking—*Applying Concepts*
8. Why was it important for people to agree on the location of the prime meridian?

GUIDED PRACTICE

Skills Development

Skill: Making maps

Students may enjoy making maps that can lead other students to "buried treasure" located somewhere in the school building or on the school grounds. Have students work in groups. Ask each group to place a "treasure" at a location of their choice. Then challenge each group to create a map that can lead another group to the treasure.

INDEPENDENT PRACTICE

Section Review 4–3

1. Maps show locations and distances on the Earth's surface. Maps can also show many different local features such as soil types, ocean currents, and city streets.
2. A globe more accurately represents the shapes of landmasses.
3. A scale is a series of marks that determines distances along a line or indicates proportional sizes of various objects.

PROBLEM Solving

Famous People—Famous Places

Famous people often make places famous. Use the following clues to locate the places on Earth being described. You will need a world atlas to discover the locations.

Interpreting Maps

1. The French artist Gauguin fled Paris to this tropical paradise, whose location is 17°S, 149°W.

2. Marie Curie discovered radium while working in a country whose capital is located at 48.5°N, 2°E.

3. Napoleon spent the last years of his life at 16°S, 5°W.

4. Ponce de Leon found the fountain of youth at 29.5°N, 81°W. The waters, alas, were not all that effective, for he died in 1521.

5. Cecil B. DeMille directed many epic films that were supposed to take place in foreign locations, but which were filmed for the most part at 34°N, 118°W.

6. Betsy Ross was supposed to have sewn the first American flag in this city, located at 40°N, 75°W.

■ Add to this list of famous places by identifying and locating some other important sites. Here are a few examples: where you live; where you were born; where your favorite sports team plays; where you would like to spend a vacation.

PROBLEM SOLVING

FAMOUS PEOPLE— FAMOUS PLACES

This feature enables students to develop and reinforce practical map-reading skills. It also provides pieces of interesting information that students may not have realized or known. If students have difficulty determining the following correct answers, explain again the method of using latitude and longitude to find specific locations on the Earth.

1. Tahiti.

2. Paris.

3. St. Helena.

4. The eastern coast of Florida.

5. California.

6. Philadelphia.

Answers will vary, depending on the student.

Integration: Use the Problem Solving feature to integrate social studies concepts into your lesson.

---

4. Longitude is the measure of distance east and west of the prime meridian, and the lines used to measure this distance are known as meridians. Latitude is the measure of distance north or south of the equator, and the lines used to measure this distance are known as parallels.

5. The international date line is an imaginary line located along the 180th meridian at which the date is adjusted, being one day later west of the line than east of the line. It is also the starting point for a day on the Earth.

6. A time zone is a longitudinal belt of the Earth in which all areas have the same local time. The Earth revolves 15° each hour, 360° in total.

7. A projection is a representation of a three-dimensional object on a flat surface; two kinds of projections are Mercator and equal-area.

8. An agreed location of the prime meridian allows a consistent system of measurement of east or west directions on the Earth.

REINFORCEMENT/RETEACHING

Monitor students' responses to the Section Review questions. If students appear to have difficulty with any of the questions, review the appropriate material in the section.

CLOSURE

▶ *Review and Reinforcement Guide*

At this point have students complete Section 4–3 in the *Review and Reinforcement Guide.*

4-4 Topographic Maps

MULTICULTURAL OPPORTUNITY 4-4

You may want to obtain a United States Geological Survey map of the area near your school. Have students locate familiar topographical features that are part of their own community.

ESL STRATEGY 4-4

Have students compare a map and a globe. Reminding them that the word *scale* can have several meanings, have them write sentences using the word as it applies to maps, fish, a science lab, thermometers, and music.

Then have students explain the following.

1. Why topographic maps are more useful to hikers than they are to motorists.
2. How a map drawn on a flat piece of paper can show the difference in elevations of a land area.

Explanations should include these terms: *contour lines, relief, contour interval, symbols,* and *legend.*

TEACHING STRATEGY 4-4

FOCUS/MOTIVATION

Begin by presenting students with the following situation.

Suppose you wanted to make a map of a park. At the north end is a hill that slopes gently at the bottom and then becomes quite steep at the top. In winter, many people enjoy sled riding on this hill. At the center of the park is a large, open field that is excellent for playing ball. Surrounding the field are narrow roads that are used by walkers, runners, bicyclists, and skaters. At the south end of the park is a swamp. The swamp is an area that you would not want to walk through. Except for a path leading to the main road at the west side of the park, the entire park is surrounded by woods.

• **What are some features of this park?** (If students have difficulty recalling the features of the park, reread the story to

---

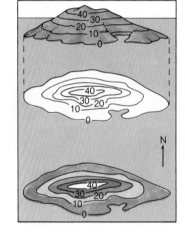

Figure 4-23 *Some topographic maps use colors to indicate different elevations. Others use contour lines to show different elevations.*

4-4 Topographic Maps

You have learned that the Earth has a varied topography. Perhaps you have even noticed some of the Earth's varied features if you have ever flown in an airplane across the United States. High above the ground, you can easily see mountains, plains, valleys, rivers, lakes, and other features. At ground level, some of these features are more difficult to observe. However, certain types of maps that show even small details of the topography of an area have been drawn. A map that shows the different shapes and sizes of a land surface is called a **topographic map.** This type of map may also show cities, roads, parks, and railroads.

Topographic maps show the relief of the land. Most topographic maps use contour lines to show relief. A **contour line** is a line that passes through all points on a map that have the same elevation. Some topographic maps show relief by using different colors for different elevations.

The difference in elevation from one contour line to the next is called the contour interval. For example, in a map with a contour interval of 5 meters, contour lines are drawn only at elevations of 0 meters, 5 meters, 10 meters, 15 meters, and so on. Look at the contour lines in Figure 4–23. What contour interval is being used here? What is the highest elevation on the hill? **❶**

Like other maps, topographic maps use symbols to represent features. Symbols for buildings and roads are usually black. Symbols for bodies of water such as rivers, lakes, and streams are blue. Green represents woods and swamps. And contour lines are brown or red. All symbols on a map are placed in a legend. The legend explains what each symbol represents. See the legend in Figure 4–24 for some common map symbols and their meanings. (Appendix D on page 169 of this textbook contains a more extensive list of map symbols.)

---

them slowly, asking them to imagine the scenes that are being read and described. Then ask the question again.)

• **Using a map, how would you describe the different features of this park?** (Accept all reasonable answers.)

You may want to have volunteers indicate on the chalkboard how they might map the park. Discuss with students some of the difficulties encountered in trying to depict the part's features. Also, point out the need for standardized symbols in

making a map that other people can understand.

CONTENT DEVELOPMENT

Use Figure 4–23 to explain to students how contour lines are read. Point out that the drawing at the top of the figure shows the actual hill. The drawing in the middle shows how the hill would be represented using contour lines. Refer students to the caption of Figure 4–23 to discover the function of the various colors.

TOPOGRAPHIC MAP SYMBOLS

Symbol	Meaning	Symbol	Meaning	Symbol	Meaning
■	House	⊠	Bridge	⋮⋮⋮	Gravel beach
⚑	School	╫	Railroad	∿	Contour line
▬▬	Primary highway	∿	Perennial stream	⊙	Depression
====	Unimproved road	⋯	Dry lake	⩩	Swamp

Figure 4–24 *The symbols in this legend are commonly found on topographic maps. What is the symbol for a school? A railroad?* ②

The first time you look at a topographic map, you may be somewhat confused. All those lines and symbols can seem awesome. But once you become familiar with contour maps and gain experience in interpreting them, a great deal of confusion will be cleared up. The information in a topographic map is quite useful, especially for people who like to hike or who enjoy camping. The following simple rules will make it easier for you to read this type of map:

- A contour line of one elevation never crosses, or intersects, a contour line of another elevation. Each contour line represents only one elevation. Contour lines can never cross because one point cannot have two different elevations.

- Closely spaced contour lines represent a steep slope. The lines are close together because the elevation of a steep slope changes greatly over a short distance. Contour lines spaced far apart represent a gentle slope. The lines are far apart because the elevation of a gentle slope changes only slightly over a short distance.

- Contour lines that cross a valley are V shaped. If a stream flows through the valley, the V will point upstream, or in the direction opposite to the flow of the stream.

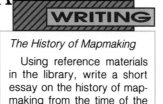

ACTIVITY

WRITING

The History of Mapmaking

Using reference materials in the library, write a short essay on the history of mapmaking from the time of the Babylonians to the present. Include information on the following:
  Gerhardus Mercator
  Christopher Columbus
  Claudius Ptolemy
  Amerigo Vespucci
  Satellite mapping
  Include drawings and illustrations with your essay.

②

I ■ 131

THE NATIONAL TOPOGRAPHIC MAP SERIES

Since 1879, the United States has maintained a topographic map program under the direction of the Geological Survey. The Geological Survey publishes the National Topographic Map Series, which provides information about the physical characteristics and human activities in all parts of the country.

■ Contour lines form closed loops around hilltops or depressions. Elevation numbers on the contour lines indicate whether a feature is a hilltop or a depression. If the numbers increase toward the center of the closed loop, the feature is a hilltop. If the numbers decrease, the feature is a depression. Sometimes elevation numbers are not given. Instead short dashes called hachures (HASH-oorz) are used to indicate a depression. Hachures are drawn perpendicular to the contour line that loops around a depression. The hachures point to the inside of the loop.

Now look at Figure 4–25. You should be able to understand all of the information on the map. What is the location of the depression? Which mountain ① has the steepest slope? In what direction does the Campbell River flow? Now look at Figure 4–26, Figure 4–27 on page 134 and Figure 4–28 on page 135. Use the legend in Figure 4–24 and the rules you have just learned to identify other topographic features.

Figure 4–25 *Once you learn the meanings of map symbols, topographic maps such as this one are easy to read. What does the symbol in green at the bottom of this map represent?* ②

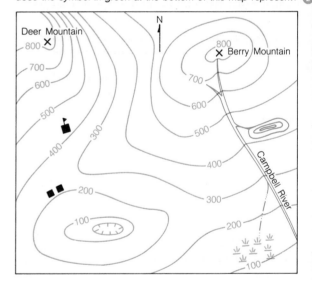

4–4 (continued)

CONTENT DEVELOPMENT

Use the rules listed on pages I131 and I132 to help students in their analysis of topographic maps. Then provide various topographic maps and have students analyze the maps. Have volunteers share their findings with the class.

GUIDED PRACTICE

▶ *Laboratory Manual*

Skills Development

Skills: Making observations, applying concepts

Students may now complete the Chapter 4 Laboratory Investigation in the *Laboratory Manual* called Using a Topographic Map. In this investigation students will use a simplified topographic map to locate a downed pilot.

REINFORCEMENT/RETEACHING

Make flashcards of the topographic-map symbols shown in Figure 4–24. On one side of each card, draw a topographic symbol. On the other side of the card, write the meaning of the symbol. Have students use the cards in small groups to reinforce their understanding of topographic symbols.

GUIDED PRACTICE

Skills Development
Skill: Interpreting maps

Have students observe the map in Figure 4–25. Ask these questions:
• **What is the contour interval used in this map?** (100 meters.)
• **How is an area of depression shown?** (With hachures.)
• **How do you know that the Campbell River originates in a mountain?** (The river is shown flowing out of an area that has an elevation of 800 meters.)
• **What feature is formed as a result of the branching of the river?** (A lake.)
• **At what elevation is the lake?** (About 450 meters.)

ENRICHMENT

▶ *Activity Book*

Students will be challenged by the Chapter 4 activity in the *Activity Book* called A Typical Topography. In this ac-

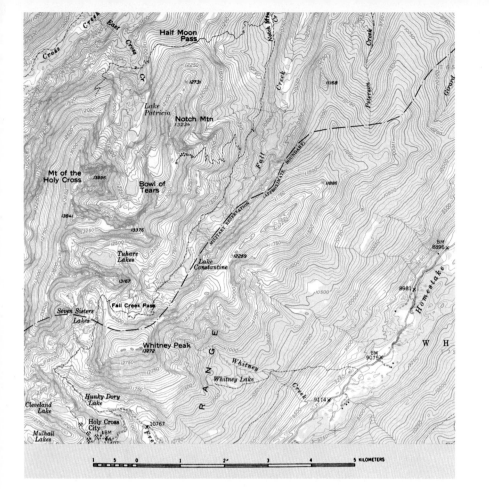

Figure 4-26 *This is a topographic map of Holy Cross Quadrangle, Colorado. What type of landscape region do you think this area is part of? How are changes in elevation shown? What is the highest point shown on this map?* ③

4–4 Section Review

1. How do topographic maps represent features of the Earth's surface?
2. What is a contour line? A contour interval?
3. Why is a map's legend important?

Critical Thinking—*Relating Concepts*

4. Why would it be difficult to show a vertical cliff on a topographic map?

I ■ 133

2. A contour line is a line on a map that passes through various points that all have the same elevation; the difference in elevation from one contour line to the next is a contour interval.
3. The legend explains the meaning of each map symbol.
4. A vertical cliff would require many contour intervals in one location.

tivity students will create a profile, or cross section, of a landform.

INDEPENDENT PRACTICE

▶ *Activity Book*

Students who need practice with the vocabulary and definitions associated with Earth's landmasses should complete the chapter activity Science Concentration. In this activity students will match vocabulary words and definitions.

INDEPENDENT PRACTICE

Section Review 4-4

1. Like other maps, topographic maps use symbols to represent features. Symbols for buildings and roads are usually black. Symbols for bodies of water such as rivers, lakes, and streams are blue. Green symbols represent woods and swamps. Contour lines are brown or red. All symbols of a topographic map are placed in a legend.

REINFORCEMENT/RETEACHING

Monitor students' responses to the Section Review questions. If students appear to have difficulty with any of the questions, review the appropriate material in the section.

CLOSURE

▶ *Review and Reinforcement Guide*

At this point have students complete Section 4–4 in the *Review and Reinforcement Guide.*

THE NATIONAL TOPOGRAPHIC MAP SERIES, PART II

All the maps in the National Topographic Map Series use the same symbols—which number more than 100 in variety—to depict various natural and human-made features. An important part of the symbols is their color. Black is used to indicate all human-made objects other than major roads. Black is also used for all names and labels. Blue is used to depict water features, including marshes. Contour lines and numbers indicate water depths. Brown is used for land-surface contour lines, for indications of land surface such as sand or mine tailings, and for certain elevation figures. Green is used to indicate vegetation, including forests, woodlands, orchards, and vineyards. Red is used for major roads and land-survey lines. Pink is used to indicate densely populated urban areas in which only landmark buildings are indicated individually. Purple appears on interim maps to indicate changes that have occurred since the previous edition.

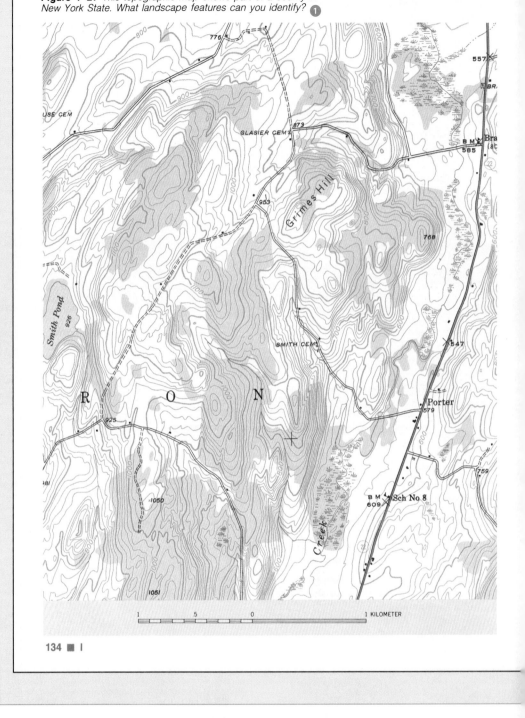

Figure 4–27 This topographic map shows part of a county in New York State. What landscape features can you identify? ❶

134 ■ I

4-4 (continued)

GUIDED PRACTICE

Skills Development

Skill: Interpreting maps

Have students observe the maps in Figures 4–27 and 4–28. Ask the following questions.

• **What obvious differences do you see as you look at these maps?** (The map in Figure 4–27 shows a region that is very hilly, whereas the map in Figure 4–28 shows an area that is relatively flat. The area shown in Figure 4–27 is an inland area, whereas the area shown in Figure 4–28 is a coastal area surrounded on three sides by water.)

• **What is the contour interval in Figure 4–27?** (20 meters.)
• **How can you tell?** (The elevation figures are 100 meters apart. In between each pair of elevation figures are four contour lines.)

• **What is the contour interval in Figure 4–28?** (80 meters.)
• **How can you tell?** (The contour lines are widely spaced, with no extra lines between the elevation figures. The elevation figures are 80 meters apart.)

ENRICHMENT

Have students work in small groups. Challenge each group to use the map in Figure 4–27 to plan a hike that takes them through Hebron County. Groups may wish to make photocopies of Figure 4–27 and then use a crayon or marker to draw their trail on the map. Have groups determine the length of their hike in kilometers and ask them to be able to justify their choice of trail based on the topography of the land surface.

Figure 4–28 *This topographic map shows part of the shoreline of California. What type of landscape region is this area part of?* 2

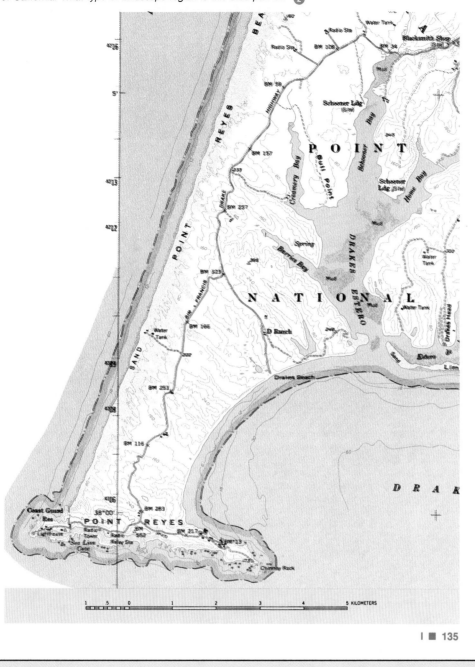

I ■ 135

REINFORCEMENT/RETEACHING

Have students work in small groups. On slips of paper, mark various topographic-map symbols. Place the symbols in a box or basket and have each group draw ten symbols at random out of the basket. Challenge each group to use the symbols they have drawn to create a topographic map.

GUIDED PRACTICE

Skills Development

Skill: Applying concepts

Divide the class into two teams. Using either Figure 4–27 or Figure 4–28, invite teams to participate in the following activity.

Begin by calling out a feature that appears on the map—for example,

"School" or "Elevation 1000 km." Allow each team to search for the feature. Repeat the procedure again with different map features.

Laboratory Investigation

MAKING A TOPOGRAPHIC MAP

BEFORE THE LAB

1. At least one day prior to the investigation, gather enough materials for your class, assuming six students per group.
2. In order to save time during the lab, you may want to have students build the model the day before and then allow the model to dry overnight.

PRE-LAB DISCUSSION

Have students read the complete laboratory procedure.
• **What is a contour line?** (It is a line connecting locations of equal elevation on a topographic map.)
• **What is a contour interval?** (The difference in elevation from one contour line to the next.)
• **Should the contour intervals that we draw remain consistent throughout all parts of the map?** (Yes.)
• **Will we be using any topographic symbols in the activity other than contour lines?** (No.)

TEACHING STRATEGY

1. Explain to students that there is no correct or incorrect way to construct a clay model of a hill. Their model hill can assume any shape, given the limits of the amount of clay and the size of the container.
2. Remind students to be very careful when handling the sheet of glass. Caution them not to place any object on the glass and to always lay the glass down flat when it is not on top of the aquarium or pan. Also, stress to students that they should report any cracked or broken glass immediately.

Laboratory Investigation

Making a Topographic Map

Problem

What information can a topographic map provide about the surface features of the Earth?

Materials (per group)

modeling clay	glass-marking pencil
metric ruler	1 L water
rigid cardboard	pencil
pane of clear glass	sheet of unlined,
aquarium tank or	white paper
deep-sided pan	

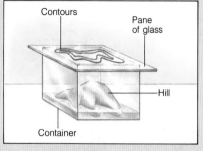

Contours
Pane of glass
Hill
Container

Procedure ⚠️

1. Cut the cardboard to fit the bottom of the tank or pan.
2. On top of the cardboard, shape the clay into a model of a hill. Include on the model some gullies, a steep slope, and a gentle slope.
3. When the model is dry and hard, place the model and cardboard into the tank or pan. Pour water into the container to a depth of 1 cm. This will represent sea level.
4. Place the pane of glass over the container. Looking straight down into the container, use the glass-marking pencil to trace the outline of the container on the glass. Also trace on the glass the contour, or outline, of the water around the edges of the model. Carefully remove the pane of glass from the container.
5. Add another centimeter of water to the container. The depth of the water should now be 2 cm. Place the glass in exactly the same position as before. Trace the new contour of the water on the pane of glass.

6. Repeat step 5, adding 1 cm to the depth of the water each time. Stop when the next addition of water would completely cover the model.
7. Remove the pane of glass. With a pencil, trace the contours on the glass onto a sheet of paper. This will be your topographic map.
8. Assume that every centimeter of water you added to the first centimeter (sea level) equals 100 m of elevation on the map. Label the elevation of each contour line on your topographic map.

Observations

1. What is the approximate elevation of the top of the hill?
2. How can you determine if the hill has a steep slope by looking at the contour lines?
3. How can you determine if the hill has a gentle slope by looking at the contour lines?
4. How do contour lines look when they show gullies on the model?

Analysis and Conclusions

What information can a topographic map provide about the Earth's surface?

DISCOVERY STRATEGIES

Discuss how the investigation relates to the chapter by asking open questions similar to the following.
• **Why do scientists build models?** (Lead students to suggest that a model is used to represent something that cannot be seen or measured directly—analyzing, relating.)
• **Can models also be used to make a concept clearer or to present that concept in a more meaningful way?** (Yes.

Point out to students that this is the function of this modeling activity—analyzing, relating.)
• **Predict what you think your topographic map will look like.** (Accept all reasonable predictions—predicting.)
• **What do you think a model of a hill might look like if its map had contour lines that were very close together?** (The model would change elevation quickly or the contour interval of its map was very small—predicting, analyzing.)
• **What do you think a model of a hill**

Study Guide

Summarizing Key Concepts

4–1 The Continents

▲ There are seven continents on Earth: Africa, Antarctica, Asia, Australia, Europe, North America, and South America.

4–2 Topography

▲ The shape of the Earth's surface is called its topography.

▲ The different physical features of an area are called its landscape.

▲ The three main types of landscape regions are mountains, plains, and plateaus.

▲ One characteristic of a landscape region is elevation. The difference in a region's elevations is called its relief.

▲ Mountains have high elevations, and are areas of high relief.

▲ Mountains are usually part of larger groups called mountain ranges, mountain systems, and mountain belts.

▲ Plains are flat land areas that are not far above sea level. They are areas of low relief.

▲ Low, flat areas along the coast are called coastal plains. Low, flat areas found inland are called interior plains.

▲ Plateaus are broad, flat areas that rise more than 600 meters above sea level.

4–3 Mapping the Earth's Surface

▲ A map is a drawing of the Earth, or part of the Earth, on a flat surface. The most accurate representation of the Earth is a globe.

▲ The Earth is divided by lines that run from north to south, called meridians, and by lines that run from east to west, called parallels.

▲ Meridians are used to measure longitude. Parallels are used to measure latitude.

▲ The Earth is divided into 24 time zones.

4–4 Topographic Maps

▲ Topographic maps show the different shapes and sizes of land surfaces.

▲ Topographic maps use contour lines to show relief.

Reviewing Key Terms

Define each term in a complete sentence.

4–1 The Continents
island
continent

4–2 Topography
topography
landscape
elevation
relief
mountain
mountain range
mountain system
mountain belt

plain
coastal plain
interior plain
plateau

4–3 Mapping the Earth's Surface
map
globe
scale
meridian
prime meridian
longitude

time zone
international date line
parallel
equator
latitude
projection
Mercator projection
equal-area projection

4–4 Topographic Maps
topographic map
contour line

I ■ 137

GOING FURTHER: ENRICHMENT
Part 1

Have students "reverse" the investigation by finding a topographic map, then building a model hill to represent a portion of the map. Have students use the contour lines they drew in this investigation to determine the relationship between the contour lines on the map and the various elevations of their model hill.

Part 2

Have students think of situations from everyday life in which a topographic map would be useful. For example, hikers use topographic maps in order to assess the difficulty of the trails they will be hiking. People building a house might want to consider the topography of the region in which they will be building. Someone wishing to establish a farm or industrial complex in a particular area might be concerned about the topography of that area.

---

might look like if its map had contour lines that were very far apart? (The model would not change elevation quickly or the contour interval of its map was very large—predicting, analyzing.)

OBSERVATIONS

1. Answers will vary, depending on the model students construct.
2. The contour lines will be close together.
3. The contour lines will be spaced farther apart.

4. The contour lines have a slight V-shaped indent where they cross the gully.

ANALYSIS AND CONCLUSIONS

1. Students should conclude that topographic maps can show the shapes and sizes of landscape features. Topographic maps also show the land's relief using contour lines.

Chapter Review

Chapter Review

ALTERNATIVE ASSESSMENT

The *Prentice Hall Science* program includes a variety of testing components and methodologies. Aside from the Chapter Review questions, you may opt to use the Chapter Test or the Computer Test Bank Test in your *Test Book* for assessment of important facts and concepts. In addition, Performance-Based Tests are included in your *Test Book*. These Performance-Based Tests are designed to test science process skills, rather than factual content recall. Since they are not content dependent, Performance-Based Tests can be distributed after students complete a chapter or after they complete the entire textbook.

CONTENT REVIEW

Multiple Choice

1. b
2. c
3. c
4. a
5. b
6. b
7. d
8. a
9. b

True or False

1. F, North America
2. F, plateaus
3. F, Plateaus
4. T
5. F, equator
6. T

Concept Mapping

Row 1: Form continents
Row 2: Africa, Australia, North
  America, South America,
  Antarctica

Content Review

Multiple Choice

Choose the letter of the answer that best completes each statement.

1. The smallest landmass that is still considered a continent is
   a. North America.   c. Africa.
   b. Australia.   d. Greenland.
2. Large areas of very old, exposed rock that form the core of a continent are called
   a. icecaps.   c. shields.
   b. mountains.   d. meridians.
3. Tops of mountains are called
   a. gorges.   c. summits.
   b. elevations.   d. projections.
4. Individual mountains are usually
   a. volcanic mountains.
   b. mountain systems.
   c. plateaus.
   d. none of these.
5. The landscape region with the lowest overall elevation is a(an)
   a. mountain belt.   c. plateau.
   b. coastal plain.   d. interior plain.

6. Broad, flat areas of land more than 600 meters above sea level are called
   a. plains.   c. farmland.
   b. plateaus.   d. mountains.
7. The measure of distance east or west of the prime meridian is called
   a. latitude.   c. projection.
   b. parallel.   d. longitude.
8. A map projection that shows the correct shape of coastlines but distorts the sizes of regions far from the equator is called a(an)
   a. Mercator projection.
   b. topographic map.
   c. equal-area projection.
   d. contour projection.
9. Lines on a map that pass through points with the same elevation are called
   a. meridians.   c. parallels.
   b. contour lines.   d. lines of relief.

True or False

If the statement is true, write "true." If it is false, change the underlined word or words to make the statement true.

1. Central America is part of the continent of <u>South America</u>.
2. The three main types of landscape regions are mountains, plains, and <u>continents</u>.
3. <u>Plains</u> are flat areas of land that rise more than 600 meters above sea level.
4. The distance around the world is measured in <u>degrees</u>.
5. The <u>prime meridian</u> divides the parallels of north latitude from those of south latitude.
6. The time in a city one time zone <u>west</u> of another city will be one hour earlier.

Concept Mapping

Complete the following concept map for Section 4–1. Refer to pages 16–17 to construct a concept map for the entire chapter.

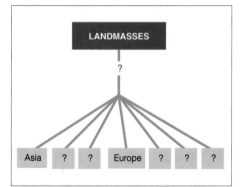

CONCEPT MASTERY

1. Asia, Africa, Antarctica, Australia, North America, South America, Europe; Australia; Antarctica; North America and South America, and Asia, Europe, and Africa.

2. Moving water can erode crevices into the sides of mountains, can smooth rugged areas, or can create flat areas by releasing the sediments it carries.

3. The difference in a region's elevations is called its relief; a steep mountain will display high relief; a flat coastal plain will display low relief.

4. Both plains are relatively flat areas with low relief. Coastal plains, however, reach only about 150 meters above sea level, whereas interior plains have an elevation of about 450 meters above sea level.

5. The international date line is the place where a day begins in the Earth's timekeeping system.

6. Maps and globes are useful for displaying Earth's landmasses and bodies of

Concept Mastery

Discuss each of the following in a brief paragraph.

1. List the continents. Which continent is also a country? Which continent is almost completely covered by a thick icecap? Which continents are joined to form larger landmasses?
2. How is the topography of an area changed by moving water?
3. Define relief as it relates to Earth's topography. What landscape feature would have high relief? Low relief?
4. What are the similarities and differences between interior plains and coastal plains?
5. Why is the international date line important to travelers?
6. In what ways are maps and globes useful?
7. Why is a map's legend important? What kinds of information can you find in a map's legend?

Critical Thinking and Problem Solving

Use the skills you have developed in this chapter to answer each of the following.

1. **Applying concepts** Explain why the distance measured by degrees of latitude always stays the same, while the distance measured by degrees of longitude varies.
2. **Making predictions** Most of the Earth's ice is found on or around Antarctica. Suppose the temperature of the area around the South Pole climbs above freezing and all of Antarctica's ice melts. Which landscape regions in the rest of the world would be most affected? Why?
3. **Interpreting maps** In Figure 4–27, what contour interval is used? At what elevation is School Number 8? If you wanted to take an easy climb up Grimes Hill, which slope would you choose to climb? Why? Why would you not want to hike in the area located just west of the major highway? Locate the unpaved road west of Grimes Hill. How many kilometers would you walk if you walked from one end of the road to the other? Does the stream flow in or out of Smith Pond? How can you tell?
4. **Relating concepts** Suppose you are the captain of a large ocean liner sailing across the Pacific Ocean from Asia to North America. You notice that the maps in your cabin have the same projection as the map shown in Figure 4–21 on page 127. Are you in trouble? Why?
5. **Applying concepts** You want to go camping with some friends in a national park. You plan to hike into the park on a highway, then leave the road to make your own trails in the forest. How would a road map help you? How would a topographic map of the area help you?
6. **Making maps** Draw topographic maps of three imaginary areas. The first area has a mountain landscape; the second has a plains landscape; the third has several plateaus separated by rivers.
7. **Using the writing process** You are lost in the deep woods with only a scrap of paper, a pencil, a small amount of supplies, and your faithful homing pigeon, Homer. You plan to send Homer for help. Write a note to tie to Homer's leg. Include a map of your location.

I ■ 139

KEEPING A PORTFOLIO

You may want to assign some of the Concept Mastery and Critical Thinking and Problem Solving questions as homework and have students include their responses to unassigned questions in their portfolio. Students should be encouraged to include both the question and the answer in their portfolio.

ISSUES IN SCIENCE

The following issues can be used as springboards for discussion or given as writing assignments.

1. Throughout the Earth's history, the surface of the Earth has changed many times. Since the beginning of civilization, human activities have contributed to these changes, Sometimes when people hear the word *change*, they automatically think of something negative. But are changes always negative? Think of the ways in which the Earth's surface has changed. Then think of what the Earth would be like if there had been no changes. Present your opinion as to whether you think the Earth is better or worse off as a result of the many changes that have taken place.

2. Each type of map projection is accurate in some ways and distorted in other ways. Do you think it would be possible to design a map projection that compensates for all distortions? For example, could the distortion of land area in a Mercator projection be corrected by such adjustments as making Greenland smaller? Learn about the advantages and disadvantages of as many different types of projections as you can. Then offer your opinion as to whether a totally accurate projection could be designed.

---

water and for giving distances along straight lines, and they are somewhat useful for showing the general proportions of features.

7. The legend of a map makes sense of the symbols used on that map; the information contained in a legend will vary, depending on the particular map.

CRITICAL THINKING AND PROBLEM SOLVING

1. Lines of latitude are parallel and equidistant; lines of longitude are not equidistant because they converge into one point at each pole.

2. The coastal regions would be most affected because they are low-lying areas located next to major bodies of water. These areas would become flooded quite easily.

3. Contour interval: 20 feet; elevation: 600 feet; go up the southwest slope; it is least steep; the area west of the highway is covered by swamps; distance: 2.6 kilometers; stream flows out of the lake toward the south; you can tell because the

SECTION	HANDS-ON ACTIVITIES
5–1 The Earth's Core pages I142–I145 Multicultural Opportunity 5–1, p. I142 ESL Strategy 5–1, p. I142	**Student Edition** ACTIVITY (Doing): What Is the Cause of Earthquakes? p. I142 **Laboratory Manual** A Model of the Earth's Interior, p. I55 **Teacher Edition** The Movement of Waves, p. I140d
5–2 The Earth's Mantle pages I146–I147 Multicultural Opportunity 5–2, p. I146 ESL Strategy 5–2, p. I146	**Student Edition** ACTIVITY (Doing): A Model of the Earth's Interior, p. I147 **Laboratory Manual** Observing the Action of Gases in a Magma, p. I47 **Teacher Edition** Plasticity, p. I140d
5–3 The Earth's Crust pages I148–I151 Multicultural Opportunity 5–3, p. I148 ESL Strategy 5–3, p. I148	**Student Edition** LABORATORY INVESTIGATION: Simulating Plasticity, p. I152 ACTIVITY BANK: How Hard Is That Rock? p. I172 **Laboratory Manual** Determining the Density of the Earth, p. I51
Chapter Review pages I152–I155	

OUTSIDE TEACHER RESOURCES

Books

Jacobs, J. A. *The Earth's Core,* Academy Press.

Sawkins, Frederick J., et al. *The Evolving Earth* (2nd ed.), Macmillan.

Sparks, John, and Arthur Bourne. *Planet Earth: Earth's Atmosphere and Crust,* Doubleday.

Audiovisuals

Earth in Change—The Earth's Crust, 16-mm film, Encyclopaedia Britannica

The Earth's Crust, filmstrip with cassette, SVE

Strata—The Earth's Changing Crust, 16-mm film, BFA

What Moved the Mountains? What Shaped the Seas?, 16-mm film, UEVA

OTHER ACTIVITIES	MEDIA AND TECHNOLOGY
Student Edition ACTIVITY (Writing): Shake and Quake, p. I144 ACTIVITY (Calculating): The Speed of Seismic Waves, p. I145 **Activity Book** CHAPTER DISCOVERY: Exploring the Earth's Interior, p. I141 ACTIVITY: Richter Scale, p. I145 ACTIVITY: How Does the Intensity of an Earthquake Change With Distance? p. I153 **Review and Reinforcement Guide** Section 5–1, p. I47	**Interactive Videodisc** Planet Earth: The Force Within **Transparency Binder** S and P Waves **English/Spanish Audiotapes** Section 5–1
Activity Book ACTIVITY: The Earth's Interior, p. I149 ACTIVITY: Making a Scale Model of the Earth's Interior, p. I151 **Review and Reinforcement Guide** Section 5–2, p. I49	**English/Spanish Audiotapes** Section 5–2
Student Edition ACTIVITY (Calculating): How Many Earths? p. I149 **Activity Book** ACTIVITY: Layers of the Earth, p. I147 ACTIVITY: Determining How Fast Some Crustal Plates Move, p. I157 **Review and Reinforcement Guide** Section 5–3, p. I51	**Interactive Videodisc** ScienceVision: TerraVision **English/Spanish Audiotapes** Section 5–3
Test Book Chapter Test, p. I99 Performance-Based Tests, p. I119	**Test Book** Computer Test Bank Test, p. I105

*All materials in the Chapter Planning Guide Grid are available as part of the Prentice Hall Science Learning System.

CHAPTER OVERVIEW

Scientists divide the Earth into four layers: the inner core, the outer core, the mantle, and the crust. The region that separates the mantle from the crust is called the Moho. The Earth is divided into these layers based on the characteristics of the materials that make up each layer. Such factors as the type of rock, whether the material is solid or liquid, and the intensity of temperature and pressure are all taken into account. As one moves from the surface of the Earth to the inner core, both the temperature and pressure increase.

For the most part, scientists have been able to learn about the Earth's interior only by indirect evidence. Nearly all that scientists know about the inner Earth has come from the study of earthquake, or seismic, waves.

The characteristics of the layers of the Earth allow the uppermost solid layers, those in the lithosphere, to move. The lithosphere is broken up into large sections called plates. The movement of the lithospheric plates underlies the theory of continental drift.

5-1 THE EARTH'S CORE
THEMATIC FOCUS

The purpose of this section is to explain to students how scientists use seismic waves to gather information about the Earth's interior. They will discover that the movement of P waves and S waves have provided much of our knowledge about the inner Earth.

Because S waves cannot travel through liquids, the termination of S waves at a depth of 2900 kilometers indicates the beginning of a liquid layer of Earth at this level. The fact that P waves slow down as they travel through liquid supports this conclusion and also indicates that the Earth becomes solid once again at a depth of 5150 kilometers.

The themes that can be focused on in this section are energy, patterns of change, and systems and interactions.

*Energy: The energy released during an earthquake generates seismic waves. These waves have been used by scientists to gather information about the Earth's interior.

*Patterns of change: Pressure and temperature increase as you approach the Earth's center.

*Systems and interactions: Iron in the Earth's inner core is believed to be the source of the Earth's magnetic field.

PERFORMANCE OBJECTIVES 5-1

1. **Explain how the Earth's structure has been determined from seismic evidence.**
2. **Describe the properties of P waves and S waves.**
3. **Describe the composition of the Earth's inner and outer core.**

SCIENCE TERMS 5-1

seismic waves p. I142
seismograph p. I143
inner core p. I144
outer core p. I145

5-2 THE EARTH'S MANTLE
THEMATIC FOCUS

The purpose of this section is to introduce students to the features of the Earth's mantle. They will learn that the mantle extends to a depth of 2900 kilometers below the Earth's surface and lies above the Earth's outer core. They will also learn about the composition of the mantle and how the density, pressure, and temperature of the mantle increase with depth.

Students will discover that the boundary between the Earth's crust and the mantle is called the Moho. They will read about how this region was discovered by seismologist Mohorovicic when he observed a change in the speed of seismic waves at a depth of 32 to 64 kilometers below the Earth's surface.

The themes that can be focused on in this section are evolution and scale and structure.

Evolution: Over time, the crust of the Earth changes as materials produced within the Earth's interior come to the surface.

*Scale and structure: There are four layers in the Earth's interior. Most of the mass and volume of the Earth is contained within the mantle.

PERFORMANCE OBJECTIVES 5-2

1. **Describe the location and composition of the Earth's mantle.**
2. **Explain what is meant by the Moho.**
3. **Describe changes of temperature and pressure at increasing depths in the mantle.**

SCIENCE TERMS 5-2

mantle p. I146
Moho p. I146
plasticity p. I147

5-3 THE EARTH'S CRUST
THEMATIC FOCUS

The purpose of this section is to introduce students to the chief characteristics of the Earth's crust. This is the most familiar part of the Earth. All life on Earth exists on or within a few hundred meters above the crust.

Students will learn that the crust is made up of three types of solid rock—igneous, sedimentary, and metamorphic. They will also learn that the crust under the continents, which is called continental crust, differs from the crust under the oceans, which is called oceanic crust. Continental crust is about four times thicker than oceanic crust.

Students will discover that the Earth's crust forms the upper part of what is called the lithosphere, the topmost solid part of the Earth.

The themes that can be focused on in this section are unity and diversity and stability.

Unity and diversity: The Earth's inner core is made mostly of iron and nickel. The mantle and the crust contain other elements in addition to iron and nickel.

*Stability: Conditions of temperature and pressure within the layers of the Earth's interior remain relatively stable.

PERFORMANCE OBJECTIVES 5–3

1. Describe the composition of the Earth's crust.
2. Compare continental crust with oceanic crust.
3. Define lithosphere.

SCIENCE TERMS 5–3

crust p. I148
lithosphere p. I149
asthenosphere p. I150

Discovery Learning

TEACHER DEMONSTRATIONS MODELING

The Movement of Waves

Use a Slinky toy to demonstrate the movement of P waves and S waves. While moving the Slinky along a horizontal path, alternatively stretch and contract the Slinky. Explain that this movement is similar to that of a longitudinal wave, which vibrates parallel to the direction of travel. The seismic waves known as P waves are longitudinal waves.

In order to demonstrate S waves, ask a student to help you by holding one end of the Slinky while you hold the other end. Vibrate the Slinky up and down while moving it along a horizontal path. Explain that this movement is similar to that of transverse waves, which vibrate perpendicular to the line of travel. The seismic waves known as S waves are transverse waves.

Plasticity

Use plastic putty to demonstrate the property of plasticity. Before showing the putty to the class, roll the putty into a smooth ball or egg shape.
- **Is this substance a liquid or a solid?** (Most students will answer solid.)
- **Why do you say solid?** (It has a definite shape; it is not runny or wet.)

Begin to pull and stretch the putty and then mold it into a very different shape.
- **Do you still think this substance is a solid?** (Answers will vary.)

- **How is its behavior different from that of most solids?** (It can be stretched, bent, and easily molded into different shapes.)

Explain that this special quality of the putty is called plasticity. Although considered a solid, a plastic material has the ability to flow.

If a refrigerator is available in or near your classroom, you may want to leave the putty in the freezer overnight and then let the class see what happens to the putty's plasticity. (The putty should lose all or most of its plasticity, become brittle, and break easily.)
- **Can you determine a relationship between temperature and plasticity?** (Plasticity decreases as temperature decreases and increases as temperature increases.)

CHAPTER 5
Earth's Interior

INTEGRATING SCIENCE

This earth science chapter provides you with numerous opportunities to integrate other areas of science, as well as other disciplines, into your curriculum. Blue numbered annotations on the student page and integration notes on the teacher wraparound pages alert you to areas of possible integration.

In this chapter you can integrate earth science and earthquakes (p. 143), language arts (p. 144), mathematics (pp. 145, 149), and earth science and rocks and minerals (p. 151).

SCIENCE, TECHNOLOGY, AND SOCIETY/COOPERATIVE LEARNING

Earth scientists have developed a more detailed model of the Earth's interior by using the geological equivalent of a CAT scan. Making use of medical technology has allowed scientists to develop a three-dimensional model of the Earth. In computerized tomography, X-rays penetrate the human body from all directions and provide doctors with a three-dimensional image of the body. Bones, tumors, and organs are easily identified because they have different densities and absorb X-rays differently.

Similarly, in seismic tomography, X-rays are used in place of seismic waves. Explosions are used to generate the seismic waves that provide scientists with data to analyze. As you know, seismic waves travel at different speeds in the Earth, depending on the temperature and density of the rock through which they travel. By examining seismic tomograms, scientists have learned that the layers of the Earth are not uniform. The tomograms used in conjunction with other measurements and data have enabled scientists to map the location and shape of the hot (less dense) and cool (more dense) regions of the Earth's interior.

INTRODUCING CHAPTER 5

DISCOVERY LEARNING

▶ *Activity Book*

Begin your introduction to this chapter by using the Chapter 5 Discovery Activity from the *Activity Book*. Using this activity, students will have an opportunity to speculate about conditions in the interior of the Earth.

USING THE TEXTBOOK

Have students examine the photograph and read the chapter introduction.
• **How would you describe this photograph?** (Accept all answers.)
• **How far into the Earth do you think the scientists in the photograph will be able to descend?** (Accept all answers, but lead students to understand that intense heat and pressure would prevent any very deep descent.)
• **How far underground did the char-**

Earth's Interior

In 1864, Jules Verne wrote *Journey to the Center of the Earth*. In this exciting and imaginative tale, Verne describes his idea of what lies hidden beneath the surface of planet Earth.

Verne was not the only person to be fascinated by this unknown world. For many years, scientists have explored the interior of the Earth. But they have not been able to use mechanical probes such as those that explore outer space. The tremendous heat and pressure in the Earth's interior make this region far more difficult to explore than it is to explore planets millions of kilometers away.

In this chapter you will learn about the structure and composition of each layer of the Earth. Afterward, you may want to read *Journey to the Center of the Earth*—and compare Jules Verne's description with the scientific model of the Earth's interior.

Journal *Activity*

You and Your World Have you ever visited a cave or a cavern? If so, in your journal write about your feelings upon first entering the cave's depths. If you have never visited a cave, use your imagination to describe what you think it might be like to walk beneath the surface of the Earth.

◀ *Dangling by what appears to be a slender thread, a group of scientists descend into the Earth.*

I ■ 141

The analysis of seismic tomograms is enabling scientists to better understand the interior of the Earth and how it relates to plate tectonics—both areas of subduction and sea-floor spreading.

Cooperative learning: Using preassigned lab groups or randomly selected teams, have groups discuss the following questions prior to a classroom discussion.

- What are some other ways in which scientists might use seismic tomography?
- Do you feel it is important to spend money researching the Earth's interior? Give reasons to support your position.
- Seismic tomography results from the application of medical science in the area of geology. What other types of scientific technology or products have been applied in new ways? (Possible answers are spinoffs from space technology, spinoffs and the use of seismographs in monitoring nuclear explosions.)
- See Cooperative Learning in the *Teacher's Desk Reference*.

JOURNAL ACTIVITY

You may want to use the Journal Activity as the basis of class discussion. After students have completed their journal entries, discuss how their experiences might have changed if a small earthquake had occurred while they were in the cave. Students should be instructed to keep their Journal Activity in their portfolio.

---

acters in Jules Verne's novel go? (To the center of the Earth.)

Point out that when we hear the word *exploring,* we usually think of going to a new place—the way Columbus went to the New World or the astronauts journeyed to the moon. Sometimes, however, direct exploration of an area is not possible.

- **Do you think anyone has ever explored the center of the Earth? Explain.** (No. Intense heat and pressure make it impossible for anyone to reach the center of the Earth.)

- **What do you think causes such great heat and pressure?** (Accept all logical answers.)

- **Why is it easier for scientists to reach far into outer space than to reach deep into the Earth?** (Satellites and spaceships can be built to withstand the conditions in outer space, but no scientific device can withstand the conditions in the interior of the Earth.)

Explain that scientists use indirect evidence to study the interior of the Earth.
- **Can you think of other situations in which indirect evidence has been used in scientific research?** (Answers will vary. Possible answers include gathering information about the atom and subatomic particles and gathering information about places in outer space that have not yet been explored directly.)

As you continue with this chapter, keep in mind that the study of the Earth's interior is an excellent example of the use of indirect evidence. Guide students to recognize that gathering indirect evidence is an important part of the scientific method when something cannot be observed or measured directly.

5-1 The Earth's Core

MULTICULTURAL OPPORTUNITY 5-1

Have students investigate some of the world's well-known earthquakes, including the disaster in San Francisco in 1906. Where are earthquakes most likely to occur? If you have students from other countries, ask them to tell the class about any earthquakes that have occurred in those regions.

ESL STRATEGY 5-1

Write the words and the sentences below on the chalkboard. Ask for volunteers to complete each sentence by choosing words from the box. Words may be used more than once. The answers are given in parentheses.

melt	slower	core	begin
radio	5150	iron	stop
outer	seismic	2900	
faster	inner	liquid	
solid	waves	nickel	

1. Scientists use _____ _____ to find out what the inside of the Earth is like. (Seismic, waves.)
2. P waves (primary waves) travel _____ and S waves (secondary waves) _____ at _____ kilometers deep. The Earth's _____ _____, which is believed to be _____, begins at this depth. (Slower, stop, 2900, outer, core, liquid.)
3. At a depth of _____ kilometers, P waves travel _____ in a temperature of 5000°C. Heat often causes solids to _____; however, increased pressure keeps the _____ _____ _____. (5150, faster, melt, inner, core, solid.)
4. Elements of _____ and _____ are found in both layers of the Earth's interior. (Iron, nickel.)

Guide for Reading

Focus on this question as you read.

▶ How do seismic waves provide evidence about the structure of the Earth's interior?

What Is the Cause of Earthquakes?

1. Obtain four carpet samples of different colors.
2. Stack the samples on top of one another.
3. Place one hand on each side of the carpet pile and gently press toward the center. Describe what happens.

If the layers of carpet were actually layers of rock, what would happen?

Figure 5-1 *An earthquake in San Francisco twisted and cracked this highway (left). An earthquake in Armenia reduced buildings to rubble (right).*

5-1 The Earth's Core

Scientists use telescopes and space probes to gather information about the planets and the stars. They use microscopes to examine unseen worlds of life on Earth. They use computers and other instruments to gather information about atoms, the building blocks of all matter. So you might find it surprising to learn that most of the information scientists have gathered about the Earth's interior has not come from complex instruments but from earthquakes.

Earthquakes and Seismic Waves

Earthquakes are produced when a part of the Earth's uppermost layer moves suddenly. During an earthquake, the ground shakes and trembles. Sometimes the movement is so violent that buildings crash to the ground and roads and highways are destroyed. Earthquakes produce shock waves that travel through the Earth. These shock waves, which are actually waves of energy, are called **seismic** (SIGHZ-mihk) **waves.** You can make a simple model to show how shock waves move. Fill a sink or basin half full with water and then drop a small pebble onto the center of the water's surface. You will observe waves that move outward from the pebble's point of impact in circles of ever-increasing size.

All earthquakes produce at least two types of seismic waves at the same time: P waves and S waves. These waves are detected and recorded by a special

---

TEACHING STRATEGY 5-1

FOCUS/MOTIVATION

Have students observe the photographs in Figure 5-1.
• **What caused the bridge and houses to collapse into the Earth?** (Earthquakes.)
• **Have any of you ever experienced an earthquake?** (Answers will vary. Have students share any experiences they may have had and any results of an earthquake that they may have seen.)

Point out that although the photographs show very obvious results of an earthquake, some effects of an earthquake are not so obvious. The movement of P waves and S waves do not cause houses to tumble into the ground, but they do show up on sensitive instruments called seismographs.

Media and Technology

An alternative way to begin the lesson is to have students use the Interactive

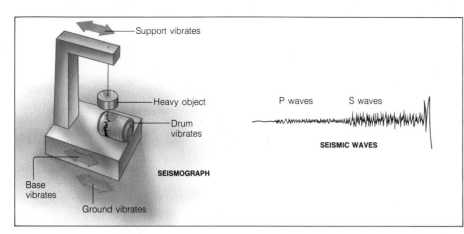

SEISMOGRAPH

SEISMIC WAVES

P waves   S waves

Support vibrates

Heavy object

Drum vibrates

Base vibrates

Ground vibrates

instrument called a **seismograph** (SIGHZ-muh-graf). Figure 5–2 describes what a seismograph looks like and how it works. Seismic waves penetrate the depths of the Earth and return to the surface. During this passage, the speed and direction of the waves change. The changes that occur in the movement of seismic waves are caused by differences in the structure and makeup of the Earth's interior. By recording and studying the waves, scientists have been able to "see" into the interior of the Earth.

Exactly how have P waves and S waves helped scientists develop a model of the Earth's inner structure? At a depth of 2900 kilometers below Earth's surface, P waves passing through the Earth slow down rapidly. S waves disappear. Scientists know that P waves do not move well through liquids and that S waves are stopped completely. So the changes in the movement of the two seismic waves at a depth of 2900 kilometers indicate something significant. Do you know what it is? You are right if you say that 2900 kilometers is the beginning of a liquid layer of the Earth. At a depth of 5150 kilometers, P waves increase their speed. This increase indicates that P waves are no longer traveling through a liquid layer. Instead, P waves are passing through a solid layer of the Earth.

After observing the speeds of P waves and S waves, scientists have concluded that the Earth's center, or core, is actually made up of two layers with different characteristics.

Figure 5–2 *A seismograph (left) detects and records earthquake waves, or seismic waves. A typical pattern of seismic waves is shown (right). What are the two types of seismic waves?* ❶

Figure 5–3 *P waves push together and pull apart rock particles in the direction of the wave movement. The slower S waves move rock particles from side to side at right angles to the wave movement.*

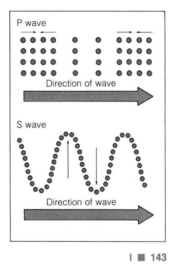

P wave

Direction of wave

S wave

Direction of wave

I ■ 143

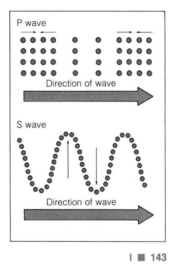

A C T I V I T Y
D O I N G

WHAT IS THE CAUSE OF EARTHQUAKES?

Skills: Manipulative, making observations, predicting
Materials: carpet samples

This simple hands-on activity allows students to make a simple model that illustrates folding in the Earth's crust. Students should observe that pressure exerted on the sides of the carpets causes the carpet samples to mound up in the middle. Students should infer that pressure on portions of Earth's crust may cause crustal movements elsewhere. If the layers of carpet were layers of rock, pressure from the sides would cause the rocks to move or break.

Videodisc called Planet Earth: The Force Within.

After students have used the videodisc, have them prepare written reports comparing the forces that cause earthquakes with those that cause volcanoes.

CONTENT DEVELOPMENT

Explain to students that a wave is a rhythmic disturbance that transmits energy from one place to another.
• **In the case of earthquake waves, where does the energy come from?** (From the breaking and sliding of rocks under the Earth.)
• **What indirect method have scientists used to learn about the Earth's interior?** (Scientists have studied earthquake waves that have been recorded on seismographs around the world.)

● ● ● ●   **Integration**   ● ● ● ●

Use the discussion of seismic waves to integrate earthquakes into your lesson.

REINFORCEMENT/RETEACHING

▶ *Activity Book*
You may wish to use the Chapter 5 activity called Richter Scale to help students understand how earthquakes are measured.

🏛 Media and Technology

Use the transparency in the *Transparency Binder* called S and P Waves to help develop the concepts in this section.

SHAKE AND QUAKE

This activity reinforces vocabulary and composition skills while allowing students to use their knowledge of the Earth's core in a creative way.

Before students write their compositions, you may want them to read Jules Verne's *Journey to the Center of the Earth* or a similar story to find out how a writer mixes scientific theories with fictional ideas.

Integration: Use this Activity to integrate language arts into your science lesson.

5-1 (continued)

FOCUS/MOTIVATION

Place a pane of thin glass over a bar magnet. Sprinkle some iron filings over the top of the glass. Tap it gently. The tapping moves the filings, and they form a pattern around the magnet. The pattern of the iron filings shows the invisible lines of force that are between the north and south poles of a bar magnet.

Scientists think the solid iron in the inner core produces an effect similar to the effect around the magnet. The Earth acts like a giant bar magnet with lines of force in the same pattern as the bar magnet.

CONTENT DEVELOPMENT

• **What behavior of P waves and S waves convinced scientists that the Earth's outer core is liquid?** (S waves stopped completely at the outer core, and P waves slowed down.)

• **What convinced scientists that the Earth's inner core is solid?** (The P waves, which had slowed down as they passed through the outer core, began to speed up.)

Have students examine Figure 5–4.

Figure 5–4 *The paths of seismic waves change as they travel through the Earth. P waves slow down as they pass through the liquid outer core. As they leave the outer core and pass through the inner core, P waves speed up. This change in speed bends the waves. S waves disappear as they enter the outer core. Why? Notice* **(1)** *that a wave-free shadow zone extends all the way around the Earth. The shadow zone is produced by the bending of seismic waves.*

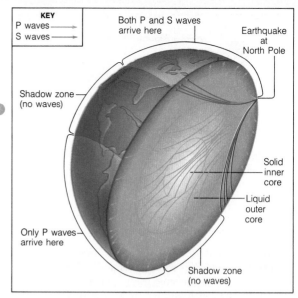

KEY
P waves →
S waves →

Both P and S waves arrive here

Earthquake at North Pole

Shadow zone (no waves)

Solid inner core

Liquid outer core

Only P waves arrive here

Shadow zone (no waves)

The Earth's Core

Both layers of the Earth's core are made of the elements iron and nickel. The solid, innermost layer is called the **inner core.** Here iron and nickel are under a great deal of pressure. The temperature of the inner core reaches 5000°C. Iron and nickel usually melt at this temperature. The enormous pressure at this depth, however, pushes the particles of iron and nickel so tightly together that the elements remain solid.

The radius, or distance from the center to the edge, of the inner core is about 1300 kilometers. The inner core begins at a depth of about 5150 kilometers below the Earth's surface. The presence of solid iron in the inner core may explain the existence of the magnetic fields around the Earth. Scientists think the iron produces an effect similar to the effect around a magnet—that is, a magnetic field. Have you ever experimented with iron filings and a bar magnet? If so, were you able to observe the pattern of the filings around the magnet? This pattern identifies the magnetic field. Perhaps your teacher can help you do this activity so that you can see a magnetic field for yourself.

ACTIVITY
WRITING

Shake and Quake

(1) Write a 250-word horror story describing the disaster that would occur in the aftermath of a fictitious earthquake that levels a major American city. Make your story as descriptive as you can.

Explain that a wave-free shadow zone that extends all the way around the Earth is produced by the bending of seismic waves.

ENRICHMENT

▶ *Activity Book*

Students who have mastered the concepts in this section will be challenged by the Chapter 5 activity called How Does the Intensity of an Earthquake Change With Distance?

GUIDED PRACTICE

▶ *Laboratory Manual*

Skills Development

Skills: Applying concepts, making comparisons

At this point you may want to have students complete the Chapter 5 Laboratory Investigation in the *Laboratory Manual* called A Model of the Earth's Interior. In the investigation students will compare two models of the Earth's

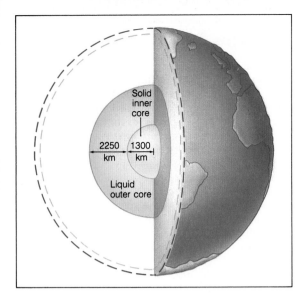

Figure 5–5 *This cross section of the Earth shows the location and radius of the inner core and the outer core. What is each core made of?* ❷

Surrounding the inner core is the second layer of the Earth, called the **outer core.** The outer core begins about 2900 kilometers below the Earth's surface and is about 2250 kilometers thick. The outer core is also made of iron and nickel. In this layer, the temperature ranges from about 2200°C in the upper part to almost 5000°C near the inner core. The heat makes the iron and nickel in the outer core molten, or changed into a hot liquid.

5–1 Section Review

1. What evidence has caused scientists to conclude that the Earth's core is made of two different layers?
2. Name two types of seismic waves. How are these waves the same? How are they different?
3. How are the inner and the outer cores of the Earth alike? How do they differ?

Critical Thinking—*Making Predictions*
4. Predict what would happen to P waves and S waves if the Earth's outer core were solid and its inner core were liquid.

$\mathcal{A}$CTIVITY

CALCULATING

The Speed of Seismic Waves

Some kinds of seismic waves travel at 24 times the speed of sound. The speed of sound is 1250 km/hr. How fast do such seismic waves travel? ❷

5-2 The Earth's Mantle

MULTICULTURAL OPPORTUNITY 5-2

On a world map, have students plot the location of the most violent volcanic eruptions as well as the location of the most violent earthquakes; they can find this information in an encyclopedia. They should note that both occurrences coincide in an area of the Pacific Ocean called the Ring of Fire.

The Ring of Fire is an area where tectonic plates are meeting, with tremendous movement of landmasses and buildup of pressure. Ask students to imagine what life is like for people living in the Ring of Fire, an area prone to natural disasters.

ESL STRATEGY 5-2

Ask students to use their dictionaries to find and copy the general definition of the word *mantle*. Then have them explain why mantle is such an appropriate name for this layer of the Earth. (Possible definition is an enveloping robe or cloak. The mantle of the Earth surrounds, or envelops, it in a way similar to the way a robe covers a person.)

Have students list the names of the elements that the mantle contains and explain how the rock located there can be described as having plasticity. (The mantle is made mostly of silicon, oxygen, iron, and magnesium. The rock in the mantle flows like a thick liquid because of great temperature and pressure. Solids with the ability to flow have plasticity.)

5-2 The Earth's Mantle

Guide for Reading

Focus on these questions as you read.

▶ What are the main elements found in the mantle?
▶ What are the features of the Earth's mantle?

The layer of the Earth directly above the outer core is the **mantle.** The mantle extends to a depth of about 2900 kilometers below the surface. About 80 percent of the volume of the Earth and about 68 percent of the planet's mass are in the mantle.

In 1909, the Yugoslav scientist Andrija Mohorov-ičić (moh-hoh-ROH-vuh-chihch) observed a change in the speed of seismic waves as they moved through the Earth. When the waves reached a depth of 32 to 64 kilometers below the Earth's surface, their speed increased. The change in the speed of the waves at this depth indicated a difference in either the density (how tightly together the particles of material are packed) or the composition of the rock. Mohorovičić discovered a boundary between the Earth's outermost layer and the mantle. In his honor, this boundary is now called the **Moho.**

Scientists have made many attempts to determine the composition of the mantle. They have studied rocks from volcanoes because these rocks were formed deep within the Earth. They have also studied rocks from the ocean floor. **After studying rock samples, scientists have determined that the**

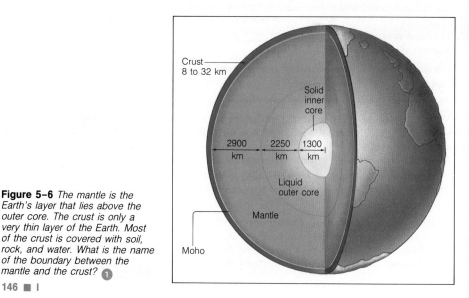

Figure 5–6 *The mantle is the Earth's layer that lies above the outer core. The crust is only a very thin layer of the Earth. Most of the crust is covered with soil, rock, and water. What is the name of the boundary between the mantle and the crust?* ❶

146 ■ I

TEACHING STRATEGY 5-2

FOCUS/MOTIVATION

Have students, either orally or in writing, imagine what it would be like to be the first explorers to travel to the center of the Earth. Allow any imaginative, fanciful stories students may come up with, even if they contain scientific inaccuracy.

CONTENT DEVELOPMENT

Have students observe the pictures of volcanoes in Figure 5–8. Point out that volcanoes can be thought of as "windows" into the interior of the Earth because the lava that flows out of a volcano is formed from magma deep within the Earth.

INDEPENDENT PRACTICE

▶ *Activity Book*

Students will better understand the concepts of this section if they use the Chapter 5 activity called Making a Scale Model of the Earth's Interior.

REINFORCEMENT/RETEACHING

▶ *Activity Book*

Students who have difficulty understanding the concepts of this section should be provided with the Chapter 5 activity called The Earth's Interior.

mantle is made mostly of the elements silicon, oxygen, iron, and magnesium. The lower mantle has a greater percentage of iron than the upper mantle has.

The density of the mantle increases with depth. This increase in density is perhaps due to the greater percentage of iron in the lower mantle. The temperature and the pressure within the mantle also increase with depth. The temperature ranges from 870°C in the upper mantle to about 2200°C in the lower mantle.

Studies of seismic waves suggest that the rock in the mantle can flow like a thick liquid. The high temperature and pressure in the mantle allow the solid rock to flow slowly, thus changing shape. When a solid has the ability to flow, it has the property of **plasticity** (plas-TIHS-uh-tee).

Figure 5–7 *Kilauea is an active volcano in Hawaii. Here you can see lava being thrown into the air as the volcano erupts (right). Lava, either from a volcano or from a rift valley in the ocean floor, forms these "pillow" shapes when it is rapidly cooled by ocean water (left).*

5–2 Section Review

1. What elements make up most of the mantle?
2. Where is the mantle located? How far does it extend below the Earth's surface?
3. What is the Moho?
4. What is plasticity?

Connection—*You and Your World*

5. In areas where earthquakes are common, the foundations of buildings are constructed so that they can move slightly on special slippery pads. Architects believe that these buildings will not be damaged during an earthquake. How would this type of construction make a building safer during an earthquake?

ACTIVITY

A Model of the Earth's Interior

1. Obtain a Styrofoam ball 15 cm or more in diameter.
2. Carefully cut out a wedge from the ball so that the ball is similar to the one in Figure 5–6.
3. Draw lines on the inside of the ball and on the inside of the wedge to represent the four layers of the Earth.
4. Label and color each layer on the ball and wedge.

ACTIVITY
DOING

A MODEL OF THE EARTH'S INTERIOR

Skills: Making models, applying concepts, relating concepts

Materials: Styrofoam ball, knife, 4 different-colored felt-tip markers

This activity provides students with the opportunity to take information from the chapter to construct a stratigraphic model of the Earth's interior.

Students should use the following scale to make their model: inner core from the center out to 1.5 cm, outer core from 1.5 cm to 4 cm, mantle from 4 cm to the edge of the ball. The crust is the surface of the ball.

GUIDED PRACTICE

▶ *Laboratory Manual*

Skills Development

Skills: Making observations, making inferences, relating cause and effect

At this point you may want to have students complete the Chapter 5 Laboratory Investigation in the *Laboratory Manual* called Observing the Action of Gases in a Magma. In the investigation students will create a simulation of the magma, or molten rock, inside the Earth.

INDEPENDENT PRACTICE

Section Review 5–2

1. Silicon, oxygen, iron, and magnesium.

2. Above the outer core. About 2900 kilometers.

3. Boundary between the crust and the mantle.

4. Ability of a solid to slow or change in shape.

5. The slippery pads allow the building to sway slightly with the moving Earth.

Architects also build a system of "dampers" that dampen this sway.

REINFORCEMENT/RETEACHING

Review students' responses to the Section Review questions. Reteach any material that is still unclear, based on students' responses.

CLOSURE

▶ *Review and Reinforcement Guide*

Have students complete Section 5–2 in the *Review and Reinforcement Guide*.

5-3 The Earth's Crust

148 ■ I

MULTICULTURAL OPPORTUNITY 5-3

Suggest that students research the life of Dr. Burton Richter, a California seismologist who invented the Richter scale. The Richter scale is used to measure the magnitude of earthquakes. Have students investigate how earthquakes were predicted in different parts of the world throughout history, as well as the work that is being done now.

Interested students may want to investigate what a career in seismology entails.

ESL STRATEGY 5-3

Ask students to use their dictionaries to find and copy the definition of the word *crust*. Then have them explain why crust describes the fourth and final layer of the Earth so well.

Suggest that students make a chart like the following to list the differences between the oceanic and continental crusts.

Crust's Name		
Location		
Thickness		
Composition		

Have students use the information in their charts to write a paragraph in which they compare the crusts in the two areas. Ask volunteers to read their paragraphs to the class.

ECOLOGY NOTE

A NEIGHBOR'S WARNING

The atmosphere on the planet Venus holds 350,000 times as much carbon as does the atmosphere of the Earth. A cloud-wrapped planet with a surface temperature hot enough to melt lead, Venus is sometimes used as a warning. If the global warming that results from our releasing carbon into the atmosphere continues, we may be headed in the same direction as Venus. The greenhouse effect on Venus not only prevents the evolution of life, it also stifles the evolution of the lithosphere, the solid crust of the planet.

Figure 5–8 *Natural rock formations, such as these in Big Bend National Park, Texas, often take beautiful, and sometimes surprising, forms. The elements that make up the Earth's crust are listed in this chart. What two elements are the most abundant?* ❷

ELEMENTS IN THE EARTH'S CRUST	
Element	**Percentage in Crust**
Oxygen	46.60
Silicon	27.72
Aluminum	8.13
Iron	5.00
Calcium	3.63
Sodium	2.83
Potassium	2.59
Magnesium	2.09
Titanium	0.40
Hydrogen	0.14
Total	99.13

5-3 The Earth's Crust

The Earth's crust is its thin outermost layer. The **crust** is much thinner than the mantle and the outer and inner cores. You can think of the crust as being similar to the peel on an apple. All life on Earth exists on or within a few hundred meters above the crust. Most of the crust cannot be seen. Do you know why? It is covered with soil, rock, and water. There is one place, however, where the crust can be seen. Where do you think that might be? ❶

The crust is made of three types of solid rocks: igneous rocks, sedimentary rocks, and metamorphic rocks. Igneous rocks form when hot liquid rock from deep within the Earth cools and hardens as it reaches the surface. The word igneous means "born of fire," a term that explains with accuracy how these rocks are formed. Sedimentary rocks form when sediments—small pieces of rocks, sand, and other materials—are pressed and cemented together by the weight of layers that build up over long periods of time. Metamorphic rock forms when igneous and sedimentary rocks are changed by heat, pressure, or the action of chemicals.

The thickness of the Earth's crust varies. Crust beneath the oceans, called oceanic crust, is less than 10 kilometers thick. Its average thickness is only about 8 kilometers. Oceanic crust is made mostly of silicon, oxygen, iron, and magnesium.

TEACHING STRATEGY 5-3

FOCUS/MOTIVATION

Display an apple.

• **How do you think the thickness of the apple peel compares to the thickness of the entire apple?** (Answers may vary, but most will probably say that the peel is very thin compared to the thickness of the entire apple.)

Point out that the thickness of the

Earth's crust compared to the thickness of the entire Earth is very much the same as the peel of an apple compared to the whole apple.

• **Do you think that the Earth's crust is a very important part of the Earth?** (Answers may vary, but the correct answer is yes.)

CONTENT DEVELOPMENT

Begin by pointing out to students that the crust is the one part of the Earth that

Layer	Composition and Temperature	Depth
Earth's surface	Oxygen, silicon, aluminum, calcium, iron, sodium, potassium, magnesium	0 km
Crust		
Moho		32 km
	870°C	
Mantle	Silicon, oxygen, iron, magnesium	
	2200°C	
	2200°C	2900 km
Liquid outer core	Iron, nickel	
	5000°C	
	5000°C	5150 km
Solid inner core	Iron, nickel	
		6500 km

Figure 5–9 *This diagram summarizes the major characteristics of the Earth's layers. Which layers are solid? Which layer is liquid?* ③

Activity Bank

How Hard Is That Rock?, p.172

Crust beneath the continents, called continental crust, has an average thickness of about 32 kilometers. Beneath mountains, continental crust is much thicker. Under some mountains, the crust's thickness is greater than 70 kilometers. Continental crust is made mostly of silicon, oxygen, aluminum, calcium, sodium, and potassium.

The Earth's crust forms the upper part of the **lithosphere** (LIHTH-uh-sfeer). The lithosphere is the

ACTIVITY

CALCULATING

How Many Earths?

The distance from the center of the Earth to the surface is about 6450 kilometers. The distance from the Earth to the sun is 150 million kilometers. How many Earths lined up in a row are needed to reach the sun? ①

I ■ 149

A C T I V I T Y
C A L C U L A T I N G

HOW MANY EARTHS?

Skills: Making comparisons, computational, calculator

This activity involves a computation, by division, that helps not only to reinforce mathematical skills but also to reveal the enormity of astronomical distances, even when compared with very great geologic distances.

To solve the problem, students first multiply the radius of the Earth (6450 km) by 2 to find that the diameter of the Earth is 12,900 km. They then divide 150 million km by 12,900 km. The answer to the question is about 11,628 Earths.

Integration: Use this Activity to integrate mathematics into your science lesson.

scientists have been able to explore directly. Much of this direct exploration has been done by drilling. The deepest holes, however, have been drilled only about 8 kilometers deep.

REINFORCEMENT/RETEACHING

▶ *Activity Book*

Students who are having difficulty understanding the concepts of this chapter should be provided with the Chapter 5 activity called Layers of the Earth.

GUIDED PRACTICE

Skills Development

Skills: Applying concepts, making observations, making comparisons

At this point have students complete the in-text Chapter 5 Laboratory Investigation: Simulating Plasticity. In the investigation students will use cornstarch to make a model of the material in the Earth's mantle.

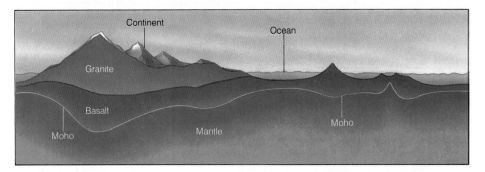

Figure 5–10 *The Earth's crust consists of two layers. The top layer is made of granite and is found only under the continents. The bottom layer is made of basalt and is found under both the continents and the oceans.*

solid topmost part of the Earth. It is between 50 and 100 kilometers thick and is broken up into large sections called lithospheric plates. There are at least seven major plates.

The layer directly beneath the lithosphere is called the **asthenosphere** (az-THEEN-oh-sfeer). The asthenosphere, which is 130 to 160 kilometers thick, is actually considered to be the upper edge of the mantle. The asthenosphere is made of hot, molten material. This material has the property of plasticity and thus can flow easily. The lithospheric plates move on the hot molten material that forms the asthenosphere. You can get a better idea of this concept by making your own model of the lithosphere and the asthenosphere. Try the following: Use a slice of bread to represent a lithospheric plate and a layer of jelly spread on a piece of cardboard to represent the asthenosphere. Place the bread on top of the jelly. Move the slice of bread back and forth slightly. What do you observe? ❶

5–3 Section Review

1. What is the Earth's crust?
2. Compare oceanic crust with continental crust.
3. What are the characteristics of the asthenosphere? What floats on this layer?

Critical Thinking—*Relating Concepts*
4. Explain why metamorphic rock could not form before igneous or sedimentary rock.

150 ■ I

5–3 (continued)

FOCUS/MOTIVATION

Have interested students build a clay model of the continental and oceanic crust overlying the mantle. Figure 5–11 will be helpful in building the model. Use reference books in geology for additional illustrations.

CONTENT DEVELOPMENT

In the area of the Earth called the asthenosphere, which is located below the lithosphere, rocks have the property of plasticity. The asthenosphere is a region of low activity for seismic waves.

• **Why do you think the asthenosphere is a region of low seismic activity?** (Rocks that are plastic are able to bend with—bounce back from—the movements of seismic waves. Because the rocks can "flow with" the waves, the waves have little effect on this region.)

GUIDED PRACTICE

▶ *Laboratory Manual*

Skills Development

Skills: Measuring, making calculations, calculator, making comparisons, making inferences

At this point you may want to have students complete the Chapter 5 Labora-

tory Investigation in the *Laboratory Manual* called Determining the Density of the Earth. In the investigation students will use various rock samples to estimate the average density of the Earth.

ENRICHMENT

▶ *Activity Book*

Students who have mastered the concepts in this chapter will be challenged by the Chapter 5 activity called Determining How Fast Some Crustal Plates Move.

INDEPENDENT PRACTICE

📀 **Media and Technology**

At this point students can begin an exploration into the Earth's crust by using the Interactive Videodisc called Terra-Vision. Using the videodisc, students examine the forces in the Earth's crust and relate them to earthquakes, volcanoes, and tsunamis. After completing the videodisc, instruct students to write a brief report in which they describe a particular

---

CAREERS

Geologist

People who study the structure, composition, and history of the Earth are called **geologists.** Geologists spend some of their time examining rocks and other structures in the crust. Geologists usually specialize in a particular area of geology. To learn more about this field, write to the American Geological Institute, 5202 Leesburg Pike, Falls Church, VA 22041.

CONNECTIONS

Beauty From Beneath ❶ the Earth's Surface

The Smithsonian Institution in Washington, D.C., has often been called the nation's attic. But you should not think of a dusty attic filled with unwanted and unused objects. For the Smithsonian Institution is a treasure-filled attic: a storehouse of items of great artistic merit made by talented women and men, as well as of treasures from the Earth itself. Here you will find diamonds, rubies, sapphires, and other gems valuable beyond price—all handcrafted by the forces of nature in a "laboratory" you know as the Earth.

For example, scientists believe that diamonds form within the upper part of the Earth's mantle. Here the pressure is tremendous—about 65,000 times the pressure at the Earth's surface—and the temperature is close to 1500°C! Under these extreme conditions of pressure and temperature, carbon can be transformed into diamonds. Diamond-laden molten rock is forced to the surface of the Earth by volcanic explosions. Mines cut into the crust expose

the diamonds formed long ago in the Earth's mantle. These rough diamonds vary in quality. Those that are gem quality are cut and shaped into precious stones used in jewelry. Those that are not fine enough to be made into jewelry are used to make drills and saws. Such *industrial-grade diamonds* are so strong that they cut through many materials, including steel. Small bits of diamond are often used in the dental drills that remove decayed parts of teeth and in the needles that follow the grooves in a record to produce the sounds of music.

If you are able to visit the Smithsonian Institution at some future time, keep this in mind: Not all the great treasures preserved and protected within the walls of this great museum were made by the hands of people; many were shaped by forces at work deep within the Earth.

Gemstones, like this green beryl, are quite beautiful. Diamonds, highly valued for their beauty, also have important uses in industry. Small diamond particles are often imbedded in drills (left) and in saws (right).

CONNECTIONS

BEAUTY FROM BENEATH THE EARTH'S SURFACE

In this Connections feature students will learn of the formation and uses of diamonds. Diamonds are made of carbon atoms that are very close together. The close arrangement of the atoms is what makes diamonds so hard. Diamonds are not only valued for their beauty, but their hardness allows them to be used as abrasives, substances that can grind down other softer substances.

Graphite is also composed of carbon atoms, but in a different and looser arrangement. Because graphite is much more common and less expensive than diamond, many people have tried to apply the necessary pressure to turn carbon into diamond. One man who came close was an American inventor, Edward Goodrich Acheson. In 1891, he heated carbon with clay and created a new and very hard compound called Carborundum.

It was not until 1955 that scientists found the right combination of very high temperature and extreme pressure that is needed to turn graphite into the modern synthetic diamonds we have today.

If you are teaching thematically, you may want to use the Connections feature to reinforce the themes of patterns of change or scale and structure.

Integration: Use the Connections feature to integrate rocks and minerals into your lesson.

type of natural disaster, such as an earthquake, and how that disaster is related to forces in the Earth's crust.

INDEPENDENT PRACTICE

Section Review 5–3

1. Thin outermost layer.

2. Oceanic crust is thinner than continental crust. Oceanic crust is mostly silicon, oxygen, iron, and magnesium. Continental crust is mostly silicon, oxygen, aluminum, calcium, sodium, and potassium.

3. Hot, molten material with property of plasticity. Lithosphere floats on asthenosphere.

4. Heat and pressure form metamorphic rock from previously existing igneous, sedimentary, or metamorphic rock.

REINFORCEMENT/RETEACHING

Review students' responses to the Section Review questions. Reteach any ma-

terial that is still unclear, based on students' responses.

CLOSURE

▶ *Review and Reinforcement Guide*

Have students complete Section 5–3 in the *Review and Reinforcement Guide.*

Laboratory Investigation

SIMULATING PLASTICITY

BEFORE THE LAB

1. Gather all materials at least one day prior to the investigation. You should have enough supplies to meet your class needs, assuming six students per group.

2. Note that the key to this experiment is for students to add just the right amount of water to the cornstarch.

PRE-LAB DISCUSSION

Review with students the concept of plasticity. Have students read the complete laboratory procedure. Discuss the procedure by asking questions similar to the following:

• **Why is the Earth's mantle said to have plasticity?** (The solid rock has the ability to flow.)

• **What causes the plasticity?** (The high temperature and pressure in the mantle.)

Point out that in this laboratory investigation, rather than working with a single substance that has plastic properties, they will be creating a plastic substance by combining a solid and a liquid. Explain that this investigation will make students aware of the relationship between pressure and plasticity.

Laboratory Investigation

Simulating Plasticity

Problem

How can the plasticity of the Earth's mantle be simulated?

Materials *(per group)*

> 15 g cornstarch
> 2 small beakers
> 10 mL cold water
> medicine dropper
> metal stirring rod or spoon

Procedure 🔬

1. Put 15 g of cornstarch in one of the beakers. Into the other beaker, pour 10 mL of cold water.

2. Use the medicine dropper to gradually add one dropperful of water to the cornstarch. Stir the mixture.

3. Continue to add the water, one dropperful at a time. Stir the mixture after each addition. Stop adding the water when the mixture becomes difficult to stir.

4. Try to pour the mixture into your hand. Try to roll the mixture into a ball and press it.

Observations

1. Before the addition of water, is the cornstarch a solid, liquid, or gas? Is the water a solid, liquid, or gas?

2. When you try to pour the mixture into your hand, does the mixture behave like a solid, liquid, or gas?

3. When you try to roll the mixture into a ball and apply pressure, does the mixture act like a solid, liquid, or gas?

Analysis and Conclusions

1. How is the mixture of cornstarch and water similar to the Earth's mantle? Different from the Earth's mantle?

2. How might the plasticity of the mantle influence the movement of the Earth's lithospheric plates?

3. **On Your Own**   Make a model of a lithospheric plate. Devise a way to show how the plasticity of the mantle allows the Earth's lithospheric plates to move.

TEACHING STRATEGY

1. Have teams follow the directions carefully as they work in the laboratory.

2. Circulate through the room, assisting students with the various setup aspects of the procedure.

3. Students will be able to observe that cornstarch mixed with water behaves like a solid and a liquid, depending on how much pressure is applied to the mixture. When they squeeze it in their hands or roll it into a ball with consistent pressure, it has the characteristics of a solid. When they release the pressure, the mixture flows like a liquid. The trick to achieving this effect is in adding just the right amount of water to the cornstarch.

DISCOVERY STRATEGIES

Discuss how the investigation relates to the chapter ideas by asking open questions similar to the following.

• **Can a mixture have properties of both a liquid and a solid?** (The mixture you pour on your hand has properties of a

Study Guide

Summarizing Key Concepts

5–1 The Earth's Core

▲ An earthquake is a sudden movement of the Earth's outermost layer.

▲ Shock waves produced by an earthquake are called seismic waves.

▲ Seismic waves are detected and recorded by an instrument called a seismograph.

▲ Seismic waves called P waves and S waves are used to study the structure and composition of the Earth's interior.

▲ The core of the Earth is made of a liquid outer core and a solid inner core. Both core layers are composed of iron and nickel.

▲ Although the temperature is high enough to melt iron and nickel, the inner core is solid because of the enormous pressure.

▲ The dense iron and nickel in the inner core may be the cause of the Earth's magnetic field.

▲ The temperature range of the Earth's outer core is from about 2200°C to almost 5000°C.

▲ P waves do not move very well through liquids. S waves do not move through liquids at all. This information has helped scientists determine that the outer core is liquid and the inner core is solid.

5–2 The Earth's Mantle

▲ The mantle is the layer of the Earth that lies above the outer core.

▲ The mantle makes up about 80 percent of the Earth's volume and 68 percent of the Earth's mass.

▲ The boundary between the Earth's outermost layer and the mantle is called the Moho.

▲ The mantle is made mostly of silicon, oxygen, iron, and magnesium.

▲ Pressure and temperature increase with depth in the mantle.

▲ Because of the tremendous heat and pressure in the mantle, rocks in the mantle exhibit the property of plasticity.

5–3 The Earth's Crust

▲ The crust is the thin outermost layer of the Earth.

▲ The crust is made of igneous, sedimentary, and metamorphic rocks.

▲ The most abundant elements in the crust are oxygen, silicon, aluminum, iron, calcium, sodium, potassium, and magnesium.

▲ Oceanic crust is about 8 kilometers thick. Continental crust is about 32 kilometers thick.

▲ The crust forms the upper part of the lithosphere. The lithosphere contains large sections called lithospheric plates.

▲ Lithospheric plates move about on the asthenosphere, the outermost edge of the mantle. The asthenosphere exhibits the property of plasticity.

Reviewing Key Terms

Define each term in a complete sentence.

5–1 The Earth's Core	5–2 The Earth's Mantle	5–3 The Earth's Crust
seismic waves	mantle	crust
seismograph	Moho	lithosphere
inner core	plasticity	asthenosphere
outer core		

tle. Students can see this happening when they roll the mixture into a ball and press it. The mixture, however, is not under intense heat and pressure.

2. Accept all logical responses. Because the plates move about on the mantle, a mantle that acted entirely like a solid would greatly impede the movement of the lithospheric plates. Plasticity, or the ability of a solid to flow like a liquid, greatly enhances the ability of the plates to move about atop the mantle.

3. Students' models will vary. One possible experiment is as follows:

Put jelly on top of a piece of cardboard that represents the asthenosphere. Use a piece of bread for the lithospheric plate. Put the bread layer on top of the jelly. Make a second model without the jelly. Place both models on a tray. Shake the tray sideways and note any movements of the bread.

GOING FURTHER: ENRICHMENT

Part 1

Students may be interested in finding other substances that have the property of plasticity. Some of these substances include paraffin, clay, and baking dough. Have students investigate these substances by subjecting them to various temperatures and pressures.

Part 2

Materials that have the properties of both a solid and a liquid are often called amorphous. Have students find out more about amorphic solids and the conditions under which they exist as either a solid or a liquid.

---

liquid. The mixture rolled into a ball has properties of a solid—relating concepts.)

• **How do the changes in the cornstarch mixture compare with the plasticity of the Earth's mantle?** (A cornstarch mixture with liquid properties can act like a mixture with solid properties as pressure changes. In the mantle, under increased pressure, solid material takes on properties of a liquid and flows slowly—making comparisons.)

OBSERVATIONS

1. Before the addition of water, cornstarch is a solid. The phase of the water is a liquid.

2. When pouring the mixture, it has the properties of a liquid.

3. When the mixture is rolled into a ball, it acts like a solid.

ANALYSIS AND CONCLUSIONS

1. The mixture has the property of plasticity, which is characteristic of the man-

Chapter Review

Chapter Review

ALTERNATIVE ASSESSMENT

The *Prentice Hall Science* program includes a variety of testing components and methodologies. Aside from the Chapter Review questions, you may opt to use the Chapter Test or the Computer Test Bank Test in your *Test Book* for assessment of important facts and concepts. In addition, Performance-Based Tests are included in your *Test Book*. These Performance-Based Tests are designed to test science process skills, rather than factual content recall. Since they are not content dependent, Performance-Based Tests can be distributed after students complete a chapter or after they complete the entire textbook.

CONTENT REVIEW

Multiple Choice

1. b
2. b
3. a
4. a
5. d
6. a
7. b
8. c

True or False

1. F, asthenosphere
2. T
3. T
4. F, P waves
5. T
6. T
7. F, iron

Concept Mapping

Row 1: Seismic waves
Row 2: Inner core, Outer core

CONCEPT MASTERY

1. Scientists learn about the composition of the Earth's interior by studying volcanic rocks, rocks from the ocean floor, and seismic waves created by earthquakes.

2. Oceanic crust is made of silicon, oxygen, iron, and magnesium, and it has an average thickness of about 8 kilometers. Continental crust is made of silicon, oxygen, aluminum, calcium, sodium, and potassium, and it has an average thickness of 32 kilometers.

3. Temperature and pressure increase. Materials change from liquid to solid.

4. Mohorovicic studied the movement of seismic waves as they travel through the interior of the Earth. He noticed a change in the speed of the waves at a depth of 32 to 64 kilometers and thus discovered a boundary between the Earth's outermost layer and the mantle. This boundary is called the Moho.

5. Igneous rock is formed when hot liquid rock cools and hardens; sedimentary rock is formed from sediments that are pressed together; metamorphic rock is formed from existing rock by heat, pressure, or chemical fluids.

6. The asthenosphere is made of hot, molten material that can flow easily. Thus, the lithospheric plates on top of

---

Chapter Review

Content Review

Multiple Choice

Choose the letter of the answer that best completes each statement.

1. The shock waves produced by an earthquake are measured with a
  a. radiograph.   c. sonograph.
  b. seismograph. d. laser.

2. The Earth's inner core is made of
  a. oxygen and silicon.
  b. iron and nickel.
  c. iron and silicon.
  d. copper and nickel.

3. The boundary between the mantle and the outermost layer of the Earth is called the
  a. Moho.   c. lithosphere.
  b. outer core. d. bedrock.

4. The crust of the Earth is made mostly of
  a. oxygen and silicon.
  b. iron and silicon.
  c. iron and nickel.
  d. copper and nickel.

5. When P waves and S waves reach the Earth's outer core,
  a. both keep moving at the same speed.
  b. both stop completely.
  c. P waves stop and S waves slow down.
  d. S waves stop and P waves slow down.

6. The layer that makes up most of the Earth's mass and volume is the
  a. mantle.   c. crust.
  b. magma. d. core.

7. The ability of a solid to flow is called
  a. ductility.   c. seismology.
  b. plasticity. d. porosity.

8. The thin outermost layer of the Earth is called the
  a. mantle.   c. crust.
  b. Moho. d. core.

True or False

If the statement is true, write "true." If it is false, change the underlined word or words to make the statement true.

1. The <u>atmosphere</u> is the outermost layer of the mantle on which the plates move.

2. The innermost layer of the Earth is called the <u>inner core</u>.

3. The outer core is <u>molten</u>.

4. <u>S waves</u> slow down as they pass through liquids.

5. The outermost layer of the Earth is called the <u>crust</u>.

6. The topmost solid part of the Earth is broken up into <u>lithospheric plates</u>.

7. The presence of <u>copper</u> in the inner core may explain the magnetic field that exists around the Earth.

Concept Mapping

Complete the following concept map for Section 5–1. Refer to pages I6–I7 to construct a concept map for the entire chapter.

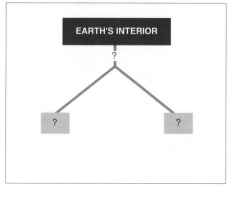

Concept Mastery

Discuss each of the following in a brief paragraph.

1. How have scientists learned about the composition of the Earth's interior?
2. How does oceanic crust differ from continental crust?
3. How do temperature and pressure change as you move from the Earth's crust to the inner core? How do temperature and pressure affect the properties of materials found in the Earth?
4. Briefly describe the work of Andrija Mohorovičić. What did this scientist discover?
5. What is igneous rock? Sedimentary rock? Metamorphic rock?
6. How does the property of plasticity shown by the asthenosphere account for the movement of lithospheric plates?

Critical Thinking and Problem Solving

Use the skills you have developed in this chapter to answer each of the following.

1. **Analyzing data** The temperature of the inner core reaches about 5000°C. The temperature of the outer core begins at 2200°C. Explain why the outer core is liquid and the inner core is solid.
2. **Relating concepts** It has been said that "Every cloud has a silver lining." What could be the "silver lining" in an earthquake?
3. **Analyzing illustrations** This illustration shows the layers of the Earth. Something is wrong with this artist's ideas, however. Identify the errors and describe what you would do to correct them.

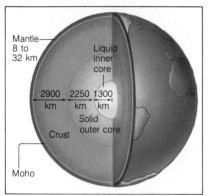

4. **Making models** Use the information in this chapter to make a model of the four layers of the Earth's interior. You may use clay of different colors, papier-mâché, or other materials to make your model. Keep the depth and thickness of each layer of your model in scale with the actual depth and thickness of the Earth's layers. Include a key to the scale you use to construct your model. For example, 1 centimeter in your model might equal 1000 kilometers in the Earth.
5. **Interpreting diagrams** Look at Figure 5–4 on page 144. You will notice an area of the Earth labeled the shadow zone. Use this diagram and your knowledge of seismic waves and the structure of the Earth's interior to explain what the shadow zone is.
6. **Using the writing process** Write a short story about an imaginary trip taken in a machine that is able to drill through the Earth. Make your destination an exotic country on the side of the Earth opposite the city or town in which you live. Use a globe to help. You might like to illustrate this story with appropriate pictures.

I ■ 155

---

cm to the edge of the ball. The crust is the surface of the ball.

5. The shadow zone is a wave-free zone extending all the way around the Earth. It is produced by the bending of seismic waves.

6. Check students' stories for scientific accuracy. They should include the correct names for the various layers of the Earth.

KEEPING A PORTFOLIO

You might want to assign some of the Concept Mastery and Critical Thinking and Problem Solving questions as homework and have students include their responses to unassigned questions in their portfolio. Students should be encouraged to include both the question and the answer in their portfolio.

ISSUES IN SCIENCE

The following issues can be used as springboards for discussion or given as writing assignments.

1. Some scientists believe that the composition of meteorites lends support to the theory that the Earth's inner core is made of iron. This is because meteorites, which contain iron, are believed to be metallic fragments that were left in space during the formation of the universe. Find out more about this idea and decide whether you feel there is enough evidence to support a relationship between meteorites and the composition of the Earth's inner core.

2. For many years, scientists believed that the Earth's magnetic field was caused by the presence of iron in the Earth's inner core. In recent years, however, some scientists have questioned this theory. They claim that the Earth's magnetic field is due to giant belts of electric current in the atmosphere and in the Earth's crust. Find out more about this issue and take a stand on what you think causes the Earth's magnetic field.

---

the asthenosphere can move because they are resting on this molten material.

CRITICAL THINKING AND PROBLEM SOLVING

1. The inner core is a solid at such high temperatures as a result of the extreme pressures found in the inner core.

2. Accept all logical answers. One possible response is that people band together to solve problems, increasing the sense of community spirit.

3. The artist has incorrectly labeled layers of the Earth. The crust, not the mantle, is 8 to 32 km deep. The inner core is solid, and the outer core is liquid. Relabel the diagram.

4. Students' models will vary in size and materials. The relative sizes of the layers, however, should be consistent with the actual thicknesses of the various layers. For example, students might use the following scale to make their model: inner core from the center out to 1.5 cm, outer core from 1.5 cm to 4 cm, mantle from 4

ALAN KOLATA AND
OSWALDO RIVERA
THE MYSTERIOUS CANALS
OF BOLIVIA

Background Information

Alan Kolata and Oswaldo Rivera first visited Tiwanaku to explore the ruins of the pre-Incan society that flourished in the area on the southern shores of Lake Titicaca. The culture of the ancient Tiwanakans endured from about AD 100 to AD 1000. At first, Kolata and Rivera concentrated their efforts on archaeological excavations, particularly of the most sacred temple of the ancient Tiwanakans, the Akapana Pyramid. They soon became fascinated by a pattern of ridges and depressions in the area. After studying the area, they came to believe that the ridges and depressions were the remains of an ancient agricultural system involving canals and raised land. Through their efforts and an agreeable farmer, they revolutionized farming in the area by instituting the ancient farming techniques.

Although the discoveries made by Kolata and Rivera helped to provide new and more detailed information about the ancient Tiwanakans, they were not the first archaeologists to visit the area. In the 1860s, E. George Squier, an American archaeologist, visited the area. He, too, explored the temples, but he left the area convinced that Tiwanaku was a sacred site of temples but had not been a thriving community. He would have been surprised by the evidence supplied by Bolivian archaeologist Carlos Ponce in the 1950s. Ponce found evidence that Tiwanaku had been the capital city of the Tiwanaku civilization. At its height, Tiwanaku was a thriving center of government probably populated by 50,000 people.

Kolata and his students and colleagues continue to work in Tiwanaku, and as they do, more will be learned about the way of life of an ancient people who taught modern people how to farm the floodplains of Bolivia.

Alan Kolata & Oswaldo Rivera
THE MYSTERIOUS CANALS OF BOLIVIA

he Pampa Koani, a treeless plain in northern Bolivia, was rich in strange ridges and depressions but poor in crops. The Aymara Indians, the inhabitants of this flood plain, were forced to watch as their crops succumbed to frost and their potatoes rotted in the boggy soil. The Aymara knew that nearly one thousand years ago their ancestors had farmed the land successfully. That powerful pre-Incan civilization, called the Tiwanaku state, had flourished from 200 to 1000 AD. What farming methods did the Tiwanakus know so many years ago that the Aymara lacked today?

In 1981, two archaeologists suggested a possible answer. Alan Kolata (bottom left), a professor of archaeology and anthropology at the University of Chicago, and Oswaldo Rivera (bottom right), an archaeologist at Bolivia's National Institute of Archaeology, had been studying the Tiwanaku culture since the late 1970s. The two scholars believed that the secret lay in the ridges and ruts that ran across the flood plain. They had observed similar topographical patterns in Mayan and Aztec farming sites in the jungles of Central America. The archaeologists suggested that the patterns were part of a sophisticated system of canals and raised planting surfaces that had allowed the Tiwanakus to grow their crops successfully.

Kolata and Rivera needed to test their hypothesis. A proven, correct theory would be more than simply a credit to the archaeologists' research abilities. It would also be

TEACHING STRATEGY: ADVENTURE

FOCUS/MOTIVATION

Ask students to imagine that they are archaeologists from the future who have just excavated a portion of a community from the 1990s.

• **What might the excavation tell you about life in the 1990s?** (Answers may include the way people worked and lived, what goods they used, their clothing, and so on.)

• **How do today's archaeologists learn about ancient societies?** (By gathering evidence from excavations and by interpreting meanings supplied by the evidence.)

CONTENT DEVELOPMENT

Kolata and Rivera began working together at Tiwanaku in 1978. Through their work, they not only learned a great deal about the way of life of the ancient Tiwanakans, but they also applied that in-a way to rejuvenate the failing Aymara farms and produce hardy crops. In 1981, the archaeologists' first attempt to rehabilitate the Aymara fields was met with a severe drought. It was not until 1987 that Kolata and Rivera were able to convince the Aymara to try again. At first, only one man agreed to cooperate. As a result, he was scorned by his neighbors, who thought the archaeologists were meddling foreigners who would only harm Aymara agriculture. The Aymaras continued to plant their crops away from the rutted fields on nearby hillsides. But the archaeologists and the lone Aymara farmer persevered. Together, the three redug the channels, planted the potato crop, and watched excitedly as the plants grew to record heights.

Then, only a few days before the first harvest, frost struck the area. The Aymara farmers looked on helplessly as 90 percent of their hillside crops were lost. They expected the same fate for the crops Kolata and Rivera had helped to cultivate. The coldest, heaviest air, they thought, would flow downhill onto the flood plain, killing every plant.

The archaeologists hoped for a different outcome. And indeed, when they went out before dawn to investigate, they beheld a remarkable sight! Across the entire flood plain, a white mist lay like a blanket over the potato crops. With the first rays of sunlight, the mist disappeared, revealing undamaged potato plants. Almost the entire crop had survived the killing frost! It was then that Kolata and Rivera, along with the Aymara farmers, recognized the ingenuity of the early Tiwanakus. These ancient people knew how to use the system of canals and ridges to protect their harvest. Can you guess how they did it?

During the day, the soil absorbs heat from the sun. But the soil quickly loses its warmth during the cold night, putting the crops at risk. Water, however, retains heat for a much longer time than soil does. A temperature difference between the water in the canals and the air causes the water to evaporate. This causes a protective, blanketlike mist to form over the crops. In addition, warm water is drawn by capillary action into the

▲ These Bolivian farmers are harvesting potatoes produced in raised fields bordered by canals.

raised platforms, conducting warmth into the soil and into the plants' root systems.

Kolata and Rivera were pleased with their discovery—and particularly with the fact that the Aymara began to trust them and treat them like friends. But nobody was more pleased than the Aymara people themselves. With the "new" farming system, their crops began to prosper, yielding bountiful harvests of potatoes, barley, oats, lettuce, and onions. As a bonus, algae and nitrogen-fixing bacteria began to thrive in the canals, providing a useful source of fertilizer after the crops were harvested and the canals were drained. And the Aymara had done all this by returning to the ways of their ancestors!

Meanwhile, Kolata and Rivera continue to research the Tiwanaku culture, which reached its peak in 600 AD. They are especially interested in the daily life of the Tiwanaku people—what they ate, what they wore, and how their society was structured. With a team that includes hydrologists and computer scientists, they study the sophisticated Tiwanaku temples and pyramids as well as their canal system. But Kolata and Rivera are just as interested in the present as in the past. The raised-field technology they helped the Aymara to implement can be used in other areas of Bolivia to help feed a hungry population.

GAZETTE ■ 157

Additional Questions and Topic Suggestions

1. Use reference materials to trace one of these civilizations that affected the Tiwanaku area of Bolivia since the time of the ancient Tiwanakans—the Incas and the Spanish.

2. The potato crop is an important one to the farmers of the Tiwanaku area. Find out where the potato originated and how it became a popular crop in other areas of the world.

3. Research information about archaeology. What tools are used? What are the goals of archaeological explorations? Write a short report about this field of study.

Critical Thinking Questions

1. The ancient Tiwanakans were able to produce excess crops using their farming methods. How do you think the ability to produce excess crops affected the civilization? (Accept all logical answers. Students may conclude that the ability to produce excess crops enabled people to diversify the type of work they did because farmers could produce enough food to support nonfarmers.)

2. At its height, Tiwanaku was a strong, powerful, sophisticated civilization. Why do you think the civilization died out? (Answers may vary; students might suggest through conquest.)

3. How might abundant food supplies have affected the size of a population of the Tiwanaku civilization? (Because food was readily available, the population would be able to grow because the people could be fed.)

formation to help the modern-day people in the area. By adapting ancient farming methods, the farmers of the area have been able to produce abundant crops and improve their lifestyles.

Emphasize that the original goal of the archaeologists in experimenting with the farming method of the ancients was to learn more about the ancient people, but as they did, they also helped the people of today.

• **How do you think the archaeologists felt about their role in helping the people?** (Accept all logical answers. It is likely that the successful results of the adaptation of ancient farming methods made the work of the archaeologists even more gratifying.)

INDEPENDENT PRACTICE

▶ *Activity Book*

After students have read the Science Gazette article, you may want to hand out the reading skills worksheet based on the article in the *Activity Book*.

WHO GIVES A HOOT FOR THE SPOTTED OWL?

Background Information

In the late 1980s and early 1990s, the northern spotted owl became a symbol representing a classic confrontation between conservationists and industry in the Pacific Northwest. The owl's population had been depleted by 80 percent, with only 3000 to 6000 pairs left in their natural habitat of old-growth forests. As the battle raged between the need to preserve the owl's environment for the sake of the owl but also for the protection of the environment itself and the need to protect jobs and to meet the demand for wood, a court-ordered study was undertaken by the federal agencies of the Forest Service, the Fish and Wildlife Service, and the Bureau of Land Management.

The study was led by an agency biologist, Jack Ward Thomas, who was authorized to conduct the study without political interference. The report titled "Conservation Strategy for the Northern Spotted Owl" was released in April 1990. It recommended a ban on logging on 30 to 40 percent of public timberland. The limited ban could result in the loss of about 50 percent of the remaining spotted-owl population. The report presented a compromise. The owl would not become extinct, and loggers could still work on the remaining 60 to 70 percent of the public timberland. The report was assailed by conservationists and the logging industry alike. The recommendations of the team of biologists were not adopted, and the northern spotted owl was put on the threatened species list. The battle rages on as the government tries to balance economic needs versus preservation of the American wilderness.

Who Gives a Hoot for the Spotted Owl?

▲ Logging in the old growth forests in the Pacific Northwest threatens the survival of this pair of northern spotted owls.

It is the still of the night in the Pacific Coast's Cascade Mountain range. A small owl swoops out of the upper reaches of a Douglas fir tree, taking advantage of the dark to find its dinner. This bird, the northern spotted owl, is a delicate creature, shy of the daylight and of too much human attention. But recently, it has been forced into the middle of an environmental controversy.

The controversy centers on the logging industry in the Pacific Northwest, for the spotted owl's natural habitat is also a prime source of commercial timber. A century of logging has removed roughly 90 percent of the region's ancient trees. Firs, pines, cedars, and oaks—all at least 250 years old—make up "old-growth" forests. In the process of harvesting wood necessary for houses, buildings, and paper products, the logging industry has also cleared away trees that are the home of the spotted owl. As its habitat dwindled, so did the bird's numbers. The result: a clash between conservationists concerned with the survival of the owl and the logging industry concerned with its employees and its profitability.

In the early 1990s, after much discussion, the United States Fish and Wildlife Service declared the bird a threatened species. This government agency also adopted plans to limit logging in the old-growth areas in order to protect the owl's habitat. Up until that time, the United States Forest Service, which is responsible for overseeing America's

---

TEACHING STRATEGY: ISSUE

FOCUS/MOTIVATION

Exhibit photographs or illustrations of threatened or endangered species from around the world. You might include pictures of the California condor, the panda bear, and the black rhinoceros. Ask students what these animals have in common. Lead students to understand that each of these is a member of a threatened or endangered species. Ask students to consider methods for preventing the extinction of the species. You might point out the efforts to save the California condor by breeding the bird in captivity and then releasing adult pairs of birds into the wild. Ask how laws and law enforcement might be used to protect the species.

CONTENT DEVELOPMENT

Display a map of the United States. Point out the Pacific Northwest. Help

forests, had been selling the equivalent of 12 billion board feet of lumber a year to logging companies. That is equal to about 400,000 acres of forest and $1.5 billion. Today, restrictions protect some 50,000 of these acres a year. But conservationists argue that this is not enough. They want the United States Government to exert even tighter controls on the timber industry to protect the owl's habitat. Logging officials claim that environmentalists are exaggerating the threat to the bird.

Although much national attention is focused on the plight of one specific (and cute) creature, it is not simply the owl that is at stake in the debate over logging. At stake, say some ecologists and conservationists, is nothing less than an entire forest ecosystem. At stake, say some officials in the timber industry, is nothing less than 30,000 jobs and the economies of Oregon, Washington State, and northern California. The debate over the spotted owl, then, is really a debate about the role of people and their responsibility for the Earth's environments.

Old-growth forests contain tremendous ecological diversity. The ancient trees used as lumber play an essential role in preserving that ecosystem. They provide a home for a large number of different insect, bird, mammal, and plant species. They also play an important role in cleaning the air and in conserving soil and water in the forest. Moisture on the trees' leaves helps trap dust and other particles to cleanse the air. Root systems absorb water and prevent runoff and soil erosion.

▼ **Standing tall and true, these trees are home for many organisms. They are also a source of jobs and lumber for people.**

Finally, fallen logs and needles provide the soil with rich nutrients to nourish young tree seedlings and other forest plants.

But the old-growth trees play an important role in the economy. Bark and sawdust from the huge trees are used as fuel to generate electricity and produce particle board. Lumber is used for a variety of construction purposes. And pulp, which is wood from a layer just inside the bark, is used to make a variety of paper products. Finally, this industry represents hundreds of thousands of jobs in the Pacific Northwest and billions of dollars in income.

Logging officials say that they have been respectful of the environment they have a right to use. In fact, it is in their best interests, they say, to protect the trees that quite literally feed and house them. They add that they are careful to replace the trees they have harvested. Because of reforestation, they say, they have reduced the number of trees in the area by only 25 percent, not 90 percent. Logging officials also argue that the logging industry in the United States meets important demands of the entire industrialized world. They say that strict limitations on logging will cost some 30,000 jobs and hundreds of millions of dollars in the coming decade.

But conservationists say the timber industry does much more harm than good. They fear that the industry has overstepped "natural" bounds and rights in its cutting down of the forests. Reforestation, they explain, cannot replace the old-growth trees that foresters

Additional Questions and Topic Suggestions

1. Environmentalists hope to preserve not only the old-growth forests of the Northwest, but also other natural environments in danger of disappearing. Research information about the efforts to save the American wetlands.

2. In their efforts to protect the environment, environmental activists around the world have used many strategies ranging from court cases to physical intervention. Use reference sources to identify the methods used by such organizations as Greenpeace and the Oregon Natural Resources Council. What techniques do they use? Do you agree with their methods? Why or why not?

3. Many of the logs and lumber cut in the Pacific Northwest are exported to other countries. Japan is one of the biggest importers of American wood. Find out what other products or resources are exported abroad. About what percentage of American exports is represented by the products of the logging industry?

gered or threatened species and preserving ecosystems.)
• **How might "New Forestry" methods help to meet the needs of both the logging industry and the environmentalists?** (The methods would permit logging to continue while preserving the old-growth forests and protecting their inhabitants.)

ENRICHMENT

People can affect the existence of other species through recreational pursuits as well as through their work. Find out about the plight of the manatee in Florida. How is this animal being harmed? How can it be protected?

students understand that northern California, as well as Washington and Oregon, is considered part of the Pacific Northwest.

GUIDED PRACTICE

Skills Development

Skills: Making and interpreting charts, comparing

On the chalkboard, write the headings Preserving the Environment and Meeting Economic Needs. Ask students to read through the article to identify information supporting each side of the issue. As students identify relevant information, ask volunteers to write the supporting information under the appropriate headings on the chalkboard.

• **What are the major concerns of the logging industry?** (The loss of jobs, economic hardship, and the right to make a living.)
• **What are the major concerns of the environmentalists?** (Protecting endan-

Class Debate

Use the questions raised in the article as a springboard for debate. Have teams take positions in support of meeting economic needs of people over the conservation of the forestland and in support of preserving the old-growth forest over the economic hardships such conservation may lead to. Make sure students support their arguments with facts based on the issues.

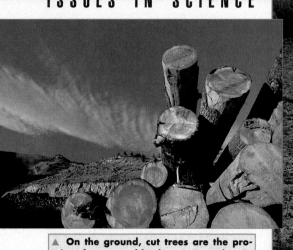

▲ On the ground, cut trees are the promise of paper and lumber. ▶ From the air, you can see how clear-cutting lumber produces a new environment. What effects does harvesting lumber in this way have on the environment?

cut. Loggers may replant trees, but they cannot replace the old-growth ecosystem and its diversity. They also argue that the logging industry is recklessly abusing the environment, as well as destroying itself—it will use up harvestable forest land in 30 years.

Caught in the midst of this conflict are the people of the Pacific Northwest. They want to respect nature's bounty that surrounds them, but many of them are dependent upon the logging industry for their livelihoods. For them, it is not necessarily a philosophical question of the place of humans in the environment. It is a question of food on their tables and clothes for their children.

One compromise that appeals to a variety of groups is a different kind of logging called "New Forestry." Conventional logging techniques use the "clear-cut" method. Clear-cutting removes all the trees in swatches of about 40 acres. From the air, regions of the Pacific Northwest look like a huge checkerboard made of cleared and uncleared areas of trees. New Forestry offers a different approach. Instead of cutting all the trees in a

small area, the new method proposes to harvest larger areas, leaving 20 to 70 percent of the trees standing. The plan also demands that loggers leave some cut trunks on the floor of the forest to add nutrients to the soil and to provide food for plants and animals. According to ecologists, New Forestry techniques resemble ways that forests are affected by natural catastrophes such as forest fires. By leaving a large portion of the trees in a given area still standing, scientists hope to protect and preserve the health and diversity of the forests.

Both the logging industry and environmentalists have expressed concerns about New Forestry, however. Timber officials say that this new method is costly and less effective than clear-cutting. They also say that any change is unnecessary at this time. Conservationists argue that the plan does not offer a complete solution to the problems of logging, but instead detracts attention from these problems. Do you think there can be a "complete resolution" to this debate over logging?

160 ■ GAZETTE

ISSUE (continued)

CONTENT DEVELOPMENT

Old-growth forests have an impact on the ecosystems in a variety of ways. They help to clean the air by trapping dust and other particles in water molecules condensed from the air on their needles. They provide biodiversity by serving as a habitat for many species. Birds nest in

the holes of broken trees, deer feed on lichen that grows on the trunks of trees, and rodents such as moles eat the fungi growing around the roots of trees. The root systems of the trees help to prevent erosion, and the decomposition of fallen logs and needles enriches the soil. The old-growth trees prevent runoff that could cause flooding and could threaten spawning areas of fish by excessive sediments in the water.

INDEPENDENT PRACTICE

▶ *Activity Book*

After students have read the Science Gazette article, you may want to hand out the reading skills worksheet based on the article in the *Activity Book*.

CITIES UNDER THE SEA

FUTURES
IN SCIENCE

CITIES UNDER THE SEA

"Oh no," I groaned, "that ends our plans for surfacing."

I gazed sadly at the three-dimensional image that floated in the middle of my room. The picture my holovision produced showed towering waves and sheets of falling rain. The voice of the weather forecaster could be heard describing the violent storm that raged 70 meters above my head. The "weather" where I lived was, of course, perfectly calm. It always was since the effects of storms disappear just a few meters below the sea's surface.

"Off," I said sharply to the control computer, taking my anger and disappointment out on the machine.

"Now what?" I thought. As if in answer to my question, the communications system chimed.

"Yes?" I said as I eagerly turned toward the computer console.

GAZETTE ■ 161

Background Information

Underwater habitats have existed for about 20 years. The purpose of the habitats thus far has been to enable scientists to conduct undersea research. A habitat named Hydrolab has operated since 1970 in the Caribbean. Another habitat, called the Western Regional Undersea Laboratory (WRUL), is planned for the waters off Catalina Island, California. WRUL, which will be run by the University of California's Institute of Marine and Coastal Studies, will allow six people to work on the sea floor for up to two weeks at a time.

The WRUL is to be a large cylinder with three chambers: living quarters, labs, and a "wet room" that holds diving gear and provides access to the sea. Necessities such as water and breathing gas will be supplied via connecting tubes from the surface. The WRUL will also have an on-board computer. Aquanauts will frequently leave the undersea laboratory to conduct experiments.

The greatest problem involved in placing humans at the bottom of the ocean is the tremendous pressure that increases with depth. As a result of this pressure, nitrogen from the bloodstream is forced into the body's tissues. When a diver wants to surface, he or she must slowly decompress so that the nitrogen can reenter the blood safely. The deeper the diver goes, the more time it takes to decompress; and because the air in the supply tank of scuba equipment is limited, the working time of a diver is very short.

Underwater habitats overcome this problem by saturating the body's tissues with nitrogen. This is accompanied by pressurizing the habitat to the level of the surrounding water and giving the aquanaut a special gas mixture to breathe that differs from air in its oxygen and nitrogen content. Before surfacing, the aquanaut needs to decompress only once.

TEACHING STRATEGY: FUTURE

FOCUS/MOTIVATION

Begin by asking students the following questions.

• **Where do you think you might be living 40 years from now?** (Accept all answers.)

• **What are some factors that might influence the place that you choose to live?** (Accept all answers.)

• **Have you ever considered the possibility that you might live in a city under the ocean?** (Accept all answers.)

Additional Questions and Topic Suggestions

1. Farming in the ocean is called aquaculture. Find out what countries are currently involved in aquaculture and the types of "crops" they raise.

2. Write a short story in which you cast yourself as a member of an undersea community.

3. Get together with several classmates. Using this article as inspiration, create a wall mural that shows various scenes entitled "Life Under the Ocean."

Critical Thinking Questions

1. How might undersea colonies help to solve the Earth's environmental problems? (Accept all logical answers. Perhaps the most obvious answer is that creating cities under the sea would help to alleviate overpopulation on the Earth and enable some of the Earth's land to remain untouched. In addition, minerals and other resources from under the sea would reduce the drain on the Earth's resources and alleviate such problems as land damage from mining and overfarming.)

2. Express your opinion about the following statement: "All this talk of undersea colonies is very exciting from a technological perspective, but when all is said and done, how many people are going to leave their comfortable homes and live several kilometers under the ocean?"

3. Another idea that scientists have proposed for ocean living is floating communities. These cities would be small human-made islands on the ocean's surface. What would be some of the advantages and disadvantages of floating cities compared with undersea communities? (Accept all logical answers.)

My friend Willie's image appeared on the screen. "I guess we're not going to picnic on an island after all," she said. "Disappointed?"

"Of course. I've been to the surface only a few times. I was really looking forward to today's trip, in spite of what's up there: the danger of sunlight to my skin and eyes, air pollution, storms, hot days and cold ones."

"Well cheer up," Willie quickly replied. "Old Professor Melligrant has another plan in mind. She's going to take us to the site of a wreck. It's many kilometers from here, so we're going to use scooters. Grab your gill and get going!"

PREPARING FOR TRAVEL

With my spirits high at the thought of an adventure, I slipped on my water suit. It felt stiff and warm while I remained in my underwater home. But I knew I'd appreciate its warmth and protection in the cool watery world outside. Then I reached into a drawer for my goggles and the all-important gill. I looked at the thin membrane that would fit comfortably over my nose and mouth. And I marveled that such a small, simple device could enable a person to work and travel for countless hours under water.

The material the gill is made of contains proteins. These proteins separate oxygen from water. And we breathe the oxygen. The gill material is used in many ways throughout our underwater city—in our homes, work stations, and transportation vehicles—to provide oxygen for breathing. Without it, human cities beneath the sea would be impossible.

Dressed in my water suit and holding my gill and goggles, I pressed a button that would call a transporter. Seconds later, a blue lamp glowed above the door. My vehicle had arrived. When the door opened, I stepped into the car and pressed the button that indicated where I wanted to go. Whizzing through the transparent tubes that linked various parts of the underwater city, I could see dozens of other cars moving in one direction or another.

At last my car pulled into the transport station located next to the great dome of our school. Professor Melligrant and nine students were already at the school. Melligrant waved me over.

I couldn't help laughing to myself when I saw John. In addition to the usual gear everyone was wearing for this trip, John was loaded down with camera, lights, sonic probe, and a long-range communicator. The sonic probe, which he held in his hand, gave off sounds that could be heard by fish, but not by humans. It was often used to round up or drive away fish. The long-range communicator would come in handy if our little group of explorers got into trouble far from home.

Professor Melligrant unfolded a large map. As we clustered around, she pointed to the general area of the wreck. We walked to the school's exit chamber, a room that would fill with water when we were ready to go. In the dimness of the exit chamber, our suits glowed. So did the water scooters parked nearby. Both the suits and scooters contain

162 ∎ GAZETTE

CONTENT DEVELOPMENT

In this article students are given an idea of what life might be like in a city under the ocean. Explain to students that scientists have been experimenting with underwater habitats for about 20 years. At the present time, these habitats are basically underwater laboratories that are used for the purpose of conducting scientific research. Eventually, however, the same principles used to construct undersea labs may be used to construct entire cities.

Stress that putting humans on or near the sea floor is a difficult task.

• **What makes the ocean such an unfriendly place for human exploration?** (Answers may vary. The main factor is tremendous pressure, which increases dramatically with depth.)

Point out that underwater habitats are built to withstand such pressure, thus making it possible for humans to stay underwater for considerable periods of time.

GUIDED PRACTICE

Skills Development

Skill: Making comparisons

Have students compare life in an undersea colony with life in a space colony. Point out that some of the problems encountered in each place are the same,

materials that react chemically with sea water and give off light. So it would be easy to spot our band of adventurers in the darkness of the ocean.

EXPLORING THE DEPTHS

When everyone was finally ready, the switches were flipped and water flooded into the exit chamber. We turned on the engines of our scooters and followed Professor Melligrant out into the open ocean. After traveling about 1 kilometer, the lights of the city's power station came into view. From the ocean floor, the station rises almost to the surface of the water. Here electricity is generated for the entire city. And at a nearby station, some of that electricity is used to separate hydrogen from water. The hydrogen is used as fuel.

Next came the farms. Although we could not see them, we knew that sonic fences surrounded the area. These invisible fences send out sounds that fish can hear. The fish do not pass through these sound fences. And as a result, huge schools of fish remain penned in fish farms. As we passed by, a lone herder waved to us. Just a short distance away, flashing lights indicated the location of thick wire cables. At the top of these cables, which extended to just below the ocean surface, are the huge kelp beds. Kelp, a kind of seaweed, is an important food substance. And kelp farming is a popular occupation.

A few kilometers beyond the kelp farms, we came across the first signs of seabed mining. According to the older inhabitants of our city, the prospect of seabed mining had first brought people to live under the sea. Robot miners, which looked like big horseshoe crabs, slowly moved along the sea floor scooping up lumps of the metals titanium and manganese.

Beyond the mining area were several large canyons, which we speedily crossed. Then, as we approached an extremely wide canyon, Professor Melligrant's scooter slowed down. She turned to the right and gradually descended. We followed.

The searchlight beam on Professor Melligrant's scooter probed the canyon floor. Then it came to a stop at what looked like a big rock. We had reached the wreck. We parked our scooters around it. Our searchlights brightened the whole area.

Professor Melligrant had never told us exactly what type of ship the wreck was. So I had expected to see the funnels and decks of an old oceanliner. Instead, what I gazed at was part of a sausage-shaped object covered with sea organisms.

Using a portable communicator, Professor Melligrant explained to us that the wreck was a submarine of the twentieth century. In this type of vehicle, people without gills had ventured beneath the surface of the sea.

Unlike other explorers of the deep, the people in this submarine had not come in peace. But that had been long, long ago. Today, the only enemy a person can find under water is a curious shark. And it can quickly be sent swimming away with the silent toot of a sonic probe.

GAZETTE ■ 163

such as the lack of an atmosphere and the need for protective suits and breathing apparatus when venturing outside the colony. Other characteristics of the two places are quite different. For example, in space people must deal with weightlessness, whereas under the ocean people must deal with great pressure.

ENRICHMENT

An alternative to undersea cities is underground cities. Have interested students research the underground community in Siwa, Egypt, and report their findings to the class.

REINFORCEMENT/RETEACHING

Review with students some of the aspects of undersea life described in this article. Write the following headings on the chalkboard: Food, Air, Transportation, Energy. Under each heading have students discuss the way this need is met.

For example, food is provided at least in part by fish and kelp farms. Transportation is accomplished by transport vehicles that move through transparent tubes.

INDEPENDENT PRACTICE

▶ *Activity Book*

After students have read the Science Gazette article, you may want to hand out the reading skills worksheet based on the article in the *Activity Book*.

For Further Reading

If you have been intrigued by the concepts examined in this textbook, you may also be interested in the ways fellow thinkers—novelists, poets, essayists, as well as scientists—have imaginatively explored the same ideas.

Chapter 1: Earth's Atmosphere

Carson, Rachel. *Silent Spring.* Boston, MA: Houghton Mifflin.

Randolph, Blythe. *Amelia Earhart.* New York: Watts.

Seuss, Dr. *The Lorax.* New York: Random House.

Silverstein, Alvin, and Virginia B. Silverstein. *Allergies.* Philadelphia, PA: Lippincott.

Verne, Jules. *Around the World in Eighty Days.* New York: Bantam Books.

Verne, Jules. *From the Earth to the Moon.* New York: Airmont.

Young, Louise B. *Sowing the Wind: Reflections on the Earth's Atmosphere.* New York: Prentice Hall Press.

Chapter 2: Earth's Oceans

Berill, N.J., and Jacquelyn Berrill. *1001 Questions Answered About the Seashore.* New York: Dover.

Coleridge, Samuel Taylor. *The Rime of the Ancient Mariner.* New York: Dover.

Dejong, Meindert. *The Wheel on the School.* New York: Harper & Row.

Hemingway, Ernest. *The Old Man and the Sea.* New York: Macmillan.

Heyerdahl, Thor. *Kon-Tiki: Across the Pacific by Raft.* New York: Washington Square Press.

McClane, A.J. *McClane's North American Fish Cookery.* New York: Henry Holt.

O'Dell, Scott. *The Black Pearl.* Boston, MA: Houghton Mifflin.

Peck, Richard. *Those Summer Girls I Never Met.* New York: Delacorte Press.

Verne, Jules. *Twenty Thousand Leagues Under the Sea.* New York: New American Library.

Wade, Wyn Craig. *The Titanic.* London, England: Penguin.

Chapter 3: Earth's Fresh Water

Garden, Nancy. *Peace, O River.* New York: Farrar, Straus & Giroux.

Grahame, Kenneth. *The Wind in the Willows.* New York: Macmillan.

Moorehead, Alan. *The White Nile.* New York: Harper & Row.

Moorehead, Alan. *The Blue Nile.* New York: Harper & Row.

Pringle, Laurence. *Water: The Next Great Resource Battle.* New York: Macmillan.

Thomas, Charles B. *Water Gardens for Plants and Fish.* Neptune, NJ: TFH Publications.

Twain, Mark. *Life on the Mississippi.* New York: Harper & Row.

Walton, Izaak. *The Compleat Angler.* London, England: Penguin.

Chapter 4: Earth's Landmasses

Adams, Ansel. *Photographs of the Southwest.* New York: New York Graphic Society.

Lasky, Kathryn. *Beyond the Divide.* New York: Dell.

Parkman, Francis. *Oregon Trail.* New York: Airmont.

Riffel, Paul. *Reading Maps.* Northbrook, IL: Hubbard Science.

Rugoff, Milton. *Marco Polo's Adventures in China.* New York: Harper & Row.

Seredy, Kate. *The White Stag.* New York: Viking.

Twain, Mark. *Roughing It.* New York: Airmont.

Chapter 5: Earth's Interior

Asimov, Isaac. *How Did We Find Out About Oil?* New York: Walker.

Goor, Ron, and Nancy Goor. *Exploring a Roman Ghost Town.* New York: Harper & Row Junior Books.

Jackson, Julia. *Treasures From the Earth's Crust.* Hillside, NJ: Enslow.

Lauber, Patricia. *Volcano: The Eruption and Healing of Mount St. Helens.* New York: Bradbury.

Rossbocker, Lisa A. *Recent Revolutions in Geology.* New York: Watts.

Traven, B. *The Treasure of the Sierra Madre.* New York: Farrar, Straus & Giroux.

Wilder, Laura. *West from Home: Letters of Laura Ingalls Wilder.* New York: Harper & Row Junior Books.

Activity Bank

Welcome to the Activity Bank! This is an exciting and enjoyable part of your science textbook. By using the Activity Bank you will have the chance to make a variety of interesting and different observations about science. The best thing about the Activity Bank is that you and your classmates will become the detectives, and as with any investigation you will have to sort through information to find the truth. There will be many twists and turns along the way, some surprises and disappointments too. So always remember to keep an open mind, ask lots of questions, and have fun learning about science.

Activity Bank

COOPERATIVE LEARNING

Hands-on science activities, such as the ones in the Activity Bank, lend themselves well to cooperative learning techniques. The first step in setting up activities for cooperative learning is to divide the class into small groups of about 4 to 6 students. Next, assign roles to each member of the group. Possible roles include Principal Investigator, Materials Manager, Recorder/Reporter, Maintenance Director. The Principal Investigator directs all operations associated with the group activity, including checking the assignment, giving instructions to the group, making sure that the proper procedure is being followed, performing or delegating the steps of the activity, and asking questions of the teacher on behalf of the group. The Materials Manager obtains and dispenses all materials and equipment and is the only member of the group allowed to move around the classroom without special permission during the activity. The Recorder, or Reporter, collects information, certifies and records results, and reports results to the class. The Maintenance Director is responsible for cleanup and has the authority to assign other members of the group to assist. The Maintenance Director is also in charge of group safety.

For more information about specific roles and cooperative learning in general, refer to the article "Cooperative Learning and Science—The Perfect Match" on pages 70–75 in the *Teacher's Desk Reference.*

ESL/LEP STRATEGY

Activities such as the ones in the Activity Bank can be extremely helpful in teaching science concepts to LEP students—the direct observation of scientific phenomena and the deliberate manipulation of variables can transcend language barriers.

Some strategies for helping LEP students as they develop their English-language skills are listed below. Your school's English-to-Speakers-of-Other-Languages (ESOL) teacher will probably be able to make other concrete suggestions to fit the specific needs of the LEP students in your classroom.

• Assign a "buddy" who is proficient in English to each LEP student. The buddy need not be able to speak the LEP student's native language, but such ability can be helpful. (**Note:** *Instruct multilingual buddies to use the native language only when necessary, such as defining difficult terms or concepts. Students learn English, as all other languages, by using it.*) The buddy's job is to provide encouragement and assistance to the LEP student. Select buddies on the basis of personality as well as proficiency in science and English. If possible, match buddies and LEP students so that the LEP students can help their buddies in another academic area, such as math.

• If possible, do not put LEP students of the same nationality in a cooperative learning group.

• Have artistic students draw diagrams of each step of an activity for the LEP students.

You can read more about teaching science to LEP students in the article "Creating a Positive Learning Environment for Students with Limited English Proficiency," which is found on pages 86–87 in the *Teacher's Desk Reference.*

Activity Bank

A MODEL OF ACID RAIN

BEFORE THE ACTIVITY

You might want to set up this activity a week before you plan on doing it in class. Show the students your set-up after they have completed their work. Students will then be able to see some longer term effects of "acid rain" on the pennies. You should use a cheap white vinegar available in a supermarket in this activity.

PRE-ACTIVITY DISCUSSION

Have students read the complete activity before they begin. Ask the following questions.

• **What is a model? Has anyone in the class ever made a model?** (Some students will describe model planes, or cars, or other models they have constructed.)

• **How is a model useful to a scientist?** (A model can help scientists research a problem that may be too large or too complicated to study easily.)

• **Have any of you ever heard of acid rain?** (Some students might be aware that acid rain is a problem for the natural world.)

• **What is being explored in this activity?** (The effects of acid rain on a copper penny.)

TEACHING STRATEGY

Tell students that this activity is a model of how acid rain affects metal sculptures. You might be able to show students photographs of the effects of acid rain on stone or metal works of art or parts of buildings.

DISCOVERY STRATEGIES

Ask students:

How do you think the activity you completed is like acid rain that occurs in nature? How does it differ? (The activity is like acid rain in nature because students study ways vinegar, an acid, affects metal. It differs in that acid rain in nature is not vinegar [acetic acid] and most statues are not made of copper, although some decorative parts of buildings and some gutters and drain pipes—especially in older buildings—are made of copper.)

OBSERVATIONS

The penny placed in plain water and the penny left alone will not change. The

---

In many parts of the country, rain contains chemical pollutants that produce harmful effects. You may have read about acid rain. Acid rain can kill fishes in lakes and damage the leaves of trees. In cities, acid rain can damage statues and buildings. You can make a model of acid rain and observe some of the harmful effects acid rain produces.

Materials

3 saucers
3 pennies
vinegar
teaspoon

Procedure

1. Place one penny in each of the three saucers.
2. Place two teaspoons of water on the penny in the first saucer.
3. Place two teaspoons of vinegar on the penny in the second saucer. Leave the third penny alone.

4. Set the three saucers aside and observe the three pennies the next day. (You may want to cover the saucers with a piece of plastic wrap to keep the liquids from evaporating.)

Observations

Describe the appearance of the three pennies. You may want to draw a picture of each penny.

Analysis and Conclusions

1. Explain the changes that occurred in the appearance of the three pennies.
2. What do you think happens to rocks and other objects that are exposed to acid rain over a period of time?

Going Further

With your classmates, see if you can devise a plan to protect the pennies from acid rain. Assume that you cannot stop acid rain from occurring. Present your ideas to your teacher before you test them out.

---

penny in the vinegar will begin to show color changes, usually a green film.

ANALYSIS AND CONCLUSIONS

1. The penny that was covered with vinegar, an acid, began to turn green. The other pennies remained copper-colored. Students actually made a model that shows the effects of acid rain on metal.

2. Over time, acid rain will cause changes to occur in objects. Metals will corrode, statues made of stone will erode.

GOING FURTHER

Answers will vary. Some students will suggest ways of preventing acid rain from occurring. Other students might suggest ways of putting a protective coating over objects to prevent acid rain from reaching them. Accept all reasonable answers.

SINK OR SWIM—IS IT EASIER TO FLOAT IN COLD WATER OR HOT?

Can you float? You may already know that it is easier to float in salt water than in fresh water. Salt water is denser than fresh water. Is it easier to float in warm water or cold? Try this investigation to find out.

Materials
large, deep pan
cold tap water
hot tap water
food coloring
dropper bottle

Procedure

1. Fill a large pan three-quarters full of cold water.

2. Put a few drops of food coloring in a dropper bottle and fill the bottle with hot tap water. **CAUTION:** *Be careful not to scald yourself. The hot water from some taps is very hot indeed!*

3. Place your finger over the opening of the dropper bottle. Carefully place the bottle on its side in the pan of cold water. The dropper bottle should be submerged completely.

4. Slowly take your finger off the opening of the bottle. Observe what happens.

Observations

1. Describe what happened to the hot water.

2. Why did you add food coloring to the hot water?

Analysis and Conclusions

1. Which water, cold or hot, was more dense? Why?

2. Which water, cold or hot, would be easier to float in? Why?

Going Further

Suppose you had placed cold water and food coloring in the dropper bottle and hot water in the pan. What do you think would have happened when you removed your finger from the dropper bottle? With your teacher's permission, test your hypothesis.

Food coloring

I ■ 167

Activity Bank

SINK OR SWIM—IS IT EASIER TO FLOAT IN COLD WATER OR HOT?

BEFORE THE ACTIVITY

If the water in your classroom is not very hot, you might want to heat some water on a hot plate before this activity begins. Be careful not to heat the water so that it is hot enough to scald the skin.

PRE-ACTIVITY DISCUSSION

Have students read the complete activity procedure.
• **Has anyone ever gone swimming in the ocean?** Ask the students who answered yes: **Has anyone ever gone swimming in a lake or pool? Describe differences you noticed in staying afloat in salt water and fresh water.** (Students should respond that it was easier to remain afloat in salt water rather than fresh.)
• **Is salt water more dense than fresh water?** (Yes. Salt water is denser than fresh water.)

TEACHING STRATEGY

Emphasize that the ability of an object to sink or float in water is related to density. Point out that an object that may not float in water may float in a denser liquid. Students should be able to infer that if two types of water—salt and fresh, for example—have different densities, then it will be easier to float in the denser of the two.

DISCOVERY STRATEGIES

Discuss how the activity relates to the chapter content by asking questions similar to the following.
• **Would you expect all objects to float on water?** (No. Objects that are denser than water will not float on water.)
• **Why is the density of substances important?** (Scientists can predict the behavior of certain substances if they know their density.)
• **Would knowing about the densities of different materials help you to design a good ship?** (Yes, it would be important to know about the densities of certain materials to design a ship. Although steel is more dense than water, a steel ship still floats. Much of the interior of a ship is filled with air. Thus the overall density of a ship is lighter than water.)

OBSERVATIONS

1. The hot water moved upward in the pan of cold water.
2. To make it easier to see.

ANALYSIS AND CONCLUSIONS

1. Cold water is denser than hot water. The warm-colored water moved up toward the surface of the cold water.
2. The cold, denser water would be easier to float in. It would support a person's weight better than the less dense hot water. Actually the difference in density is very slight so there would probably be little, if any, difference in the ability of a person to float in water of either temperature.

GOING FURTHER

The cold, colored water would sink in the warm water.

Activity Bank

BACKGROUND INFORMATION

You may have heard the question: How are organisms adapted to a certain environment? In this activity students will explore ways fish are adapted to life in fresh water. This activity can also be used in the previous chapter to show some of the adaptations fish have to life in an ocean environment.

BEFORE THE ACTIVITY

You should purchase several goldfish a day or two before you schedule this activity. Many pet stores sell "feeder" goldfish. These fish are smaller and less expensive than larger fish.

TEACHING STRATEGY

You can also make this activity the basis of a field trip to an aquarium. If students are encouraged to share the information they gather, this activity can easily be set up as a Cooperative Learning experience.

SAFETY TIPS

If you use glass aquaria or jars, caution students about possible breakage. Do not attempt to move an aquarium filled with water. You can also let students observe fish in small jars or containers.

DISCOVERY STRATEGIES

Discuss how the investigation relates to the chapter content by asking questions similar to the following.
• **What kind of animals live on land? What kind live in water?** (Answers will vary.)
• **What are some things that animals that live on land need to survive?** (Students should suggest that animals need food, oxygen, and a place to live.)
• **What are some things that animals that live in water need to survive?** (Students should be able to infer that animals that live in water need the same things animals that live on land need.)

OBSERVATIONS

1. The tail fin is primarily used for forward motion. Other fins may cause the fish to move forward too.

Fishes are well adapted for life in water. In this activity you will observe a fish and discover for yourself how fishes are suited to live in water.

Materials

small goldfish
aquarium
fish food
thermometer

watch or clock
several sheets of
unlined paper

Procedure

1. On a sheet of unlined paper, draw an outline of the fish from the side. On the same sheet of paper, draw an outline of the fish as seen head-on. On the same sheet of paper, draw an outline of the fish as seen from the top.
2. As you observe your fish, draw its fins on your outlines. Use arrows to show how each fin moves. If a fin doesn't appear to move, indicate this on your drawing.
3. Feed the fish. Record its reaction to food.
4. Take the temperature of the water. Enter the temperature reading in a data table similar to the one shown here. Now count the number of times the fish opens and closes its gills in 1 minute. (The gills are located at the front end

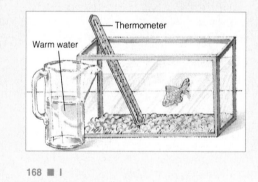

Thermometer

Warm water

168 ■ I

of the fish just behind its eyes. In order to live, fish take oxygen from the water. They swallow water through their mouth and pass it out through their gills.)
5. Add a little warm water to the aquarium. You want to raise the temperature of the water only a few degrees, so be careful. Do not make too drastic a change in the water temperature. Count the number of times the gills open and close in the warmer water in 1 minute.

Observations

1. What fin or fins move the fish forward in the water?
2. What fins help the fish turn from side to side?
3. How does the movement of the gills relate to the temperature of the water?

DATA TABLE

	Gills open and close
Temperature 1	
Temperature 2	

Analysis and Conclusions

What special structures and behaviors enable fishes to survive in a water world?

Going Further

You might like to set up an aquarium that reflects a fish's natural environment more accurately. For example, add a gravel layer to the bottom of the aquarium. Place some rocks and plants in the aquarium. You should then examine your fish's behavior after you have completed this task. What changes, if any, do you note?

---

2. The pectoral fins, located on the sides of the fish near the gills, turn the fish from side to side. The tail fin also can help the fish turn.
3. The gills open and close more rapidly in warm water than in cold.

ANALYSIS AND CONCLUSIONS

Students should mention the gills that remove oxygen from, and give off carbon dioxide to, the water; and the fins that aid a fish in moving. Other answers are possible. For example, some students might mention the streamlined shape of fish, their protective scales, and their colors.

GOING FURTHER

Students will observe fish explore a more natural environment. Supplying places for the fish to hide makes fish more secure. Some fish might also eat plants placed in the water. Accept all other reasonable answers.

WHAT IS THE EFFECT OF PHOSPHATES ON PLANT GROWTH?

Sometimes seemingly harmless chemicals have effects that are not easily predictable. For example, detergents are often added to water to clean clothes and dishes. When the clothes and dishes are rinsed, the detergents in waste water enter home septic systems or town sewage systems. Detergents in water may eventually be carried to streams, lakes, and sources of groundwater. So far this story seems unremarkable.

However, some detergents contain phosphates. Because of their effects on plant growth, detergents that contain phosphates have been banned by some communities. In this investigation you will measure the effects of phosphates on plant growth. You will uncover reasons why communities try to keep phosphates out of water supplies, and thus ban the use of certain detergents used to clean clothes and dishes.

Materials

2 large test tubes with corks or stoppers to fit	2 sprigs of *Elodea*
test-tube rack, or large plastic jar or beaker	detergent that contains phosphates
	sunlight or a lamp
	small scissors

Before You Begin

Make sure that the detergent you will be using contains phosphates; many do not. *Elodea* is a common water plant used in home aquariums. A local pet store is a good source of supply.

Procedure 🧪

1. Take two sprigs of *Elodea* and use your scissors to cut them to the same length. Measure the length of the sprigs and record the length in a data table similar to the one shown on the next page. Place a sprig of *Elodea* into each test tube.

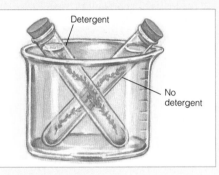

2. Add enough water to each test tube to fill it nearly to the top. Be sure the *Elodea* sprig is covered with water.
3. Place a small pinch of detergent into one test tube. Gently swirl the test tube to mix the water and detergent. Leave plain water in the other test tube.
4. Stopper each test tube.
5. Place the test tubes in a test-tube rack or plastic jar or beaker. Place the rack (or jar or beaker) in a sunny window or under another source of light.

(continued)

Activity Bank

WHAT IS THE EFFECT OF PHOSPHATES ON PLANT GROWTH?

BACKGROUND INFORMATION

Water can be polluted by many things. Phosphates are one example of a water pollutant. It may seem strange that phosphates, used by farmers to enhance the growth of their crop plants, may also cause serious water pollution. When phosphates enter rivers and streams, they cause water plants to increase their rate of growth. Eventually the increase in plants uses up the available nutrients in the water. The increased number of plants also use up the oxygen in the water. The plants begin to die. Fish and other water organisms also begin to die. Eventually the water becomes foul.

In an effort to protect water supplies, many communities now prohibit the sale of detergents that contain phosphates. This is especially true of communities that tap aquifers as water sources. Some communities on Long Island in New York state use aquifers as a water supply. For many years, detergents that contain phosphates have been banned. The concern here is that pollutants will be carried over a large area once they enter an aquifer.

BEFORE THE ACTIVITY

You can have students add a small pinch of detergent to a test tube, or you can make a weak detergent solution by adding a half-teaspoon of detergent to a liter of warm water. Stir to dissolve. You may have to do some scouting to find a detergent that contains phosphates. If you live in a community that bans their sale, you will have to travel elsewhere. Remember that no liquid detergent contains phosphates.

If you cannot find a detergent that contains phosphates you can make a detergent. Add a half-teaspoon of super phosphate, a fertilizer sold in garden supply stores, to a liter of water. Add a pinch of detergent to this. You should tell the class that you have mixed up the detergent they need because it was not possible to purchase a suitable detergent locally. You might make this a plus by telling the class that after this activity they will understand some reasons why detergents that contain phosphates are not available locally.

Elodea is a good plant to use because it is commonly available in pet stores. It also grows by increasing in length from the tip and rarely branches. When students cut their pieces of *Elodea,* make sure they cut the end away from the growing tip. A small piece fits quite nicely in a large test tube. However it does need light to grow. If you do not have a source of natural sunlight, you can use an electric lamp or a plant-growth bulb.

PRE-ACTIVITY DISCUSSION

Have students read the complete activity procedure.
• **What is the variable in this activity?** (The detergent is the variable.)
• **How will we determine the effect of detergent on plant growth?** (By measuring the length of a piece of *Elodea* grown in a solution that contains detergent and comparing this growth to a length of a piece of *Elodea* grown in plain water.)

Remind students to handle glassware carefully.

TEACHING STRATEGY

You may want to make solutions of differing strengths for this activity. You can than make this a Cooperative Learning experience by having students pool their data. Try to make sure that all other variable are controlled. All *Elodea* should receive the same intensity and duration of light. All should be kept at the same temperature. Keep in mind that an electric lamp used as a source of light can increase the temperature of the water in a test tube.

DISCOVERY STRATEGIES

Discuss how the investigation relates to this chapter by asking questions similar to the following.

• **Why is it necessary to protect our water supply from pollutants?** (People need water for drinking and many other uses. This water must be protected.)

• **Why have some communities banned the sale of detergents that contain phosphates?** (In water, phosphates act as fertilizers and stimulate plant growth. Increased plant growth is not a plus in water that may be used by people.)

• **What can we do to protect our water supply?** (We can avoid using detergents that contain phosphates. By making wise choices we can limit potential damage to the environment and can protect our supply of drinking water.)

OBSERVATIONS

1. Students were testing for the effects of detergent on plant growth, so the control was the plant that was placed in plain water.

2. It increased in length.

3. It should have shown a greater increase in length than the *Elodea* that was placed in plain water.

4. It is important to place the sprigs back in the correct tubes so that the effects of the detergent on plant growth are confined to one plant.

ANALYSIS AND CONCLUSIONS

1. Yes, the *Elodea* that was placed in the water that contained detergent showed greater growth.

6. Every three days for a month, carefully remove each *Elodea* sprig and measure it. Record your measurements in your data table. Place the sprigs back into the test tubes they were removed from each time. Do not mix up the sprigs!

Observations

1. What was the control in this experiment? Why?

2. Describe the *Elodea* that was placed in plain water.

3. Describe the *Elodea* that was placed in water that contained the detergent drops.

4. Why was it important to return each sprig to the correct tube?

Analysis and Conclusions

1. Did the detergent affect the *Elodea's* growth?

2. How do you explain the results of this investigation?

3. How might the effect of phosphates on water plants affect a community's water supply?

Going Further

Design an investigatation that compares the effects of detergents and fertilizers on plant growth. Have your teacher check the design of your investigation before you begin.

DATA TABLE

Day	Detergent	No Detergent
1		
4		
7		
10		
13		
16		
19		
22		
25		
28		
31		

2. Phosphates in detergents act as plant fertilizers. Phosphates are used by plants as they grow.

3. If large amounts of phosphates enter a community's water supply, plant growth in the water can increase rapidly. The increased number of plants may use all available nutrients and gases in the water. If this happens, the plants begin to die. The water becomes fouled. Fish and other organisms in the water may also die.

GOING FURTHER

Answers will vary. Check to make sure that students have included a control plant that recieves neither detergent nor fertilizer.

MAKING SOIL

Soil is a substance that is certainly taken for granted by most people. This common substance, often underfoot and easy to see, contributes greatly to human survival. Plants need soil to grow well—it is good, fertile soil that makes our croplands so productive. In this activity you will "make" some soil. Keep in mind, however, that what you can accomplish in an afternoon takes nature's forces many years to produce.

Materials

rocks
sand
magnifying glass
dried leaves

plastic pan or
  bucket
soil sample

Procedure

1. Use the magnifying glass to examine the rocks and the sand. Draw what you observe on a separate sheet of paper.

2. Place a thick layer of sand in the bottom of the plastic pan or bucket.

3. Break up the dried leaves into tiny pieces. You might even grind the dried leaves between two flat rocks.

4. Add a layer of the ground-up plant material to the sand. Use your hands to gently mix the sand and dried leaves together.

5. Use the magnifying glass to compare the soil mixture you made with the soil sample provided by your teacher. Draw what you observe.

Observations

1. How does the sand compare with the rock samples?

2. Did you observe leaves or other pieces of plant material in the soil sample provided by your teacher?

3. In what ways did the soil you made resemble the soil sample? In what ways was it different?

4. How could you make your soil more like the soil in the sample?

Analysis and Conclusions

1. Where does sand come from in natural soil?

2. Where does the plant material come from in natural soil?

3. Why is plant material an important part of soil?

4. Why are sand and other rock material important parts of soil?

Going Further

Design an experiment to compare the growth of plants in the soil you made with the growth of plants in natural soil. Discuss your plan with your teacher, and get his or her permission before you begin.

Activity Bank

MAKING SOIL

BEFORE THE LAB

You can use potting soil sold in plastic bags in garden centers as a source of soil. This soil is often sterilized (treated with heat) to kill weed seeds and insects.

TEACHING STRATEGY

Have students read the section on topography. This section discusses areas where good soil supports crop growth. Use the maps of the United States to relate topography to soil and farming.

DISCOVERY STRATEGIES

Discuss with the class how this activity relates to the chapter content. You might want to ask questions similar to the following to begin a discussion.

• **In what areas of the United States can you find good places to grow crops?** (Plains are areas of good soil and thus are fertile areas that produce good crops.)

• **Why is soil important to people?** (Crops are grown in soil. Animals and people are dependent upon these crops.)

• **How is soil formed?** (Soil forms when rocks break down into small particles by natural processes. The remains of plants and animals that break down in the soil contribute chemical nutrients that support the growth of plants.)

• **How can we protect soil?** (We must prevent soil from erosion by wind and water. Preventing erosion will protect a vital link in our food supply.)

OBSERVATIONS

1. Sand is much smaller than the rock samples. Rocks break down into smaller and smaller particles during natural weathering processes that occur in nature. The smaller particles, consisting of compounds that made up the original rocks, are known as sand. Beach sand is made of silicon and oxygen.
2. Answers will vary. Soil samples will contain plant material.
3. Answers will vary. All samples should contain a mixture of material from non-living (rocks and minerals) sources and plant materials.
4. Answers will vary, but students should suggest that better analysis of the components of the soil sample would result in soil more like the sample.

ANALYSIS AND CONCLUSIONS

1. Sand results when rocks are broken down into very small particles.
2. The plant material in soil comes from plants that have died and decayed. Students might suggest falling leaves or soil additives such as peat moss as sources of plant material.
3. Decaying plant material supplies nutrients that enhance the growth of other plants. Decaying plant materials can be considered a kind of "natural" fertilizer.
4. Sand and rock material improve soil drainage and porosity.

GOING FURTHER

Student proposals will vary. Make sure that students include a control.

Activity Bank

BEFORE THE ACTIVITY

Gather some rock samples several days before this activity is scheduled. You might be able to borrow a Mohs hardness sample kit from the local high school. If you are able to get a kit, you will be able to make more accurate assessments of the hardness of the rock samples you are testing. This activity is perfect for Cooperative Learning and ESL. The tests are simple, and the vocabulary in this activity is limited.

PRE-ACTIVITY DISCUSSION

Have students read the complete activity procedure.
• **List some hard substances.** (Answers will vary, but students should name rocks as one example of a hard substance.)
• **Are all rocks equally hard?** (Accept all answers. After this investigation students will realize that some rocks are very hard, while others are soft enough to be scratched with a fingernail.)

SAFETY TIPS

Caution students about breakable glass and the safe use of a kitchen knife.

TEACHING STRATEGY

Emphasize that there are many types of rocks on Earth that differ in the amounts and types of substances that make them up.

Have students list ways rocks are used in a modern society. Students should say that rocks are used for buildings, to make roads, and to make sculptures. Many other answers are possible.

DISCOVERY STRATEGIES

Discuss how this activity relates to the chapter by asking questions similar to the following.
• **Where are rocks found?** (In the crust of the Earth.)
• **Why do rocks differ in hardness?** (Different rocks are made up of different substances. These substances give different properties to the rocks. Hardness is one property that depends upon the chemical substances that are found in rocks. Hard-

---

Activity Bank

Hardness is a property that is often used to identify rocks. In this activity you will determine the hardness of several rock samples relative to each other and to several common substances. Geologists often use the Mohs hardness scale to determine the hardness of a rock specimen. But if you are collecting rocks in the field, it may not be easy to carry the ten mineral specimens that represent the Mohs hardness scale along with you. It is often easier to use commonly available substances to perform a hardness test.

For example, a fingernail has a hardness of about 2.5, a penny a hardness of 3.0, a steel knife blade a hardness of about 5.5, and a piece of glass a hardness of 5.5 to 6.0.

Materials

selection of rock samples
square glass plate
steel kitchen knife
penny

Procedure 🔬 🧰

1. Select two rock specimens. Try to scratch one with the other. Keep the harder of the two specimens. Put the softer one aside.
2. Select another rock and use the same scratch test. Keep the harder of these two rocks and set the other aside.
3. Keep repeating the procedure until you have identified the hardest rock specimen you have.
4. Compare the rocks to find the second hardest rock. Continue this procedure until all the rock specimens have been put in order from the hardest to the softest.

5. Now compare the rock specimens to the other materials of known hardness to determine the actual hardness of as many of your specimens as possible. **CAUTION:** *Use care when handling sharp materials. Your teacher will show you the proper way to proceed.* Share your results with your classmates. Use their findings to confirm yours.

Observations

1. Did you find any rocks that were softer than your fingernail?
2. Did any rocks scratch the penny?
3. Were any rocks unscratched by the steel blade?
4. Did any rocks scratch the glass plate?

Analysis and Conclusions

1. Calcite has a rating of 3 on the Mohs scale. Would calcite be scratched by a penny?
2. Many people think that diamond (10 on the Mohs scale) is the only mineral that can scratch glass. Is this correct? Why?

---

ness can be determined by comparing rocks with rocks and other substances whose hardness is known.)

OBSERVATIONS

Answers will vary depending upon the rock specimens that were available to students.

ANALYSIS AND CONCLUSIONS

1. No, it would not.
2. No, it is not correct. Diamond has a hardness of 10, glass has a hardness of 5.5 to 6.0. Any rock with a hardness greater than 6 will scratch glass.

Appendix A

The metric system of measurement is used by scientists throughout the world. It is based on units of ten. Each unit is ten times larger or ten times smaller than the next unit. The most commonly used units of the metric system are given below. After you have finished reading about the metric system, try to put it to use. How tall are you in metrics? What is your mass? What is your normal body temperature in degrees Celsius?

Commonly Used Metric Units

Length   The distance from one point to another

meter (m)   A meter is slightly longer than a yard.
1 meter = 1000 millimeters (mm)
1 meter = 100 centimeters (cm)
1000 meters = 1 kilometer (km)

Volume   The amount of space an object takes up

liter (L)   A liter is slightly more than a quart.
1 liter = 1000 milliliters (mL)

Mass   The amount of matter in an object

gram (g)   A gram has a mass equal to about one paper clip.

1000 grams = 1 kilogram (kg)

Temperature   The measure of hotness or coldness

degrees $0°C$ = freezing point of water
Celsius (°C) $100°C$ = boiling point of water

Metric–English Equivalents

2.54 centimeters (cm) = 1 inch (in.)
1 meter (m) = 39.37 inches (in.)
1 kilometer (km) = 0.62 miles (mi)
1 liter (L) = 1.06 quarts (qt)
250 milliliters (mL) = 1 cup (c)
1 kilogram (kg) = 2.2 pounds (lb)
28.3 grams (g) = 1 ounce (oz)
$°C = 5/9 \times (°F - 32)$

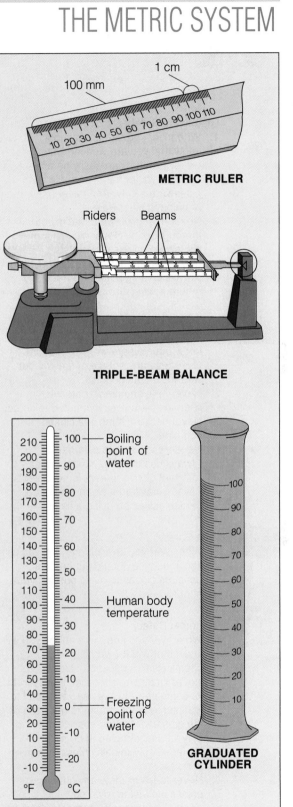

METRIC RULER

TRIPLE-BEAM BALANCE

THERMOMETER

GRADUATED CYLINDER

Appendix B

Glassware Safety

1. Whenever you see this symbol, you will know that you are working with glassware that can easily be broken. Take particular care to handle such glassware safely. And never use broken or chipped glassware.
2. Never heat glassware that is not thoroughly dry. Never pick up any glassware unless you are sure it is not hot. If it is hot, use heat-resistant gloves.
3. Always clean glassware thoroughly before putting it away.

Fire Safety

1. Whenever you see this symbol, you will know that you are working with fire. Never use any source of fire without wearing safety goggles.
2. Never heat anything—particularly chemicals—unless instructed to do so.
3. Never heat anything in a closed container.
4. Never reach across a flame.
5. Always use a clamp, tongs, or heat-resistant gloves to handle hot objects.
6. Always maintain a clean work area, particularly when using a flame.

Heat Safety

Whenever you see this symbol, you will know that you should put on heat-resistant gloves to avoid burning your hands.

Chemical Safety

1. Whenever you see this symbol, you will know that you are working with chemicals that could be hazardous.
2. Never smell any chemical directly from its container. Always use your hand to waft some of the odors from the top of the container toward your nose—and only when instructed to do so.
3. Never mix chemicals unless instructed to do so.
4. Never touch or taste any chemical unless instructed to do so.
5. Keep all lids closed when chemicals are not in use. Dispose of all chemicals as instructed by your teacher.

6. Immediately rinse with water any chemicals, particularly acids, that get on your skin and clothes. Then notify your teacher.

Eye and Face Safety

1. Whenever you see this symbol, you will know that you are performing an experiment in which you must take precautions to protect your eyes and face by wearing safety goggles.
2. When you are heating a test tube or bottle, always point it away from you and others. Chemicals can splash or boil out of a heated test tube.

Sharp Instrument Safety

1. Whenever you see this symbol, you will know that you are working with a sharp instrument.
2. Always use single-edged razors; double-edged razors are too dangerous.
3. Handle any sharp instrument with extreme care. Never cut any material toward you; always cut away from you.
4. Immediately notify your teacher if your skin is cut.

Electrical Safety

1. Whenever you see this symbol, you will know that you are using electricity in the laboratory.
2. Never use long extension cords to plug in any electrical device. Do not plug too many appliances into one socket or you may overload the socket and cause a fire.
3. Never touch an electrical appliance or outlet with wet hands.

Animal Safety

1. Whenever you see this symbol, you will know that you are working with live animals.
2. Do not cause pain, discomfort, or injury to an animal.
3. Follow your teacher's directions when handling animals. Wash your hands thoroughly after handling animals or their cages.

One of the first things a scientist learns is that working in the laboratory can be an exciting experience. But the laboratory can also be quite dangerous if proper safety rules are not followed at all times. To prepare yourself for a safe year in the laboratory, read over the following safety rules. Then read them a second time. Make sure you understand each rule. If you do not, ask your teacher to explain any rules you are unsure of.

Dress Code

1. Many materials in the laboratory can cause eye injury. To protect yourself from possible injury, wear safety goggles whenever you are working with chemicals, burners, or any substance that might get into your eyes. Never wear contact lenses in the laboratory.

2. Wear a laboratory apron or coat whenever you are working with chemicals or heated substances.

3. Tie back long hair to keep it away from any chemicals, burners and candles, or other laboratory equipment.

4. Remove or tie back any article of clothing or jewelry that can hang down and touch chemicals and flames.

General Safety Rules

5. Read all directions for an experiment several times. Follow the directions exactly as they are written. If you are in doubt about any part of the experiment, ask your teacher for assistance.

6. Never perform activities that are not authorized by your teacher. Obtain permission before "experimenting" on your own.

7. Never handle any equipment unless you have specific permission.

8. Take extreme care not to spill any material in the laboratory. If a spill occurs, immediately ask your teacher about the proper cleanup procedure. Never simply pour chemicals or other substances into the sink or trash container.

9. Never eat in the laboratory.

10. Wash your hands before and after each experiment.

First Aid

11. Immediately report all accidents, no matter how minor, to your teacher.

12. Learn what to do in case of specific accidents, such as getting acid in your eyes or on your skin. (Rinse acids from your body with lots of water.)

13. Become aware of the location of the first-aid kit. But your teacher should administer any required first aid due to injury. Or your teacher may send you to the school nurse or call a physician.

14. Know where and how to report an accident or fire. Find out the location of the fire extinguisher, phone, and fire alarm. Keep a list of important phone numbers—such as the fire department and the school nurse—near the phone. Immediately report any fires to your teacher.

Heating and Fire Safety

15. Again, never use a heat source, such as a candle or burner, without wearing safety goggles.

16. Never heat a chemical you are not instructed to heat. A chemical that is harmless when cool may be dangerous when heated.

17. Maintain a clean work area and keep all materials away from flames.

18. Never reach across a flame.

19. Make sure you know how to light a Bunsen burner. (Your teacher will demonstrate the proper procedure for lighting a burner.) If the flame leaps out of a burner toward you, immediately turn off the gas. Do not touch the burner. It may be hot. And never leave a lighted burner unattended!

20. When heating a test tube or bottle, always point it away from you and others. Chemicals can splash or boil out of a heated test tube.

21. Never heat a liquid in a closed container. The expanding gases produced may blow the container apart, injuring you or others.

22. Before picking up a container that has been heated, first hold the back of your hand near it. If you can feel the heat on the back of your hand, the container may be too hot to handle. Use a clamp or tongs when handling hot containers.

Using Chemicals Safely

23. Never mix chemicals for the "fun of it." You might produce a dangerous, possibly explosive substance.

24. Never touch, taste, or smell a chemical unless you are instructed by your teacher to do so. Many chemicals are poisonous. If you are instructed to note the fumes in an experiment, gently wave your hand over the opening of a container and direct the fumes toward your nose. Do not inhale the fumes directly from the container.

25. Use only those chemicals needed in the activity. Keep all lids closed when a chemical is not being used. Notify your teacher whenever chemicals are spilled.

26. Dispose of all chemicals as instructed by your teacher. To avoid contamination, never return chemicals to their original containers.

27. Be extra careful when working with acids or bases. Pour such chemicals over the sink, not over your workbench.

28. When diluting an acid, pour the acid into water. Never pour water into an acid.

29. Immediately rinse with water any acids that get on your skin or clothing. Then notify your teacher of any acid spill.

Using Glassware Safely

30. Never force glass tubing into a rubber stopper. A turning motion and lubricant will be helpful when inserting glass tubing into rubber stoppers or rubber tubing. Your teacher will demonstrate the proper way to insert glass tubing.

31. Never heat glassware that is not thoroughly dry. Use a wire screen to protect glassware from any flame.

32. Keep in mind that hot glassware will not ap-pear hot. Never pick up glassware without first checking to see if it is hot. See #22.

33. If you are instructed to cut glass tubing, fire-polish the ends immediately to remove sharp edges.

34. Never use broken or chipped glassware. If glassware breaks, notify your teacher and dispose of the glassware in the proper trash container.

35. Never eat or drink from laboratory glassware. Thoroughly clean glassware before putting it away.

Using Sharp Instruments

36. Handle scalpels or razor blades with extreme care. Never cut material toward you; cut away from you.

37. Immediately notify your teacher if you cut your skin when working in the laboratory.

Animal Safety

38. No experiments that will cause pain, discomfort, or harm to mammals, birds, reptiles, fishes, and amphibians should be done in the classroom or at home.

39. Animals should be handled only if necessary. If an animal is excited or frightened, pregnant, feeding, or with its young, special handling is required.

40. Your teacher will instruct you as to how to handle each animal species that may be brought into the classroom.

41. Clean your hands thoroughly after handling animals or the cage containing animals.

End-of-Experiment Rules

42. After an experiment has been completed, clean up your work area and return all equipment to its proper place.

43. Wash your hands after every experiment.

44. Turn off all burners before leaving the laboratory. Check that the gas line leading to the burner is off as well.

Boundaries

National . . . .

State or territorial . . . .

County or equivalent . . . .

Civil township or equivalent . . . .

Incorporated city or equivalent . . . . . .

Park, reservation, or monument . . . . . .

Small park . . . .

Roads and related features

Primary highway . . . .

Secondary highway . . . .

Light-duty road . . . .

Unimproved road . . . .

Trail . . . .

Dual highway . . . .

Dual highway with median strip . . . . . .

Bridge . . . .

Tunnel . . . .

Buildings and related features

Dwelling or place of employment: small;
 large . . . .

School; house of worship . . . .

Barn, warehouse, etc.: small; large . . . .

Airport . . . .

Campground; picnic area . . . .

Cemetery: small; large . . . .

Railroads and related features

Standard-gauge single track; station . . .

Standard-gauge multiple track . . . .

Contours

Intermediate . . . .

Index . . . .

Supplementary . . . .

Depression . . . .

Cut; fill . . . .

Surface features

Levee . . . .

Sand or mud areas, dunes, or shifting
    sand . . . .

Gravel beach or glacial moraine . . . .

Vegetation

Woods . . . .

Scrub . . . .

Orchard . . . .

Vineyard . . . .

Marine shoreline

Approximate mean high water . . . .

Indefinite or unsurveyed . . . .

Coastal features

Foreshore flat . . . .

Rock or coral reef . . . .

Rock, bare or awash . . . .

Breakwater, pier, jetty, or wharf . . . .

Seawall . . . .

Rivers, lakes, and canals

Perennial stream . . . .

Perennial river . . . .

Small falls; small rapids . . . .

Large falls; large rapids . . . .

Dry lake . . . .

Narrow wash . . . .

Wide wash . . . .

Water well; spring or seep . . . .

Submerged areas and bogs

Marsh or swamp . . . .

Submerged marsh or swamp . . . .

Wooded marsh or swamp . . . .

Land subject to inundation . . . .

Elevations

Spot and elevation . . . . X_{212}

Glossary

abyssal (uh-BIHS-uhl) **plain:** large flat area on the ocean floor

abyssal zone: open-ocean zone that extends to an average depth of 6000 meters

air pressure: push on the Earth's surface caused by the force of gravity pulling on the layers of air surrounding the Earth

aquifer (AK-wuh-fuhr): layer of rock or sediment that allows ground water to pass freely

asthenosphere (az-THEEN-oh-sfeer): layer of the Earth directly beneath the lithosphere

atmosphere (AT-muhs-feer): envelope of gases that surrounds the Earth

atoll: ring of coral reefs surrounding an island that has been worn away and has sunk beneath the surface of the ocean

barrier reef: coral reef separated from the shore of an island by an area of shallow water called a lagoon

bathyal (BATH-ee-uhl) **zone:** open-ocean zone that begins at a continental slope and extends down about 2000 meters

benthos (BEHN-thahs): organisms that live on the ocean floor

cavern (KAV-uhrn): underground passage formed when limestone is dissolved by carbonic acid in ground water

coastal plain: low, flat area along a coast (place where the land meets the ocean)

condensation (kahn-duhn-SAY-shuhn): process by which water vapor changes back into a liquid; second step of the water cycle

continent: major landmass that measures millions of square kilometers and rises a considerable distance above sea level

continental glacier: thick sheet of snow and ice that builds up in polar regions of the Earth; also called polar ice sheet

continental margin: area where the underwater edge of a continent meets the ocean floor

continental rise: part of a continental margin that separates a continental slope from the ocean floor

continental shelf: relatively flat part of a continental margin that is covered by shallow ocean water

continental slope: part of the continental margin at the edge of a continental shelf where the ocean floor plunges steeply 4 to 5 kilometers

contour line: line that passes through all points on a map that have the same elevation

convection (kuhn-VEHK-shuhn) **current:** movement of air caused by cool, dense air sinking and warm, less dense air rising

coral reef: large mass of limestone rocks surrounding a volcanic island in tropical waters near a continental shelf

crest: highest point of a wave

crust: thin, outermost layer of the Earth

deep current: ocean current caused mainly by differences in the density of water deep in the ocean

deep zone: area of extremely cold ocean water below the thermocline

elevation: height above sea level

equal-area projection: projection in which area is shown correctly, but shapes are distorted

equator: imaginary line around the Earth that divides the Earth into two hemispheres; parallel located halfway between the North and South Poles

evaporation (ih-vap-uh-RAY-shuhn): process by which energy from the sun causes water on the surface of the Earth to change to water vapor, the gas phase of water; first step of the water cycle

exosphere (EHKS-oh-sfeer): upper part of the thermosphere that extends from about 550 kilometers above the Earth's surface for thousands of kilometers

fringing reef: coral reef that touches the shoreline of a volcanic island

glacier: huge mass of moving ice and snow

globe: spherical, or round, model of the Earth

groundwater: water that soaks into the ground and remains in the ground

guyot (gee-OH): flat-topped seamount

hard water: water that contains large amounts of dissolved minerals, especially calcium and magnesium

hemisphere: northern or southern half of the Earth

hydrosphere: part of the Earth's surface consisting of water

iceberg: large chunk of ice that breaks off from a continental glacier at the edge of the sea and drifts into the sea

impermeable: term used to describe material through which water cannot move quickly; opposite of permeable

inner core: solid, innermost layer of the Earth's core

interior plain: low, flat area found inland on a continent; somewhat higher above sea level than a coastal plain

international date line: line located along the 180th meridian; when the line is crossed going west, one day is added; when it is crossed going east, one day is subtracted

intertidal zone: region that lies between the low- and high-tide lines

ion: electrically charged particle

ionosphere (igh-AHN-uh-sfeer): lower part of the thermosphere that extends from 80 kilometers to 550 kilometers above the Earth's surface

island: small landmass completely surrounded by water

jet stream: strong, eastward wind that blows horizontally around the Earth

landscape: physical features of the Earth's surface found in an area

latitude: measure of distance north and south of the equator

lithosphere: part of the Earth's surface covered by land; solid, topmost part of the Earth

longitude: measure of distance east and west of the prime meridian

magnetosphere (mag-NEET-oh-sfeer): area around the Earth that extends beyond the atmosphere, in which the Earth's magnetic force operates

mantle: layer of the Earth directly above the outer core

map: drawing of the Earth, or a part of the Earth, on a flat surface

Mercator projection: projection used for navigation in which the correct shape of coastlines is shown, but the sizes of land and water areas far from the equator become distorted

meridian (muh-RIHD-ee-uhn): line that runs between the points on a globe or map which represent the geographic North and South Poles of the Earth

mesosphere (MEHS-oh-sfeer): layer of the Earth's atmosphere that extends from about 50 kilometers to about 80 kilometers above the Earth's surface

midocean ridge: mountain range located under the ocean

Moho: boundary between the Earth's outermost layer (crust) and the mantle

mountain: natural landform that reaches high elevations with a narrow summit, or top, and steep slopes, or sides

mountain belt: large group of mountains including mountain ranges and mountain systems

mountain range: roughly parallel series of mountains that have the same general shape and structure

mountain system: group of mountain ranges in one area

nekton (NEHK-ton): forms of ocean life that swim

neritic (nuh-RIHT-ihk) **zone:** area that extends from the low-tide line to the edge of a continental shelf

oceanographer (oh-shuhn-NAHG-ruh-fuhr): scientist who studies the ocean

outer core: second layer of the Earth surrounding the inner core

ozone: gas in the Earth's atmosphere formed when three atoms of oxygen combine

parallel: line going from east to west across a map or globe that crosses a meridian at right angles

permeable (PER-mee-uh-buhl): term used to describe material through which water can move quickly

plain: flat land area that does not rise far above sea level

plankton (PLANGK-tuhn): animals and plants that float at or near the surface of the ocean

plasticity (plas-TIHS-uh-tee): ability of a solid to flow, or change shape

plateau: broad, flat area of land that rises more than 600 meters above sea level

polarity (poh-LAR-uh-tee): property of a molecule with oppositely charged ends

pore space: space between particles of soil

precipitation (prih-sihp-uh-TAY-shuhn): process by which water returns to the Earth in the form of rain, snow, sleet, or hail; third step of the water cycle

prime meridian: meridian that runs through Greenwich, England

projection: representation of a three-dimensional object on a flat surface

relief: difference in a region's elevations

reservoir (REHZ-uhr-vwahr): artificial lake used as a source of fresh water

salinity (suh-LIHN-uh-tee): term used to describe the amount of dissolved salts in ocean water

scale: used to compare distances on a map or globe with actual distances on the Earth's surface

seamount: underwater volcanic mountain on the ocean floor

seismic (SIGHZ-mihk) **wave:** shock wave produced by earthquakes that travels through the Earth

seismograph (SIGHZ-muh-grahf): instrument used to detect and record P waves and S waves produced by earthquakes

shoreline: boundary where the land and the ocean meet

soft water: water that does not contain minerals

solution: substance that contains two or more substances mixed on the molecular level

solvent (SAHL-vuhnt): substance in which another substance dissolves

stratosphere (STRAT-uh-sfeer): layer of the Earth's atmosphere that extends from the tropopause to an altitude of about 50 kilometers

submarine canyon: deep, V-shaped valley cut in the rock through a continental shelf and slope

surface current: ocean current caused mainly by wind patterns

surface runoff: water that enters a river or stream after a heavy rain or during a spring thaw of snow or ice

surface zone: zone where ocean water is mixed by waves and currents

thermocline (THER-muh-klighn): zone in which the temperature of ocean water drops rapidly

thermosphere (THER-moh-sfeer): layer of the Earth's atmosphere that begins at a height of about 80 kilometers and has no well-defined upper limit

time zone: longitudinal belt of the Earth in which all areas have the same local time

topographic map: map that shows the different shapes and sizes of a land surface

topography (tuh-PAHG-ruh-fee): shape of the Earth's surface

trench: long, narrow crevice, or crack, along the edge of the ocean floor

troposphere (TRO-poh-sfeer): layer of the atmosphere closest to the Earth

trough (TRAWF): lowest point of a wave

tsunami (tsoo-NAH-mee): ocean wave caused by an earthquake

turbidity (ter-BIHD-uh-tee) **current:** flow of ocean water that carries large amounts of sediments

upwelling: rising of deep, cold currents to the ocean surface

valley glacier: long, narrow glacier that moves downhill between the steep sides of a mountain valley

Van Allen radiation belts: layers of high radiation around the Earth, in which charged particles are trapped

water cycle: continuous movement of water from the oceans and freshwater sources to the air and land and finally back to the oceans; also called the hydrologic cycle

water table: surface between the zone of saturation and the zone of aeration that marks the level below which the ground is saturated, or soaked with water

watershed: land area in which surface runoff drains into a river or a system of rivers and streams

wavelength: horizontal distance between two consecutive crests or two consecutive troughs

zone of aeration (ehr-AY-shuhn): relatively dry underground region in which the pores are filled mostly with air

zone of saturation (sach-uh-RAY-shuhn): underground region in which all the pores are filled with water

Index